STRUCTURAL INTERDEPENDENCE AND
ECONOMIC DEVELOPMENT

Structural Interdependence
and
Economic Development

PROCEEDINGS OF
AN INTERNATIONAL CONFERENCE
ON INPUT-OUTPUT TECHNIQUES,
GENEVA, SEPTEMBER 1961

EDITED BY

TIBOR BARNA

IN COLLABORATION WITH
WILLIAM I. ABRAHAM and
ZOLTÁN KENESSEY

LONDON
MACMILLAN & CO LTD
NEW YORK · ST MARTIN'S PRESS
1963

MACMILLAN AND COMPANY LIMITED
St Martin's Street London WC 2
also Bombay Calcutta Madras Melbourne

THE MACMILLAN COMPANY OF CANADA LIMITED
Toronto

ST MARTIN'S PRESS INC
New York

PRINTED IN GREAT BRITAIN

Preface

by WASSILY LEONTIEF

The papers brought together in this book were presented at the Third International Input-Output Conference held in September 1961 in Geneva. The meetings were sponsored jointly by the Secretariat of the United Nations and the Harvard Economic Research Project. Over two hundred economists and statisticians, coming from forty-one different countries, took part in them.

The first international conference on interindustrial relations met in 1951 in Driebergen, Holland; its programme centered on the construction and empirical implementation of the basic theoretical systems [1]. Continued work on analytical, statistical and computational procedures is reflected in the proceedings [2] of the second conference which took place in 1954 in Varenna, Italy. The application of the input-output techniques to economic *projection* and developmental *planning* appeared on its programme among other 'special applications.' The title of the present volume indicates that the proceedings in Geneva were dominated by these two subjects.

For the first time experts from the Soviet Union and other socialist countries and planners from underdeveloped areas shared their ideas and practical experiences in the study of interindustrial relationships with economists working on the same problems in countries of private enterprise.

Direct and indirect interdependence between the input and the output flows of all goods and services governs the intersectoral balance of every economic system. In one way or another such a balance is maintained in industrialized countries as well as in countries still in the early stages of economic growth. The same is true of the necessary intertemporal connection between capital accumulation, i.e., investment in productive capacities of specific kind and the expansion rates of various outputs. Depending on the nature of the social and economic institutions of the particular country, such a balance is established and such an intertemporal dependence maintained either through a more or less effective operation of the impersonal forces of the market mechanism, through a more or less efficient planning action or through some combination of both. In either case the input-output method is used as an effective projection or a planning tool.

In the development of this analytical technique and of its variou-applications, economists and statisticians from private enterprise econos mies and from socialist states, from highly industrialized areas as well as

v

from areas that are just entering the steep path of economic growth, can profitably work together since the scientific problems they are facing are, in this particular instance, essentially the same.

The present exchange of methodological ideas should naturally lead to international cooperation of a more substantive kind.

A national input-output table permits us to analyse the interindustrial relationships between the sectors of the economy of a given country in great detail, but when it comes to the description of the flow of goods and services connecting that economy with the economies of other countries, it traces them up to the geographic border — but not beyond. Thus, the analytical schemes based on such data must of necessity be kept 'open' in respect to external trade: the foreign demand for any good or service exported from a given country is treated not as an integral element of the picture, but rather as a part of its external frame, and so is the supply of imports obtained from abroad. This procedure restricts severely the analytical power and consequently also the practical usefulness of national input-output computations, particularly for the small and the developing economies in whose internal balance exports and imports play an important and frequently even a dominant role.

Establishment of effective statistical and analytical links between the national input-output tables of countries trading with each other would obviously increase the usefulness of the factual information contained in each one of these tables. The lively discussion of the international standardization of input-output statistics summarized in the last chapter of this volume deserves, because of that, particular attention. A proper conceptual and numerical alignment of the import and export figures entered in the tables of interindustrial flows prepared for individual countries would represent a most significant advance in the development of input-output techniques.

In the name of the Sponsoring Committee of the Geneva Conference I want to thank Professor Tibor Barna for the effective discharge of his responsibilities as Chairman of the Editorial Committee; Dr. Zoltán Kenessey and Professor William Abraham cooperated with him in the performance of that demanding task.

REFERENCES

[1] The Netherlands Economic Institute, ed., *Input-Output Relations*, Proceedings of a Conference on Inter-industrial Relations held at Driebergen, Holland. (Leiden, 1953.)

[2] Barna, Tibor, ed., *The Structural Interdependence of the Economy*, Proceedings of an International Conference on Input-Output Analysis, Varenna, 27 June–10 July 1954. (New York and Milano, 1956.)

Contents

List of Contributors

*The position of contributors given is that at the
time of the conference*

ABDEL MEGUID, A. R., Director of Research, Bank of Alexandria, Cairo.

ABRAHAM, WILLIAM I., Statistical Office, United Nations.

AUKRUST, ODD, Director of Research, Central Bureau of Statistics of Norway.

BALBOA, MANUEL, Director, Economic Development and Research Division, Economic Commission for Latin America.

BARNA, TIBOR, Assistant Director, National Institute of Economic and Social Research, London.

BRUNO, MICHAEL, Research Department, Bank of Israel.

CAO-PINNA, VERA, Lecturer, University of Rome.

CARTER, ANNE P., Senior Research Associate, Harvard Economic Research Project, Harvard University, U.S.A.

CHENERY, HOLLIS B., Professor of Economics, Stanford University, U.S.A.

DAY, RICHARD H., Economic Research Service, U.S. Department of Agriculture.

DELANGE, GEORGES, Department of Economic and Financial Research, Ministry of Finance, Paris.

ELEISH, GAMAL, Head of Input-Output Unit, National Planning Commission, Cairo.

FOX, KARL A., Head, Department of Economics and Sociology, Iowa State University, U.S.A.

GHOSH, AMBICA, Reader in Economics, Jadavpur University, Calcutta, India.

GOLDMAN, MORRIS, Office of Business Economics, U. S. Department of Commerce,

HIRSCH, WERNER Z., Professor of Economics and Director of the Institute for Urban and Regional Studies, Washington University, St. Louis, U.S.A.

HOFFENBERG, MARVIN, Operations Research Office, Johns Hopkins University, U.S.A.

ISARD, WALTER, Professor of Regional Science, Wharton School of Finance and Commerce, University of Pennsylvania, U.S.A.

KENESSEY, ZOLTÁN, Chief of Section, Hungarian Central Statistical Office

KOMIYA, RYUTARO, Assistant Professor, Faculty of Economics, University of Tokyo.

LEONTIEF, WASSILY, Professor of Economics and Director of Harvard Economic Research Project, Harvard University, U.S.A.

LIEBLING, HERMAN, Director of Economic Studies, National Science Foundation, Washington.

MATHUR, PURUSHOTTAM N., Professor, Gokhale Institute of Politics and Economics, Poona, India.

MYCIELSKI, JERZY, Institute of Physics, Polish Academy of Sciences.

NEMCHINOV, V. S., Director of the Laboratory of Economic-Mathematical Sciences, Academy of Sciences of the U.S.S.R.

NOVAK, ANTE, Director, Federal Statistical Office, Belgrade.

REY, KRZYSZTOF, Economic Adviser, Computing Centre, Polish Academy of Sciences.

ROELANTS DU VIVIER, B., O.E.E.C., Paris.

SENGUPTA, J. K., Fulbright Fellow at Iowa State University (U.S. Educational Foundation in India).

SEVALDSON, PER, Central Bureau of Statistics of Norway

SMOLENSKY, EUGENE, Assistant Professor of Economics, Haverford College, U.S.A.

STROUT, ALAN, Technical Associate, Harvard Economic Research Project, Harvard University, U.S.A.

TRZECIAKOWSKI, WITOLD, Head of Research Project, Polish Ministry of Foreign Trade.

UCHIDA, TADAO, Assistant Professor, Faculty of General Education, University of Tokyo.

WATANABE, TSUNEHIKO, Research Center in Economic Growth, Stanford University, U.S.A.

Introduction

by TIBOR BARNA

The title of this volume of papers, *Structural Interdependence and Economic Development*, underlines the most important aspect of the use made today of the techniques associated with the name of Wassily Leontief, that is, their application to studies and to programmes of economic development.

In retrospect, Leontief's input-output method appears to have been one of the most fruitful contributions to both theoretical and empirical economics, and one which has exercised, ever since the publication of his first results in 1936, a stimulating influence on economists and statisticians in many countries. As is the case of inventions in other fields, Leontief's invention was brought to full fruition by a combination of favourable circumstances and the energy of the inventor himself.

An invention achieves success if, on the one hand, it meets a social need, and, on the other, if there are suitable materials and processes available for its application. In many instances it takes a long time for an invention to bear fruit if the materials and processes needed for its application are still primitive; but often the invention itself stimulates research into the required materials and processes.

When Leontief, in 1931, began his study for the United States, 'the objective prospects of completing it successfully were anything but bright.'[1] And the success of the method, when the results were first presented, was by no means immediate. The post-war period, however, made circumstances favourable. In countries like Norway, the Netherlands and Italy, much use was made of the input-output method in the reconstruction period. Further, as countries in Asia and Africa embarked on development programmes, they mostly used input-output techniques from the beginning.

Just when the need for the input-output method was growing, the development of electronic computers made possible the practical application of input-output models to empirical problems. It became less necessary for economists to limit their efforts because of difficulties in computation; they could now embark on more ambitious compilations of statistics and on a fuller analysis of the economy.

[1] Quoted from a letter written by Leontief in 1947 when the study for Britain was started.

It is in the field of statistics that the most interesting results are observable, for the input-output method not only made use of the growing volume of economic statistics which became available in the post-war period but, by its very nature, stimulated the ❨collection and organization of statistics in a consistent, rational manner. This is said to be one of the important advantages of the input-output table in a statistically advanced country like Norway. But even in countries, like Egypt, where previously some authorities believed that not enough statistics existed for an analysis of the economy, the actual application of the input-output method demonstrated that 'the data necessary for an input-output table were dispersed rather than scarce'.[1]

The spread of Leontief's ideas and methods is evident from an examination of the attendances at the three *ad hoc* international input-output conferences which have taken place. In 1950, at Driebergen, in the Netherlands, there were 15 non-Dutch participants; the papers eventually published were contributed by authors from the United States, the Netherlands, Norway and Britain. In 1954, at Varenna, in Italy, there were 25 non-Italian participants, and authors from Denmark, France and Italy also contributed to the proceedings. In 1961, at the Geneva conference the attendance was some 240, with about 100 actively participating in the discussions. And they came from 41 countries; from capitalist and communist countries, from developed and underdeveloped countries alike. They represented an international fraternity of economists and statisticians, trying to talk a common language and trying to learn from each other irrespective of political divisions.

The years between these international conferences have witnessed not only a geographical expansion of the method but also a considerable shift in emphasis and interest. For one thing, the development of electronic computers has greatly lessened the effort devoted to computational problems which are now cheaply and efficiently solved by machines. Further, in recent years there has been much less discussion about abstract problems, such as the constancy of the input-output coefficients, and more empirical research into actual variations in these coefficients, as represented by papers in Part IV of this volume. But the most important development is the practical application of the input-output model to national economic planning, as described in papers on communist, capitalist, and underdeveloped countries in Part III. This preoccupation with a forward-looking application of the method is admirable since at each stage one is forced to ask whether a possible

[1] See p. 202 below.

theoretical refinement in the model is capable of being implemented, or is indeed necessary, and whether for practical purposes a simple form of the model will work.

It is in fact the compromise between an elaborate theoretical structure and an oversimplified statistical description of the economy which is the essence of the input-output and related techniques. Until recently the gap between the theoretical economist, with his general model containing innumerable parameters and variables, and the working statistician, with his global national income or output estimates, has appeared unbridgeable. The method used by all papers in this volume represents a great simplification of theoretical models but a considerable elaboration and refinement of statistical data, to the point where theory and empirical implementation meet. On the theoretical side we have had in the past general equilibrium models like that of Walras and on the empirical side, among the most elaborate early attempts, the Soviet national accounts for 1923–4; as Nemchinov points out 'Leontief's merit consists in expressing the interindustry production relations mathematically, and especially in the synthesis of the balance-sheet method and linear programming.'[1]

The application of the synthesis mentioned in the above paragraph is well illustrated in Chapter 1 by Chenery. While some years ago the relative merits of input-output analysis and linear programming were hotly debated, Chenery now suggests a compromise between the two methods. For the purposes of development programming input-output models of the classical type are not satisfactory; but, on the other hand, it is not practicable to expect to find in the less developed countries the full amount of information needed for a linear programming framework. Chenery shows how the input-output and the programming techniques may be used jointly so as to check and to modify each other's results. While Chenery's results are applicable particularly to the long-term development of non-industrial countries, in Chapter 2 Mycielski, Rey and Trzeciakowski deal with a short-term planning problem. Their paper is a notable example of the application of rigorous mathematical techniques to the solution of economic problems in socialist countries; again, a compromise is sought between the cruder input-output analysis and the programming techniques which in themselves are too ambitious to be practicable. The three Polish authors attempt to devise rules whereby in a centrally planned economy decentralised decisions may be taken; for instance, managers of enterprises have to take decisions on

[1] See p. 177 below.

imports and exports in such a way that the trading pattern of the country should be optimal from a national point of view. The authors solve the problem, in the short-term case, in an abstract form but, as they point out, the organizational problem of decentralization is still unsolved.

Mathur, in Chapter 3, also deals with an important problem in a highly abstract form. He poses the problem of a less developed country like India adopting the technology of a developed country like the United States. He then examines the efficient path of transformation from the old to the new technology under alternative definitions of an optimum solution. He shows, by way of illustration rather than by way of actual examples, how the pattern of investment changes if profits including interest instead of profits excluding interest are maximised. He also illustrates the important role which foreign loans could play in development.

Chapter 4 by Fox and Chapter 5 by Sengupta both investigate a common problem: whether it is valid for certain purposes to divide the economy into two sectors, agriculture and allied industries on the one hand and the rest of the economy on the other. Fox argues that in the advanced economy of the United States the agricultural complex is relatively independent from the rest of the economy and thus it is possible to analyse agricultural problems without paying close attention to interdependence between agriculture and industry. Sengupta makes the same point for the less developed economy of India, although there agriculture supplies inputs to industry rather than the other way round. (However, Day argues that in both cases there is interdependence via the household sector.) Having stated the case for partial analysis within the input-output framework, Fox deals with some of the problems that arise in a fine analysis of the agriculture and food complex; he shows the possibility of reconciling process analysis for agriculture with an input-output model for the whole economy. Sengupta, on the other hand, is interested in the application of two-sector models for a study of economic growth. The behaviour of agriculture, in an underdeveloped country in particular, is less predicatable than that of industry; he shows that in a two-sector model it is not difficult to allow for the stochastic elements. Like Fox, although from a different point of view, Sengupta also elaborates the combination of programming and input-output techniques.

The five chapters on models of the economy thus adopt a very similar attitude. The authors, although writing in abstract terms, are each concerned with real problems of economic planning and decision taking. They do not consider that the input-output model is sufficient for their purposes, nor do they consider that programming techniques on a full scale are feasible; hence in each case they elaborate methods which are more complicated than the simple input-output method, but not so complicated as to defy empirical implementation. There is no doubt that the eyes of each of the authors are focussed on the eventual empirical implementation of their models.

The papers in Part II are also concerned with models but here the interest is in regional application. This aspect of input-output and related techniques has gained increasing attention in a number of countries. The three papers illustrate three different techniques: Isard and Smolensky are concerned with the role of input-output analysis in over-all regional planning; Leontief attempts a description of a multi-regional system and explores the validity of simplifying working assumptions for such a system; Hirsch is interested in application to particular urban problems such as local finances.

In Part III the emphasis of the papers is switched from theory to application on a national scale. The interest of each of the authors is in the use of input-output techniques in a forward-looking analysis of the national economy. All modern governments are planning the future of the economy, although the content of planning and the framework in which planning takes place vary enormously from country to country, and the authors put forward the view that for this purpose input-output and related techniques are useful. This is true, perhaps obviously so, for the Soviet Union; true for capitalist countries which engage in long-term planning exercises, here represented by France; and also true, as the authors stress, for developing economies like Egypt, Israel and the Latin American countries.

Nemchinov's authoritative statement covers wide ground, the application of statistical and mathematical techniques in the process of planning in the Soviet Union. It is made clear that these are techniques which are not pursued for their own sake but as aids towards the achievement of political and social objectives.

The Soviet Union has a record of some 35 years of practical planning, and by now a vast amount of experience has been built up. It is, however, only in recent years that this experience has been systematized and that empirical models of the economy have been built. Soviet economist may have been slow in developing such models and in the application of electronic computers to them, but Nemchinov's paper leaves no doubt that work is now proceeding on a wide front and with the use of large resources. Much of the methods described here, such as the analysis of regional economies, are to be employed for the first time in the Soviet Union.

The experience of France with central planning is of more recent origin, beginning with the Monnet plans after the war, but it is already such that other countries, like Britain, are attempting to draw upon it. In the course of a few years the French have adapted the input-output technique to their own purposes, having in view its practical use in short-term forecasting and longer-term planning. Delange's paper deals mainly with the technical side of the methods, most of which were developed in the Ministry of Finance; for a description of the broader aspects of planning in France reference should be made to other publications.[1]

Tha papers on Egypt, Israel and the Latin American countries show remarkable similarities in the use which is made of input-output models in development programming. In each case development implies industrialization and in each case industrialization requires imports of machinery and equipment but is leading to the creation of import-saving industries in other directions. The input-output table is of great help in judging the nature of the expected development and in analysing discrepancies between plans and their realization.

The papers included in this volume describe the use of input-output analysis in a few countries only. Similar work is proceeding in other countries also. Current research in Hungary and neighbouring countries was described in papers read at an international conference in Budapest in June 1961, and among the less developed European countries, research is in an advanced state in Greece and Spain.

Turning to the papers on problems of estimation and statistics, in Part IV, here again it is interesting to note the common ground between the authors. It is by now generally recognized that input-output coefficients are not constant. But there is a great deal of stability in these coefficients and the practical question is to what extent and with what modifications the input-output model may be used in empirical applications. Chapters 14, 15 and 16 are in fact addressed to this practical question. In Japan there is a well-known difference between large and small establishments, and Komiya and Uchida explore the variation in the labour coefficients in two industries. Anne Carter examines the effects of a changing technology on the coefficients for some American industries. She presents a mathematical formulation of alternative approaches to the problem of estimation and then tests empirically, with a few detailed examples, which method appears most suitable. Sevaldson

[1] See p. 198 below.

studies the variation of some of the main coefficients in two Norwegian industries in an attempt to give a systematic explanation of such variations. These papers deal with small areas of the economy in microscopic detail and are in fact excellent examples of the methods by which a rigorous analysis of empirical evidence may contribute to a better understanding of structural changes in the economy and to more accurate forecasting of such changes.

Finally, in the last chapter we have a debate between those who advocate a great deal and those who advocate only a limited degree of international standardization of input-output statistics. The need for some form of international agreement on concepts, definitions and classification is obvious, and it would be a pity if in this relatively new field of economic and statistical research no such agreement were to be reached. The method of interregional analysis could then be applied on the international scale. For instance, all developing countries are planning import-saving industries and are planning additional exports to the rest of the world. There is some danger that import saving may be carried too far, at the expense of international specialization, as well as some danger that they may not be able to export to each other the commodities and the quantities planned.

The more extreme view in favour of standardization is expressed by authors connected with international organizations; their impatience with differences in national practices is understandable. The more modest approach is favoured by statisticians working in national offices. Already much practical exchange of views between statisticians has taken place in the Conference of European Statisticians, meeting under the auspices of the U.N. Economic Commission for Europe. Irrespective of national and political differences working statisticians are striving towards common goals: the better understanding of economic processes and the supply of better information for those taking decisions.

PART I

Models of Economic Development

CHAPTER 1

The Use of Interindustry Analysis in Development Programming[1]

by HOLLIS B. CHENERY

1. *Introduction*

The current efforts to promote the growth of the less developed economies have stimulated great interest in interindustry analysis, and input-output studies have been completed in more than a dozen such countries. The main purpose of this research has been to analyse development possibilities and to provide a better basis for government policy.

Increasing experience with policies of deliberate economic development has shown the difficulty of anticipating the changes that take place in the composition of demand, production and trade as income rises. Since conventional methods of aggregate and partial analysis are inadequate to deal with these interrelated changes, bottlenecks frequently accompany efforts to promote more rapid growth. Experience with structural imbalance, in which shortages occur in some sectors and surpluses in others, is one of the most persuasive arguments for studies of structural interdependence.

Although the need for interindustry analysis is now widely recognized, there is general dissatisfaction with the use of the classical input-output model for underdeveloped economies. It is commonly believed that the establishment of new industries, the adoption of new techniques in place of old, and rapid change in the composition of output within sectors will more seriously affect the stability of input coefficients in developing economies than in mature industrial countries. Furthermore, a more flexible analytical technique is required to determine which structural changes are most desirable.

The need to study alternative allocations of investment and other resources suggests the use of a linear programming framework instead of the Leontief model. This method has not yet been adopted in any country, although several small-scale experiments have been made with

[1] I am indebted to Tsunehiko Watanabe for helpful comments.

mathematical programming techniques. Instead, it is customary to introduce changes in the input structure of the Leontief model on the basis of partial analysis. It is unlikely, however, that this piecemeal modification of the input structure will lead to the best estimate of development possibilities.

The main purpose of this paper is to rationalize the *ad hoc* programming procedures that have been developed and to suggest ways in which they can be carried out more systematically. The proposed methods take into account existing limitations on statistical resources in less developed countries, in which the feasible industry breakdown rarely exceeds 40 to 50 sectors. One of the central problems is to relate this sector framework to the detailed project analysis which is required in implementing development plans.

2. *Evolution of the Interindustry Structure*

Since it is sometimes implied that underdeveloped economies are so simple that interindustry analysis is not needed,[1] it is useful to consider first the typical structure of a low-income country and its evolution as income rises. Countries having *per capita* incomes of under $100 — a category which includes much of Asia and Africa — normally derive only 10 to 12 per cent of their income from manufacturing and 50 to 60 per cent from primary production.[2] More than half of manufacturing industry consists of food processing and textiles, whose main inputs come directly from agriculture. Of the remaining intermediate goods, more than half are imported. As a result of these factors, intermediate demand for manufactured goods accounts for only 5 to 6 per cent of the total demand for goods and services in the economy, and only half of this amount is supplied from domestic sources. Intermediate demand for primary products and services comprises another 20 per cent or so of total demand, but these sectors have less feedback to the rest of the economy and so are less important to interindustry analysis.

As *per capita* income rises, a number of structural changes take place whose combined effect is to increase the intermediate demand for manufactured goods very rapidly. (i) Final demand for manufactured goods (for consumption and investment) increases considerably more rapidly than *per capita* income, with an average income elasticity of

---

[1] This view is found in Peacock and Dosser [1] and in the first ECAFE report on development planning [2].

[2] These and other estimates of the typical industry structure are taken from my 'Patterns of Industrial Growth' [3], which was based on regression analyses of a sample of 50 countries at all income levels.

about 1·35 [3, Table 6]; (ii) Factory production replaces handicraft methods, producing an increase in demand for machinery and other producer goods; and (iii) Domestic production of manufactured goods replaces imports, and manufacturing output therefore rises more rapidly than total demand.

These factors result in a combined elasticity of manufacturing output with respect to income level of about 1·9 at income levels below $200 and of about 2·3 for investment goods and intermediate products.

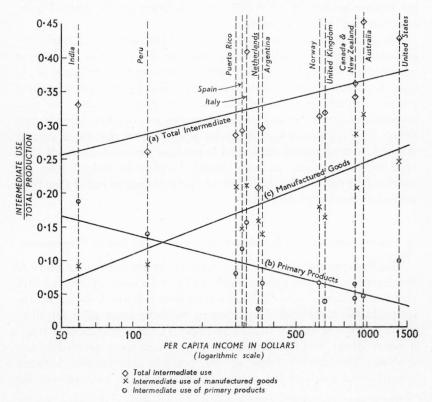

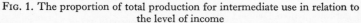

FIG. 1. The proportion of total production for intermediate use in relation to the level of income

The effects of industrialization on intermediate demand are summarized in the regression lines of Figure 1 for a sample of countries at various income levels.[1] Although input-output studies vary somewhat

[1] These figures result from a recalculation of the regressions in [3] for 27 countries having incomes less than $200 *per capita*.
Equations for the regression lines shown are:

in concept and are not strictly comparable, the rapid increase in intermediate demand for manufactured goods with higher income level is
clearly shown by the regression line (c). The rise of domestic production
is even more rapid. Without disputing the conclusion of Peacock and
Dosser [1] as to the limited usefulness of input-output analysis in
primitive economies like Tanganyika, it can be asserted that the industrial
sectors become much more interdependent as income levels rise and
that interindustry analysis may be quite important for countries having
per capita incomes of $200–300, or even lower in the case of large
countries like India and Pakistan.

The share of intermediate demand in total production understates the
proportion of total capital formation that is needed to supply increases in
intermediate demand. Here the relevant measure is the *increase in the
domestic output* of intermediate goods multiplied by the capital required
per unit of increase in output. On this basis, probably half of the total
investment in even very low income countries goes to satisfy intermediate
demands. This proportion contrasts sharply with the much smaller
share of existing capital stock used to produce intermediate goods. The
need for interindustry analysis should therefore be judged from the
nature of the demand for the output of new investments rather than from
the present economic structure.

3. *Compromises between Input-Output Analysis and Linear Programming*

The changes that typically take place in the productive structure of
developing economies, together with the limited amount of interindustry
statistics available, indicate the characteristics that are desirable for the
interindustry framework. In particular, the latter must allow for alternative sources of supply (including imports), for aggregation of interindustry effects, and for specific connections with more detailed project
analysis. This section takes up the possible compromises between
input-output and activity analysis models and the next section the

---

(a) $\dfrac{\text{Total Intermediate Demand}}{\text{Total Production}} = W_T = 0\cdot1038 + 0\cdot0869 \log Y$
$\qquad\qquad\qquad\qquad\qquad\quad (0\cdot0177)\quad (0\cdot0110)$

(b) $\dfrac{\text{Primary Intermediate Demand}}{\text{Total Production}} = W_I = 0\cdot3276 - 0\cdot0930 \log Y$
$\qquad\qquad\qquad\qquad\qquad\quad (0\cdot0433)\quad (0\cdot0268)$

(c) $\dfrac{\text{Manufactured Intermediate Demand}}{\text{Total Production}} = W_M = -0\cdot1718 + 0\cdot1378 \log Y$
$\qquad\qquad\qquad\qquad\qquad\qquad (0\cdot0516)\quad (0\cdot0319)$

where Y is *per capita* income. Based on data from Watanabe [4].

properties of the aggregated models that result. Section 5 takes up the choice of projects within the interindustry framework.

Linear programming differs from Leontief's input-output model [5] in its consideration of alternative sources of supply for given commodities and in its use of a comprehensive optimizing procedure to determine the best combination of supply activities. In development planning the most important generalization of the input-output model is the addition of alternative activities, including the alternative of importing. It will usually be necessary, however, to use a rough approximation to the programming procedure for choosing among activities. The result will be a compromise between the original input-output formulation and thoroughgoing linear programming.

In Table 1 four possible stages between input-output and linear programming are suggested. They differ in the method used to select activities or projects within each sector and in the extent to which the interindustry model is used to calculate prices (or total factor use) for this purpose. The four stages suggested are as follows:

TABLE 1

Suggested Compromises between Input-Output Analysis and Linear Programming

Nature of model	Price calculations	Choice criterion	Feasibility of quantity solution
1. Input-Output	None	Partial analysis for each sector	Commodities only
2. Mixed	Exogenously determined accounting prices for foreign exchange, labour, capital	Profitability of projects using accounting prices for direct inputs	Commodities only
3. Mixed	Accounting prices calculated from the model for factors only	Same	Commodities and primary factors
4. Linear programming	Shadow prices for factors and commodities calculated from the model	Profitability of activities (Simplex Criterion)	Commodities and factors

(1) The first model assumes that there are a number of activities for producing or importing the commodities included in a given industrial sector. Starting from the combination used in the base year, as observed in the input-output table, changes in production techniques and in the proportions of production and imports are

introduced on the basis of an independent analysis for each sector. A similar method has been used by Leontief and Carter[1] to study past technological change, using input-output tables at successive dates. The empirical methods of analysing import substitution described in Section 5 are examples of this procedure in that a new average input structure is determined from a set of decisions on the proportion of demand for each commodity to be supplied from domestic sources.

(2) The second step toward linear programming is the application of a uniform criterion to the choice of activities in each sector. The criterion used in linear programming is the profitability of each activity as determined by the shadow prices corresponding to a given solution. The simplest approximation is to estimate accounting prices for direct factor inputs only, as suggested by Tinbergen [6], and then to evaluate the profitability of alternative sources of supply of each commodity (including imports) on this basis. Capital intensity or other partial investment criteria can also be used.[2]

The combination of activities or projects selected for each sector results in a new ratio of domestic production to imports and can also be used to determine new average input coefficients where necessary. From this data, an input-output solution can be calculated that is consistent with the demand limitations in the model. It may or may not be consistent with the assumed supply of capital and labour or the balance of payments limitation.

(3) The next step toward linear programming consists in further adjusting the choice of activities to be consistent with the factor limitations. This can be done on the basis of new accounting prices for the primary factors determined from the excess demands revealed in step (2), using an iterative procedure outlined in [8]. In practice, a number of other elements of judgment also enter into the revision process at this point. The new accounting prices can also be used to evaluate any activities not considered previously.

(4) The last step consists in computing shadow prices for commodities as well as for primary inputs. This permits the application of the simplex criterion of linear programming to all inputs instead of considering only the costs of the factors used directly. At this point, the model may properly be called a linear programming model, although it retains the aggregation into industries

---

[1] Suggested in [5] and described in Chapter 15 below.
[2] Alternative partial criteria are discussed in [7].

that is characteristic of input-output analysis. This type of model is discussed more fully in [8] and [9].

After the fourth step, progress toward a more complete programming model is largely a question of disaggregation. It is, however, in my judgment not desirable to disaggregate the interindustry framework of a development programme beyond 40 to 50 sectors because it becomes increasingly hard to relate it to the decision-making units and sources of data and to evaluate the results.[1] Instead of a single comprehensive programming model, an interindustry framework combined with a series of separate sector analyses is likely to be more workable.[2]

Two types of error are introduced by retaining an industry basis for programming instead of utilizing a more detailed commodity breakdown: (i) errors in determining profitability (efficiency), and (ii) errors in determining supply and demand (consistency). The nature of these errors is discussed in the next section. Offsetting them is the fact that sector studies of important industries will complement the interindustry analysis and will serve to correct the more important changes in input structure.

4. *Properties of an Aggregated Programming Model*

It was suggested in the preceding section that the extremely detailed industry model that would be needed for specific resource decisions probably would not be an efficient analytical tool, and it would certainly not be statistically feasible in the less developed countries. An intermediate stage of sector analysis is needed to prevent the intersector model from becoming too unwieldy and to introduce other factors that do not fit readily into interindustry analysis. Although this two-stage procedure has been followed in several cases in which input-output methods have been used in formulating development programmes [12, 13, 14, 15 and Chapter 12 below], there seems to have been no attempt to formalize the relationship between interindustry analysis on the one hand and sector and project analysis on the other.

The elements that must be fitted together in an analysis of development possibilities are: (i) individual projects,[3] or units of resource use;

---

[1] Frisch in [10] is an advocate of more thoroughgoing use of linear programming. The programming model of Sandee [11] fits, however, my stage 4.

[2] This applies to the form in which this model is used rather than to the collection of basic data. For the latter purpose, a breakdown into several hundred commodities is desirable.

[3] For analytical convenience, any practical resource unit may be defined as a 'project', whether it is the construction of a new plant, the extension of an old one, or the introduction of a new agricultural technique.

(ii) projections of demand and supply for individual commodities, and
(iii) economy-wide analyses of intersector relations, balance of payments,
and factor use. The commodity breakdown in (ii) must be sufficiently
detailed to enable decisions to be made on the choice of projects and the
scale of output, which may require the subdivision of an input-output
model of 30 or 40 sectors into 20 or 30 commodities per sector.[1] For
some commodities, it will be possible (and desirable) to break down
intermediate use by commodity; for others only a breakdown of total
intermediate use will be feasible.

This type of interindustry framework is useful for two purposes: to
determine intermediate demands for commodities and to estimate
accounting prices and requirements for labour, capital and imports.
Different types of aggregation error are introduced in each case, as may
be shown by comparison with a more detailed model. For the demand
analysis, the prediction of total demand D_i in a hypothetical input-
output model having n commodities and n corresponding sub-sectors
would be:

$$D_i = Y_i + \sum_j a_{ij}^k X_j^k \qquad \begin{aligned} &(k=1, \dots, m) \\ &(i=1, \dots, n) \\ &(j=1, \dots, n) \end{aligned} \qquad (1)$$

If we form an $n \times m$ matrix by combining all sub-sectors with a superscript k into sector k, but do not aggregate commodities, the predicted
demand for commodity i would be:

$$D_i = Y_i + \sum_k A_{ik} X_k \qquad \begin{aligned} &(i=1, \dots, n) \\ &(k=1, \dots, m) \end{aligned} \qquad (2)$$

where A_{ik} is the weighted average of the input coefficients of commodity
i in the sub-sectors that are combined into industry k, using base-year
outputs as weights:

$$A_{ik} = \frac{X_{ik}}{X_k} = \frac{\sum_j a_{ij}^k X_j^k}{\sum X_j^k}.$$

The summation is carried out for all sub-sectors in industry k.

According to the usual principles of aggregation if the rate of growth
of each sub-sector of industry k is the same or if all the a_{ij} in industry k

[1] In the most detailed published statement of this type of analysis that is known to me,
that of the Economic Commission for Latin America for Peru [15], manufacturing was
broken down into 17 industries for purposes of interindustry analysis, and these were
in turn broken down into several hundred commodities to determine domestic production possibilities. In most plans only the aggregate results are published, so it is
difficult to make detailed comparisons.

are the same, the intermediate demand predicted by equation (2) will be the same as that predicted by equation (1).[1] If not, the magnitude of the error depends on the differences in the growth rates and in the a_{ij}^k.

Aggregation of commodities into sectors has a similar effect on the estimate of factor use in different activities or projects. Assume the same hypothetical $n \times n$ input-output model with a direct use of capital per unit of output in activity j of k_j and a total use of capital per unit of output of K_j. The equation for the total use of capital K_j is then analagous to equation (1) for total demand:

$$K_j = k_j + \sum_i a_{ij}^l K_i^l \qquad (i = 1, \dots, n) \qquad (3)$$

where k_j is the direct capital-output ratio. When the i commodities are aggregated into m sectors, in which sector l is composed of the inputs having the superscript l, the equation for total capital use in activity j becomes:

$$K_j = k_j + \sum_l A_{lj} K_l \qquad (l = 1, \dots, m) \qquad (4)$$

where $A_{lj} = \sum_i a_{ij}^l$. The result will be the same as that of equation (3) if the aggregate unit capital use K_l is equal to the weighted average of the unit capital use K_i^l calculated for the component commodities of industry l in the detailed model; i.e. if:

$$K_l = \frac{\sum_i a_{ij}^l K_i^l}{\sum_i a_{ij}^l}.$$

Equations (2) and (4) are symmetrical in form; they combine a detailed analysis of direct (final) demand and direct factor use with an aggregated analysis of indirect (intermediate) demand and indirect factor use. The averaging effect that is introduced by aggregation reduces the differences among commodities and activities in the same sector. It will preserve differences due to the fact that direct factor use and direct demand are a large proportion of total factor use and total demand.

5. *Project Analysis and Overall Balance*

The initial attempts at planning in most countries have started from a consideration of individual projects. This starting point has led to

---

[1] For commodities in which a within-sector breakdown is only made of total intermediate demand, the average proportion of commodity i in sector k is applied to all intermediate uses, and the effects of changes in the composition of intermediate demand for each commodity are averaged out.

an extensive discussion of investment priorities for underdeveloped countries, which has been conducted almost exclusively in terms of partial analysis. Where it has been used, input-output analysis has usually been added later as a way of making the projects that had been selected initially by partial analysis consistent with each other. In the centrally planned economies, the method of material balances, which establishes balances of supply and demand in physical terms for a large number of commodities, is used for the same purpose [16]. Neither of these procedures ensures that an optimum result has been attained, however, unless the initial assumptions of the project analysis are re-examined.

The formulation of a development programme by starting from a study of individual projects has sometimes been called the 'bottom up' approach [2], in contrast to the 'top down' method which starts from aggregate projections and an overall analysis of economic interdependence. Inconsistencies between the two are inevitable because each takes into account some information that is ignored in the other. The final development programme must reconcile the specific aspects of project analysis — scale and location of plants, effects of natural resources, etc. — with the requirements of consistency and balance that are inherent in overall programming. This section examines the effect on the procedures for project analysis using the programming framework outlined in the previous section.[1]

Project analysis and linear programming

The main criteria used in the two contrasting approaches to planning may be summarized as: (i) the requirement that for all commodities and productive factors supply should be at least as great as demand and (ii) the requirement that each commodity should be supplied at lowest social cost. If the welfare objectives of the economy can be described in terms of an objective function with a quantitative set of restraints, the two sets of requirements can be reconciled by methods of mathematical — linear or non-linear — programming.

The principal obstacle to the adoption of the programming solution is the lack of information and the high cost of increasing it.[2] Given the existing lack of data, the mathematical programming formulation does not correspond to the planner's view of his problem. The simplex

---

[1] I shall not discuss the many alternative approaches to project evaluation and investment priorities, which I have surveyed in [7]. The relation of the accounting price procedure used in this paper to other methods of partial analysis is indicated there.

[2] The rapid advances in computers and computing techniques in the past few years make the problems of calculation much less important.

method and other procedures for solving programming models determine the optimum choice among specified activities of production, importing, investment, etc. Only a few of these potential activities can be described by the planner with any accuracy, however, and the available engineering and economic research facilities only permit him to extend his knowledge to a limited degree in formulating a given programme. Under these circumstances, the relations between project analysis and overall programming assume great importance. If all of the information were provided at the start, the choice among various optimizing techniques could be made on the basis of computational convenience alone. However, if the programming procedure must also serve as a guide to further research into technological and economic alternatives, the basis for choice becomes quite different.

Under these circumstances, it is very likely that project analysis based on informed judgment will give a better first approximation than a mechanical procedure such as the simplex method. One approach that has been used in practice in several countries is to start from an existing input-output model for the base year and to assume a probable value for the maximum rate of growth. This permits the maximizing problem to be converted into a (simpler) problem of minimizing the use of one of the inputs — capital or foreign exchange — subject to restrictions on the final demand and the labour and other resources available. The next step is to utilize the partial analysis of investment projects to guess at the optimum proportions of production and imports in each sector. In some sectors, this estimate may require a revision if the input-output coefficients of the industry did not exist or if it produced a very different set of products; otherwise the initial input coefficients can be used as an approximation to the future structure of the industry. On the basis of these assumptions, an input-output solution can be made in order to test the consistency of the assumptions with the limitations on the balance of payments and the supply of capital and labour.

The result of this first approximation will be a set of surpluses and deficits for the primary inputs. As shown in [8], these can be used with some version of the Arrow-Hurwicz gradient method to revise the prices of the primary inputs, which are then used to recompute the profitability of investment projects in each sector. For this purpose, the 'simplex criterion' for activity j (which is assumed to produce one unit of output j) can be stated either in terms of the prices of inputs, as in equation (5), or in terms of the total use of capital and labour, as in equation (6):

$$\pi_j = P_j - [\sum_i A_{ij} P_i + n_j P_n + k_j P_k] \tag{5}$$

$$\pi_j = P_j - [N_j P_n + K_j P_k] \qquad (6)$$

where π_j is the social profitability of activity j; P_l, P_n and P_k are shadow prices of commodity l, labour and capital; N_j and K_j are the total direct and indirect use of labour and capital in activity j. In this procedure, the same criterion is applied to the choice of techniques for producing a given commodity and the choice between projects in different sectors. The latter choice involves a comparison of each project to the alternative of importing, and so the estimate of the shadow price of foreign exchange plays a critical role, as shown in [9].

This general procedure can be used with any of the compromises between input-output analysis and linear programming that were suggested in Section 3, above. In the crudest approximation, the choice of projects for import substitution and exports is made intuitively in the light of the magnitude of the payments deficit shown in the input-output solution. A new input-output solution can be computed to determine how large the remaining deficit in the balance of payments is and whether the supply of investment resources has been exhausted. This is roughly the procedure followed in the input-output projections for Colombia [13], Argentina [14], Peru [15], and Israel (Chapter 12 below) and set out more explicitly in an ECAFE report on industrial programming methods [17].

Increased accuracy requires that greater use be made of accounting prices for primary factors (stage 2 and 3 of the sequence in Table 1) and for commodities (stage 4). When commodity prices are estimated, it can be shown that the optimum solution is obtained by successive revisions in the profitability of the projects [18].

Effects of economies of scale

It is generally recognized that economies of scale are of much greater importance in underdeveloped countries than in advanced ones because of the smaller markets of the former. The crucial element in the choice between domestic production of a new commodity and continued imports is often the scale at which it can be produced. For intermediate goods, the demand must be determined from interindustry analysis. When such choices exist in several interrelated sectors, the analysis may become quite complex.

The choice among different techniques of production also frequently hinges on the scale of the market. In most types of manufacturing processes — chemical, metallurgical, metal fabricating, etc. — there is a choice between a continuous flow sequence, which can only be used with a given minimum scale of output, and more intermittent types of production. In many industrial sectors, therefore, there will be at least three supply activities to choose from for each commodity; imports, small scale manufacture, and large scale manufacture. The relation of total cost to output level and the variation in the choice of activity with scale are indicated in Figure 2 for a hypothetical industry.[1]

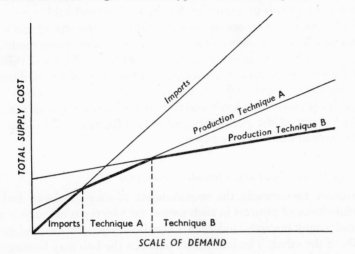

FIG. 2. The effects of economies of scale on the choice of activity in a hypothetical industry

It is well known that economies of scale upset the marginal mechanism for resource allocation, both in a market economy and in mathematical programming. It is necessary to take into account the level of output and total cost as well as marginal cost in determining the optimum solution to a model containing significant economies of scale. While there is as yet no general method of solving programming models embodying scale economies, apart from the enumeration of all possible combinations of production activities, in practice workable approximations can probably be developed. Economies of scale present no problem in the simple input-output model, since there is no choice of activities and the non-linear input functions apply mainly to capital and labour. It is in sectors where there is a choice among imports and several production processes, each having different scale characteristics, that the problem is particularly difficult. Haldi [20] has shown that in this case the optimum pattern of investment over time is likely to be unbalanced since it will pay to continue importing in one sector in order to build a large plant and reap the economies of scale in another.

[1] Based on [19 Fig. 1].

To allow for the effects of economies of scale, it is desirable to consider different production capacities and output levels in sectors where scale economies are important. Projects should be designed for the range of output levels that seems probable on the basis of the preliminary programming solution, and a comparison should be made of alternative programmes (or sub-programmes) for the sectors involved.[1]

The discussion of economies of scale illustrates the type of factor that cannot be adequately allowed for in an overall programming model, but which also cannot be analysed in isolation. Other problems of this type are location, use of natural resources, and use of overhead facilities. In studying these specific aspects, the interindustry analysis provides an indication of production levels and factor use in related sectors, but more detailed study of the peculiarities of particular projects is required to judge the desirability of investments.

The sequence of project and interindustry analysis

In order to reconcile the requirements of sector balance and the optimal choice of projects in each sector, the two types of analysis must proceed simultaneously and each must be revised to incorporate the results of the other. The interaction between the two may be suggested by the following sequence:

(*A*) *Initial interindustry analysis*
1. Final demand estimates.
2. Initial estimates of input-output coefficients and import ratios by sector.
3. Input-output solution based on 1 and 2.
4. Calculation of excess demand for foreign exchange and primary inputs.

(*B*) *Initial project analysis*
1. Initial estimates of accounting prices for labour, capital, and foreign exchange based on A-4.
2. Use of A-3 and B-1 to select the best projects in each sector.
3. Revision of input coefficients and import proportions in A-2.

(*C*) *Revised interindustry analysis*
1. Programming solution(s) based on B-3 and revision of accounting prices after each solution. Change in import proportions based on B-1.

---

[1] A more detailed process analysis approach to this interdependence among plants is outlined in [21].

   2. Revision of initial income and demand targets if necessary and repetition of C-1.

(D) *Revised project analysis*

   1. Use of accounting prices for primary factors and key commodities to re-evaluate the profitability of the projects.

   2. Test of consistency of import substitution and export projects using revised prices.

   3. Analysis of alternative levels of output in sectors having economies of scale.

   4. Adjustment of results of project analysis for technical interrelations among projects.

In any actual planning procedure, these successive revisions go on simultaneously at both the overall and project level.[1] The important aspect is to have the results of one analysis systematically incorporated in the other so that the optimal solution will be approached. In the absence of economies of scale, it can be shown that revision of the project selections and overall programme on this basis will ultimately lead to the best solution. With economies of scale the tests ensure an improvement but there is no guarantee of optimality.

6. *Conclusion*

This paper has been concerned with ways of applying the logic of interindustry analysis to developmental programming, introducing more flexible methods of solution to allow for deficiencies in the data and for the need to exercise judgment. Given the margin of error that exists in estimates of crucial parameters, such as the capital requirements of individual techniques of production, it would be misleading to suggest that mathematical programming can be directly applied to most of the underdeveloped countries. On the other hand, formal programming procedures do furnish a guide to the development of more systematic pragmatic methods that allow for judgment at each step of the analysis. I have tried to show that the logic of programming can be followed with different degrees of precision and can be modified to allow for the possibility of improving the available information at each step. Most of this discussion is of necessity rather speculative, since few underdeveloped countries have reached a stage beyond that of constructing their first input-output table. It is clear, however, that the special characteristics of underdeveloped countries will require substantial

---

[1] This type of iterative procedure is discussed in more detail in [17].

modification in the projection techniques developed for advanced countries. These new techniques are now emerging from practical efforts to increase the flexibility of input-output analysis.

REFERENCES

[1] PEACOCK, A. T. and DOSSER, D., 'Input-Output Analysis in an Under-developed Country, A Case Study,' *Review of Economic Studies*, Oct. 1957, p. 21.

[2] UNITED NATIONS, ECAFE, 'Economic Development and Planning in Asia and the Far East,' *Economic Bulletin for Asia and the Far East*, Vol. VI, No. 3, 1955.

[3] CHENERY, H. B., 'Patterns of Industrial Growth,' *American Economic Review*, 1960, p. 624.

[4] WATANABE, T., 'A Test of the Constancy of Input-Output Coefficients Among Countries,' *International Economic Review*, 1962.

[5] LEONTIEF, W., 'Structural Change,' in Leontief *et. al.*, *Studies in the Structure of the American Economy*, New York, 1953.

[6] TINBERGEN, J., 'The Relevance of Theoretical Criteria in the Selection of Investment Plans,' in M. Millikan, ed., *Investment Criteria and Economic Growth*, Cambridge, Mass. 1955.

[7] CHENERY, H. B., 'Comparative Advantage and Development Policy,' *American Economic Review*, 1961, p. 18.

[8] CHENERY, H. B. and UZAWA, H., 'Non-Linear Programming in Economic Development,' in Arrow, Hurwicz and Uzawa, *Studies in Linear and Non-Linear Programming*, Stanford, 1958.

[9] CHENERY, H. B., 'The Role of Industrialization in Development Programs,' *American Economic Review*, Proceedings, 1955, p. 40.

[10] FRISCH, R., 'A Method of Working Out a Macroeconomic Plan Frame with Particular Reference to the Evaluation of Development Projects, Foreign Trade and Employment,' Oslo, 1958. (Mimeo.)

[11] SANDEE, J., *A Long-Term Planning Model for India*, United Nations, 1959.

[12] CHENERY, H. B., CLARK, P. G. and CAO-PINNA, VERA, *The Structure and Growth of the Italian Economy*, Rome, 1953.

[13] UNITED NATIONS, *Analyses and Projections of Economic Development*, III, *The Economic Development of Colombia*, Geneva, 1957.

[14] UNITED NATIONS, *Analyses and Projections of Economic Development*, V, *The Economic Development of Argentina*, Mexico City, 1960.

[15] UNITED NATIONS, *Analyses and Projections of Economic Development*, VI, *The Industrial Development of Peru*, Mexico City, 1959.

[16] MONTIAS, J. M., 'Planning with Material Balances in Soviet-type Economies,' *American Economic Review*, 1959, p. 963.

[17] UNITED NATIONS, ECAFE, *Formulating Industrial Development Programmes with Special Reference to Asia and the Far East. Report of the Second Group of Experts on Programming Techniques*, Bangkok, 1961.

[18] CHENERY, H. B., 'Development Policies and Programmes,' *Economic Bulletin for Latin America*, March 1958, p. 51.

[19] CHENERY, H. B., 'The Interdependence of Investment Decisions,' in Abramovitz *et. al.*, *The Allocation of Economic Resources*, Stanford, 1959.

[20] HALDI, J., *Economies of Scale and Economic Development*, Stanford, 1960. (Mimeo.)

[21] ISARD, W., SCHOOLER, E. W. and VIETORISZ, T., *Industrial Complex Analysis and Regional Development: A Case Study of Refinery-Petrochemical-Synthetic-Fiber Complexes and Puerto Rico*, New York, 1959.

CHAPTER 2

Decomposition and Optimization of Short-Run Planning in a Planned Economy

by JERZY MYCIELSKI, KRZYSZTOF REY
and WITOLD TRZECIAKOWSKI

1. *Introduction*

Drafting central plans cannot be avoided in any economy striving for planning. The fact that such plans are put into practice proves that it is possible to find a feasible solution even applying traditional methods. However, the feasible solution obtained in practice is usually far from being optimal; the utilization of productive capacities and of foreign trade opportunities is bound to be more or less inefficient. Therefore, to find the optimal solution for the economy as a whole is of specific interest for the underdeveloped countries in view of their limited productive capacities.

To formulate the optimization problem for the economy as a whole is simple, at least in theory. It consists of a set of balance equations for particular commodities and foreign currencies — well known from the input-output technique — supplemented by the objective function. However, because of the huge number of commodities and possible techniques of production, the problem is practically untractable in this form. Two different ways of approach are possible.

The aggregation method consists in reducing the number of equations and variables by aggregating commodities and activities. This however makes the model practically useless for short-run planning since the concepts of production constrains, material inputs, unit costs of production, foreign prices, demand and supply, concern specific goods and not aggregate groups of commodities. Moreover, aggregation involves proceeding with a fixed structure within particular groups. This necessarily reduces drastically the number of degrees of freedom. It is obvious that a loss in the number of degrees of freedom involves losses in capacity utilization.

In order to avoid this deficiency we adopt the second way of approach. The economy can be decomposed into its parts or even into particular enterprises. Then inserting some parameters, having the dimension of prices (and exchange rate), the optimization problems for these parts can be formulated and the method of obtaining the values of the parameters can be given. In this way an optimum for the whole economy can be attained, solving numerous, relatively small, partial problems. This is the topic we shall deal with.

2. *The General Model of Short-Run Planning*

The starting point of the present argument is the necessity to satisfy final demand, for consumption and investment, established in the central plan of development, while minimizing social outlays of labour. The levels of production and foreign trade are the variables, while final demands and the required balance of trade with particular markets are the given constants. Production capacity in the short run is assumed to be fixed.

The general model of the volume and technique of production, as well as the commodity structure of foreign trade and its regional allocation, is described below.

We shall use the following notation:

x_j = The level of productive activity j.

y_k^{Er} = Exports of commodity k to market r (in physical units).

y_k^{Ir} = Imports of commodity k from market r (in physical units).

a_{kj} = The output (with positive sign) or input (with negative sign) of commodity k per unit of activity j.

P_k = Domestic demand for commodity k for consumption and investment.

d_k^{Er} = Export price of a unit of commodity k in foreign currency on the market r (f.o.b. frontier).

d_k^{Ir} = Import price of a unit of commodity k in foreign currency from market r (c.i.f. frontier).

λ_r = The planned balance of trade with market r.

b_j = Maximum capacity of activity j.

π_k^{Er} = Demand on market r for the export of commodity k of the given country.

π_k^{Ir} = Supply on the market r of the commodity k imported by the country.

c_j = Domestic processing costs (labour cost) per unit of activity j in the last stage of processing (costs of raw material and depreciation omitted).

p = The number of productive activities.
m = The number of foreign markets.
n = The number of commodities.

Therefore $\sum_{j=1}^{p} a_{kj}x_j$ is the final product of commodity k.

The condition of satisfying final demands for each consumption and investment good is:

$$\sum_{j=1}^{p} a_{kj}x_j + \sum_{r=1}^{m} y_k^{Ir} - \sum_{r=1}^{m} y_k^{Er} = P_k \quad (k=1, \dots, n). \tag{1}$$

The condition of balancing trade in each foreign market r is:

$$\sum_{k=1}^{n} d_k^{Er} y_k^{Er} - \sum_{k=1}^{n} d_k^{Ir} y_k^{Ir} = \lambda_r \quad (r=1, \dots, m). \tag{2}$$

The boundary conditions are that production is kept within the limits of:

$$0 \leqslant x_j \leqslant b_j \quad (j=1, \dots, p); \tag{3}$$

that exports of commodity k to market r cannot exceed the demand for this commodity in that market:

$$0 \leqslant y_k^{Er} \leqslant \pi_k^{Er}; \tag{4}$$

and that imports of commodity k from market r cannot exceed the supply of this commodity in that market:

$$0 \leqslant y_k^{Ir} \leqslant \pi_k^{Ir} \quad (k=1, \dots, n; r=1, \dots, m). \tag{5}$$

The optimization criterion consists of minimizing aggregate domestic costs

$$\sum_{j=1}^{p} c_j x_j = \text{minimum}. \tag{6}$$

This model, just as other global economic models, cannot be used in such form for practical purposes because of unsurmountable computational difficulties. As it was pointed out above, the way of decomposition of the economy into groups of interrelated activities should be chosen.

In a paper by one of the authors [1], a method of dividing the economy into groups of interrelated commodities was suggested. Optimizing separate groups leads to general optimization through:

(a) deriving from the general model a set of global parameters M^r, which ensure balancing trade with separate foreign currency markets r (the parameters M^r express the marginal amount of domestic currency paid for a unit of the currency of market r);

(b) introducing technical interrelations which limit the production of many groups of commodities.

The solution presented in [1] was however based on the simplifying assumptions that commodities belonging to the group of interrelated activities under consideration are not raw materials for the rest of the economy; and that raw materials used in such a group and originating from outside of this group are produced domestically and do not limit the outputs based on them. These simplifying assumptions are now rejected and we seek for such an optimal solution within the given group which leads to the optimization of the general solution for the economy as a whole. For this purpose we shall give in the next section a simple proof of a decomposition theorem on the basis of Kantorovich's theorem.

3. *The Decomposition Theorem*

Kantorovich's problem of optimization [2] is the following. Suppose we have the real numbers

$$A_{is} \qquad (i=1, \ldots, N; s=1, \ldots, \nu), \tag{7}$$

$$B_i \qquad (i=1, \ldots, \mu), \tag{8}$$

$$K_j > 0 \qquad (j=1, \ldots, N-\mu), \tag{9}$$

$$D_s > 0 \qquad (s=1, \ldots, \nu). \tag{10}$$

The variables $z_s \, (s=1, \ldots, \nu)$ fulfil the conditions

$$D_s \geqslant z_s \geqslant 0 \qquad (s=1, \ldots, \nu), \tag{11}$$

$$\sum_{s=1}^{\nu} A_{is} z_s \geqslant B_i \qquad (i=1, \ldots, \mu). \tag{12}$$

We intend to find the variables z_s in such a way as to give the maximal value to the expression

$$\min_{1 \leqslant j \leqslant N-\mu} \left(\frac{1}{K_j} \sum_{s=1}^{\nu} A_{\mu+js} \, z_s \right). \tag{13}$$

Such set of z_s's is called the optimal plan.

Kantorovich's theorem states that the necessary and sufficient condition for optimality of the plan z_s which fulfils the conditions (11) and (12), is the existence of the Lagrange multipliers ('shadow prices') $l_i \, (i=1, \ldots, N)$ fulfilling the following conditions

(*a*) $l_i \geqslant 0$ $\quad (i=1, \ldots, N)$, $\quad \max_{1 \leqslant j \leqslant N-\mu} l_{\mu+j} > 0$,

(b) $\sum_{i=1}^{N} l_i A_{is} \begin{cases} \leqslant 0 \text{ if } z_s=0, \\ =0 \text{ if } D_s>z_s>0, \\ \geqslant 0 \text{ if } z_s=D_s, \end{cases}$ $(s=1, \ldots, \nu)$,

(c) $l_i=0$ if $\sum_{s=1}^{\nu} A_{is}z_s>B_i$ $(1\leqslant i\leqslant\mu)$, or

$$\sum_{s=1}^{\nu} A_{is} z_s > K_{i-\mu} \min_{1\leqslant j\leqslant N-\mu} \left(\frac{1}{K_j}\sum_{s=1}^{\nu} A_{\mu+js}z_s\right) \quad (\mu+1\leqslant i\leqslant N).$$

Let us now specify Kantorovich's theorem in the case

$$N=\mu+1 \tag{14}$$

and denote $A_{\mu+1s}$ by $-C_s$. Then Kantorovich's problem reduces to

$$0\leqslant z_j\leqslant D_j \quad (j=1, \ldots, \nu), \tag{15}$$

$$\sum_{j=1}^{\nu} A_{kj} z_j\geqslant B_k \quad (k=1, \ldots, \mu), \tag{16}$$

$$\sum_{j=1}^{\nu} C_j z_j=\min. \tag{17}$$

From part (a) of Kantorovich's theorem we have

$$l_{\mu+1}>0. \tag{18}$$

We can put $l_{\mu+1}=1$ and conclude that the necessary and sufficient condition for optimality of the plan z_s, which fulfils the conditions (15) and (16), is the existence of l_k $(k=1, \ldots, \mu)$ fulfilling the conditions

$$l_k\geqslant 0 \quad (k=1, \ldots, \mu), \tag{19}$$

$$\sum_{k=1}^{\mu} l_k A_{kj} \begin{cases} \leqslant C_j \text{ if } z_j=0, \\ =C_j \text{ if } 0<z_j<D_j, \\ \geqslant C_j \text{ if } z_j=D_j, \end{cases} \quad (j=1, \ldots, \nu), \tag{20}$$

$$l_k=0 \quad \text{if } \sum_{j=1}^{\nu} A_{kj}z_j>B_k \quad (1\leqslant k\leqslant\mu). \tag{21}$$

Now we investigate the problem

$$\sum_{j=1}^{\nu} A_{kj}z_j=B_k \quad (k=1, \ldots, \mu; \mu<\nu), \tag{22}$$

$$0\leqslant z_j\leqslant D_j \quad (j=1, \ldots, \nu), \tag{23}$$

$$\sum_{j=1}^{\nu} C_j z_j=\min. \tag{24}$$

The equalities (22) can be written

$$\left. \begin{array}{l} \sum_{j=1}^{v} A_{kj} z_j \geqslant B_k , \\[2mm] \sum_{j=1}^{v} (-A_{kj}) z_j \geqslant -B_k . \end{array} \right\} \quad (k=1,\dots,\mu) \qquad (25)$$

The problem (22)–(24) is then of the type (15)–(17).

We use the theorem (19)–(21), inserting l'_k and l''_k respectively for the first and second type of the inequalities (25) and denoting $l_k = l'_k - l''_k$. We then conclude that the necessary and sufficient condition for optimality of the plan z_s which satisfies the conditions (22) and (23), is the existence of l_k $(k=1, \dots , \mu)$ satisfying the conditions (20). In this way we arrive at the well-known theorem of the shadow prices.

Applying this theorem, we can formulate the method of obtaining the optimal solution of the problem (22)–(24). We choose a set of numbers l_k $(k=1, \dots , \mu)$ and take the values of z_j $(j=1, \dots , v)$ in accordance with the conditions (20). If such a solution does not satisfy the conditions (22), we have to repeat the procedure with another set of l_k's, until (22) will be satisfied. In the given step of iteration the inequality $\sum_{j=1}^{v} A_{kj} z_j > B_k$ suggest that l_k must be lowered, the opposite one suggests that it must be raised.

This method, although simple in principle, is not convenient because of the great number of iterations which are required for larger problems. This difficulty arises from the great number of l_k's (equal μ) which have to be chosen and then changed. Because of that, we shall write the theorem in a different form which is more elastic in practical application. For this purpose let us consider the following problem:

$$\sum_{j=1}^{v} A_{kj} z_j = B_k \qquad (k=1, \dots , k'-1, k'+1, \dots , \mu), \qquad (26)$$

$$0 \leqslant z_j \leqslant D_j \qquad (j=1, \dots , v), \qquad (27)$$

$$\sum_{j=1}^{v} C_j z_j - l_{k'} \sum_{j=1}^{v} A_{k'j} z_j = \min. \qquad (28)$$

We shall prove that, first, if $l_{k'}$ is the shadow price of the problem (22)–(24), then the optimal solution of the problem (22)–(24) is the optimal solution also for the problem (26)–(28); the shadow prices of the problem (22)–(24) are the shadow prices also for the problem (26)–(28). Second, if the optimal solution of the problem (26)–(28), with some number $l_{k'}$, satisfies the condition

$$\sum_{j=1}^{v} A_{k'j} z_j = B_{k'}, \tag{29}$$

then it is also the optimal solution of the problem (22)–(24); the shadow prices of the problem (26)–(28) and the number $l_{k'}$ give the complete set of shadow prices for the problem (22)–(24).

We shall now prove the first part of the theorem. The optimal solution of (22)–(24) is of course a feasible solution of (26)–(28), i.e. it satisfies the conditions (26) and (27). The sufficient condition for this solution for being also the optimal solution of (26)–(28) is the existence of such l'_k $(k=1, \ldots, k'-1, k'+1, \ldots, \mu)$ that:

$$\sum_{\substack{k=1 \\ k \neq k'}}^{\mu} l'_k A_{kj} \begin{cases} \leqslant C_j - l_{k'} A_{k'j} \text{ if } z_j = 0, \\ = C_j - l_{k'} A_{k'j} \text{ if } 0 < z_j < D_j, \\ \geqslant C_j - l_{k'} A_{k'j} \text{ if } z_j = D_j. \end{cases} \quad (j=1, \ldots, v). \tag{30}$$

Such l'_k exist: they are by definition the shadow prices of the problem (22)–(24).

We now treat the second part of our theorem. The optimal solution of (26)–(28), satisfying (29), is the feasible solution of (22)–(24). The sufficient condition for this solution for being also the optimal solution of (22)–(24) is the existence of such l'_k $(k=1, \ldots, \mu)$ that:

$$\sum_{k=1}^{\mu} l'_k A_{kj} \begin{cases} \leqslant C_j \text{ if } z_j = 0, \\ = C_j \text{ if } 0 < z_j < D_j, \\ \geqslant C_j \text{ if } z_j = D_j. \end{cases} \quad (j=1, \ldots, v). \tag{31}$$

If we put

$$l'_{k'} = l_{k'}, \tag{32}$$

we see that such l''_k's $(k=1, \ldots, k'-1, k'+1, \ldots, \mu)$ exist: they are, by definition, the shadow prices for the problem (26)–(28). (Compare conditions (30).) This completes the proof of our theorem.

The theorem proved can easily be generalized, simply by iteration, for the case in which not only one but several conditions (22) are omitted, i.e. for the problem:

$$\sum_{j=1} A_{kj} z_j = B_k \quad (k=1, \ldots, k_1-1, k_1+1, \ldots, k_\sigma-1, k_\sigma+1, \ldots, \mu), \sigma \leqslant \mu,$$
$$\tag{33}$$

$$0 \leqslant z_j \leqslant D_j \quad (j=1, \ldots, v), \tag{34}$$

$$\sum_{j=1}^{v} C_j z_j - \sum_{i=1}^{\sigma} l_{ki} \sum_{j=1}^{v} A_{kij} z_j = \min. \tag{35}$$

If l_{ki} $(i=1, \ldots, \sigma)$ are the shadow prices of the problem (22)–(24), then the optimal solution of this problem is the optimal solution also for the problem (33)–(35); the shadow prices of the problem (22)–(24) are the shadow prices also for the problem (33)–(35). On the other hand, if the optimal solution of the problem (33)–(35), with some numbers l_{ki} $(i=1, \ldots, \sigma)$, satisfy the conditions

$$\sum_{j=1}^{\nu} A_{kij} z_j = B_{k_i} \qquad (i=1, \ldots, \sigma), \qquad (36)$$

then it is also the optimal solution of the problem (22)–(24); the shadow prices of the problem (33)–(35), and the numbers l_{ki} $(i=1, \ldots, \sigma)$ give the complete set of shadow prices for the problem (22)–(24).

On the basis of this theorem we can solve the problem (22)–(24) in the following way. We can drop some of the equations (22) which are most inconvenient, e.g. because they tie together several subsets of z_j's, these subsets being otherwise independent on each other. The problem takes then the form (33)–(35). We choose the values of l_{ki} $(i=1, \ldots, \sigma)$ and solve the problem by any standard method. If the solution does not satisfy the conditions (36) we must repeat the procedure of solving (33)–(35) with another set of l_{ki}'s, until (36) will be satisfied. On the given step of iteration the inequality $\sum_{j=1}^{\nu} A_{kij} z_j > B_{ki}$ suggest that l_{ki} must be lowered, and the opposite one that it must be raised. The shadow prices and l_{ki} $(i=1, \ldots, \sigma)$ obtained in the last step of iteration are the right shadow prices for the problem (22)–(24).

Let us now consider the problem (33)–(35) in which some of the unknown z_{j_t} (for $t=1, \ldots, \theta; \nu-\theta > \mu-\sigma$) were fixed on their optimal values $z_{j_t}^0$. The problem is:

$$\sum_{\substack{j=1 \\ j \neq j_t(t=1,\ldots,\theta)}}^{\nu} A_{kj} z_j = B_k - \sum_{t=1}^{\theta} A_{kj_t} z_{j_t} \qquad (k=1,\ldots,k_1-1,k_1+1,\ldots,k_\sigma-1,k_\sigma+1,\ldots,\mu), \qquad (37)$$

$$0 \leqslant z_j \leqslant D_j \qquad (j=1, \ldots, \nu; j \neq j_t \text{ for } t=1, \ldots, \theta), \qquad (38)$$

$$\sum_{\substack{j=1 \\ j \neq j_t(t=1,\ldots,\theta)}}^{\nu} C_j z_j - \sum_{i=1}^{\sigma} l_{ki} \sum_{\substack{j=1 \\ j \neq j_t(t=1,\ldots,\theta)}}^{\nu} A_{kij} z_j = \min. \qquad (39)$$

It is obvious that the optimal solution of z_j $(j \neq j_t$ for $t=1, \ldots, \theta)$ of the problem (33)–(35) is the optimal solution also for this problem, and that the shadow prices for the problem (33)–(35) are also the shadow prices for (37)–(39). This leads to some possible modification of our method of obtaining the optimal solution of the problem (22)–(24). We start from some feasible or even unfeasible solution of (22)–(23), and treat these z_j's $(j=1, \ldots, \nu)$ for a moment as z_j^0. We choose also the values of l_k's $(k=1, \ldots, \mu)$. Taking then an arbitrary subset of equations and a subset of z_j, we find by any standard procedure the solution of the problem (37)–(39). We obtain then a new set of values z_j^0 $(j \neq j_t, t=1, \ldots, \theta)$ and shadow prices l_k $(k \neq k_i, i=1, \ldots, \sigma)$. We now go to another subset of equations and unknowns and repeat the procedure. We can thus go through the whole problem and stop when the iterations do not give any more changes in z_j^0's and l_k's. These will be the optimal solution and shadow prices. Some of the equations must not be taken into account in any problem of the type (37)–(39) but their l_k's must be then changed during the iteration procedure so as to obtain the fulfilment of these equations.

4. *Decomposition of Short-run Planning*

Let us now go back to our model of short-run planning. The problem (1)–(6) is of the form (22)–(24). We denote the shadow prices for commodities by l_k and for foreign currency by M^r (exchange rates). We drop the foreign trade balance equations and make the appropriate change in the expression (6). Choosing some subset of productive activities x_j (e.g. $j=1, \ldots, \alpha$), domestic demand P_k (e.g. $k=1, \ldots, \beta$) and trade $y_k^{E,Ir}$ $(k=1, \ldots, \beta; r=1, \ldots, m)$ we can write the problem of the form (37)–(39) but now for maximization:

$$\sum_{j=1}^{\alpha} a_{kj}x_j + \sum_{r=1}^{m} y_k^{Ir} - \sum_{r=1}^{m} y_k^{Er} = P_k - \sum_{j=\alpha+1}^{p} a_{kj}x_j^0 \qquad (k=1, \ldots, \beta), \qquad (40)$$

$$0 \leqslant x_j \leqslant b_j \qquad (j=1, \ldots, \alpha), \qquad (41)$$

$$\left.\begin{array}{l} 0 \leqslant y_k^{Er} \leqslant \pi_k^{Er} \\ 0 \leqslant y_k^{Ir} \leqslant \pi_k^{Ir} \end{array}\right\} \quad (k=1, \ldots, \beta; r=1, \ldots, m), \qquad \begin{array}{l}(42)\\(43)\end{array}$$

$$\sum_{r=1}^{m} M^r \sum_{k=1}^{\beta} (d_k^{Er}y_k^{Er} - d_k^{Ir}y_k^{Ir}) - \sum_{j=1}^{\alpha} (c_j - \sum_{k=\beta+1}^{p} l_k a_{kj})x_j = \max. \qquad (44)$$

x_j^0 express activities in the rest of the economy. The procedure described for obtaining the optimal solution for the problem (22)–(24) can now be used here to obtain the optimal solution of (1)–(6). We start from some feasible or even unfeasible solution of (1)–(5): x_j^0 $(j=1, \ldots, p)$, y_k^{Er0} and y_k^{Ir0} $(r=1, \ldots, m; k=1, \ldots, n)$. We choose also the values of l_k $(k=1, \ldots, n)$ and M^r $(r=1, \ldots, m)$. Taking different subsets of activities and commodities, we solve by any standard procedure the problems of the form (40)–(44), obtain new x_j's, $y_k^{E,Ir}$'s and l_k's for activities and commodities from these subsets, use them in the next problems and thus go through the whole economy. M^r's must be changed during this procedure in order to obtain the fulfilment of equations (2). We stop when the iterations do not give any more changes in x_j's, $y_k^{E,Ir}$'s, l_k's and M^r's. The optimal solution of (1)–(6) is then reached.

The above method is more general than that presented in [1] since: (*a*) it allows for several techniques of production of a given commodity; (*b*) it allows for inputs of commodity k for production of other groups ($-\sum\limits_{j=\alpha+1}^{p} a_{kj}x_j^0$); and (*c*) it opens the possibility of using for the production of a commodity inputs of domestic or imported raw materials, the production capacity or import possibilities of which limit other alternative uses of that raw material.

It is obvious that in practical planning the number of iteration steps ought to be limited as far as possible. Therefore, from the practical point of view, to find for the first step of the iteration process values of x_j^0's, $y_k^{E,Ir0}$'s, l_k's, M^r's as close to optimal as possible is of the greatest importance. Different methods of obtaining such values from statistical data may be proposed. Some of these methods are under investigation; as an example we give the outline of one of them.

It can easily be proved that for the optimal solution the following simple conditions hold:

$$
l_k \begin{cases} \geqslant M^r d_k^{Er} & \text{if } y_k^{Er}=0, \\ = M^r d_k^{Er} & \text{if } 0<y_k^{Er}<\pi_k^{Er}, \\ \leqslant M^r d_k^{Er} & \text{if } y_k^{Er}=\pi_k^{Er}, \end{cases} \tag{45}
$$

$$
l_k \begin{cases} \geqslant M^r d_k^{Ir} & \text{if } y_k^{Ir}=\pi_k^{Ir}, \\ = M^r d_k^{Ir} & \text{if } 0<y_k^{Ir}<\pi_k^{Ir}, \\ \leqslant M^r d_k^{Ir} & \text{if } y_k^{Ir}=0. \end{cases} \tag{46}
$$

From the above conditions we can obtain a reasonable first approximation for l_k's for the first step of the iteration process if we assume that the current solution of foreign trade is not too far from the optimal one and that we have approximate values of marginal exchange rates M^r.[1]

The relation of the planning prices l_k and prices of consumption goods on the domestic market is a problem on its own and is not discussed here.

The model presented above solves a well-known problem about the possibility of economic calculus and objective price systems in planned economies.[2] The above considerations lead to the conclusion that in a

---

[1] For more complete discussion of the methods of obtaining l_k's see Piaszczyński [3].
[2] This topic was raised in the Lange-Mieses controversy [4].

planned economy there is not only scope but also need for economic calculus and an objective planning price system. Moreover, the introduction of the proposed price system in planning simplifies the management of the economy and provides for optimal levels of activities.

It should be stressed that prices l_k, though determined basically by domestic productive capacities, costs, planned demand and investment targets, depend also (as do also exchange rates M^r) on demand and prices in foreign markets. Although the model deals with the individual optimum of one country, the optimal solution cannot be reached by neglecting these relations. It is obvious that by removing some constraints on international trade the number of degrees of freedom increases and the optimal solution can be improved.

An important component of the planning process — as it is presented above — is 'operational research' on particular parts of the economy or on enterprises. Appreciable improvement of capacity efficiency can be reached — as it is well known — at this level of planning. The use of the objective function (44) for operational research programmes is consistent with the maximization of savings of social labour.

The method of planning presented here in principle consists, for any part of the economy, in satisfying the demands of the rest of the economy for commodities manufactured in this part, and in charging 'own' prices for these commodities. Techniques of production and foreign trade activities are also decided in the partial solutions — taking into account of course the exchange rates M^r derived from the national balance of trade. Thus the method allows for a high degree of decentralization of planning. But the problem of the optimal degree of decentralization is of an organizational nature and is still unsolved.

REFERENCES

[1] TRZECIAKOWSKI, W., 'Problemy Kompleksowego Systemu Analizy Bieżacej Efektywności Handlu Zagranicznego' (Problems of a System of Complex Analysis of Current Effectiveness of Foreign Trade) in *Studia KPZK Pan*, Tom II, Warsaw, 1961.

[2] KANTOROVICH, L. V., *Ekonomicheskij Raschot Nailutshevo Ispolzovanija Resursov* (Economic calculus of the optimal use of resources), Moscow, 1959.

[3] PIASZCZYŃSKI, W., 'Ceny Efektywności w Gospodarce Planowej' (Shadow Prices in a Planned Economy), in *Studia KPZK PAN*, Warsaw, 1962.

[4] LIPPINCOTT, B. (ed.), *On the Economic Theory of Socialism*, Minneapolis, 1938. (Contributions by LANGE, O. and TAYLOR, F. M.)

CHAPTER 3

An Efficient Path for the Technological Transformation of an Economy[1]

by PURUSHOTTAM NARAYAN MATHUR

1. *Introduction*

In this study we attempt to find out how the tools of input-output analysis and of linear programming could be together employed to trace an efficient path for the transformation of an economy when a new technology appears on the horizon.

Economic progress, in the sense of increasing per capita income, is primarily the resultant of the structural and/or technological transformation of the economy. The structural changes may be defined as the changing proportionate shares of various sectors or industries in the national economy while technological transformation refers to changes in the input-output relations of various activities.[2]

A purely structural change[3] will lead to economic progress when the shift is from industries requiring more labour inputs per unit of income (in the 'value added' sense) to industries requiring less of it, other things being equal. This may be a result of changes in the pattern of demand, internal and international.[4]

The role of suitable inventions and their adoption — in short of 'innovations' — has long been recognized as a harbinger of economic growth by economic historians and theorists alike. But, apart from the notable exception of Schumpeter, hardly any theoretical economist has

---

[1] This paper is dedicated to Professor D. R. Gadgil on the occasion of his sixtieth birthday. I am grateful to Professor Wassily Leontief for his continuous encouragement and critical interest in my work. My thanks are also due to Dr. R. Bharadwaj, Dr. A. Daniere and Mr. V. Bhatia for their helpful suggestions. Mrs. P. M. Anderson assisted me in programming.

[2] The words sectors, industries and activities are used here interchangeably.

[3] The structural change has become the cornerstone of some descriptive theories of economic growth, for instance, those of Kuznets and Colin Clark. But they do not distinguish whether the observed structural change is due to technological changes or to some other causes. As such, these theories have not much to offer towards causal understanding of the process.

[4] Marshall was so impressed by the international aspect that he wrote, 'The causes which determine the economic progress of nations belong to the study of International Trade.'

D   B.S.I.E.D.

entered into the complicated analysis of the process of adoption of a new technology. Schumpeter himself was handicapped by the lack of tools by which the repercussions of technological changes throughout the economy could be handled. Neither the apparatus of partial analysis nor that of national aggregatives lend themselves to such an undertaking. It was Leontief who provided the tool of input-output analysis which seems suited for the purpose. After his pioneering work a lot of data has been collected on the existing structure of economies in various countries. But historical series of such data which can be used for studying technological transformations are simply non-existent. In the absence of historical series it may be helpful to construct artificial series, under various assumptions, and attempt to understand their behaviour. The present paper is a small effort in this direction. However, lots of similar studies and hard economic thinking will have to go into the economic phenomenon of technological transformation of an economy before the outline of the process begins to emerge.

Incidentally, this leads to the formulation of a planning model, where the chief efforts of planning are concentrated on transforming the traditional techniques of production into modern ones, and which, under various assumptions, can provide answers to such questions as the following:

(*a*) Which of the existing technologies should be adopted by the country?

(*b*) How much time will the economy take for complete transformation?

(*c*) What will be its rate of growth at various periods?

(*d*) What will be the magnitude of unemployment over the period of transition?

(*e*) What will be the requirements of various types of trained personnel in different years?

(*f*) To what extent can the process be accelerated by foreign loans or aid of the right type?

(*g*) When should the repayment of these loans begin?

(*h*) What is the most desirable commodity composition of foreign trade?

In an economy defined by a unique technological matrix and a stationary structure of consumption, government expenditure and international trade, economic growth is likely to take the form of a uniformly expanding economy at a unique rate of development, provided the availability of natural resources is not a bottleneck. In such a model growth is essentially a result of capital accumulation and the rate of growth is determined by the values of the input-output and capital coefficients. Normally, this rate of growth will be greater than or equal to the rate of growth of population except probably in such artificial cases as a colonial economy.

It is evident that an economy with fixed labour coefficients cannot grow uniformly at a rate faster than the rate of growth of the working force. It can be easily shown that an economy that can grow at a uniform given rate of growth can also grow at any lower rate of growth if free disposal of goods is allowed. The amounts of this necessary free disposal show up as the final demand vector in the open Leontief Dynamic System and in the real world they are absorbed as additions to government and/or private consumption.

The process of growth will proceed differently if we allow for the transformation of the initial economy into one with a different technology, having a higher per capita income. Such transformation is achieved by the instrumentality of the accumulation of the right type of capital. In the real world, before this process is completed a new technological horizon may become visible, superimposing a new path for the economy over the one previously chalked out. Accordingly, a study of this transformation path in the first few years will be of particular interest.

Hundreds of paths are possible that may lead from one such single technology economy to another. In constructing an artificial series it is necessary to select one in accordance with certain efficiency criteria. One obvious criterion may be to minimize the time required for such complete transformation. But this cannot be easily handled arithmetically.

Alternatively, therefore, we have chosen to maximize such variables as income or profits at the end of a certain arbitrarily given time period, and have used linear programming technique to determine an efficient way of capital accumulation for doing so. By increasing this arbitrarily given time period further and further, the time necessary for achieving the complete transformation, i.e. a situation in which the whole of the available labour force is employed and works under the new technology, could also be derived. It is obvious that no further purpose can be served by increasing the horizon further once such an equilibrium is achieved. Beyond this, the economy will follow the uniform and balanced rate of growth equivalent to that of the labour force until and unless a new technology of production and/or a new structure of consumption, governmental expenditure or international trade emerges. And as such there will be no further problem of optimization.

In the following section, we define the various concepts and enumerate the simplifying assumptions used, together with their rationale. In Section 3 we outline the mathematical properties of the model; and we give the artificial series constructed in Section 4.

2. *Assumptions Relating to the Coefficients*

A flow coefficient, a_{ij}, may be defined as the amount of the ith commodity required for the production of a unit of the jth commodity. The unit of commodity measurement may be taken as the amount of the commodity that can be purchased for, say, one rupee in the base period. We can distinguish two sets of flow coefficients in a developing economy. One set may consist of those coefficients which are associated with the new technique of production and the other may be taken as the average of the flow coefficients of the previous techniques still in use. The latter may be taken as a weighted average of the various techniques in use in proportion to their contribution to the total. If, however, it is felt that this will distort the picture significantly, especially when taking unused capacity into account, it may be advisable to explicitly account for more than two techniques. Here, however, such differences are ignored both for the sake of simplicity and because of lack of data.

The flow coefficients do not take into account consumption demand from the various sectors. When an industry develops, it employs more workers; they may be new entrants to the labour force, or they may come from some other sector. In any case, we can assume that once he has joined the industry the newcomer's consumption will follow the level and pattern associated, on the average, with a person of his position in that industry. Thus, if we assume that, for a particular technique in a sector, the pattern of income distribution remains the same irrespective of the size of the sector or the proportion of the particular technique used in it; and if we further assume that the level and the pattern of consumption, given prices, depends on income only, we can assume a fixed pattern and level of consumption demand generated by every unit of each commodity produced by each technology. This of course assumes direct proportionality between the number of workers employed in each industry and its output under a given technology.

The assumption that the pattern of consumption, given prices, depends on income alone, does not, however, preclude other factors like wealth, education, etc., from affecting the consumption behaviour of the families. It only means that the effects of such factors are independent of the particular sector of the economy to which the person belongs, apart from that portion which is also accounted for by income. However, the assumption of constant consumption coefficients does not preclude the consumption level from rising, if commodities are available in the requisite quantities. In that case the extra consumption of that commodity can be accounted for in the final demand sector.

Leontief, in his closed model, has built consumption demand into the model itself by assuming a separate household sector. That assumes the pattern of demand of the household sector to be practically independent of both the patterns and the techniques of production. That type of approach is more suitable for economies where the productivities of the two technologies are not very different, so that a shift in the pattern of production and its technique is not likely to effect income distribution to a significant extent. Otherwise, such a shift in favour of the newer industries and techniques is likely to generate more income in the higher income brackets, which in its turn may significantly affect the level and pattern of consumption. In these circumstances, Leontief's technique may not meet the requirements of the situation.

It has been assumed that all new capacity that is being created is geared to the new technique of production available for each individual industry. The input of the ith commodity required to create a unit capacity for the production of the jth commodity may be designated by b_{ij}. It is further assumed that the capacity created in a particular period is utilized only in the succeeding period. This capacity, it may be added parenthetically, can be created from the production of the same period.

Sometimes it may be found more advantageous to leave some capacity unutilized rather than to work at full capacity. This will release some current inputs of commodities as well as of labour to be utilized in a more profitable way. It is assumed that capacity created under the new technology will always be fully utilized, while that previously in existence under the old technology may or may not be.

The best solution along these lines may have undesirable consequences for the employment position during the transition period. It may be profitable, according to this solution, to make the extent of unutilized capacity so much that the labour released by it, plus the natural increase of the labour force, may together be greater than the labour requirements of the new investment, thereby creating unemployment.

Under various assumptions about entrepreneural behaviour, this may provide a prognostication of impending unemployment, but a lot of work will have to be done on these lines to make the model correspond to reality more closely. For purposes of planning, we may have to introduce unemployment benefits as costs in the model. Then the model will tell us whether it is better to provide unemployment benefits and discard the old technology quickly, or whether it is profitable for the economy to continue using the old technology for some more time.

Final Demand and Foreign Trade

Both demand for capital formation and that for consumption by persons employed in the different sectors have been built into the model, instead of being included in final demand. Final demand consists of government demand, demand by other non-economic bodies (i.e. those not included in the sectors within the model, like religious, social and educational institutions), demand for consumption by employees of the government and of these institutions, and demand for export. An important point to note is that if we estimate the future expenditure of, say, government, for assessing its effects on the various economic sectors, we shall also have to estimate simultaneously the consumption expenditure of extra government servants employed, to be included in the final demand.

Turning to international trade, as is well known foreign trade plays a large part in easing the constraints imposed by interindustry balances on the working of an economy. In the ideal case, where there is infinite elasticity of exports and imports, interindustry balances do not put any constraints on the economy. For that particular case, an aggregative analysis will as well serve the purpose; anything not available in sufficient quantities in the economy can always be imported in exchange for any other commodity that can be spared. But reality is far from that ideal. It is very difficult to increase one's exports, especially if the country is mainly a primary producer. Further, the effects of an export drive cannot be easily predicted. For these reasons, in the present model exports are taken as given, and thus form a part of final demand.

However, in the case of imports, there is normally greater freedom. Quantitative import restrictions are a recognized method of governmental promotion of various economic policies. In this model, we have assumed complete substitutability between different imports, subject only to the condition that they are not to exceed a stipulated amount in total. This total may be taken as equivalent to the exports plus any other amount for which credit is likely to be available.

Thus we shall attribute an extra availability I_i to each industry in the form of an imported amount of the ith commodity, the restriction being that the sum of all these I's should be less than a given amount.

This, as we shall see later, serves as a good guide in judging the value of foreign exchange for the purpose of the transformation. Rates of growth can be calculated with and without the availability of extra foreign exchange. Similarly, it can be found whether the export of any particular item is worthwhile to earn the foreign exchange. At the margin, this can be seen easily by comparing the shadow price of a unit of foreign exchange and that of the item in question.

3. *The Model*

The above considerations give us the following balance equations:

$$X_i^0 + \sum_{k=1}^{p-1} \Delta_k X_i + I_i^p - U_i^p \geqslant \sum_{j=1}^{n} (a_{ij} + c_{ij}) X_j^0 + \sum_{j=1}^{n} (a_{ij}' + c_{ij}') \sum_{k=1}^{p-1} \Delta_k X_j$$

$$+ \sum_{j=1}^{n} b_{ij} \Delta_p X_j - \sum_{j=1}^{n} (a_{ij} + c_{ij}) U_j^p + Y_i^p \quad (1)$$

$$(p = 1, 2, \ldots, m; i = 1, 2, \ldots, n),$$

where $X_i^0 =$ Total output of ith commodity at the initial capacity level.

$\Delta_k X_i =$ Increase in the capacity of the ith industry in the kth period.

$I_i^p =$ Import of the ith commodity in the pth period.

$U_i^p =$ Unutilized capacity of the ith industry[1] in the pth period.

$a_{ij} =$ Current input requirement of ith commodity for the production of one unit of jth commodity by the initial technology.

$a_{ij}' =$ Current input requirement of ith commodity for the production of one unit of jth commodity by the new technology.

$c_{ij} =$ Consumption requirement of the ith commodity by persons employed in the jth industry per unit of output of jth industry by the initial technology.

$c_{ij}' =$ Consumption requirement of the ith commodity by persons employed in the jth industry per unit of output of jth industry by the new technology.

$b_{ij} =$ Requirements of the ith commodity for the creation of one unit capacity[2] in the jth industry.

$Y_i^p =$ Final demand of ith commodity in the pth period.

The system (1) above represents inequalities for each commodity and for each of the m periods which are within the horizon. Apart from these $n.m$ inequalities, there will be m inequalities denoting the import

---

[1] ith industry stands for the industry producing the ith commodity.
[2] Capacity creation is assumed, as indicated earlier, to be in the new technology only.

constraints, and another m inequalities denoting the labour constraints. They are:

$$\sum_{i=1}^{n} I_i^p \leqslant E^p \tag{2}$$

$$\sum_{i=1}^{n} \left\{ l_i X_i^0 + l_i' \sum_{k=1}^{p-1} \Delta_k X_i - l_i U_i^p \right\} \leqslant L^p \tag{3}$$

$$p = 1, 2, \dots, m.$$

where E^p and L^p are fixed values dependent on other considerations and given to the system, and l_i and l_i' represent the labour requirement of the ith industry per unit of its output in old and new technologies respectively. As unutilized capacity is assumed to be only of that of the old technology, it cannot be more than the initial capacity of the economy. This gives us $n.m$ further constraints of the form:

$$U_i^p \leqslant X_i^0 \qquad (p = 1, 2, \dots, m; i = 1, 2, \dots, n) \tag{4}$$

The constraints given by the $2m(n+1)$ relations (1), (2), (3), (4) are in terms of inequalities. As such, we can assume as many slack variables that will turn them into equalities. For the equations (1) these $n.m$ slack variables will denote the extra quantities of the various commodities produced at different periods which are required neither for consumption in the period nor for the production of current or capital goods. Let us denote by r_i^p the extra quantity of the ith commodity produced in the pth year.

This extra product can as well be stored if, by that process, it is possible to meet the requirements of some processes in the next year. This storage activity will have some cost. Here, however, for the sake of simplicity, no cost for storage activity has been assumed. Thus, accumulating foreign exchange (with no interest) by postponing imports or by importing immediately and storing with no cost would have the same effect. This assumption allows us not to have any slack variable for imports.

The slack variable in unutilized activity constraint denotes utilized old capacity in the period. The slack variable in labour constraints gives the estimate of unemployment in the particular year. This unemployment series will in itself give an important characteristic of the path of transformation of an economy from one set of techniques to another under different assumptions.

A uniformly expanding terminal economy, which can be described symbolically in terms of the fundamental equation of Leontief's Open Dynamic Model in period analysis form, can be written as:

$$X^t = (1 - A - \lambda B)^{-1} Y^t \Big\}$$
$$Y^t = Y^{t_1}(1+\lambda)^{t-t_1} \Big\}$$

$$t = t_1, t_1 + 1, t_1 + 2, \ldots$$

(5)

where X^t is the vector giving the production in the tth year; Y^t is the final demand vector in the year t; λ is the yearly rate of uniform increase which should be equal to the rate of increase of the labour force, and A and B are, respectively, flow and capital coefficient matrices relating to the terminal technology; t_1 is the year from which the economy has started working as a single technology with full employment.

In the above equation, Y^t should be such that the production vector X^t, derived from it, should employ the whole of the labour force available in the year t; viz., it should satisfy

$$A'_{n+1}(1 - A - \lambda B)^{-1} Y^t = L^t$$

(6)

$$t = t_1, t_1 + 1, t_1 + 2 \ldots$$

where A_{n+1} is the employment vector $(l_1, l_2, l_3, \ldots, l_m)$ and L^t is the labour force available in the year t, excluding that employed by the exogenous sector, and which is assumed to be increasing at the rate λ per year. It can easily be seen that if (6) is true for any t, it is true for all the t's.

From (5), it can be seen that for $t \geqslant t_1$

$$\Delta_{t+1} X = \lambda \Delta_t X$$

(7)

where $\Delta_t X$ is the vector $(\Delta_t X_i)$ $(i = 1, 2, \ldots, n)$.

Equation (7) may be used as a terminal condition in the case where the horizon is so large as to achieve complete transformation. However, in the case of a smaller horizon we can have any reasonable terminal condition. We have assumed, in the example below, that the capital formation in the last year in each of the sectors will not be less than that in the previous year as the terminal condition.

The Maximizing Function

Let vector G^t represent the demand of the exogenous sector, which increases at the rate λ, the rate at which the economy expands. It is evident that G^t is feasible if

$$A'_{n+1}(1 - A - \lambda B)^{-1} G^t \leqslant L^t$$

(8)

If the sign of equality holds good in the above equation, a maximizing function having positive values associated with the total capacity of at least one sector in the new technology and non-negative values with other sectors of it, and a non-positive value for the capacity of the old technology, will serve the purpose for the linear programming problem envisaged here. For, once the complete transformation with full employment to the new technology has been achieved, and the economy follows the path given by equation (5), there is no further maximizing problem; and if it is feasible to achieve this transformation for a given t, any such maximizing function will draw a path leading to its achievement. However, it will not ensure that the path chosen is such as to lead to the complete transformation in the least possible time.

Alternatively, if:

$$A'_{n+1}(1 - A - \lambda B)^{-1}G^t < L^t \qquad (8a)$$

we have another optimizing problem. In the year t the economy can attain any Y^t on the hyperplane given by (6). Out of all these Y^t's, we are interested in those which are not less than G^t. Let $C^t \equiv Y^t - G^t$ represent extra availability that can be used for extra consumption either by individuals or by the government. Out of the feasible C^t's we may choose one with the aid of some criterion like the social welfare function. For any t, the set of Y^t defined by the equation (6) and the conditions that $Y^t \geqslant G^t$, and equation (8), is an n-cornered $(n-1)$ dimensional hyperplane in which each corner is given by the intersection of the n hyperplanes given by equation (6) and any $(n-1)$ of the following n equations:

$$Y^t = G^t \qquad (9)$$

Such n possible permutations of (9) define such corners.

All the vectors Y^t which are attainable, given G^t, are the weighted sum of these n vectors, defining these corners.

In a linear programming set-up, such as ours, any linear maximizing function will lead in general to one of the n corners, depending upon the weight given to the various sectors in the objective function. Thus there are two possible approaches. One is to determine first D^t and then get the efficient path as a solution to the linear programming problem by putting $D^t = Y^t$. Alternatively, find n efficient paths to all the corner points and then determine an efficient path to any attainable point, including the optimum one as a weighted average of these n paths. In both cases the exact coefficients in the maximizing form do not matter provided they are within certain broad limits.

However, in a planning problem in which the horizon is not so large as to encompass a complete transformation, the exact coefficients in the objective function are very relevant. In the following section, three such objective forms have been maximized for the terminal year:

(a) The total value added by the use of the New Technology,
(b) Total gross profits (including interest) of all firms using the New Technology, and
(c) Profits (not including interest) of all firms using the New Technology.

Only final year values have been taken because the products available in the intervening years have been used up in the economy as intermediate goods. And final year capacity really represents a stream available to all future years by the capacity created during the planning period.[1]

4. *An Illustrative Transformation Path*

In this section we illustrate certain problems of the technological transformation of an economy. Although the example is numerical and is based on actual data for India and the United States, it is purely of an illustrative character. It is important to underline this quality — namely that the example is an artificial time path worked out by us — because no effort has been made to verify whether the technology given by the U.S.A. input-output table can ever be adopted under Indian conditions. The validity of the premise, that the old technology of the Indian economy depicted by the Indian input-output table can and should be changed to the new technology as given by the input-output table for the U.S.A. depends of course on a great variety of factors. First, the pattern of availability of natural resources is very different for the two countries. Second, in the case of a real solution, it is necessary to work out various engineering blueprints as warranted by Indian conditions. Third, it should also be taken into account that the analysis given here has been carried out at a highly aggregative level.

The economy has been divided into the following five sectors:

1. Agriculture (Food), Textiles, Leather, and Miscellaneous Manufactures.

---

[1] The complicating effects of depreciation have been ignored. However, in a single-technology economy they can easily be introduced as additions to flow coefficients. They can also be easily introduced in the linear programming model by changing total old capacity limit in various years and junking the new capacity created after its useful life.

2. Lumber, Wood Products, Paper and Printing, Construction, Non-Metallic Minerals and Fabricated Metal Products.
3. Machinery and Transport Equipment.
4. Power, Chemicals, Iron and Steel and Non-Ferrous Metals.
5. Transportation, Trade, Communication, Services, etc.

Tables 1 and 2 below give input-output coefficients for India and the U.S.A.,[1] and Table 3 gives capital coefficients for the U.S.A.

TABLE 1

Input-Output Coefficients, India, 1953

FROM	TO				
	Sector				
Sector	1	2	3	4	5
1	0·2907	− 0·3220	− 0·1063	− 0·1980	− 0·5064
2	− 0·0147	0·8605	− 0·0187	− 0·0408	− 0·3331
3	− 0·0028	− 0·0316	0·9618	− 0·0209	− 0·0191
4	− 0·0208	− 0·0839	− 0·2351	0·7614	− 0·0265
5	− 0·1992	− 0·2503	− 0·0956	− 0·1774	0·7514

TABLE 2

Input-Output Coefficients, U.S.A., 1947

FROM	TO				
	Sector				
Sector	1	2	3	4	5
1	0·4801	− 0·0653	− 0·0684	− 0·0570	− 0·1287
2	− 0·0422	0·7289	− 0·0918	− 0·0408	− 0·0837
3	− 0·0238	− 0·0492	0·7128	− 0·0189	− 0·0410
4	− 0·0475	− 0·1056	− 0·1486	0·5821	− 0·0612
5	− 0·2420	− 0·2340	− 0·1472	− 0·1251	0·6641

[1] Household consumption by persons earning their living in a sector has been taken as an input of that sector.

TABLE 3

Capital Coefficients, U.S.A.
(5-Yearly Period)[1]

FROM	TO				
	Sector				
Sector	1	2	3	4	5
1	0·0498	0·0023	0·0025	0·0017	0·0061
2	0·1044	0·0780	0·0662	0·1260	0·1330
3	0·0020	0·0268	0·0536	0·0602	0·0690
4	0·0562	0·0022	0·0078	0·0234	0·0023
5	0·0120	0·0060	0·0098	0·0143	0·0156

Table 6 below gives the path under the above assumption. Capital formation has been traced for five periods.[2] Exogenous expenditure has been taken as constant and, as such, foreign exchange available for imports has also been taken as constant. But it is assumed that it is possible to allocate imports for various sectors, excluding No. 5. The values of exogenous expenditure are as follows:

TABLE 4

Exogenous Expenditure
(billions of rupees)

Sector	1	2	3	4	5
Exogenous Expenditure	7·798	0·868	0·222	0·716	3·231

It has been sought to maximize value added in the last period (at constant prices) generated by investment in new technology over the

---

[1] With a view to cover a larger number of years, we have taken five-yearly periods. This may lead to an underestimation of the possible growth as the capacity created in one period is utilized only in the subsequent periods.

[2] For this purpose balance equations for six periods were constructed and it was assumed that in each of the sectors capital formation in the sixth period will not be less than that in the fifth period.

period. The following are the 'value added' coefficients for different sectors:

TABLE 5

'Value Added' Coefficients

Sector	1	2	3	4	5
Value Added Coefficient	0·3975	0·4689	0·4163	0·4341	0·6740

TABLE 6

Capacity Creation in Various Sectors in Different Periods for an Efficient Path

(in terms of capacity for a billion rupees worth of production per year in 1953 prices)

Sector	Period					Total new capacity created
	1	2	3	4	5	
1	—	—	23·65	107·6	238·9	370·1
2	1·84	45·96	66·06	175·6	705·9	995·4
3	8·08	13·34	30·32	80·9	87·4	220·0
4	5·25	18·63	40·80	97·6	210·7	373·0
5	4·33	33·91	81·30	152·8	394·5	566·8
Total	19·50	111·83	242·13	614·4	1627·4	2625·3
National product[1] per annum generated by new investment	9·43	58·04	125·50	304·1	819·6	1316·7

While the capacity created in the first period has been from the products of the old technology and imports, which are assumed to be constant throughout the period, those in the subsequent periods are from the products of firms employing the new technology also. If we consider the contribution of the products of the old technology as equivalent to the investment created in the first year (viz. 19·50 billion rupees worth), the remaining may be considered as a contribution of the products of the new technology. The following table gives these

[1] It may be noted that the national product in the initial period was Rs. 105 billion.

contributions as well as the rate of growth of new-technology capacity on these assumptions:

TABLE 7
Rate of Growth of New Technology

Period (1)	New capacity created (2)	Of which attributable to products of new technology firms (3)	Total new capacity working (4)	Rate of growth of new technology (3 ÷ 4) (5)
1	19·5	nil	nil	nil
2	111·8	92·3	19·5	4·73
3	242·1	222·6	131·3	1·70
4	614·4	594·9	373·5	1·59
5	1627·4	1607·8	987·9	1·64

For an efficient programme, it was found expedient to utilize the whole of the old capacity for sectors 1, 3 and 4 throughout the period. They are worth 101·4, 1·8, and 4·5 billions of rupees of product per annum respectively. However, for sector 2 it was found more efficient to junk the whole of the old capacity worth Rs. 12·0 billions of product after two periods. The whole old capacity of sector 5 of Rs. 37·3 billions of product has to be utilized for the first two periods, while for the third period utilization of only a part of that capacity, 25·5 billion rupees worth of product, is efficient. For the remaining periods it was found better not to utilize any of the old capacity of this sector.

For the efficient programme the only storage activity found useful was that of the products of sector 2 in the first period, to the extent of 4·58 billion rupees worth of product. Further 0·27, billion worth of product of sector 5 may have to be disposed of outside the system in the same period. Interestingly enough, no such storage or disposal problem arises in any other period. Tentatively we can say that it is only at the beginning of the period of transformation that storage and/or disposal activities are useful in changing the pattern of availability of the goods of various sectors in a way more suited to new types of requirements. After that, new capacity is created in such a way as not to require any such adjustments.

The availability of foreign exchange per annum has been taken as equivalent to Indian exports in the year 1953, 5·16 billion rupees. For the first period it was found that to meet the current input requirements and exogenous demand 2·14 billion rupees worth of yearly imports were required, leaving just 1·22 billion rupees worth of foreign exchange for allocation to capital creation in different sectors. Of this, Rs. 0·06 billion was allocated for sector 1, Rs. 0·96 billion for sector 3 and Rs. 0·20 billion for sector 4.

In the second period 4·04 billion rupees worth of yearly foreign exchange is allotted to sector 1 and 1·12 billion worth to sector 4. In all other periods, all foreign exchange goes to sector 1. The shadow price of foreign exchange gives, at the margin, its contribution to the national product at the end of the period; this works out to be as high as 308 for the first period, decreasing to 57, 28, 12, and 5 for the succeeding periods. This clearly illustrates the important role that foreign loans can play in the development of such economies. The marginal gains from the loans in the first period that are to be repaid in the next will be equal to $308-57 \ (1+i)^5$ where i is the rate of interest p.a., which will really be substantial for almost any reasonable value of i. These shadow prices also give an idea of the commodity on whose export promotion efforts should be concentrated to earn foreign exchange. The lowest shadow price has been found to be for the goods of sector 2;[1] it was as low as 45 in the first period, which gives an indication of the gains in earning foreign exchange that can be reaped by exporting the goods of sector 2.

To find the effects of foreign loans in speeding up this process, we have worked out the path under the assumption that foreign loans worth 5 billion rupees per year are available in the first two periods. It was found that national product can be increased by 65 per cent in the final year if such loans were available. The following table compares the progress achievable under the two conditions:

TABLE 8

Capacity Formation with and without Foreign Loans

(in billions of rupees)

Capacity Formation	Period					
	1	2	3	4	5	Total
With foreign loans	50·1	184·1	300·3	1010·3	2692·1	4237·0
Without foreign loans	19·5	111·8	242·1	614·4	1627·4	2625·3

[1] Apart from that of sector 5 whose goods were not readily exportable.

The path described above has been traced so as to maximize total 'value added' in the terminal year. As stated earlier, such a path was also traced with the objective of maximizing total gross profits (including, as well as excluding, interest payments) in the terminal year using the new technology.

The following table gives the values of all the three objective functions when each of them is maximized in turn:

TABLE 9

Values of Objective Functions

(in billions of rupees)

On Maximizing	Total Value Added	Total Profits (including interest)	Total Profits (excluding interest)
Value Added	1316·7	517·6	427·3
Total Profits (including interest)	1121·8	520·4	417·4
Total Profits (excluding interest)	1316·6	518·3	427·9

When the objective function of total profits (excluding interest) is substituted for that of 'value added', only slight changes are made in the example. But the pattern of investment changes when total profit (including interest) is maximized instead. Instead of sector 2, sector 4 becomes the most desired. We seem to be heading towards another corner of the attainable hyperplane of the new technology.[1] The table below gives the total new capacity envisaged in various sectors under the two plans.

TABLE 10

Total Capacity Creation by Sector with Different Objective Functions

(in billions of rupees)

Sector	New Capacity with Value Added as Objective Function	New Capacity with Profits as Objective Function
1	370	295
2	955	370
3	220	186
4	373	934
5	667	517
Total	2625	2302

[1] See Section 3 above.

The analysis so far has been on the assumption of constant exogenous expenditure. We now compute the adverse effects on capital accumulation of increasing exogenous expenditure. This has been computed for three cases, where exogenous expenditure increases by two, three and five per cent per annum respectively; the pattern of expenditure is assumed to be the same. The 'value added' by the use of the new technology at the end of the period is given in Table 11, under various assumptions regarding exogenous expenditure:

TABLE 11

'Value Added' Achievable with Varying Exogenous Expenditure

(in billions of rupees)

	Exogenous Expenditure			
	Constant	*Increasing 2% per annum*	*Increasing 3% per annum*	*Increasing 5% per annum*
'Value Added' Achievable	1317·7	1199	1131	973
Per cent less than with constant expenditure	—	8·9	14·1	26·1

CHAPTER 4

The Food and Agricultural Sectors in Advanced Economies

by KARL A. FOX

---

1. *The Place of Agriculture in an Advanced Economy, with Special Reference to the United States*

A strong feature of input-output analysis has been its emphasis upon the interdependence of the various sectors of an economy. An input-output table is essentially a general equilibrium model. Like the Walrasian system, it warns us against naïve assumptions that everything else will remain constant when the output of a particular industry is changed. At the same time, we cannot help wishing for the convenience and flexibility of partial equilibrium models which might justify us in focusing our attention upon one sector of the economy. safe in the knowledge that events in other sectors will not *seriously* upset our prognostications.

In an advanced economy, we cannot hope to define one sector that is completely independent of all the rest. However, we may find a sector that is 'independent enough' (in some sense) or one that is unilaterally dependent upon other sectors rather than mutually interdependent with them.

This section examines the degree of interdependence between agriculture and the nonfarm economy from the perspective of conventional input-output analysis. The second section discusses the 'fine structure' of production in agriculture and closely related sectors, and suggests some applications of process analysis as logical extensions of the input-output approach. The chapter concludes with some suggestions for reconciling process analysis models of the food and agricultural sectors of an advanced economy with input-output models of the economy as a whole.

Some advantages of partial analysis

I believe that the data network for agriculture in the United States is denser, more accurate, and better designed for analysis than are the data networks for most other sectors. The long tradition (nearly a century) of data collection and research in the United States Department of Agriculture and the land-grant universities has contributed to this result.

Thus, from an analytical standpoint, it seems possible to obtain clearer explanations of economic phenomena in the food and agricultural sectors than in the economy as a whole. From the policy standpoint also, an argument can be made for a partial equilibrium approach. In this context, a partial equilibrium approach would give the Secretary of Agriculture wide latitude in determining policies for the food and agricultural sectors. Coordination of policies between Agriculture and other departments *might* be required at rather infrequent intervals and at a high level of aggregation if a partial approach were justified. In contrast, a general equilibrium approach to policy would require the Secretary of Agriculture to consider the effects of his every contemplated action upon all other sectors of the economy and to scrutinize in detail every action contemplated by other cabinet officers.

The advantages of a partial equilibrium approach would, however, be quite illusory unless favoured by an appropriate structuring of the real economy. Whether an appropriate structuring exists is a question of fact, to the investigation of which we now turn. We will approach the question first from the point of view of conventional static input-output analysis.

An appropriate sectoring of the United States economy

Table 1 shows a transactions matrix for the United States for 1947, for seven interacting sectors. Two of these, livestock products and crops, make up agriculture itself. Two others, food processing and fibre processing, stand for the most part between agriculture and final demand. The other three are manufacturing (other than food and fibre processing), energy and transportation, and trade and services.

A striking feature of Table 1 is the cluster of small figures in the upper right-hand corner of the matrix of interacting sectors. The cluster appears even more clearly in the matrix of input-output coefficients, shown in Table 2, which has been partitioned between Sectors 4 and 5. The twelve entries in the upper right-hand block show that in only two cases would a gross output of $1 billion from Sectors 5, 6 or 7 require an input of as much as $0·01 billion from Sectors 1, 2, 3 or 4.

The two blocks on the principal diagonal of Table 2 contain sizeable interindustry flows. The entries in the lower left-hand block average much larger than those in the upper right.

Other aspects of this sectoring are brought out in the series of inverse matrices shown in Tables 3, 4 and 5, and in equation (1). If A is the

TABLE 1

Input-Output Transactions Matrix, United States, 1947

(7 interacting sectors)

In billions of dollars

	1 Livestock products	2 Crops	3 Food processing	4 Fibre processing	5 Other manufacturing	6 Energy and transportation	7 Trade and services	Final Demand				Total gross output
								New construction and maintenance	Exports	Government, inventory increases, gross capital formation	Households	
1. Livestock Products	1·4	—	11·2	0·6	*	*	0·1	—	*	0·2	6·4	19·9
2. Crops	7·4	4·0	6·6	1·8	0·3	*	*	0·1	1·7	0·9	3·4	26·2
3. Food Processing	2·4	0·1	12·0	0·6	2·2	0·1	0·5	*	2·0	1·3	36·8	58·3
4. Fibre Processing	*	0·1	0·2	8·5	1·6	*	0·2	*	1·4	1·1	13·4	26·6
5. Other Manufacturing	0·2	1·5	3·2	1·9	59·7	3·3	9·5	11·2	8·0	19·5	18·4	136·5
6. Energy and Transportation	0·7	0·4	1·8	0·5	5·1	2·2	4·6	1·3	2·4	1·2	4·8	24·9
7. Trade and Services	0·9	1·0	3·3	1·2	7·5	1·3	16·3	4·0	1·3	9·2	78·6	124·8
Autonomous Inputs:												
New Construction and Maintenance	0·1	0·1	0·2	0·1	0·3	1·4	4·7	*	—	21·6	0·2	28·7
Imports	0·3	0·7	2·4	0·5	2·7	0·2	0·1	—	—	2·3	0·8	10·0
Government, Inventory Depletions	1·1	2·3	3·1	1·3	7·2	2·8	12·5	0·5	0·8	4·2	32·4	68·2
Households, Depreciation	5·4	15·9	14·3	9·8	49·8	13·4	76·2	11·5	0·9	29·5	2·1	228·9
Total Gross Outlay	19·9	26·2	58·3	26·6	136·5	24·9	124·8	28·7	18·5	91·1	197·5	753·0

* Less than $50 million.

TABLE 2

Matrix of Input-Output Coefficients, United States, 1947

(7 interacting sectors)

	1 Livestock products	2 Crops	3 Food processing	4 Fibre processing	5 Other manufac- turing	6 Energy and transporta- tion	7 Trade and services
1. Livestock Products	0·0692	—	0·1915	0·0236	*	0·0001	0·0006
2. Crops	0·3967	0·1539	0·1134	0·0659	0·0025	0·0004	0·0003
3. Food Processing	0·1210	0·0053	0·2066	0·0223	0·0163	0·0055	0·0043
4. Fibre Processing	0·0001	0·0041	0·0042	0·3196	0·0114	0·0013	0·0016
5. Other Manufacturing	0·0121	0·0587	0·0556	0·0696	0·4373	0·1342	0·0761
6. Energy and Transportation	0·0330	0·0147	0·0306	0·0169	0·0373	0·0873	0·0371
7. Trade and Services	0·0468	0·0392	0·0562	0·0441	0·0550	0·0534	0·1310

* Less than 0·00005.

TABLE 3

Inverse Matrix, United States, 1947

(7 interacting sectors)

	1 Livestock products	2 Crops	3 Food processing	4 Fibre processing	5 Other manufac- turing	6 Energy and transporta- tion	7 Trade and services
1. Livestock Products	1·1109	0·0028	0·2699	0·0489	0·0094	0·0034	0·0032
2. Crops	0·5100	1·1859	0·2952	0·1444	0·0176	0·0055	0·0043
3. Food Processing	0·1765	0·0120	1·3093	0·0554	0·0411	0·0148	0·0110
4. Fibre Processing	0·0067	0·0098	0·0138	1·4751	0·0314	0·0071	0·0058
5. Other Manufacturing	0·1250	0·1418	0·2026	0·2294	1·8237	0·2800	0·1731
6. Energy and Transportation	0·0638	0·0282	0·0723	0·0469	0·0822	1·1115	0·0551
7. Trade and Services	0·1064	0·0656	0·1305	0·1050	0·1260	0·0877	1·1664

matrix of technical coefficients, each inverse has the formula $(I - A)^{-1}$ where I is the identity matrix.

In Table 3 most of the total effects in the upper right-hand block are less than 1 per cent as large as the corresponding change in deliveries to final demand. The two largest effects are those of 'other manufacturing' upon the food processing and fibre processing sectors.

TABLE 4

Inverse Matrix, United States, 1947

(5 interacting sectors)

	1 Livestock products	2 Crops	3 Food processing	4 Fibre processing	5–7 All other industries
1. Livestock Products	1·1110	0·0026	0·2698	0·0487	0·0055
2. Crops	0·5102	1·1856	0·2951	0·1440	0·0092
3. Food Processing	0·1768	0·0114	1·3090	0·0544	0·0222
4. Fibre Processing	0·0070	0·0093	0·0136	1·4742	0·0152
5–7. All Other Industries	0·3008	0·2214	0·3992	0·3581	1·6315

In Table 4, Sectors 5, 6 and 7 are combined into a single category, 'all other industries.' A $1 billion increase in deliveries from this category to final demand calls for increases of only $0·0055 to $0·0222 billion in total gross outputs of the sectors comprising what I shall call the 'Agricultural Complex.' In sharp contrast, an increase of $1 billion in deliveries to final demand from a sector in the Agricultural Complex requires an increase of $0·2214 to $0·3992 billion in the total gross output of 'all other industries'.

TABLE 5

Inverse Matrix, United States, 1947

(4 interacting sectors)

	1–4 Agricultural complex	5 Other manufac- turing	6 Energy and transport	7 Trade and services
1–4. Agricultural Complex	1·7822	0·1002	0·0306	0·0241
5. Other Manufacturing	0·1967	1·8231	0·2799	0·1731
6. Energy and Transport	0·0616	0·0824	1·1115	0·0551
7. Trade and Services	0·1165	0·1260	0·0877	1·1664

Table 5 compresses the Agricultural Complex into a single sector. The pull of the Agricultural Complex upon each of the other three sectors is considerable, but only one of the three, 'other manufacturing', exerts a substantial pull upon the Agricultural Complex.

The final stage of compression, with the national economy divided into two interacting sectors, is given by the following matrix equation:

$$\begin{bmatrix} X_1 \\ X_2 \end{bmatrix} = \begin{bmatrix} 1\cdot7811 & 0\cdot0521 \\ 0\cdot3649 & 1\cdot6314 \end{bmatrix} \begin{bmatrix} Y_1 \\ Y_2 \end{bmatrix} \tag{1}$$

where the Y's are deliveries to final demand and the X's are total gross outputs, all measured in billions of 1947 dollars. For 1947 the values of the variables are as follows (in billion dollars):

Agricultural Complex: $X_1 = 132$; $Y_1 = 69$
All other industries: $X_2 = 286$; $Y_2 = 160$

The 2 by 2 inverse is nearly triangular. If Y_1 increases by \$1 billion, the gross output of 'all other industries' increases by \$0·36 billion. But if Y_2 increases by \$1 billion, the gross output required from the Agricultural Complex increases by only \$0·05 billion.

Some allowance should be made for the fact that the 'all other industries' sector is more than twice as large as the Agricultural Complex in terms of gross output and of deliveries to final demand. An increase of 10 per cent (\$16·0 billion) in deliveries of 'all other industries' to final demand would call for an increase of 0·6 per cent in gross output from the Agricultural Complex. And an increase of 10 per cent (\$6·9 billion) in deliveries to final demand from the Agricultural Complex would call for an increase of 0·9 per cent in the gross output of 'all other industries'.

It appears that, if only the input-output mechanism is considered, quite accurate projections could be made of output levels in the Agricultural Complex even if the output projection for 'all other industries' were in error by more than 10 per cent. The converse is also true: quite accurate projections could be made of output levels in the aggregate of 'all other industries' even if output projections for the Agricultural Complex were in error by 10 per cent or more.

These demonstrations are all based on data for the year 1947. Are they equally valid for 1961?

The 1947 transactions matrix, like the inverse, is nearly triangular:

	Agricultural Complex	All other industries
Agricultural Complex:	57	5
All other industries:	17	110

where all entries are in billions of 1947 dollars. All sectors of the economy have grown substantially since 1947. There has been a rapid substitution of machinery for labour in agriculture since 1947 and a sharp increase in the use of fertilizer and other manufactured inputs. Thus, the lower left-hand entry has grown markedly.

But the upper right-hand entry has shown little or no growth in absolute terms and has doubtless declined on a relative basis. It reflects uses of farm products and by-products in industries other than food and fibre processing. In many of these uses (soap, paint, and the like), agricultural raw materials have been partially displaced by petroleum by-products and other sources of organic compounds. Hence, changes since 1947 have made the 2 by 2 matrix even more nearly triangular.

Conventional input-output analysis therefore suggests that a partial equilibrium approach to economic analysis and policy formation in the food and agricultural sectors would be quite feasible, and that the consideration of interactions between these sectors and the rest of the economy might require only minor adjustments in the results of a partial analysis. We shall return to this point in the concluding section.

2. *The Fine Structure of the Agricultural Complex in an Advanced Economy*

This section deals with the nature of agricultural production and with some problems of classification or sectoring that arise when we try to adapt the facts of agricultural production in an advanced economy to the requirements of input-output analysis.

The nature of agricultural production

The starting point for a description of agricultural production is the physical relationship between inputs and output on a given acre of land or with respect to a particular cow, hen, or other animal unit. This is the familiar production function or surface of economic theory.[1]

The majority of these functions show diminishing returns to particular factors and relationships of substitution and/or complementarity between factors. If we know the prices of the product and of each variable factor, we can choose a particular point on the production surface which corresponds to maximum net income. This assumes, of course, that the production surface is known exactly and that all the variable inputs are

---

[1] Heady and Dillon [1] have brought together a large number of empirical production functions for agricultural products.

available in sufficient quantities to achieve the maximum net income combination.

Already we have a difficulty in adapting input-output analysis to the nature of agricultural production. Input-output analysis involves linear production functions, whereas the great majority of agricultural production functions are curved (convex). However, there are ways of reducing this inconsistency. Suppose that a farmer has 40 acres of land and has already decided to plant the entire 40 acres to a specified crop, say corn. We can imagine a 'master production surface' for 40 acres of corn which includes the various inputs that might be employed in any of the possible processes or activities for growing corn. If two inputs are direct substitutes (for example, horse power and tractor power), production activity using one of them will involve a portion of the master production surface for which inputs of the other are zero. If certain inputs are indivisible, there will be discontinuities in the production surface. However, some paths across some portions of the production surface will be smooth and curvilinear.

To make a transition from such a surface to linear production functions, we could draw a straight line or vector from the origin (at which all inputs are zero) to any point on the master production surface — in fact, we could draw as many such vectors as we liked. For example, one vector or 'activity' might differ from another only in that the first involved 20 pounds of nitrogen fertilizer per acre while the second involved 21 pounds. However, if the range of fertilizer applications worth considering runs from zero to 200 pounds, such a minute difference between activities would be an over-refinement and would lead to prohibitively expensive computations if we tried to make operational use of such linearized production functions.

In practice, we might consider a limited number of activities for producing corn, covering perhaps three or four levels of fertilizer use per acre, three or four kinds of farm machinery and/or animal-drawn equipment, and perhaps two or three levels of some other input. Then, for any given set of prices of inputs and of corn, together with such limitations as might exist upon the quantity of labour and other specific resources available, linear programming could be used to select the most profitable activity for growing corn.

The same linear programming concepts can be extended to the case of a farm that produces two or more products. As before, there may be a number of alternative processes for producing corn and a number for each other crop or livestock product that would be feasible from the standpoint of climate and soil. The farm can be subdivided into a number of fields representing different soil types and degrees of slope. The profit-maximizing production plan for the year just ahead, given an array of expected prices for all products and factors, would be subject to a number of specific resource limitations. Over a longer period, some of the short-run limitations could be removed by replacing existing types of equipment with new ones, remodelling farm buildings, and so on.

A linear programming analysis of production possibilities on a given farm also yields estimates of the marginal value products of the various limiting resources. If the technical coefficients in each of the activities were accurately specified, and if the resource limitations were spelled out in full realistic detail, then the marginal value products of the different limiting resources (compared with the market prices of additional quantities of these resources) would suggest directions in which the farmer should try to change his present array of resources. A high marginal value product for land suggests the desirability of his buying or renting additional land to combine with his present labour and capital; a high marginal value product for capital would suggest the desirability of borrowing additional funds; and so on.

Any one of the possible vectors or processes just described is a linear homogeneous production function, of the same form as a column of technical coefficients in an input-output matrix. However, a given farmer may select different activities for raising the same crop in successive years, depending upon changes in relative prices and in his stock of resources. Thus, the column of technical coefficients for the corn 'industry' on his farm would change from year to year.

It is well known that a column of technical coefficients in a national input-output matrix represents a blend of the many different techniques and production functions actually being used in individual establishments. If the proportions of the industry's output produced by different processes should change, the column of technical coefficients will also change.

Given sufficiently detailed information, we could explain changes in technical coefficients at the industry level in terms of changes in the processes selected and used on each individual farm. And the rationale of the individual farmer in adopting new techniques can be expressed in linear programming terms.[1]

Once a new type of input (for example, a mechanical cotton picker) becomes available and its performance characteristics known, one or more new activities involving its use are added to the previously existing array of possible activities. If, given the resource limitations on a farm,

---

[1] This has been demonstrated in a study by Richard Day [2].

one of the new activities would result in a higher net income than any of those previously available, it will probably be adopted.

Hence, linear programming models of individual farms can be made to generate changes in input-output coefficients as a by-product of the profit-maximizing behaviour of farm operators. Two main paths are available for making this approach operational.

One of these is to apply linear programming models to small, homogeneous agricultural regions as though each region were a profit-maximizing unit. This approach has been taken by Henderson [3], Heady and Egbert [4], and Day [2]. Day's model treats a small region at a level of detail similar to that used in linear programming studies of individual farms. Henderson and Heady and Egbert divided the United States into more than 100 regions, but their models for individual regions are much less detailed than Day's.

The other path is to take a sample of individual farms, make a linear programming model for each farm, and expand the sample responses to provide estimates for regions and for the nation as a whole.[1]

It is possible to take account of regional variations in farm product prices and to deal realistically with transportation costs and the locations of food processing activities by means of a spatial equilibrium model. Such a model could be extended to encompass several interdependent farm products or groups of products and a considerable number of regions.[2] Conceptually, a rather detailed process analysis model of the entire Agricultural Complex appears to be within reach.

Problems of commodity classification and sectoring within the Agricultural Complex

It is customary in input-output analysis to subdivide agriculture on the basis of commodities rather than of establishments. A single farm may raise products as diverse as wheat and cattle or as milk, eggs, hogs, beef cattle, corn, oats, and soybeans. The industries related to agriculture are also differentiated along commodity lines. This suggests that the significant flows to keep track of in agriculture and closely related sectors are flows of commodities rather than the sales from particular types of multi-product farms.

An input-output transactions matrix for the Agricultural Complex presents us with two main types of problems:

(1) How to deal with extra-market (or intra-firm) transactions, and

---

[1] Heady and others in the United States have work in progress based on this approach.
[2] I have discussed in [5] the problems involved in integrating such a model with the linear programming formulations of agricultural production put forward by Heady and Egbert [4] and (separately) by Henderson [3] and Day [2].

(2) How to deal with changes in the degrees of specialization and vertical integration?

Extra-market transactions

A sectoring of agriculture by commodities produces some artificialities. In the first instance, the total output of feed grains and hay is credited to the feed crops sector. But a very large proportion of this output is then delivered to the livestock sector(s). The bulk of this transfer of feed output to the livestock sector takes place on the farm which has produced the feed. In such situations, feed crop production is simply an intermediate step toward the more basic objective of livestock output.

When pasture is grazed by livestock, any fertilizer, irrigation water and other inputs applied to the pasture are regarded as direct inputs into the livestock sector (that is, they are so treated in the 1947 input-output study for the United States). However, if hay were cut from this same field — hay of a type and in a form that had some potential market value — the inputs of fertilizer and irrigation water would be attributed directly to the feed crops sector, even though the farmer fed all the hay to his own livestock.

The problem seems to arise because once feed crops are harvested they *can* be sold. Feed crops that are sold may be transferred from the original producer to a neighbouring farmer or to a local feed dealer. The dealer in turn may sell them either to nearby farmers or to firms and dealers located at various distances. But suppose the upshot is, in every case, that the feed crops, without processing, are consumed by livestock: Shall we separate the flow of feed crops to livestock into a number of different components depending on the distance of shipment and the number of middlemen involved? Or shall we regard the entire flow as a direct transfer from the crop to the livestock sector?

Suppose now that feed crops are sold to a feed manufacturer who grinds and blends them, adds vitamins, minerals, antibiotics and the like, and sells the resulting products to livestock producers. Once specialization between farms or farming regions has progressed to the point at which some farmers regularly sell feed crops and other farms regularly depend on purchased feed, it becomes possible for a feed manufacturer to introduce a blending operation in addition to the transportation and trade inputs that are already being made.

However, the operator of a very large farm could do a fairly good feed grinding and blending job on the farm. Does this activity become part of the 'grain mill products' industry? Is it an extension of the 'feed crop' industry? Or is it a part of the livestock industry?

Changes in degrees of specialization and vertical integration

The problem of dealing with intra-firm transactions is not unique to agriculture. Neither is the problem of changing degrees of vertical integration and specialization. However, changes in the organization of food production and marketing in the United States are taking place with such speed as to warrant special attention.

The most sweeping changes have occurred in the production of broilers — that is, young chickens raised for meat. Thirty years ago, a farmer might raise a few scores or hundreds of young chickens as a by-product of an egg-laying enterprise. The chicks would be hatched on his own farm.

When commercial hatcheries became skilful in sorting baby chicks by sex it became possible for some farmers to specialize in broiler production and others in egg-laying enterprises. Then, in a few areas, feed manufacturers took over the function of coordinating the various steps in broiler production and marketing. A revolution in food retailing and wholesaling technology facilitated the development of this role. The broiler industry demonstrated the feasibility of integrated production and marketing sequences in which functions traditionally performed on farms become steps in a comprehensive factory-type production sequence.

So far as technology is concerned, it would be possible for a retail food chain to establish an 'industrial complex' including, on a single site of limited area, a hatchery, a feed mill, buildings in which the broilers would be housed and fed, and a processing plant in which they would be dressed and packaged for retail sale. Egg production could be carried on at the same site. Thus, the entire poultry industry could *conceivably* be lifted out of the agricultural context with which it has traditionally been associated. It would remain a biological industry, but not an agricultural one. No one connected with the industry would need to know how to plant grain or plough a field. Similar possibilities exist with respect to the production of hogs, fluid milk, and other livestock products.

These recent trends and future prospects raise serious problems of classification, particularly if it is desired to compare successive input-output tables over ten, twenty or thirty years. To the extent that individual farmers specialize on a single livestock product, the conflict between commodity and establishment principles of classification will be reduced. But transfers of production activities from farms to industrial establishments or the disappearance of marketable intermediate products increase our difficulties.

If there is a way out of these difficulties, it lies in a much more comprehensive view of food production and marketing than has been customary in input-output tables or national income accounts. The marketing process for farm food products is typically conceived as extending from the farmer's gate to the point at which a retail store transfers the product to consumers. This is a useful demarcation for many purposes. But it is more fruitful to think of a final demand function for 'food on the table' and a sequence of factor inputs extending from that point back through the marketing system and through the production process on the farm. These boundaries should be sufficiently inclusive for our purposes, although a long chain of production processes and factor inputs extends backward from the farm into the marketing and production complex for inputs used in agricultural production.

Thus, each unit of a particular food product on the dinner table is the output of an activity or process which may be represented as a vector of technical coefficients. Inputs of labour will be made at several levels in the production and marketing sequence, and the cash or imputed costs of an hour of labour at each level may be different. The opportunity cost of the housewife's labour in the kitchen must be taken into account; it is also a factor in the capital intensity of the consumer's kitchen regarded as a food processing 'plant'.

Alternative processes exist for getting a particular kind and quality of food to the consumer's table. Some of these activities include considerable processing of food somewhere in the marketing chain; others leave most of the processing to be done in the consumer's kitchen. If the quality of the end product is identical for several processes, that process which involves the lowest cost under the given constellation of cash and imputed input prices will tend to be selected.

The problem of product quality can also be viewed in this light. Units of a product which are identical as they leave the farm may be different commodities when they arrive on the consumer's table. Certain aspects of the different processing and marketing activities affect the flavour, aroma, and texture of the product which reaches the consumer. They result in different prices for final products derived from identical raw materials. Given rough estimates of the community indifference surfaces of particular groups of consumers, price discounts associated with quality defects could be allocated back to the particular aspects of production and marketing activities which are responsible for them.

Within a decade or two we may be able to define and quantify most of the attributes of foods that are of interest to consumers. If a given food product were defined as a vector of nutrients and other measurable utilities, we might scan the available production and marketing sequences and select, by linear programming methods, the least-cost process which would meet the product specifications.

Conceptually, the process of selecting foods for a least-cost diet[1] could be linked to the process of choosing the least-cost production and marketing sequence for each food. It is too early to say whether this concept can or should be made operational. At the least it suggests the economic incentives for changes in the present activity-mix of food and agriculture.

To understand or anticipate structural changes in the food production and processing sectors, we should evidently make as detailed a separation of processes within the Agricultural Complex of an advanced economy as our data permit. At the worksheet level we might have several processes for producing each commodity. If we knew the quantities produced by each process, we could weight the process vectors to obtain a column of input-output coefficients for the commodity sector. Thus, on a descriptive level, our information could be poured into an input-output model of the economy as a whole.

TABLE 6

Change in Quantities of Inputs per Unit of Total Farm Output and Changes in Prices of Inputs, United States, 1940 to 1960

Input	(1) Input per unit of farm output	(2) Price per unit of input	Price Index
	1960 as per cent of 1940	1960 as per cent of 1940	
Manhours	32	489	Farm wage rates.
Cropland	62	353	Value of farm land per acre, with all improvements.
Trucks	189	257	Motor vehicles (price index).
Tractors	194	250	Farm machinery (price index).
Fertilizer	273	155	Fertilizer (price index).

On an analytical level, information as to the array of processes available for producing a given commodity would help us to predict changes in

[1] V. E. Smith [6], [7] has used a least-cost diet model containing nearly 100 targets or restrictions with selections to be made from a list of nearly 600 foods. The retail price of each food is taken as given; some of the restrictions are based on nutritional needs and some on food preferences as indicated by data from a consumer panel. The amount of each food included in the diet depends upon its relative efficiency in satisfying one or more of the restrictions.

F

technical coefficients in the corresponding input-output sector. Table 6 gives a hint of the tremendous speed with which technical coefficients in United States agriculture have been changing. Compared with 1940, a unit of farm output in 1960 required only 32 per cent as much labour and only 62 per cent as much land. However, each manhour of labour in 1960 was accompanied by several times as much machinery and chemical fertilizer as in 1940. Furthermore, the directions of change in the proportions of the different inputs were precisely those which would be expected from changes in relative prices.

It would be hard to find more impressive evidence of the effects of factor prices upon the selection of processes or activities. These effects can be allowed for in process analysis models.

One type of transaction which presents sectoring problems is the consumption of produce on the farm on which it is grown — the case of self-suppliers. In the United States, the products thus consumed on farms are valued at farm prices in the national income accounts. It is true, of course, that no use is made of *commercial* transportation and processing facilities in this connection. But nonfarm consumers will pay retail prices for the same commodities and will also be credited with purchasing services from the transportation and trade sectors.

It seems best to separate farm households from other households in the final demand columns and in the autonomous input rows that border the transactions matrix. This will also be an advantage if, as is likely, the income elasticities of demand for various commodity groups differ as between farm and other households. Also, the nature of capital formation and induced investment may differ between farm and nonfarm proprietors.

The boundary between agriculture and nonagriculture

The development of integrated production and marketing sequences indicates that we will have increasing difficulty in maintaining a consistent boundary between traditional agriculture and certain specialized livestock producing enterprises and services. To establish a boundary that will probably remain stable for a decade or more, we must draw a line that includes not only traditional agriculture but a cluster of food processing, fibre processing and related sectors which account for some 95 per cent of all deliveries of agricultural products and by-products to final demand. The inclusion of a few other sectors providing specialized inputs, such as farm real estate and fertilizer, would further stabilize this boundary against the effects of vertical integration.

3. *Reconciling Process Analysis Models of the Agricultural Complex with Input-Output Models of the Entire Economy*

It is clear enough that the various activities used for producing a given commodity can be aggregated into a column of technical coefficients suitable for inclusion in an input-output table. This would be a reconciliation at the descriptive level.

A reconciliation could also be effected at the analytical level. Suppose we succeeded in developing a process analysis model of the entire Agricultural Complex. If prices of all possible inputs and all possible outputs of the Agricultural Complex were specified in advance, and if various resource or capacity limitations were specified, we could compute an optimal array of outputs delivered to final demand and of inputs required from other sectors. Inputs would be transformed into outputs using optimal combinations of processes which in turn would involve optimal intersectoral flows through a transactions matrix. If we assumed that input prices were given but that the prices received for farm products would depend upon quantities produced as indicated by statistical demand functions, we should arrive at an efficient and consistent production pattern.

Different portions of the required programming computations might be handled in an iterative fashion. For example, optimal production patterns for a sample of farms could be computed assuming specified prices for farm outputs. The outputs of these farms could be expanded into national aggregates. The amounts produced would be conveyed through the processing and marketing sectors in least-cost sequences, subject to relevant capacity limits. When delivered to final demand, these quantities might result in retail prices which were inconsistent with the farm prices originally assumed. The farm prices would then be conformed to the new retail prices and the sequence of steps repeated. As all demand functions will be downward sloping and all supply functions either upward sloping or horizontal, it appears that these calculations would converge satisfactorily within a very few iterations.

These calculations would generate a detailed 'bill of goods' for inputs produced in other sectors of the economy. Let us assume that a government agency other than the Department of Agriculture has been making detailed projections of these other sectors within an input-output framework. This agency will have made tentative estimates of goods and services which will likely be required from these other sectors by the Agricultural Complex. If the two sets of estimates of inputs differ from one another (and they undoubtedly will differ in detail) the following procedure might be used:

(a) Adjust the total gross output of each nonagricultural sector so that it is consistent with the Department of Agriculture's estimates of input requirements.

(b) These adjustments will logically require slight changes in the amounts of certain farm products required for industrial uses. In themselves, the adjustments may hardly be worth making, but they can, in principle, be made.

The modest size of the adjustments is suggested by the calculations cited in Section 1 — namely, (1) that a 10 per cent change in deliveries to final demand from the Agricultural Complex would call for a change of about 0·9 per cent in the gross output of 'all other industries', and (2) that a 10 per cent change in deliveries to final demand from 'all other industries' would alter gross output required from the Agricultural Complex by about 0·6 per cent.

In reality, an input-output table does not include all the channels through which the two major sectors of the economy interact. For example, changes in nonagricultural employment lead to changes in consumer incomes which in turn cause demand curves for foods and textile products to shift. In principle it is possible to combine an input-output table with a macro-economic model connecting certain of the autonomous input sectors with components of final demand.

Also, the level of precision implied in the preceding discussion may be unnecessary for many practical purposes. This is particularly true if we are assuming a private enterprise system with active competition in most sectors of the Agricultural Complex. The decisions which result in economies of size and economies of coordination are for the most part left to private individuals, including farmers, who are accustomed to bearing some degree of risk. Year-to-year variations in crop yields and in exports also contrast with the precision of linear programming computations.

REFERENCES

[1] HEADY, E. O. and DILLON, J. L., *Agricultural Production Functions*, Iowa State University Press, 1961.
[2] DAY, R. H., *Production Response and Recursive Programming*, Amsterdam, 1962.
[3] HENDERSON, J. M., 'The utilization of agricultural land,' *Review of Economics and Statistics*, 1959, p. 242.

[4] HEADY, E. O. and EGBERT, A. C., 'Programming regional adjustments in grain production,' *Journal of Farm Economics*, 1959, p. 718.

[5] FOX, K. A., 'Spatial price equilibrium and process analysis in the food and agricultural sectors' in *Studies in Process Analysis: Economy-wide Production Capabilities*, New York, 1963.

[6] SMITH, V. E., 'Linear programming models for the determination of palatable human diets,' *Journal of Farm Economics*, 1959, p. 272.

[7] SMITH, V. E., 'Measurement of product attributes recognised by consumers,' in *Consumer preferences and market development for farm products*, Center for Agricultural and Economic Adjustment, Iowa State University, 1960 (Mimeo.).

[8] FOX, K. A., 'The study of interactions between agriculture and the nonfarm economy: local, regional and national,' *Journal of Farm Economics*, 1962, p. 1.

CHAPTER 5

Models of Agriculture and Industry
in Less Developed Economies[1]

by J. K. SENGUPTA

---

1. *The Input-Output Framework in Less Developed Economies*

Recent research into alternative designs of planning models in less developed economies has emphasized the detailed input-output type of accounting. The collection of the data required is, however, difficult, time-consuming and expensive unless confined to an occasional benchmark year. It seems, therefore, practical to inquire whether models consisting of a few rather closely integrated sectors, which can be kept up to date with little cost or difficulty, can be developed for specifying the process of economic growth.

This paper attempts to evaluate, in the light of Indian experience, the implications of models with a small number of relatively integrated sectors. After examining, in this section, the appropriateness of the input-output technique in a predominantly agricultural economy, in Section 2 the usefulness of an analysis in which industries are divided into an 'Agricultural Complex' and an 'Industrial Complex' is discussed. In Section 3 it is shown that one of the basic advantages of two-sector models is the ease or flexibility with which stochastic variations of the parameters can be introduced. Moreover, as shown in Section 4, such models could easily be combined, if desired, with the detailed accounting system of conventional input-output analysis.

The process of economic growth in a less developed economy, insofar as it involves changes in production structure, may be analysed by input-output technique, but there are some characteristics which are not treated satisfactorily in the usual analysis. First, input-output coefficients change over time due to several factors, such as the emergence of newer industries, technological change, the intersectoral allocation of planned investment and even stochastic influences. Second, while input-output coefficients in a developed economy may be interpreted as indicators of

[1] Grateful acknowledgment is due to Dr. Karl A. Fox for advice and criticism concerning an earlier draft of this paper.

optimal adjustment of output-mix, this may not hold true, in the short run, in the less developed economies, particularly for the Agricultural Complex.[1] In a less developed economy input-output coefficients are to be taken as allocation coefficients: changes in supply pre-determine changes in deliveries to final demand rather than the other way round. Third, the process of capital accumulation associated with development has a number of 'stages' (irreversibilities) due to the fact that the output configuration in a given period sets the stage for input provision in the next. This is relevant and important particularly when the input-output technique is utilized as a policy model for planning economic development over time.

There is also a basic problem encountered in empirical input-output accounting in most underdeveloped economies in that stock-flow coefficients entering into the capital account of interacting sectors are not available. Figures of capital stock over time are, however, usually available for a few aggregated sectors, such as agriculture, manufacturing and transport. This information can be utilized if the detailed input-output tables are aggregated into a few sectors.

One of the simplest divisions of the economy is into an Agricultural Complex and an Industrial Complex; the former includes primary agriculture, food and fibre processing industries, and the latter all other industries in the manufacturing, transport and energy sectors.[2] An important reason for this division is that it shows the contrast between relatively declining and growing sectors.[3] The advantage of this scheme, which can in some cases be extended to sub-sectors of the two integrated sectors, is that the two-way interdependence of the interacting part of an input-output table can be reduced to unilateral and consecutive interdependence. This may permit decentralization of an overall plan into unilaterally dependent subplans.

Changes in coefficients

As regards changing input-output coefficients, when the changes are small the balance equation of an input-output system can be reformulated as

$$\dot{X}_i = \sum_j a_{ij}\dot{X}_j + \sum_j \dot{a}_{ij}X_j + \dot{Y}_i \qquad (i, j = 1, 2, \ldots, n) \qquad (1)$$

---

[1] This term is used here in exactly the same sense as on p. 62 in Chapter 4 above.

[2] Throughout this chapter, use is made of the 19-sector tables published by the Indian Institute of Public Opinion. Trade and services are excluded from the interacting sectors. 'Fibre processing' includes textiles, wood, leather and rubber products.

[3] A closely related type of sectoring is in terms of two integrated sectors, one producing consumer goods and the other investment goods.

where X denotes gross output, Y final demand and a_{ij} the input-output coefficients; the dot over a variable denotes its time derivative.

For a two-sector economy, with an Agricultural Complex (sector 1) and an Industrial Complex (sector 2), the equation system (1) can be written as,

$$
\begin{bmatrix} \dot{X}_1(t) \\ \dot{X}_2(t) \end{bmatrix} = \begin{bmatrix} \dfrac{\dot{a}_{11}(1-a_{22})+a_{12}\dot{a}_{21}}{\varDelta} & \dfrac{\dot{a}_{12}(1-a_{22})+a_{12}\dot{a}_{22}}{\varDelta} \\ \dfrac{a_{21}\dot{a}_{11}+\dot{a}_{21}(1-a_{11})}{\varDelta} & \dfrac{\dot{a}_{12}a_{21}+\dot{a}_{22}(1-a_{11})}{\varDelta} \end{bmatrix} \begin{bmatrix} X_1(0) \\ X_2(0) \end{bmatrix}
$$

$$
+ \begin{bmatrix} \dfrac{1-a_{22}}{\varDelta} & \dfrac{a_{12}}{\varDelta} \\ \dfrac{a_{21}}{\varDelta} & \dfrac{1-a_{11}}{\varDelta} \end{bmatrix} \begin{bmatrix} \dot{Y}_1(t) \\ \dot{Y}_2(t) \end{bmatrix} \tag{2}
$$

where $\varDelta=(1-a_{11})(1-a_{22})-a_{12}a_{21}$ and $X_i(0)$ is the base period level of gross output in sector i. In particular, when $\dot{a}_{ij}$ equals zero for each i and j, we have the conventional input-output system. Denoting the first coefficient matrix on the right-hand side of equation (2) by B and the second coefficient matrix by $(I-A)^{-1}$, we may write (2) in matrix terms as

$$
\varDelta X = B(I-A)^{-1}Y + (I-A)^{-1}\varDelta Y \tag{3}
$$

The matrix B may be called the transition matrix, since it specifies the change in input-output coefficients over time (with output configuration constant at the initial level) in response to changes in final demand. A broad idea of the structural change in the Indian economy

TABLE 1

Two-Sector Transition Matrix, India

Sectors	1952–3 to 1960–1		1960–1 to 1965–6	
	Agricultural Complex	Industrial Complex	Agricultural Complex	Industrial Complex
Agricultural Complex	−0·0011	0·0353	−0·0193	−0·0297
Industrial Complex	0·0012	0·0242	0·0070	−0·0011

may be gained from the transition matrix derived from two-sector input-output tables for 1952–3, 1960–1 and forecasts for 1965–6, shown in Table 1. Although the statistical data are imperfect, a notional estimate could be made of the direction of structural change. As seen from the table, in the period 1952–3 to 1960–1 the column of technical coefficients belonging to the Industrial Complex has changed positively to a greater extent than has that of the Agricultural Complex.

Using a method developed by Rasmussen [1], an index of the change in input coefficients can be calculated for each sector.

For the Agricultural Complex the index is 0·000074 whereas for the Industrial Complex it is 0·003158; when, as in Table 2, the Agricultural Complex is disaggregated into four sectors — livestock products, all crops, food processing, fibre processing — the indices of structural change are − 0·003586, 0·000987, 0·000071, 0·002529 and 0·004846. If we assume that the input-output coefficients for a given column each come from populations with different means, but equal variances, then a criterion may be set up for distinguishing between a significant change and a non-significant change. Table 2 shows the observed change in each coefficient between 1952–3 and 1960–1 and the estimated variance of the total column coefficients on a five sector level of disaggregation.

TABLE 2

Changes in Input-Output Coefficients in India (1952–3 to 1960–1)
and Estimated Variance for Columns

Sectors	Livestock products 1	All crops 2	Food processing 3	Fibre processing 4	All other industries 5
1	− 0·0013	0·0000	0·0008	0·0003	− 0·0081
2	− 0·0077	0·0006	− 0·0024	− 0·0100	− 0·0119
3	− 0·0020	0·0000	0·0001	0·0000	− 0·0021
4	—	0·0000	0·0005	0·0015	0·0006
5	0·0001	0·0003	0·0005	0·0051	0·0167
Estimated variance	0·02315	0·00097	0·04268	0·00759	0·00680

It is remarkable that for the last two columns the change in the co-efficients is significant, implying that they lead in the process of growth.

Use in decision models

The use of the input-output technique as a policy-maker's decision model in a less developed economy raises another difficulty. Once the period of basic capital formation is completed, the Industrial Complex will have greater output flexibility than the Agricultural Complex. In the formulation of a national planning model, therefore, a planner can be more certain of a definite supply in the Industrial Complex than about future demand conditions. This fixes the future gross supply X_2^0 as a multiple of the current X_2, whereas the future final demand Y_2 for sector 2 may be such that one part (Y_{2a}^0), being the minimum average of the past levels, may be more reliably estimated and the other part (Y_{2b}) may be relatively unknown. Likewise, for the Agricultural Complex, the policy-maker could be more definite about demand, than about supply. This fixes the future level of final demand (Y_1^0) as a multiple of the current level (Y_1), whereas one part of the future level of gross supply (X_{1a}^0) could be more reliably estimated as the minimum average of past production levels, the other part (X_{1b}) being relatively unknown ($X_1 = X_{1a}^0 + X_{1b}$).

For the planning horizon, the balance equations now become

$$X_{1a}^0 + X_{1b} = a_{11}(X_{1a}^0 + X_{1b}) + a_{12}X_2^0 + Y_1^0$$
$$X_2^0 = a_{21}(X_{1a}^0 + X_{1b}) + a_{22}X_2^0 + Y_{2a}^0 + Y_{2b} \tag{4}$$

of which the solutions can be written as

$$\begin{bmatrix} X_{1b} \\ Y_{2b} \end{bmatrix} = \begin{bmatrix} \dfrac{a_{12}}{1-a_{11}} & -1 \\ (1-a_{22}) - \dfrac{a_{12}a_{21}}{1-a_{11}} & 0 \end{bmatrix} \begin{bmatrix} X_2^0 \\ X_{1a}^0 \end{bmatrix} + \begin{bmatrix} \dfrac{1}{1-a_{11}} & 0 \\ \dfrac{-a_{21}}{1-a_{11}} & -1 \end{bmatrix} \begin{bmatrix} Y_1^0 \\ Y_{2a}^0 \end{bmatrix} \tag{5}$$

Depending on the change in the coefficients a_{ij}, the national plan could in this case be divided into two segments: the 'core plan', which would be more certain to be realized; and the rest, which would depend on the change in the structural coefficients in the preceding stages. A natural extension of this case would be its reformulation in the form of multi-stage programming where some activities would be chance-constrained and some final demand may have a switch-over from one stage to another.

At the level of aggregation of a few sectors, it may be feasible to construct transactions matrices continually for several years. In such cases, mean values of each input-output coefficient may be specified and considering the deviations from the mean to be independently distributed with a finite variance, it is possible to derive the confidence interval for the gross output vector for a given change in the vector of final demand. Assuming the values of each input-output coefficient in the matrix to be randomly and independently distributed and denoting the (i, j) element of the inverse of $(I - A)$ by b_{ij}, one could compute the variance of the gross output vector as

$$\text{Var } X_i = \sum_{j=1}^{n} Y_j^2 \text{ Var } b_{ij} \qquad (i, j = 1, 2, \ldots, n) \qquad (6)$$

This type of information may be helpful in continuous planning for economic development, because in order to insure a stable rate of growth of gross output, the planning authority may allocate investment to a sector at a rate inversely proportional to the observed variance of sectoral output.

2. The Agricultural Sector in Less Developed Economies

In most of the densely populated underdeveloped economies, including India, the agricultural sector exhibits some common characteristics: a large weight in national income, relatively inflexible production and occupation structure, low rate of reinvestment, and lower rate of resource productivity than in the rest of the economy. A mature, developed economy, like the United States, presents a contrast in almost all of these aspects.

Table 3 shows a five sector transactions matrix for India for 1960–1 at 1952–3 prices. The last column indicates that the food-processing sector delivers to final demand more than 90 per cent of its gross output, 'all other industries' about 65 per cent, and other sectors percentages within these limits.

When the transactions matrix is compressed further into an Agricultural and an Industrial Complex, then, as Table 4 shows, the coefficients in the diagonal are far greater than the off-diagonal elements. Due to this diagonal dominance, the inverse of the coefficient matrix for 1960–1 shows an interesting result: an increase of one billion rupees worth of final demand for the Agricultural Complex would require an increase in gross industrial output by about Rs. 0·05 billion, whereas an identical increase for the Industrial Complex would require an increase of agricultural output by about Rs. 0·22 billion. To show that the coefficient matrix and its inverse are nearly triangular, as in a developed economy,[1] it is only necessary to interchange the two sectors so that the off-diagonal elements interchange with one another. The fact that the two sectors are of unequal size does not alter the situation much as compared with an advanced economy. For instance, an increase of 10 per cent (Rs. 2·3 billion) in deliveries of the Industrial Complex to

[1] See Chapter 4, p. 63.

TABLE 3

Five-Sector Transactions Matrix, India, 1960–1

(in Rs. millions 1952–3 prices)*

Sectors	Livestock products 1	All crops 2	Food processing 3	Fibre processing 4	All other industries 5	Total gross output	Total interindustry use as per cent of gross output
1. Livestock Products	97·8 *0·0556*	156·6 *0·0184*	64·7 *0·0553*	64·9 *0·0389*	124·4 *0·0348*	1,758·9	29
2. All Crops	563·4 *0·3202*	679·6 *0·0801*	578·9 *0·4955*	366·1 *0·2198*	207·8 *0·0582*	8,480·8	28
3. Food Processing	24·5 *0·0138*	11·2 *0·0013*	37·2 *0·0318*	2·9 *0·0017*	22·6 *0·0063*	1,167·8	8
4. Fibre Processing	—	67·5 *0·0079*	8·8 *0·0075*	167·3 *0·1005*	101·4 *0·0284*	1,664·0	21
5. All Other Industries	16·0 *0·0091*	180·5 *0·0212*	71·1 *0·0606*	128·8 *0·0772*	826·0 *0·2315*	3,567·7	34

* Input coefficients shown in italics.

TABLE 4

Two-Sector Coefficient Matrices and Inverses, India 1952–3, 1955–6, 1960–1, and projection for 1965–6

(Based on constant 1952–3 prices)

	1952–3		1955–6		1960–1		Projected 1965–6	
	Sector 1	Sector 2	Sector 1	Sector 2	Sector 1	Sector 2	Sector 1	Sector 2
				Coefficient Matrices (A)				
Sector 1	0·222	0·103	0·227	0·130	0·221	0·128	0·205	0·105
Sector 2	0·029	0·214	0·032	0·220	0·030	0·232	0·036	0·232
				Inverse Matrices*				
Sector 1	1·293	0·169	1·304	0·217	1·293	0·215	1·259	0·172
Sector 2	0·047	1·279	0·053	1·293	0·051	1·311	0·059	1·303

* This is of the form $(I-A)^{-1}$ where $I =$ identity matrix.

Sector 1, Agricultural Complex; Sector 2, Industrial Complex.

final demand would call for an increase of about 0·37 per cent in gross output from the Agricultural Complex, whereas an increase of 10 per cent (Rs. 9·7 billion) in final demand from the Agricultural Complex would call for an increase of about 1·26 per cent in the gross material output of the Industrial Complex.

As the process of development continues, the sector representing the Agricultural Complex is expected to increase its use of inputs from the Industrial Complex (e.g., more extensive use of fertilizers, mechanical power and nutrients), whereas the Industrial Complex is likely to use a lesser proportion of inputs from the Agricultural Complex. This means that a quasi-upper triangular coefficient matrix[1] would be gradually replaced by a quasi-lower triangular matrix, although the diagonal elements would retain their dominance under the given basis of aggregation.

Final demand is 74 per cent of total gross output for the Agricultural Complex and 66 per cent for the Industrial Complex. For the former, final demand is almost entirely consumption demand, for the latter it consists largely of investment, much of which is deliberately planned for in the public sector. It is not possible to indicate the impact of this investment pattern on the elements of the coefficient matrix, unless the matrix of investment allocation according to sectors of delivery is specified. The effect of unequal income elasticities of demand for the two sectors can however be easily specified by the relation

$$\Delta X_i = \sum_j b_{ij} \Delta Y_j = \sum_j b_{ij} \epsilon_j Y_j \left(\frac{\Delta Y_T}{Y_T} \right) \tag{7}$$

where ϵ_j denotes income elasticity of demand for the jth sector, Y_T denotes total net national income and b_{ij} is the (i, j) element of the inverse of the matrix $(I - A)$. Assuming income elasticities of 0·5 and 0·8 respectively for the two sectors, it is easy to show on the basis of the 1960–1 table that a 10 per cent increase of overall national income would require about a 5·1 per cent increment in gross output of the Agricultural Complex and about a 7·5 per cent increment in gross output of the Industrial Complex.

From an operational standpoint, one important question is how to specify systematically functional interrelationships between different sectors so that the process of evolution of a growing economic system

---

[1] An upper triangular matrix is such that all elements $a_{ij} = 0$ whenever $i > j$. A quasi-upper triangular matrix is such that all elements a_{ij} for $i > j$ are very small in relation to the elements on or above the main diagonal. A lower triangular matrix is such that all elements a_{ij} for $i < j$ equal zero (or very small as compared to others in the quasi-triangular case).

can be visualized. Conceptually, the ideal case would be to arrange sub-systems of an input-output matrix in an increasing scale of rates of growth: sectoring into an Agricultural Complex and an Industrial Complex (or integrated consumption-goods and investment-goods sectors), where the latter is expected to lead relatively in the process of growth, is a near approximation.

From an accounting standpoint, it may be necessary to identify as clearly as possible the growth-inducing activities by the principles of sectoring and classification. For a less diversified economy, some method for compression of a detailed input-output table into a few, relatively homogenous sectors would be immensely useful. Its advantage can be judged from the fact that in the table of 19 interacting sectors for India in 1960–1, the proportion of zero transactions (empty cells) constitutes nearly 52 per cent of the 361 possible transactions and if entries less than 1 per cent of each sector's total interindustry use are neglected, this figure would be more than 60 per cent. The table of 36 interacting sectors for 1953–4 which includes all types of trade and services in the interacting network,[1] has 46 per cent empty cells, or 55 per cent if very small entries are neglected.

3. *Framework of the Indian Planning Model*

The quasi-triangular coefficient matrix for the Agricultural and Industrial Complexes included neither autonomous inputs provided by households nor final demand. From this standpoint, an alternative principle of sectoral classification would be in terms of two integrated sectors, one producing investment goods and the other producing consumption goods.

Following Mahalanobis [2],[2] consider two 'completely integrated' sectors, Sector 1 producing consumer goods and Sector 2 producing investment goods, and assume that public-sector investment (G) is the main activating instrument for generating growth of output. Then the model is given by

$$\begin{bmatrix} \dot{Y}_1 \\ \dot{Y}_2 \end{bmatrix} = \begin{bmatrix} \beta_1 & 0 \\ 0 & \beta_2 \end{bmatrix} \begin{bmatrix} \lambda_1 G \\ \lambda_2 G \end{bmatrix} \quad (\lambda_1 + \lambda_2 = 1) \tag{8}$$

where Y_i and λ_i denote respectively the increment of *net* output and the investment allocation ratio for the ith sector.

[1] Prepared by the Indian Statistical Institute.
[2] It is interesting to note that the model used by Mahalanobis for the calculation of investment allocation in the five-year plans in India is based on a matrix of output-investment coefficients which is strictly diagonal in the two sector case and nearly triangular in the four sector case.

For a less developed economy, the ratio of investment goods to total national product is low (around 10 per cent) and a large part of investment is devoted to the needs of replacement and expansion in the consumption-goods sector. Hence, even assuming that such a two-sector breakdown is sufficiently valid as a broad approximation, some interrelation needs to be specified between the rates of growth of output of the two sectors. But so long as the total allocable investment G is considered exogenous in the model, there is no room left for introducing such flexibility. One way out may be to introduce a transactions matrix relating to gross output. Alternatively, we may break up the investment-goods sector into two parts: one part producing capital goods required for the expansion of the consumer-goods sector, the other part for further expansion of the investment-goods sector itself. The system can now be written as

$$\begin{bmatrix} \dot{Y}_1 \\ \dot{Y}_2 \\ \dot{Y}_3 \end{bmatrix} = \begin{bmatrix} \beta_{11} & 0 & 0 \\ \beta_{21} & \beta_{22} & 0 \\ 0 & \beta_{32} & \beta_{33} \end{bmatrix} \begin{bmatrix} \lambda_1 G \\ \lambda_2 G \\ \lambda_3 G \end{bmatrix} \quad (\lambda_1 + \lambda_2 + \lambda_3 = 1) \qquad (9)$$

where the coefficient matrix is strictly lower triangular.

So long as the consumption-goods sector is dominant in the subsistence economy, the first-stage decision behind the amount of allocable investment (G) concerns the proportion of additional consumer goods to be produced. The second-stage decision then involves the optimum choice between the proportions of investment to be allocated for producing capital goods either for the investment-goods sector itself or for the further expansion of consumer goods; the system has now two degrees of freedom. If the integrated consumption-goods sector itself is broken into three subsectors of production — large-scale manufacture in factories, small-scale rural enterprises, and households and the various services — then the coefficient β_{11} could be considered as a block or submatrix (with appropriate changes in the first row of (9) which would be unilaterally dependent on the other two subsectors of the investment-goods sector). The degrees of freedom in the model would now be four and the investment decisions could be taken in consecutive stages.[1]

The advantages of a triangular or block diagonal coefficient matrix are mainly twofold. First, it enables us to decompose the set of structural (or balance) equations into relatively independent subsets of equations, each subset being capable of solution in a recursive fashion. Second, it helps to make the decision-making process of national planning a decentralized one. An overall national plan can in this case be split into

[1] For a more detailed discussion, see [3].

a nucleus (a core plan) and unilaterally dependent sub-plans. The allocation model given in (8) assumes that the growth of output of the consumption-goods sector depends on that of the investment-goods sector, but not vice versa.

To show that such a recursive relation can be specified even when the two sectors are divided into n subsectors, we need to consider each β_i as the weighted average of subsector output-investment ratios,

$$\beta_i = \sum_k \lambda_{ik}\beta_{ik} \qquad (k=1, 2, \ldots, n; i=1, 2) \qquad (10)$$

The advantage of this flexible scheme is that stochastic variations of the output-investment ratios can easily be incorporated in an optimal sense in the framework of a policy model. Consider model (8) again and replace G by total planned investment (I), assuming, however, that the latter is exogenously determined. Denoting total income by Y and its rate of change by Z, it is easy to see that

$$\text{Var } Z = I^2(\lambda_1^2 \text{ var } \beta_1 + \lambda_2^2 \text{ var } \beta_2 + 2\rho\lambda_1\lambda_2\sigma_1\sigma_2) \qquad (11)$$

where ρ denotes the population correlation coefficient and σ_1, σ_2 stand for the standard deviations of the output-investment coefficients β_1 and β_2 respectively.

Suppose that the policy maker in setting the target rate of growth (T) wants to allocate total investment in such a manner that the stochastic variations in the input coefficients do not affect his target substantially. Denoting mean values by a bar over a variable and using E for the expectation of a random variable, the objective function of the policy maker can be written as

$$E(Z - T)^2 = \text{var } Z + (Z - T)^2$$

Minimization of this objective function yields the stochastic optimal allocation ratios

$$\lambda_1^* = \frac{\text{Var } \beta_2 + \left(\bar\beta_2 - \bar\beta_1\right)\left(\bar\beta_2 - \dfrac{T}{I}\right) - 2\rho\sigma_1\sigma_2}{\text{Var } \beta_1 + \text{var } \beta_2 + (\bar\beta_1 - \bar\beta_2)^2 - 4\rho\sigma_1\sigma_2}$$

$$\lambda_2^* = 1 - \lambda_1^* \qquad (12)$$

When $\bar\beta_1 = \bar\beta_2$ and $\rho = 0$, we get a simple result

$$\lambda_1^* = \frac{\text{Var } \beta_2}{\text{Var } \beta_1 + \text{var } \beta_2} \qquad (13)$$

This has a simple economic meaning, i.e., allocate more investment to that sector which in a proportional sense shows less variance of the parametric coefficient. The two-sector model (8) designed by Mahalanobis specified a value $\lambda_1 = 0\cdot33$ as the optimal one, on the basis of expected values $\bar{\beta}_1 = 0\cdot2$, $\bar{\beta}_2 = 0\cdot4$, by the condition of maximizing expected national income for a fixed planning horizon. From equation (13) it is evident that this value of $0\cdot33$ may also be stochastically optimal, in the sense of minimum variance only if $\mathrm{Var}\,\beta_1 = 2(\mathrm{Var}\,\beta_2)$.

When total investment (I) is endogenous to the system and is given by

$$I = I_0 e^{\lambda_1 \beta_1 t} \tag{14}$$

We can compute the variance of I by the approximation rule of statistical differential and then form the objective function of the policy maker as

$$F = w_1 I_0 \lambda_2 \bar{\beta}_2 e^{\lambda_1 \bar{\beta}_1 t} - w_2 (\mathrm{Var}\,I)^{1/2} \tag{15}$$

with positive fixed weights w_1 and w_2. Maximization of function F would mean a maximal rate of change of consumption goods output and a minimal dispersion of total allocable investment. The optimal allocation ratio would in this case be given by

$$\lambda_1^* = \frac{w_1 \bar{\beta}_2 (1 - \bar{\beta}_1)}{w_2 \sigma_1 + w_2 \sigma_1 \bar{\beta}_1 t - \bar{\beta}_1 \bar{\beta}_2 w_1}$$

$$\lambda_2^* = 1 - \lambda_1^* \tag{16}$$

To illustrate the nature of the probability density function for the input coefficients β_1 and β_2, we have computed in Table 5 the observed mean, variance (σ^2), skewness (γ_1) and kurtosis (γ_2) for the Indian data under two different methods.[1]

TABLE 5

Parameters of the Distribution of the net Output-Capital Ratio (marginal)

		Mean	Variance σ^2	Skewness γ_1	Kurtosis γ_2
Method I	β_1	0·2373	0·003407	−0·5075	0·0594
	β_2	0·2856	0·040247	0·1979	−2·3018
Method II	β_1	0·3352	0·031882	2·0107	4·3165
	β_2	0·7058	0·458162	1·9190	−0·3092

It is remarkable that means and variances of the input-output coefficients (β_1, β_2) are significantly different for the two sectors and the variances for the consumer goods sector (which consists very largely

[1] Method I is based on the census of manufacturing industries (1949–53). Method II is based on additional data and corrected (higher) capital values.

of the Agricultural Complex) are larger than those for the remaining sector. It is evident therefore that the optimal allocation ratios for the two sectors would be very much different when variances of the input-coefficients were considered, than in the nonstochastic case assumed by the Mahalanobis model.[1]

4. *Methods of Combining Input-Output and Programming Techniques with Macroeconomic Models*

It is now possible to indicate an outline of the way in which an appropriate combination of input-output and programming techniques with macroeconomic models could be devised for specifying the process of growth in a developing economy.

One of the earliest combinatorial methods is suggested by Sandee and Schouten in the framework of the long-run growth model outlined by the Netherlands Central Planning Bureau [5]. In this method, the parameters and coefficients used in the macromodel are tested for internal consistency and sectoral bottlenecks by means of detailed input-output accounting. In case of disagreement, the boundary conditions and the feasible values of the coefficients of the macromodel are suitably revised.

Such a method is likely to be less appropriate for a developing economy, like India, for two main reasons. First, it is the very aim of development planning to change the pattern of intersectoral interdependence itself in some manner conducive to further growth; hence the optimization considerations behind a macromodel are essentially dependent on the way the intersectoral coefficients are affected. Second, the input-output coefficients in such a framework may not always be interpreted as the optimal coefficients at a given point of time; these are intermediate between physical production coefficients and the weighted allocation coefficients, assigned through sectoral investment predetermined by the policy-maker. If demand is relatively unlimited for some sectors but there is scarcity of investible resources, then the coefficients could be largely allocation-oriented, whereas if a relative degree of excess capacity exists together with limited demand, the coefficients could be interpreted as production-oriented. In a mixed economy, but not in an advanced economy, these dual aspects are closely interrelated.

Under these conditions some different types of combinatorial methods may be appropriate. The simplest that suggests itself is a specification of the macromodel with some additional characteristics. One characteristic

[1] A dynamic stochastic programming application of this type of growth model has been considered in [4].

may be that each behaviour equation of a macromodel would include a variable representing the change in sectoral interdependence (i.e. structural change) over time. The consumption and production functions would have a time shift on account of the structural change. Another characteristic would be to incorporate the method of allocation of public investment between a few 'receiving' sectors. In those economies where public investment acts as the trigger for growth, this would mean that the allocation ratios (λ_j) would predetermine a large part of induced private investment. A third characteristic would be to specify a principle of disaggregation into a few sectors, so that the structural coefficients could be arranged in a block diagonal or nearly triangular form.

The advantage of this scheme is that it remains sufficiently flexible when it combines methods of optimization and multistage programming of an input-output system with an aggregated macromodel. For instance, consider the problem of optimal allocation of total investible resources at a given period $(I(t))$. Given the preference function and the feasibility conditions with respect to consumption propensity and resource availability, some level of investible resources would be decided upon in the first instance. In this phase, the optimization decision would involve the proportions to be devoted to the production of additional consumer goods (λ_c) and capital goods (λ_i); if the latter two sectors are considered to be nearly integrated, the relevant structural matrix is either diagonal or nearly triangular. Now with an estimate of marginal output-investment ratios for the two sectors, the optimal proportion of allocation λ_i^* for the integrated investment-goods sector could be found by maximizing national income (or a linear combination of consumption goods and investment goods) within a planning horizon, subject to certain minimum consumption requirements and other restrictions. In general, this may lead to concentrating a sizeable part of initial-period investment in a few basic sectors so as to create a greater growth impulse.

In the second phase of optimization, allocation between the subsectors of the two integrated sectors may be decided so as to maintain balance as much as possible with forthcoming marginal demand. Thus, the intra-allocation with the consumption-goods sector would give priority to the production of those commodities for which the income-elasticities of demand are estimated to be the highest, and so on. Of course, the first phase optimal values would be considered binding constraints in the second phase solution. Since any given subsector will admit of a spectrum of techniques or activities, the third phase of optimization would involve the choice of optimal activities under a closely interacting input-output type of network, subject to the preassigned solutions of the first two phases. For an economy having a very small capital-goods producing sector, such a three-phase division of the economy may prove to be a sufficiently valid approximation for a short period of time. With increasing diversification, it would be more and more difficult to secure the optimal values of each phase consecutively, because the coefficient matrices may deviate from near-triangularity or the input utilization and processing activities may gain in importance.

When the above three-phase framework is extended to successive stages, three additional decisions are involved: (*a*) an evaluation of the sequence of reinvestment over time, (*b*) the impact of structural growth on the sequential relations between the coefficients, and (*c*) an evaluation of the degree of capacity created in the sectors. As an example of (*b*), consider the growth of investible resources, as generated by the optimal allocation ratio λ_i^* for the investment-goods sector, in the first phase given the incremental output-investment ratio β_i:

$$\dot{I}(t) = \lambda_i^* \beta_i I(t) \qquad \text{(exponential solution)} \qquad (17)$$

Next assume that β_i would change over time, due to the process of industrialization itself, as $\beta_i = \beta_{i0} - \beta_{i1} I(t)$, where β_{i1} may be very small initially but with the tempo of industrialization it may gradually become more and more important. It is easily seen that the transient solution of (17) becomes logistic rather than exponential, with an upper asymptote given by (β_{i0}/β_{i1}). This means that the accumulation of investment goods *per se* would have a definite upper limit, unless demand for them, and for that matter demand for consumption goods, could be stepped up.

The most difficult task would be to optimize structural interdependence itself by a particular sequence of investment allocation.[1] It may be necessary in this case to specify in detail the objective function of the policy-maker in terms of indicators measuring sectoral interdependence, and at each stage this may have to be optimized, subject to the boundary constraints upon the output of each strategic sector. It is apparent that the near-triangular arrangement into an Agricultural Complex and an Industrial Complex may be helpful in this connection as a flexible device which permits new information and decision-making ability to be utilized at consecutive stages.[2]

[1] An approximate method has been indicated by Tintner and myself [6], assuming that the structural interdependence could roughly be measured by the ratio of investment goods to consumption goods.

[2] In 1960 Ragnar Frisch [7] has utilized a 22-sector input-output model of the Indian economy (1950–1) to find the optimal combination of sector-variables for maximizing some preassigned preference function, subject to several restrictions. He has also emphasized the need for breaking up public-sector investment into intersectoral allocation ratios (i.e., an investment matrix), as the change in the current input-output coefficients (replacement matrix) would be largely initiated by public sector investment either directly or indirectly. (See also Sandee [8].)

Short-term and long-term plans

For a developing economy with investment planning, like India, an interesting case would be to specify each short-term plan as part of the long-term scheme, when the long-term planning horizon is specified and the effects of each stage's short plan is taken into account in the next stage.[1] The multi-stage programming model can then be defined in terms of optimization of final state variables as

$$B_{11}\dot{X}_1 \qquad\qquad = I^{(1)}$$
$$B_{21}\dot{X}_1 + B_{22}\dot{X}_2 \qquad = I^{(2)}$$
$$\cdots \qquad \cdots \qquad\qquad \cdots \qquad\qquad (18)$$
$$B_{n1}\dot{X}_1 + B_{n2}\dot{X}_2 + \ldots + B_{nn}\dot{X}_n = I^{(n)}$$
$$w^{(1)}\dot{X}_1 + w^{(2)}\dot{X}_2 + \ldots + w^{(n-1)}\dot{X}_{n-1} < w^{(n)}\dot{X}_n = Z$$

where B_{ij} are matrices of output-investment ratios, $\dot{X}_1$ is the vector of gross-output increases in the first stage, $\dot{X}_2$ in the second stage and $\dot{X}_n$ in the nth stage, $I^{(1)}$ is the vector of allocated investment (constraints) in the first stage, $I^{(2)}$ in the second stage, etc., $w^{(i)}$ is a row of output weights at the ith stage and Z is the objective function.

Optimization of the final stage growth rates is reduced here to successive stages of consecutive optimization. For any given stage, the proportions of total investment allocated to different sectors could be considered as instruments (at most $n - 1$, if there are n sectors), and the targets may be the gross-output increases in some basic sectors and/or overall national output. If for a given stage there are m targets and $n - 1$ instruments, we can choose out of $(n - 1)$ instruments in $\binom{m}{n-1}$ ways, since all instruments are here comparable; hence, the optimal combination of instruments out of $\binom{m}{n-1}$ possible ways may be determined (if a unique optimal combination exists) by the policy-maker's objective function at each stage.[2]

As a matter of fact, calculations underlying the second 5-year plan in India have indicated the estimated growth of total investment up to the fifth plan stage (1976) and it has been observed that 'although for certain purposes it is convenient to divide the process of development into shorter spans, in reality it forms one continuous whole in which the

[1] See also Dantzig [9].
[2] In the general case, the output-investment ratios of one stage would have a feed-back relation with the allocated investment $I^{(i)}$ in preceding stages.

priorities and objectives for each period are linked with a larger perspective. Thus, both the first and second plan were conceived as stages in the long-term development in the country.' [10]

The flexibility of the system (18) is apparent. By the block-triangularity type of arrangement, the long-term plan for the entire planning horizon could be split into short plans at successive stages; emerging new sectors, industries or technologies could be included in consecutive stages. Even the initial stage interacting transactions could be recorded for only broad groupings such as agriculture, food-processing, fibre-processing, energy and transport and 'all other manufacturing'; and in this case there would not be much cost involved in keeping the interindustry coefficients up-to-date.

REFERENCES

[1] RASMUSSEN, P. N., *Studies in Intersectoral Relations*, Amsterdam, 1956.
[2] MAHALANOBIS, P. C., 'Approach of Operational Research to Planning in India,' *Sankhya*, Vol. 16, 1955, p. 3.
[3] SENGUPTA, J. K., *et al.*, *Planning and the Plans: A Review of India's Five Year Plans*, Calcutta, 1961.
[4] TINTNER, G. and SENGUPTA, J. K., 'Stochastic Linear Programming with Application to Planning in India,' *Metroeconomica*, 1963.
[5] SANDEE, J. and SCHOUTEN, D., 'A Combination of a Macro-economic Model and a Detailed Input-Output System,' in *Input-Output Relations*, Leiden, 1953.
[6] TINTNER, G. and SENGUPTA, J. K., *On the Design and Use of a Generalized Growth Model*, Iowa State University, 1961.
[7] FRISCH, R., *Planning for India: Selected Explorations in Methodology*, Bombay, 1960.
[8] SANDEE, J., *A Demonstration Planning Model for India*, Bombay, 1960.
[9] DANTZIG, G. B., 'On the Status of Multi-Stage Linear Programming Problems,' *International Statistical Institute Bulletin*, Vol. 36, part 3, 1957–8.
[10] PLANNING COMMISSION, GOVERNMENT OF INDIA, *Third Five-Year Plan: A Draft Outline*, New Delhi, 1960.

COMMENTS ON PAPERS BY PROFESSOR FOX AND MR. SENGUPTA

by RICHARD H. DAY

Technological change and input-output coefficients

Fox and Sengupta both emphasize the importance of changes in technical coefficients over time and suggest methods for including such changes in input-output analyses. I illustrate this aspect of their study with some empirical results.

In a study to which Fox refers[1] a dynamic regional agricultural model was developed for describing and forecasting changes of regional production, individual process levels, and investment in both new and old capital goods. By an appropriate aggregation of processes used for producing a given commodity the changes in that commodity's average input-output coefficients can be determined. Thus let $x_i(t)$ be the level or intensity in acres of the ith process for producing cotton in the year t, let $y_i(t)$ be the expected average output coefficient in lb. of lint per acre for the ith process, and let $l_i^u(t)$ and $l_i^s(t)$ be the input coefficients in hours per acre of unskilled and skilled labour respectively. Finally, let $l_u(t)$ and $l_s(t)$ be the average input-output coefficients for unskilled and skilled labour respectively involved in producing a lb. of cotton in the year t, where

$$l_u(t) = \frac{\sum_i l_i^u(t) x_i(t)}{\sum_i y_i(t) x_i(t)} \quad , \quad l_s(t) = \frac{\sum_i l_i^s(t) x_i(t)}{\sum_i y_i(t) x_i(t)}$$

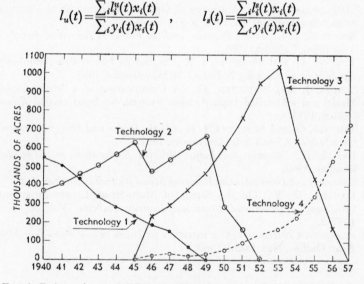

FIG. 1. Estimated use of different technologies for producing cotton in the Mississippi Delta Area

Figure 1 shows the changing magnitudes of the process levels for four distinct processes $(x_i(t), i = 1, \dots, 4)$ for producing cotton for the years $t = 1940, \dots, 1957$ in the Mississippi Delta, an important cotton producing region of the United States. Figure 2 shows the average input-

[1] Reference [2] p. 74 above. Figures 1 and 2 are based on that study.

output coefficients for unskilled and skilled labour ($l_u(t)$ and $l_s(t)$) for each year of the same period.

These average input-output coefficients show a marked shift over time. This illustrates the importance of accounting for such structural changes in a sector model of agriculture. These results also show how changes in aggregative input-output coefficients may be derived from a detailed, dynamic model of an individual sector as Fox has proposed.

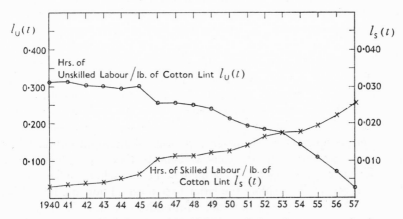

FIG. 2. Average skilled and unskilled labour coefficients for cotton production in the Mississippi Delta Area

Stability conditions for the Fox integrated model

Professor Fox outlines a scheme for integrating a detailed model of the agricultural-complex with a Leontief inter-industry model of the whole economy (p. 73, above). The result is a particular static general equilibrium model. The method which he presents for solving such a model may be regarded as a dynamic process analogous to the well-known Cobweb Model for a single commodity. As in the Cobweb Case one can consider the stability of this dynamic process. Downward sloping demand curves do not in general provide sufficient stability conditions for such a model. Instead a relation must exist between the slopes of the demand curves and the shape of the supply 'surface'. Since the latter will be a discontinuous step function (if the agricultural sector is represented by a programming model) the stability conditions will be difficult if not impossible to determine *a priori*. It is possible, therefore, as in the Cobweb Model, that the iterative process will not in fact converge to the equilibrium solution.

This is of course a purely empirical problem. Only after such a model has been constructed and effort directed towards its solution will this question be resolved. I would not be as optimistic on this point as Professor Fox. On the other hand his considerable experience with spatial equilibrium models solved by similar iterative methods lends a good deal of authority to his proposal. In any case a discovery of stability or instability in such a model is of importance in itself, perhaps of far greater importance than an equilibrium solution. Let us hope then that a model such as Professor Fox proposes can be added to the tools of input-output analysis.

The household sector and the independence of the agricultural complex

Professor Fox and Mr. Sengupta deal extensively and ingeniously with the empirically observed independence of the agricultural complex from the remaining industrial sectors of the economy. To some extent (though I think not wholly) their proposals for partial analysis rest on this observed independence. However, a perusal of the input-output tables presented (pp. 63 and 83, above) suggests that this phenomenon may depend on the exogenous treatment of the 'household' or 'consumer-labourer' sector. To explore the latter hypothesis, I added a household sector to the 2 × 2 input-output tables for both the United States and the Indian economies, giving a 3 × 3 input-output table for each economy. The resulting model remains open with respect to imports, government expenditure, etc. and so the inverse matrices can be obtained. Tables 1, 2 and 3 show respectively the resulting 'transactions', 'flow coefficients', and 'Leontief inverse matrices' for India and the United States. The contrast between these results and the 2 × 2 tables presented in Chapters 4 and 5 could hardly be more striking. In the United States case a 10 per cent increase in deliveries to final demand in 1947 of the industrial sector would call for an increase of $4\frac{1}{2}$ per cent in agricultural output. This contrasts with a corresponding increase of 0·6 per cent when households are exogenous. An increase of 10 per cent in deliveries to final demand of the agriculture complex would call for an increase of nearly 6 per cent in the output of all other industries. This contrasts with an increase of only 0·9 per cent when households are exogenous.

These illustrative results demonstrate the 'specification' error that can arise when important sectors are omitted from the structure of a Leontief model. On the other hand, for some purposes it might be reasonable to delete important sectors, particularly the household sector. But the fact that the solution including the household sector is significantly different from the solution excluding it, with a correspondingly

TABLE 1: *Transaction Matrices*

Sector	U.S.*					INDIA†				
	1	2	3	Final Demand	Total	1	2	3	Final Demand	Total
1. Agriculture	56962	5169	60073	8790	130994	2891	456	9034	690	13072
2. Industry	16558	109605	101929	58098	286190	363	826	1332	1114	3568
3. Households	36337	111580	1693	33510	183120	6383	1095	1597	1149	10224

TABLE 2: *Flow Coefficient Matrices*

Sector	U.S.*			INDIA†		
	1	2	3	1	2	3
1. Agriculture	0·4348	0·0181	0·3281	0·2213	0·1278	0·8836
2. Industry	0·1264	0·3830	0·5566	0·0303	0·2315	0·1303
3. Households	0·2774	0·3899	0·0093	0·4884	0·3067	0·1562

TABLE 3: *Leontief Inverse Matrices*

Sector	U.S.*			INDIA†		
	1	2	3	1	2	3
1. Agriculture	2·7103	1·0021	1·4603	4·9615	3·0891	5·6722
2. Industry	1·9220	3·2232	2·4472	0·7274	1·8395	1·0457
3. Households	1·5151	1·5489	2·3812	3·1358	2·4564	4·8480

* Data expressed in millions of dollars.   † Data expressed in millions of rupees.

significant difference in the economic implications, suggests that inclusion of the household sector should be seriously considered — especially if the agricultural sector is the focus of study.

To summarize, we can state as an empirically tested hypothesis the following principle: The independence of the agricultural complex within a Leontief input-output model implies and is implied by the treatment of the household sector as a component of final demand.

The household sector and economic development

Inclusion of the household sector as a part of the structure of the input-output model for these two empirical examples also leads to certain implications for economic development. The substantial demand for agricultural produce generated by increased final deliveries to the industrial sector for investment purposes suggests that economic development of agriculture may be an important correlative for any industrial development programme. In addition to the support lent to this hypothesis by Table 3 for the United States and Indian economies, there is the recent experience of China, and economic history provides further examples. In the United States, mechanization of agriculture proceeded side by side with industrial development. In the transition from the feudal agrarian economy to the commercial city-state, European agriculture experienced a corresponding development and increase in efficiency. A further argument for at least this kind of balanced growth is the immediate pay off in demand for industrial products created by a developing agriculture. This fact together with the immediate increase in welfare, and the substantial release of labour from the agricultural sector which would facilitate further industrial expansion, provides strong justifications for agriculturally oriented industrial development programmes.

A second important implication of our exercise occurs with an inspection of the household sector's inputs required for its own output in the United States and Indian economies. The United States input coefficient is about 0.01 while that of the Indian economy is about 0.16. This result indicates the high degree of dependence of the Indian household sector on domestic labour. The process of development itself can be expected to diminish this coefficient, thereby releasing labour for other purposes. On the other hand rigid institutional organizations can impede this development process. The tentative conclusion of these reflections is that including the household sector in an Input-Output Model may point up economic and technical conditions which are strongly related to institutional structures and thus show strategic areas in which a programme of economic development must be closely correlated with a programme of social development.

These comments do not detract from the methods developed by the authors. Instead, I hope that a consideration of them might, at least to a small degree, enhance the effectiveness of their contribution.

REPLY

by KARL A. FOX *and* J. K. SENGUPTA

Mr. Day has made a number of interesting suggestions. We will comment only briefly on one or two of these. But we do wish to point out some major limitations of his particular method of including households among the interacting sectors of an input-output matrix.

1. *Stability conditions for the Fox integrated model.* Mr. Day is correct in pointing out that an iterative determination of a supply and demand equilibrium in the Agricultural Complex bears some analogy to a multi-commodity Cobweb Model. However, we believe that the conditions for a normative equilibrium solution are essentially those of general equilibrium theory — except for the discontinuous character of pro-gramming formulations of supply.

We may question whether aggregative supply functions in the real world have significant discontinuities even though supply 'curves' derived by linear programming are indeed step functions. Technical coefficients will show statistical variation from farm to farm based on detailed differences in soils, topography, managerial skills and the like. The steps in the supply functions for (say) corn on a thousand different farms will occur at many different price-quantity points, so that the industry supply curve will be for all practical purposes continuous.

When we treat a relatively homogeneous agricultural region by programming methods, as if it were one big farm, we may obtain extremely valuable insights. But the size of the steps in our regional supply function depends upon how finely we are prepared to discrimin-ate among soil types, levels of fertilizer use, and other variations in production activities. If our array of activities recognizes only two soil types and two levels of fertilizer use, our regional supply function has big steps; if the array includes ten soil conditions and twenty levels of fertilizer use, our regional supply function has small steps.

2. *The household sector and the independence of the Agricultural Com-plex.* Mr. Day is correct in pointing out that the open static input-output

model of Chapter 4, Tables 1–5, understates the real interdependence between the Agricultural Complex and other sectors. However, the coefficients implicitly assumed by Mr. Day seriously overstate this interdependence.

Matrix equation (1) in Chapter 4 indicates that an increase in deliveries to final demand from 'all other industries' will require only limited quantities of farm products. But the increased activity in 'all other industries' will in fact be accompanied by increased employment and increased wage, salary and other payments to households. Thus, demand curves for foods and other products will be shifted to the right, calling for increased farm output if prices are to remain unchanged.

If value added in each sector of the economy changes in proportion to its total gross output, if disposable income of households equals 60 per cent of value added, and if income elasticities of demand for outputs of the Agricultural Complex and all other industries in the United States are 0·3 and 1·0 respectively, we find that an increase of 10 per cent in deliveries to final demand from all other industries calls for an increase of 2·3 per cent in gross output from the Agricultural Complex. Conversely, an increase of 10 per cent in deliveries to final demand from the Agricultural Complex would call for an increase of 2·8 per cent in gross output from all other industries.

For convenience, the results of the three sets of assumptions about households are tabulated below:

Effects of a 10 per cent increase in final demand	(1) *Households exogenous (Fox, Chap. 4)*	(2) *Households endogenous*	(3)
		Day's assumptions	*Fox's assumptions*
	per cent	*per cent*	*per cent*
A. *For* industrial products *upon* output from the Agricultural Complex	0·6	4·5	2·3
B. *For* food and fibre products *upon* output from all other industries	0·9	6·0	2·8

Day's model assumes an income elasticity of household demand for products of the Agricultural Sector of 1·0. It also assumes no leakages between gross national product and disposable personal income. More realistic assumptions about income elasticities and leakages lead to the results in Column (3). While they are closer to the original Fox estimates than to Mr. Day's figures, the results in Column (3) are less favourable to the hypothesis that policies could be separately designed and implemented in the Agricultural Complex than was implied in Chapter 4.[1]

A model originally presented by Fox [1, pp. 242–244] in 1954 also leads to more moderate claims for partial analysis. It was specifically designed to estimate the effects of alternative farm price support programmes upon prices and incomes in farm and nonfarm sectors. The principal mechanisms were full-cost pricing in the nonfarm sector, a partial adjustment of wage rates to increases in the consumer price index, and a consumption multiplier. If the direct effect of a new price support program were to increase prices of farm products by 10 per cent, the total effect in that model would be to increase them by 12·3 per cent. Thus, interdependence between agriculture and the nonfarm economy added an indirect effect of 2·3 per cent. If we assumed that farm price supports were being set with complete disregard for indirect consequences, we might say that the *intended* price effect of 10 per cent was supplemented by an unanticipated price effect of 2·3 per cent. The coefficients in the model were designed to reflect the structure of the United States economy in 1954.

The various calculations cited lend only limited support to the wisdom of a partial approach to policies for food and agriculture in advanced economies. If we can tolerate errors of 20 per cent or so in designing policies for these sectors we can afford to proceed on a partial basis. Less than 5 per cent of the national income of the United States originates in agriculture and less than 20 per cent originates in what we have called the Agricultural Complex. Hence, it is intuitively plausible that the unintended effects of sector policies upon the economy as a whole would be no larger than those cited.

Perhaps the chief lesson to be gained from Mr. Day's demonstration is that partial analysis can be undertaken with assurance only after the relevant general model has been correctly specified. The results in Chapter 4 are valid *if* increased income payments to households are taxed away and/or if quantities of goods available to households are held constant through rationing. In this context it is perfectly true that a big expansion in industrial output requires a very limited increase in agricultural production. The open static input-output model is designed for the analysis of intermediate, and not of final, demands.

If we are interested in appraising sector policies in an economy in which income payments and consumption expenditures are closely

---

[1] The income elasticity of 0·3 for products of the Agricultural Complex is too high for food alone under current U.S. conditions. It represents a judgment average for food, tobacco products, alcoholic beverages and cotton and woollen textiles.

linked with changes in production, we need something more comprehensive than the input-output model of Chapter 4. Suggestions for such a multisectoral model are contained in a 1956 paper by Fox [1, pp. 266–271]. The macroeconomic approach pioneered by Tinbergen can be and is being adapted to these ends in a number of countries.

REFERENCE

[1] Fox, K. A., *Econometric Analysis for Public Policy*, Iowa State University Press, 1958.

PART II

Regional Models

PART II

Regional Models

CHAPTER 6

Application of Input-Output Techniques to Regional Science

by WALTER ISARD *and* EUGENE SMOLENSKY

1. *Introduction*

This paper illustrates the central role which input-output techniques play in operational Regional Science, particularly for making projections for planning and development purposes, and suggests that for under-developed nations, encompassing several regions, national input-output analysis alone can lead to serious planning errors and may contribute to disequilibrium and unbalanced growth; for such nations interregional input-output analysis is required.[1]

We shall sketch an operational, comprehensive framework for interregional analysis that is applicable right now, for any nation which has built an interregional input-output table. We shall eschew the use of any tools of analysis which are purely conceptual or which have not yet been empirically validated.[2]

Our schematic framework will centre on regional and interregional input-output tables.

2. *The Analytical Framework*

The basic data

The first requirement is to describe the economic structure in a base year within and among the regions of a system of regions which comprises a nation. The central descriptive tool is an interregional input-output table.[3] Across the top, this table lists the regions and in each region the basic sectors; the sectors vary from region to region reflecting different economic structures. Similarly, the left hand stub is broken into regions and the sectors of each region. Going across any row indicates the distribution of the product of a sector of a given region to

[1] We are indebted to Jorgi Casanova for helpful comments on this point.
[2] For a discussion of this and a number of other points raised in this chapter, see [1].
[3] France and Yugoslavia are constructing basic elements of interregional input-output tables. A table has already been developed in Japan.

other sectors in the same region and to all sectors in all other regions. Going down any column indicates the set of inputs shipped to the sector at the head of the column from all other sectors in its region and from all sectors in all other regions. Further columns are added to the right of the structural matrix to cover the bill-of-goods sectors for each region. Also, rows for each region are added under the structural matrix to record appropriate accounting charges for sectors of all regions. Associated with this table are the basic social accounts for each region and the system (nation). Their elements are listed in or easily derived from items in the totals column and totals row of the interregional input-output table as extended above.

For operational purposes, the descriptive detail of the extended interregional input-output table must be supplemented. A whole range of socio-economic data on population, birth rates, death rates, ethnic groupings, migration, etc., are required, as well as data on income and price elasticities of demand, capital coefficients (by sector), transport rates, wages and power costs by region, labour skills, technological know-how and other basic items. The precise nature and role of these data and of derived magnitudes, such as average productivity and labour force, will become apparent shortly.

The time horizon

Against the background of a rather complete set of data, we wish to construct a comprehensive analytical framework for projection purposes. But first it is useful to consider the year for which the projection is to be made.

Since we intend to make use of comparative cost and industrial complex analyses to add strength and additional meaning to the input-output framework, certain time considerations are immediately relevant. The judicious use of comparative cost and industrial-complex techniques requires a reasonably long time horizon. Suppose, for example, a continuous rise in steel output of 10 per cent per year is envisaged. A set of one year projections (and plans based thereon) would perhaps call for continuous additions to plant at existing sites. Taking a longer-run view, however, might justify (and perhaps make imperative from the standpoint of locational efficiency) the erection of one or more fully integrated steel works. Also new fully integrated steel works, exploiting the entire range of economies of scale, might involve a fundamental change in production technique. As a consequence, impacts upon local economies — their employment levels and incomes — and upon the spatial pattern of linked industries, such as steel fabricating, might also be far different. Hence we consider our framework to be most fruitful for a date at least a decade ahead.

At the same time it is recognized that our comprehensive technique will require many assumptions about the future. The more distant the year of projection, the larger is the likely error in the forecast due to 'unrealized' assumptions.[1] We consider our framework appropriate for projecting regional structure 10 to 25 years in the future. For the purposes of this paper, we project for some 20 years into the future, in particular for year 1980.

Specification of regional and system goals

Our comprehensive analytical framework is sketched in Figure 1. For simplicity, we refer to a system of only two regions: North and South. The extended interregional input-output table, which we have already discussed, lies in the centre of the lower section and to its left. The emphasis on the bills of goods should be noted: it is into these sectors that we wish to funnel our existing knowledge about regional and system goals, efficient spatial patterns, and other relevant social science knowledge.

As indicated at the top of the figure, the analyst begins with regional and national (system) goals. It is clear that these goals are highly interrelated. In practice, national goals are sometimes set first and regional goals subsequently established; or the national goal is merely the sum of regional goals.

At the outset goals may be defined broadly so as to reflect basic national aspirations such as equality, liberty, justice, security and social welfare. From such broad objectives must proceed a chain of successive specification. It is at the intermediate levels that the inter-action of regional and national goals is clearly visible. These intermediate goals might concern such items as the level of *per capita* income, the proportion of the labour force in agriculture, the intensity with which particular resources are to be developed, a steel plant or some heavy industry in every region, a school in every village, etc. Now while national goals such as a large increase in *per capita* income may be sensible for countries in which regional differences are not great, for countries in which regional differences in *per capita* income are great, the goal of reducing such differences may have high priority, even higher priority than a rapid rise in national income *per capita*. In Italy, for example, national goals must yield at least in part to regionally oriented goals.

[1] Of course, for items of great durability, such as bridges, dams, irrigation, power works, buildings and land-use patterns, a projection over a period as long as fifty years may be required.

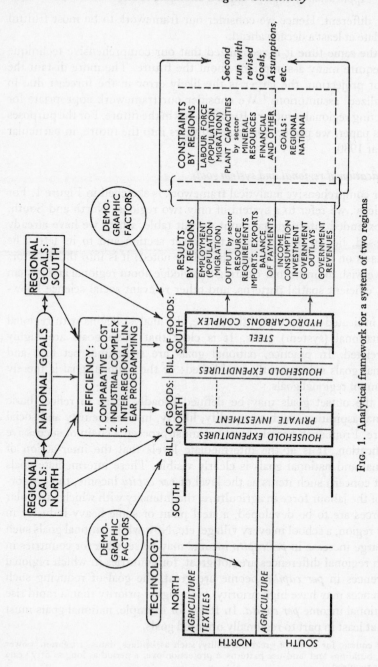

Fig. 1. Analytical framework for a system of two regions

Once an apparently consistent set of regional and national goals, such as *per capita* income levels and general investment levels, are administratively established, and once they are translated into specific targets, input requirements to meet these targets must be indicated. These input requirements are the deliveries which appear in certain of the columns in the regional bills of goods. For example, once the target of an irrigation project is set for a region, the items necessary for its construction must be included in the government capital formation sector of that region. Or, once a specific *per capita* income level for a region is set as a target, the appropriate array of consumption items must be entered into the household column in the bill of goods of that region. In estimating these, the investigator should utilize all the best demographic material available, including preliminary projections of employment opportunities in a given region since they will assist in making preliminary estimates of migration and thus of regional population. He should exploit socio-economic knowledge such as that pertaining to changing tastes and consumption patterns as household incomes change, or estimates of income distribution by size within the region.

In Figure 1 arrows indicate the direct relation of regional and national goals to the regional bills of goods.[1]

Economies of scale and comparative-cost, industrial-complex and other efficiency techniques

Efficiency is a goal that should be basic to any plan. While in Figure 1 we have indicated that some goals should by-pass the efficiency box, others must be channelled through it, that is subordinated to the efficiency criterion. It is clear, for example, that the otherwise desirable objective of a reduction in income inequality among regions may, if pushed too far, be self-defeating. In the extreme case, this objective can introduce so much inefficiency into the location and production structure that, while each region obtains its small steel plant and irrigation project, it comes to suffer an absolute decline in real income.

It is recognized that one of the major shortcomings of input-output analysis and similar techniques in linear economics is that they fail to account for scale and external economies. Fortunately, there are tools available which can take into account such economies and which at the same time can be grafted onto interregional input-output analysis via the regional bills of goods. These tools are comparative-cost and industrial-complex analysis which have historically been embedded in location theory and which have recently been reinvigorated in the field of

[1] The full exposition of these links is given in [1].

regional science. These tools are indicated in the efficiency box of Figure 1.

The essentials of the procedure for effecting this fusion is as follows. First, for a cost-sensitive industry, markets are projected on the basis of both (*a*) the regional and national goals as translated into the bill of goods vectors in standard input-output analysis, and (*b*) trend projections of the entries in the body of the base-year (1960) interregional input-output transactions table. Next, for each market, or group of markets, the cost items leading to major differentials between existing and hypothetical production sites are determined. After scale economies are fully incorporated into the analysis, this procedure yields for the entire set of markets a first approximation to the optimal spatial pattern of production. This pattern can then be viewed as a set of required production targets implied by the broader objective of efficiency; and, further, the inputs necessary to achieve these production goals may be set down as columns in the regional bill of goods sectors. If such a comparative cost study were done for the steel industry, then in the bill of goods sectors of one or more regions would appear a column headed 'steel production'.[1]

Comparative cost analysis, however, is for the most part limited to consideration of scale economies internal to the firm. It is equally important to take into account economies external to the firm (or industry), which is not easily done through the traditional comparative cost framework. For this purpose industrial-complex analysis has been developed. An industrial complex may be defined as a set of activities occurring at a given location and belonging to a group (sub-group) of activities which reap important external economies because of their close production, marketing or other linkages. As an example consider the hydro-carbons complexes which correspond to consistent sets of inputs and outputs (as may be listed in an activity matrix) in successive stages of production which follow the processing of crude oil, natural gas, or other hydro-carbon raw material.[2] Using market estimates based on established goals and trend projections of the relevant items in the transactions matrix, and then taking into account scale economies and other economies generated by (1) the fuller use of power, steam and other common facilities, (2) the exploitation of by-products, (3) savings

[1] Usually, the steel columns and rows in the structural matrix would simultaneously be deleted. However, this step is not necessary if the investigator distinguishes between new and existing steel capacity, and contends that comparative cost analysis is only relevant for the new capacity.

[2] One hydro-carbon complex for example would include as successive activities the production of gasoline (straight-run, cracked, reformed and polymerized), kerosene, diesel oil, cycle oil, coke and carbon, L.P.G., hydrogen, methane, ethylene, ethylene oxide, ethylene glycol, etc., culminating in urea, ammonium nitrate and Dacron staple.

in transport, and (4) the upgrading of the uses of hydrogen and other intermediate products, the analyst evaluates a given site's potential for the activities of a hydro-carbons complex. As with comparative cost analysis, such an analysis for all sites yields a first approximation to an optimal spatial distribution of activities covered by hydro-carbons complexes. Also, as with comparative cost analysis, required inputs for these complexes in each region can be entered into the regional bill of goods sectors in a new column headed, say, 'Hydro-carbons Complexes'.[1]

We have also listed interregional linear programming in the efficiency box of Figure 1.[2]

It is axiomatic that planning itself uses up resources, and must be performed under resource constraints. These constraints require that only the most important cost-sensitive activities be examined by those techniques aiming at efficiency. Even if all cost-sensitive industries were examined, the structural matrix would remain large and extremely useful. All those industries for which the pull of markets is overwhelming, or which are localized at a single source of a raw material, would remain in the structural matrix. In addition, the input-output matrix would house the host of foot-loose industries as well as the numerous service activities.

To summarize: goals, as modified by demographic and other factors, are used to set household expenditures, capital formation, government outlays and exports. When augmented by input requirements set via comparative-cost and industrial-complex analysis for cost-sensitive sectors, they give rise to the enlarged regional bill of goods. New industries placed in the bill of goods are struck in part or whole from the structural matrix.

The regional bill of goods having been set, some attention must be given to coefficients relating to those industries remaining in the structural matrix. These coefficients, having been derived for a base year, will clearly be inadequate twenty years later. A plan, for example, may call for a rate of increase in the capital stock which may alter the capital to labour price-ratio. Within many industries there will be expenditures for research and development expressly designed to lower the technical coefficients. Additions to the transport net and other social investments will influence regional trade coefficients. Because of these

---

[1] Again, appropriate rows and columns in the body of the input-output matrix may or may not be eliminated, depending upon the distinction which is made between new and existing capacity.

[2] The operational use of this technique, which may be viewed in part as a variant of the comparative-cost or industrial-complex technique, is currently confined to the analysis of single industries or single industrial complexes.

and many other considerations the input-output coefficients must be adjusted.

First-run results, feasibility, and re-runs

Given the bills of goods and the adjusted interregional matrix, a first-run computation is made. The results that emerge yield for each region: employment and population, output by sector, resource requirements, imports and exports, balance of payments, etc. Some of these are shown at the lower right of Figure 1.[1]

The next step is to check the first-run results for feasibility. For each region there is, for instance, a demand for labour by industry, implying demands by occupation and skill level. Will these requirements exceed the available supply in the region after allowance is made for migration, natural increase, and the education programme envisaged? Will the first-run required regional outputs by industry exceed capacity levels?; that is, over the period 1960–1979, will there have been sufficient investment by industry and region to support the required 1980 outputs? Furthermore, is the 1980 investment programme reasonable, or does it imply an infeasible saving-income ratio?

These and other checks must be supplemented with goal checks. For example, do the first-run results on income generated match the *per capita* income goal set at the outset for each region? Are government revenues generated by the computation consistent with government outlays implied by health, education, resource development and other programmes in addition to the outlays required for normal operations?

Finally, results must be checked against assumptions underlying the comparative cost and industrial-complex calculation. To illustrate: are the spatial distributions of income and markets consistent with those initially assumed? Are the resulting demands for labour, power and other inputs consistent with the prices of those inputs which were assumed at the start to prevail in each region?

Inconsistencies and non-feasibilities will abound. Specific goals will have to be revised, some comparative cost and industrial-complex analyses carried out again under new market assumptions, etc. Armed with new goals and revised estimates, a second-run computation can be made. Again results must be checked against resources, goals and initial assumptions to test for feasibility. New goals and revised market estimates and assumptions may once more be required and a third-run computation may be needed. For the sophisticated regional scientist,

---

[1] The major items of the social accounts: income, consumption, investment, government expenditures and net foreign investment for each region are easily derived.

however, only a few runs should be necessary to develop a set of goals and assumptions which lead to consistent results.[1]

3. *Disequilibrium and the Choice between National and Interregional Input-Output*

The second objective of this paper is to suggest that planning and development programming based on national input-output analysis alone may, in effect, lead to undesirable planning and disequilibrium. To illustrate the point we consider the impact of change in a developed country, the United States.[2]

Suppose a major disarmament programme is to be initiated as is assumed in a forward-looking article by Leontief and Hoffenberg [3]. The effect by sector for the nation as a whole is traced through a national input-output table. The authors also use a national input-output table to spell out the direct and indirect effects by sector of various alternative programmes designed to return aggregate expenditures to 1958 levels; they estimate the change in employment by sector that would result from an $8 billion reduction in expenditures by the military accompanied by a simultaneous $8 billion increase in other items, assuming that each of the following would be increased over the 1958 level by the same percentage: exports (except military), exports to India (except food), business investment, personal consumption, public services construction, maintenance construction, residential construction, and government (non-military) outlays.

A moment's reflection must lead to the conclusion that the analysis ought not to stop here. If for each state defence expenditure as a proportion of personal income is calculated, the state-to-state variation is very large indeed.[3]

Simply to replace $8 billion of military expenditures by $8 billion of representative non-military expenditures implies that some states such as Alaska, Hawaii, Washington and California would in all probability become large pockets of unemployment and suffer depressive forces, while other states like Oregon, Idaho, Wisconsin and Illinois would in all probability become boom areas subject to inflationary forces reflecting

---

[1] Although several runs may need to be made, most of the data of one run are usable in the next so that the cost of computations is not a linear function of the number of runs.
[2] For further discussion and information on interregional differences in the U.S.A. see [2].
[3] For Alaska the figure is 349 per cent of the national average and for Washington 235 per cent; at the other end of the scale, the figure for Oregon is 20 per cent and for West Virginia 10 per cent.

important sectoral and regional bottlenecks. To avoid such gross inequities and subsequent emergency *ad hoc* measures, there is need for regional and interregional input-output tables and analysis if a disarmament programme is to be effectively cushioned with desirable private investment, foreign aid, housing, urban redevelopment and other programmes, and if appropriate monetary and fiscal measures are to be taken.

Based on the analyses of these and many other sets of regional data we strongly feel that, in nations in which the economic differences among regions are still greater, national planning and development programmes based on national input-output analysis *must* run into the same kind of disequilibria (and regional inequities) as were just suggested for the United States. Moreover, one must also be realistic and recognize that when regional differences are large, elimination of those differences often becomes a fundamental political issue. Apart from the frequently projected goal of reducing income inequality, differences in regional economic structure will make for powerful and antagonistic political blocks on such issues as tariffs, land tenure, urban housing development, cottage industry, etc. Political agreement on national plans frequently requires balancing sectional demands, and sectional representatives must be convinced that the plan will meet a politically acceptable minimum of their needs. In such cases, the deeper insight and more extensive information which an interregional input-output table and its analysis provides becomes invaluable.

In fact, the issue may become more difficult. It is frequently recognized that the complex of forces in a free market may tend to perpetuate rather than reduce interregional inequality. In the language of location theory, the pull of markets and agglomeration economies may outweigh the pull of cheap labour and other cheap resources; industrial expansion and desirable employment opportunities may continue to concentrate in the already high-income regions. It then becomes essential to have a fused framework, such as outlined above, which combines comparative-cost, industrial-complex and interregional input-output techniques. For armed with such a framework, concessions to political pressures may be designed so as to minimize the economic inefficiencies which such concessions imply.

In sum, we strongly feel that the increasing complexity of society more and more compels the analyst to consider regional and interregional implications of growth and change. The development of the field of regional science is a manifestation of this phenomenon and, of the operational techniques available to the regional scientist, none is more vital than interregional input-output.

REFERENCES

[1] ISARD, W. *et al.*, *Methods of Regional Analysis*, Chs. 10 and 12, New York, 1960.
[2] SMOLENSKY, E., 'Industrialisation and Income Inequality — Recent United States Experience', *Papers and Proceedings of the Regional Science Association*, 1961.
[3] LEONTIEF, W. W. and HOFFENBERG, M., 'The Economic Effects of Disarmament', *Scientific American*, 1961, p. 47.

COMMENTS ON PAPER BY PROFESSORS ISARD AND SMOLENSKY

by H. I. LIEBLING

I wish to make three comments on the objective of the paper, 'to sketch an operational, comprehensive framework for interregional analysis that is applicable right now. . . .'

First, I would question the appropriateness of the phrase 'right now', because a marriage of many techniques and disciplines less advanced than input-output has been arranged with input-output and difficulties have been compounded. If a flaw exists in the paper, it is the failure to differentiate more adequately between so-called *theoretical* and *operational* areas among the various techniques and disciplines. Second, while the framework of the paper is established by reference to the need for making projections in 'operational *Regional* Science', the issues raised are not uniquely regional, a point deserving greater recognition. Third, I should also like to take issue with the linking of many disciplines as though they were necessarily part of an input-output system which has already proved its usefulness. This burdens the system unnecessarily from the viewpoint of evaluation of results. Input-output, I feel, needs to be considered on its own merits as a particular tool with sufficient problems of its own, especially in regional applications.

I should like to illustrate these general points. For example, the relationships portrayed in Figure 1 — if they are to be considered as truly analytical rather than graphic — in which the basic input-output regional relationships are related to national and regional goals of a political, social, and perhaps philosophical nature, imply a knowledge of social organization and the ability to project in this area. The figure is supported by the statement that 'it is into these sectors that we wish to funnel our existing knowledge about . . . goals, efficient spatial patterns, and other relevant social science knowledge.' At this stage it may perhaps be prudent to view goals as given by governments or certain groups rather than as 'operationally' determinable types of knowledge, against which interindustry models may be tested for feasibility. Now that many countries have accepted input-output tables as desirable and necessary, it may be timely to recognize that this powerful tool is not ideally linked with the determination of suitable social and political goals, whether national or regional; for this purpose, other and quite independent techniques may be applied, especially in democratic societies where the decision-making process is diffused.

This is not to say that economic feasibility tests are not best handled by input-output techniques along with other approaches, but means and ends need to be more clearly distinguished. Presumably the authors would like to provide a single all-inclusive system designed to solve a large variety of problems within a single framework, even if this leads to the intrusion of many disciplines. I am in complete agreement that bills of goods are affected by regional and other factors; however, I would point out that optimization techniques are not yet available in these areas and furthermore, since these factors are hardly related to input-output techniques in an integral way, concern with them may cause attention to be diverted from more pressing and solvable problems of input-output analysis. It would also seem to me that attention should be given to the possibility of securing valid measures of these factors.

It will be noted that increasing the number of factors or areas for which functional relationships are not yet determinable is reflected in a diminution of the size of the input-output matrix. Thus, the separate analysis of what Isard and Smolensky call 'cost-sensitive industries' and 'industrial complexes' results in their exclusion from the matrix to become part of specified bills of goods, thereby increasing the openness of the systems. Carried far enough this tendency would lead interindustry analysis to merge with conventional types of study. This is desirable insofar as it emphasizes the still large unknown areas of knowledge in which much work needs to be done, e.g. income and income-size distribution as they affect consumers' and investors' demand, and financial influences governing the supply of and demand for funds and goods and services; in short, the commonplace range of problems the solutions of which are on the threshold of attainment.

Turning to more specific issues, it is obvious that input-output analysis would benefit from the special treatment of 'cost-sensitive industries' and of 'industrial complexes' as noted in the paper. The authors' restriction of such treatment to only a few industries on the grounds that 'planning itself uses up resources' seems questionable. Under some circumstances, industries considered as insensitive to cost due to localized sources of supply may in fact be revealed as cost-sensitive — witness, for example, the coal and other mineral industries in the U.S. Furthermore, scale and external economies abound in developing economies. In the highly developed economies also, where significant investment is made in research and development, input-output research should be pointed towards the solution of the important problems which are encountered in a broad range of industries. This would be preferable, I think, to restricting the number of industries within the matrix to so-called non-cost-sensitive, high-demand industries.

Indeed, considering the long period of 20 years which the authors regard as appropriate for projecting regional structures, changes in the production coefficients of a large number of industries can be anticipated, especially in view of the trends in investment in scientific research and the potentialities for modifying production processes and creating new products. At the very least, attention could be given in long-term projections to the most modern rather than to the average technology. A broader type of industry analysis requires only generalization of the procedure indicated for cost-sensitive industries in the paper.

The alternative to the suggested study of trends in technology is to shorten the forecast period to, say, five years, or whatever period can be determined as reasonable for this purpose, leaving only fairly general economic relations for long-run planning. The French appear to have chosen 4 to 5 years as a suitable period.

Considering the major unsettled theoretical issues, it may seem almost trivial to comment on some of the minor problems in regional social accounting. However, they persist and are reflected in differing treatments in regional accounts by Leontief, Isard, Moore, Cumberland, and others. To the extent that they are involved in the questions posed by Isard and Smolensky on the regional impact of a reduction in defence expenditures, some observations may be in order.

To begin with, the determination of gross national product or national income by region awaits the solution of problems relating to allocation of income to factors of production; difficulties in allocating profits, the treatment of depreciation, and other matters are involved here. For rough purposes, the approximations hitherto used, such as regional personal income, may be adequate. These estimates typically represent wage and salary and other factor payments on a 'where received' rather than 'where earned' basis — the latter, however, constitutes a more appropriate basis for an analysis of income generation and reflects more accurately the 'value added' concept.

In terms of statistical implementation, value added by region as obtained from Census sources, at least in the United States, is too imprecise a measure for national income originating — differing for the country as a whole by as much as one-third in 1954. However, when an attempt is made to estimate national income by factor shares for specific regions, the allocation of the non-labour elements presents many conceptual and statistical problems. An example of the former is the determination of regional property income of interregional railroads and insurance companies; an example of the latter is the filing of income tax returns — generally the central source of income data — in the region of the home office of a corporation rather than in the region of its principal operations.

The authors illustrate the need for regional analysis by applying to states the estimates of Leontief and Hoffenberg on the impact of a cut in U.S. national defence expenditures. They find that the impact varied widely between states. The point that needs to be made is that, considering that the states are political rather than economic units, it would have been preferable to analyse the differential impacts by defining localities differently.

CHAPTER 7

Multiregional Input-Output Analysis

by WASSILY LEONTIEF
in collaboration with Alan Strout

---

1. *A System of Multiregional Relations*

In multiregional input-output analysis the economic system is described not only in terms of interdependent industries, but also in terms of several interrelated regions. The output of each region is defined as a combination of outputs of economic activities carried on within its geographic boundaries; its input accordingly comprises the direct inputs of these industries and the goods and services absorbed directly by the final demand sectors of that region.

The economic interdependence between two regions is the interdependence between the industries located within their respective boundaries. It is direct to the extent to which commodities and services produced in one region are absorbed by the industries or the final demand sectors of the other; it is indirect (from the regional point of view) to the extent to which the connection between such inputs and outputs is established through industries located in some other regions.

The movement of commodities or services from one region to another obviously reflects the existence of a direct input-output relationship between the industries — or an industry and the final demand sector — located within their respective boundaries. Indirect regional interdependence gives rise to what is commonly called triangular or multilateral trading patterns.

The multiregional input-output scheme described below is not intended to provide a systematic theoretical description of the many factors and relationships that ultimately determine the pattern of a multiregional economic system; it is designed rather as a rough and ready working tool capable of making effective use of the limited amount of factual information with which, even in the statistically advanced countries, economists have to work. It is for this reason that, after having experimented with linear programming models, we now avoid explicit use of the cost minimization or revenue maximization principle in the basic formulation of the multiregional scheme. As in the case of ordinary input-output analysis, the opportunities for formal choice between alternative production (and interregional shipments) patterns can be introduced later, step by step, as better factual information becomes available.

The peculiar theoretical problem of multiregional input-output analysis stems from the simple fact that identical goods can be, and actually are, produced and consumed in different regions. The regional origin of the particular batch of a given kind of good absorbed by its users in one particular region is as irrelevant to them as the ultimate regional destination of his output is to a producer. It is as if the producers of a specific commodity or service located in one particular region had merged their output in a single regional supply pool, and the users of that commodity or service located in a given region had ordered and received it through a regional demand pool. All interregional movements of a particular commodity or service within a multiregional economy can thus be visualized as shipments from regional supply to regional demand pools of that good. In accordance with that over-all point of view, the general equilibrium system described below consists of a set of regional interindustrial input-output systems of conventional design linked to-gether in — or rather fitted into — a separately constructed system of interregional relationships.

The system of equations

We will describe the regional input-output systems first. Let $X_{i.og}$ represent the total internal input (i.e., production + imports − exports) of good i in region g, $X_{j.go}$ the output of good j in region g, and $Y_{i.g}$ the final demand for good i in region g. The following equation describes, for any region g, the balance between the total internal input and output of good i, the outputs of all other goods and the internal final regional demand for good i:

$$X_{i.og} = \sum_{j=1}^{n} [a_{ij.g} X_{j.go}] + Y_{i.g} \qquad (i=1, 2, \ldots, n)$$
$$(g = 1, 2, \ldots, m) \qquad (1)$$

The constants, $a_{ij.g}$, are the familiar technical input coefficients describing the amount of good i required to produce one unit of good j in region g.

If the $m.n$ final demands are considered as given, the $m.n$ equations of system (1) contain $2m.n$ unknowns: $m.n$ regional outputs and $m.n$ regional internal inputs. The interdependence between the outputs and inputs of the different regions is described below.

In an isolated multiregional economy subdivided into m separate regions the interregional flows of each good i must satisfy $2m$ balance equations of the following kind:

$$X_{i.go} = \sum_{h=1}^{m} X_{i.gh} \qquad \left\{ \begin{array}{l} (i=1, 2, \ldots, n) \\ (g=1, 2, \ldots, m) \end{array} \right. \tag{2}$$

$$X_{i.oh} = \sum_{g=1}^{m} X_{i.gh} \qquad \left. \begin{array}{l} \\ (h=1, 2, \ldots, m) \end{array} \right\} \tag{3}$$

The variable, $X_{i.go}$ represents here, as before, the supply pool of good i in region g, $X_{i.oh}$ the demand pool of good i in region h, and $X_{i.gh}$ the total shipment of good i from the supply pool in region g to its demand pool in region h.

A multiregional economy trading with the world outside can be formally transformed into an isolated system by the simple device of treating the 'outside world' as its additional internal region. An alternative, well-known device for closing an open multiregional system in respect to foreign trade is the inclusion of goods exported by each region into the region's final bill of goods; imports must of course be entered on the right-hand side of (1) with a minus sign.

Summing each of these two sets of equations over all regions, we see that the aggregate supply of good i for the isolated multiregional economy as a whole equals the aggregate demand for that good:

$$\sum_{g=1}^{m} \sum_{h=1}^{m} X_{i.gh} = \sum_{g=1}^{m} X_{i.go} = \sum_{h=1}^{m} X_{i.oh} = X_{i.oo} \qquad (i=1, 2, \ldots, n) \tag{4}$$

The structural equations which we propose to use in explaining the magnitude of all interregional flows of any commodity or service i, are of the following general form:

$$X_{i.gh} = \frac{X_{i.go} X_{i.oh}}{X_{i.oo}} Q_{i.gh} \qquad \begin{array}{l} (i=1, 2, \ldots, n) \\ (g=1, 2, \ldots, m) \\ (g \neq h) \quad (h=1, 2, \ldots, m) \end{array} \tag{5}$$

The flow of the particular good i from region g to any *other* region h is assumed to be directly proportional to its total output in region g, to its total input in region h, and inversely proportional to the aggregate amount of commodity i, $X_{i.oo}\left(= \sum_{g=1}^{m} X_{i.go} = \sum_{h=1}^{m} X_{i.oh} \right)$, produced and consumed in all the regions of the economy as a whole. The coefficients, $Q_{i.gh}$, are empirical constants; their significance and determination will be discussed in Sections 2 and 3.

The multiplicative form in which the total output of good i in the exporting and its total input in the importing regions enter into (5) permits us to characterize it as a special type of Isard's Gravity or Potential Model. It implies that there can be no flow from region g to region h if either one of those two magnitudes is equal to zero. The introduction of the aggregate output of good i into the denominator implies that, if that aggregate output, as well as output $X_{i.go}$ in region g and total input $X_{i.oh}$ in region h, double, the flow of that good from region g to region h will double too.

If neither $X_{i.go}$ or $X_{i.oh}$, nor $X_{i.ho}$ or $X_{i.og}$ is equal to zero, and if the coefficients $Q_{i.gh}$ and $Q_{i.hg}$ are positive, both $X_{i.gh}$ and $X_{i.hg}$ will be positive too, i.e., good i will be shipped between regions g and h simultaneously in both directions. In an ideal system in which both regions are defined as locational points, in which good i is considered to be perfectly homogeneous and all shipments are assumed to result from strictly rational decisions based on perfect information, cross shipments could of course not occur. In actual empirical analysis, however, good i will as a rule be defined as an aggregate of several similar but not strictly identical items, while regions g and h will often represent more or less extended areas, so that the average distance (or the average unit costs of transportation) between them would necessarily conceal the actual diversity of commodity flows connecting a great many distinct pairs of sending and receiving points. Under such circumstances cross shipments should be expected, and actually are observed, nearly everywhere.

Thus the ability of equations (5) to allow for the existence of simultaneous flows of the same good i between two regions in opposite directions should be considered as a desirable characteristic, not a flaw. In those instances, however, in which the actual conditions approach the ideal and cross shipments do not occur, or are so small that they can be interpreted as being 'accidental', we can, by setting the appropriate coefficient, $Q_{i.gh}$, equal to zero, exclude the possibilities of the appearance of one of the two opposite flows (see Section 2 below).

Substituting from (5) into (2) we obtain:

$$X_{i.go} = \frac{X_{i.go} \sum_{r=1}^{m} [X_{i.or} Q_{i.gr}]}{X_{i.oo}} + X_{i.gg} \qquad \begin{aligned} &(Q_{i.gg}=0) \\ &(g=1, 2, \ldots, m) \\ &(i=1, 2, \ldots, n) \end{aligned} \qquad (6)$$

The term, $X_{i.gg}$, i.e., the internally absorbed part of the output of region g, appears on the right-hand side because equations (5) pertain only to interregional flows: the subsidiary condition, $Q_{i.gg}=0$, reduces to zero the term $X_{i.og} Q_{i.gg}$.

A substitution from (5) into (3) yields:

$$X_{i.oh} = \frac{X_{i.oh} \sum_{r=1}^{m} [X_{i.ro} Q_{i.rh}]}{X_{i.oo}} + X_{i.hh} \qquad \begin{aligned} &(Q_{i.hh}=0) \\ &(h=1, 2, \ldots, m) \\ &(i=1, 2, \ldots, n) \end{aligned} \qquad (7)$$

The multiregional system is now formally complete. It contains $3mn$ equations and an equal number of unknowns (the final demand for each good in every region being considered as given): there are mn equations in set (1), which constitutes the intraregional part of the system, and $2mn$ equations in its interregional part represented by sets (6) and (7). The unknown variables are the mn outputs $X_{i.go}$ and the mn total inputs $X_{i.oh}$ of each of n goods in each of m regions, and also the mn $X_{i.gg}$'s, which represent the internally absorbed parts of the outputs of each good in each region. The last group of variables appears explicitly only in the interregional equations (6) and (7).

Towards a numerical solution

As a first step toward a numerical solution of the system described above, the mn variables $X_{i.gg}$ (or $X_{i.hh}$) can be eliminated and the number of equations which have to be treated simultaneously reduced from $3mn$ to $2mn$.

By substituting g for h, re-write (7) in the notation used in (6):

$$X_{i.og} = \frac{X_{i.og} \sum_{r=1}^{m} [X_{i.ro}Q_{i.rg}]}{X_{i.oo}} + X_{i.gg} \quad \begin{array}{l} (Q_{i.gg}=0) \\ (g=1, 2, \dots, m) \\ (i=1, 2, \dots, n) \end{array} \quad (7a)$$

From (6) and (7a) we have:

$$X_{i.go}X_{i.oo} - X_{i.go} \sum_{r=1}^{m} [X_{i.or}Q_{i.gr}] = X_{i.og}X_{i.oo} - X_{i.og} \sum_{r=1}^{m} [X_{i.ro}Q_{i.rg}] \quad (8)$$

$$\begin{array}{l} (Q_{i.gg}=0) \\ (i=1, 2, \dots, n) \\ (g=1, 2, \dots, m) \end{array}$$

Equation (4) can be transcribed as,

$$\sum_{g=1}^{m} X_{i.og} = \sum_{g=1}^{m} X_{i.go}(\equiv X_{i.oo}) \quad \begin{array}{l} (i=1, 2, \dots, n) \\ (g=1, 2, \dots, m) \end{array} \quad (4a)$$

Now let $\sum_{g=1}^{m} X_{i.og}$ be substituted for $X_{i.oo}$ on the left-hand side of (8) and $\sum_{g=1}^{m} X_{i.go}$ on its right-hand side, and let the constants $Q_{i.gr}$ be replaced by new constants $L_{i.gr}$ defined as

$$L_{i.gr} = 1 - Q_{i.gr} \quad (L_{i.gg}=1) \quad \begin{array}{l} (i=1, 2, \dots, n) \\ (g=1, 2, \dots, m) \\ (r=1, 2, \dots, m) \end{array} \quad (9)$$

Thus we arrive at the following new set of interregional equations:

$$X_{i.go} \sum_{r=1}^{m} [X_{i.or}L_{i.gr}] = X_{i.og} \sum_{r=1}^{m} [X_{i.ro}L_{i.rg}] \qquad (L_{i.gg}=1)$$
$$(i=1, 2, ..., n)$$
$$(g=1, 2, ..., m) \qquad (10)$$

This set contains mn equations and $2mn$ variables $X_{i.og}$ and $X_{i.go}$ (the $X_{i.gg}$'s having been eliminated). However, n of these equations are redundant — one in each set of m describing the interdependence between all the regional outputs and inputs of one particular good i. To demonstrate this let us form a new equation by summing over regions g, the left-hand and the right-hand sides of such a sub-group of equations (10) corresponding to any one particular commodity i:

$$\sum_{g=1}^{m} \sum_{r=1}^{m} [X_{i.go}X_{i.or}L_{i.gr}] = \sum_{g=1}^{m} \sum_{r=1}^{m} [X_{i.og}X_{i.ro}L_{i.rg}] \qquad (11)$$

This is in fact an identity: by interchanging the subscripts g and r on the right-hand side (which leaves the double sum essentially unchanged) one can show it to be identical with the expression on the left-hand side. It follows that any one of the m equations, which have been added together to form (11), can be derived from the other $m-1$ and consequently could be omitted.

From the set (10) as a whole we can, for example, omit the n equations identified by the subscript $g=m$. This reduces the number of (independent) equations in that set to $mn-n$. On the other hand, the n balance equations (4a) — which were redundant so long as (6) and (7) were not yet combined into (7a) — must now be considered as imposing additional constraints on our system and, consequently, must be included in it.

Thus after elimination of the mn unknowns $X_{i.gg}$, the multiregional system in its new compressed form comprises mn regional input-output equations (1), $mn-n$ structural interregional equations of set (10) and n interregional balance equations (4a), i.e., a total of $2mn$ equations. The mn total regional outputs $X_{i.go}$, and the mn total regional inputs $X_{i.og}$, make up the corresponding set of $2mn$ unknowns.

With the mn final demands $Y_{i.g}$, — for n different goods in m different regions — considered as given, a general solution of this system can show, for example, what effect a change in any one $Y_{i.g}$ would have on the total output and the total input of each good in every region. Having computed the magnitudes of all the $X_{i.go}$'s and $X_{i.og}$'s we can insert them in (6) and (7a) to determine the values of $X_{i.gg}$ for any i and g; the magnitudes of all the interregional flows, $X_{i.gh}$ $(g \neq h)$, can be similarly derived from the basic set of structural interregional equations (5).

The conventional input-output equations of set (1), as well as the interregional balance equations (4a), are linear. The interregional structural equations (10) are non-linear; for purposes of numerical computation they can, however, be linearized by means of a first order approximation.

Let the value of each variable be split into two parts, its base year magnitude and its deviation from that. The system can be solved for the deviations of all dependent variables from their base-year magnitudes, on the assumption that the base-year magnitudes are known and that the deviations of the regional final demands $Y_{i.g}$ from their base-year magnitudes are given.

Below we will use a bar to identify the magnitude of each variable in the base-year and, up to the end of this section, the increment sign Δ to mark the deviations of all variables from their respective base year values.

To obtain a linear approximation of (10), we substitute in it $(\bar{X}_{i.go} + \Delta X_{i.go})$ for $X_{i.go}$, and $(\bar{X}_{i.og} + \Delta X_{i.og})$ for $X_{i.og}$. In the resulting expression all terms containing a product of two barred letters will cancel out, because equation (10) holds for the base year, and all the products of two deviations of variables can be dropped because they represent second-order terms. Thus the first-order approximation of (10) takes the form of the following set of linear relationships:

$$\sum_{r=1}^{m} [\Delta X_{i.or} M_{i.gr}] - \sum_{r=1}^{m} [\Delta X_{i.ro} N_{i.rg}] = 0 \qquad (i=1, 2, \dots, n)$$
$$(g=1, 2, \dots, m-1) \qquad (12)$$

The new constants are introduced to simplify the form of these equations; they can be computed from the previously used constants and the base year values of the regional inputs and outputs:[1]

[1] In terms of the constants appearing in basic structural equations (5),

$$M_{i.gr} = \begin{cases} \bar{X}_{i.go}(1 - Q_{i.gr}) & (\text{if, } r \neq g) \\[2ex] \bar{X}_{i.go} - \bar{X}_{i.oo} + \sum_{q=1}^{m} [\bar{X}_{i.qo} Q_{i.qg}] & (\text{if, } r = g) \end{cases}$$

$$(13b)$$

$$N_{i.rg} = \begin{cases} \bar{X}_{i.og}(1 - Q_{i.rg}) & (\text{if, } r \neq g) \\[2ex] \bar{X}_{i.og} - \bar{X}_{i.oo} + \sum_{q=1}^{m} [\bar{X}_{i.oq} Q_{i.gq}] & (\text{if, } r = g) \end{cases}$$

$$(Q_{i.gg} = 0)$$

$$M_{i.gr} = \begin{cases} \overline{X}_{i.go}L_{i.gr} & \text{(if, } r \neq g) \\ \overline{X}_{i.go} - \sum\limits_{q=1}^{m} [\overline{X}_{i.qo}L_{i.qg}] & \text{(if, } r = g) \end{cases}$$

(13)

$$N_{i.rg} = \begin{cases} \overline{X}_{i.og}L_{i.rg} & \text{(if, } r \neq g) \\ \overline{X}_{i.og} - \sum\limits_{q=1}^{m} [\overline{X}_{i.oq}L_{i.gq}] & \text{(if, } r = g) \end{cases}$$

In passing from (10) to (12) we have dropped the n equations with the subscript $q = m$ because, as is demonstrated above, they can be considered to be redundant.

Equations (1), (4a) and (12) constitute a complete linear system which enables us to determine the dependence of changes in total outputs and total inputs of all goods in all regional subdivisions of a multiregional economy on given changes in the regional vectors of final demand. The corresponding changes in all intraregional flows $\Delta X_{i.gg}$, and interregional flows $\Delta X_{i.gh}$, can of course be determined by inserting the previously computed values of $\Delta X_{i.go}$ and $\Delta X_{i.oh}$ into equations (5) and (6), or (7a).

The magnitude of the errors resulting from the linearization of the non-linear interregional relationships can be assessed through insertion of the computed $\Delta X_{i.go}$'s and $\Delta X_{i.og}$'s into the original system (10). The differences between the left-hand and right-hand terms of each equation will indicate how close an approximation has actually been attained. Since all these quadratic equations are homogeneous of the first degree, the errors caused by the linear approximation would be nil (for any given i) if all the computed increments $\Delta X_{i.go}$ and $\Delta X_{i.og}$ happened to be strictly proportional to the base year levels $\overline{X}_{i.go}$ and $\overline{X}_{i.og}$ of the corresponding variable, i.e., if $\dfrac{\Delta X_{i.go}}{\overline{X}_{i.go}} = \dfrac{\Delta X_{i.og}}{\overline{X}_{i.og}} = \lambda$ for all g's, where λ is some constant. This means that the linearization error depends not on the absolute, but only on the relative magnitude of incremental changes of these variables.

In case the first order approximation, by which equation (12) has been derived from the non-linear set (8), proves to be insufficient, a higher degree of approximation could most likely be attained through an iterative procedure in which the total value of the variables obtained in one round of computations are used to determine their 'base values' for the next round.[1]

2. *The Interregional Coefficients*

Having presented the analytical basis of the entire system and its overall design, we turn now to the discussion of the constants $Q_{i.gh}$ appearing in (5) and all interregional equations derived from it. The three subscripts attached indicate that equations describing a system with n goods and m regions will contain nm^2 such constants. They can be best visualized arranged in n square matrices. Each of these matrices contains the constants characterizing the structure of the interregional flows of one particular good and has m rows and columns, the row number g indicating the origin, and the column number h the destination of the specific interregional flow characterized by the particular $Q_{i.gh}$. Since they all refer to the same good, the coefficients contained in each such matrix will naturally have the same i-subscript.

Equations (5), (6) and (7), which make up the basis of the interregional part of our system, can also be conveniently subdivided into n groups, each group containing m^2 equations from set (5), m equations from set (6), and m equations from set (7), all pertaining to one particular good i.

---

[1] A purely linear multiregional system is obtained if, instead of deriving its interregional part from structural equation (5), one substitutes for it the following set of analogous relationships between variables describing each region's external trade:

$$X_{i.gh} = \frac{Z_{i.go} Z_{i.oh} Q_{i.gh}}{Z_{i.oo}} \qquad (g \neq h) \qquad \begin{aligned} &(i = 1, 2, \dots, n) \\ &(g = 1, 2, \dots, m) \\ &(h = 1, 2, \dots, m) \end{aligned} \qquad (5')$$

Where $Z_{i.go}$ and $Z_{i.oh}$ represent respectively the 'gross exports' of good i from region g and the 'gross imports' of that good into region h:

$$\begin{aligned} Z_{i.go} &= X_{i.go} - X_{i.gg} \\ Z_{i.oh} &= X_{i.oh} - X_{i.hh} \end{aligned}$$

From (4) it also follows that,

$$\sum_{r=1}^{m} Z_{i.or} = \sum_{r=1}^{m} Z_{i.ro} = X_{i.oo} - \sum_{r=1}^{m} X_{i.rr} \qquad (4')$$

When the values of $X_{i.gh}$ as defined by (5') are substituted in (2) and (3), the interregional balance equations, corresponding to the non-linear equations (6) and (7) above, turn out to be of a linear form:

$$\sum_{r=1}^{m} Z_{i.or} = \sum_{r=1}^{m} [Z_{i.or} Q_{i.gr}] \qquad (Q_{i.gg} = 0) \qquad \begin{aligned} &(i = 1, 2, \dots, n) \\ &(g = 1, 2, \dots, m) \end{aligned} \qquad (6')$$

$$\sum_{r=1}^{m} Z_{i.ro} = \sum_{r=1}^{m} [Z_{i.ro} Q_{i.rh}] \qquad (Q_{i.hh} = 0) \qquad \begin{aligned} &(i = 1, 2, \dots, n) \\ &(h = 1, 2, \dots, m) \end{aligned} \qquad (7')$$

All variables in each one of such subsets of interregional equations must carry the same subscript, i, as will the constants $Q_{i,gh}$ that will appear in these equations; these constants will accordingly belong to one of the distinct coefficient matrices mentioned above.

In the analysis that follows we will concern ourself with one such single group of equations describing the structure and the balance of the interregional flows of one particular good, say 'steel' or 'electrical machinery'. To simplify notation in formulae presented in this section, the subscript i under all variables and constants is omitted; e.g. instead of $X_{i,gh}$ we write X_{gh}.

In case the available base-year statistics comprise not only information on regional output and inputs $\bar{X}_{go}$ and $\bar{X}_{og}$ but also on interregional flows $\bar{X}_{gh}$ $(g \neq h)$, a direct estimate of any constants Q_{gh} can be obtained through insertion of the base-year values of the appropriate variables in the corresponding equation (5).[1] This is a procedure analogous to that which is conventionally used to derive the matrix of the technical coefficients a_{ij} from an input-output table compiled for some base year. In Section 3 below this method of deriving the magnitude of interregional constants from complete base-year information will be referred to as the 'Single Point Estimate'.

Systematic statistical information on the interregional flows of many, if not most, goods and services is, however, unavailable in many countries. To overcome this major obstacle to the practical application of the multiregional input-output system presented in Section 1 above, an analytical procedure is described in this section which makes it possible to apply that system even in those instances in which no base-year information on interregional flows is available. The constants Q_{gh} can in this case be estimated indirectly from the base-year magnitudes of total regional inputs and outputs; supplemental information on interregional distances or, more generally, on unit transportation costs can also be utilized in these indirect estimates of the structural parameters.

For the purpose of the following analysis each of the constants Q_{gh} will be described in terms of four subsidiary parameters appearing on the right hand side of (14):

[1] This observation and all that follows applies to cases in which the number of inter-related regions is greater than 3. With only three regions — if the three total regional exports, $X_{go} - X_{gg}$, and the three total regional imports, $X_{oh} - X_{hh}$, are given — the magnitudes of all the six possible interregional flows X_{gh} $(g, h = 1, 2, 3)$ can be derived immediately i.e. without recourse to any structural equations, from the six balance equations (2) and (3). In case of only two interrelated regions even the total exports and the total imports of each one of them cannot be considered as 'exogenously' given, since from (2) and (3) it follows that $X_{10} = X_{12} = X_{02}$ and $X_{20} = X_{21} = X_{01}$.

$$Q_{gh}=(C_g+K_h)d_{gh}\delta_{gh} \qquad \begin{aligned}(g&=1, 2, \ldots, m)\\(h&=1, 2, \ldots, m)\end{aligned} \qquad (14)$$

(5) can accordingly be rewritten as:

$$X_{gh}=\frac{X_{go}X_{oh}(C_g+K_h)d_{gh}\delta_{gh}}{X_{oo}} \qquad \begin{aligned}(g&\neq h)\\(g&=1, 2, \ldots, m)\\(h&=1, 2, \ldots, m)\end{aligned} \qquad (5a)$$

For the time being let δ_{gh} be assumed to be equal to 1. (We shall see that the only other value assigned to this parameter will be 0.)

The constant d_{gh} is intended to be a measure of the inverse of the 'per unit' transportation costs that would be incurred in moving the good in question from region g to region h. For lack of better information, it might for example represent the *reciprocal* of the distance between these two regions; however, in general d_{gh} is not necessarily equal to d_{hg}.

The constants C_g and K_h are parameters characterizing in a summary way the relative position of region g *vis-à-vis* all other regions as a supplier, and of region h as a user, of good i. The introduction of these essentially summary parameters emphasizes the fundamental difference between this system and the analytically more explicit, and empirically more demanding, linear programming models.

The C_g's and K_h's cannot be observed, they can be computed only indirectly. In partial analysis — i.e., in an analysis that does not take into account the interregional balance equations (6) and (7) — these parameters can be derived statistically through the application of the least squares or some other conventional curve-fitting procedure (see Section 3 below). Within the framework of a consistent interregional equilibrium system, of which (6) and (7) constitute a part, the values of C_g and K_h can also be determined through solutions of a set of simultaneous linear equations involving the use of factual information concerning the magnitudes of total output X_{go}, inputs X_{oh}, and the internal use of the domestic production X_{hh} of the particular good in each region in a given *base year*.

Let us rewrite equations (6) and (7) describing all Q_{gh}'s in terms of the four new parameters and substituting for all the unknown regional inputs and outputs their observed base year values:

$$X_{go}\sum_{r=1}^{m}[X_{or}(C_g+K_r)d_{gr}\delta_{gr}]=(X_{go}-X_{gg})X_{oo} \qquad \begin{aligned}(\delta_{gg}&=0)\\(g&=1, 2, \ldots, m)\end{aligned} \qquad (6a)$$

$$X_{oh}\sum_{r=1}^{m}[X_{ro}(C_r+K_h)d_{rh}\delta_{rh}]=(X_{oh}-X_{hh})X_{oo} \qquad \begin{aligned}(\delta_{hh}&=0)\\(h&=1, 2, \ldots, m)\end{aligned} \qquad (7b)$$

The magnitudes of all barred variables can thus be considered as given, as well as the magnitudes of the transportation costs or distances (d_{gh}). The subsidiary conditions, $\delta_{gg}=0$ and $\delta_{hh}=0$, correspond to the subsidiary conditions, $Q_{gg}=0$ and $Q_{hh}=0$, in the original equations, (6) and (7); for all other subscripts δ_{gh} can still be assumed to equal 1.

Combined together (6a) and (7b) can be viewed as representing a system of $2m$ simultaneous linear equations with $2m$ variables: the unknown parameters C_g and K_h. Since the observed base-year values of the regional outputs and inputs necessarily satisfy the overall relationship (4), one of the $2m$ balance equations in system (6a) and (7b) is redundant. In other words, a set of variables that can satisfy any $2m-1$ of these equations will necessarily satisfy the last equation too. This means that one (any one) of these equations must be dropped and that only if the value of one of the unknowns is arbitrarily fixed, can the remaining $2m-1$ equations be solved for all the other C_g's and K_h's.

Examining the structural equations (5a) we can, moreover, see that if some particular set of C_g's and K_h's, say C_g^0 and K_h^0, can satisfy them, the set $C_g^0+\alpha$, $K_h^0-\alpha$ (where α is an arbitrary constant) will satisfy them too. This means that, if structural relationships of that form do actually hold, $2m-1$ and not $2m$ of these parameters could determine uniquely the magnitudes of all the interregional flows. Thus before solving the linear system (6a)–(7b), we not only must eliminate one of its component equations, but also fix arbitrarily the value of one of the $2m$ unknown C_g's or K_h's. We will drop the first equations (corresponding to $h=1$) in (7b) and set $K_1=0$.

For computational purposes it is convenient to consider not the parameters C_g and K_h but rather the products $\bar{X}_{go}C_g$ and $\bar{X}_{oh}K_h$ as our unknowns. For the same reason the units in which all $\bar{X}_{go}$'s and $\bar{X}_{oh}$'s are measured can be redefined so as to make the total base-year output, $\bar{X}_{oo}(=\sum_g \bar{X}_{gr}=\sum_h \bar{X}_{oh})$ of good i in the entire system equal to 1.

The structure of the resulting system of $2m-1$ linear equations can best be shown by writing it in determinantal form. The variables in (15) are written out in the form of a horizontal vector on the top. To each one of them there corresponds a column of constants in the square matrix below. The constants from the right-hand side of all equations make up the vertical column vector to the right.

The system can be solved and the base year values of the constants, C_g and K_h (for g, $h=1, 2, \ldots , m$), determined through inversion of the square matrix on the left-hand side.

$$
\begin{array}{c}
\begin{array}{cccc|cccc}
X_{02}K_2 & X_{03}K_3 & \cdots & X_{om}K_m & X_{10}C_1 & X_{20}C_2 & X_{30}C_3 & \cdots & X_{mo}C_m
\end{array}\\[4pt]
\left[
\begin{array}{cccc|cccc}
\dfrac{\sum_r X_{ro}d_{r2}\delta_{r2}}{X_{02}} & 0 & \cdots & 0 & d_{12}\delta_{12} & 0 & d_{32}\delta_{32} & \cdots & d_{m2}\delta_{m2}\\[10pt]
0 & \dfrac{\sum_r X_{ro}d_{r3}\delta_{r3}}{X_{03}} & \cdots & 0 & d_{13}\delta_{13} & d_{23}\delta_{23} & 0 & \cdots & d_{m3}\delta_{m3}\\[6pt]
\vdots & & & \vdots & \vdots & & & & \vdots\\[4pt]
0 & 0 & \cdots & \dfrac{\sum_r X_{ro}d_{rm}\delta_{rm}}{X_{om}} & d_{1m}\delta_{1m} & d_{2m}\delta_{2m} & d_{3m}\delta_{3m} & \cdots & 0\\[10pt]
\hline
d_{12}\delta_{12} & d_{13}\delta_{13} & \cdots & d_{1m}\delta_{1m} & \dfrac{\sum_r X_{or}d_{1r}\delta_{1r}}{X_{10}} & 0 & 0 & & 0\\[10pt]
0 & d_{23}\delta_{23} & \cdots & d_{2m}\delta_{2m} & 0 & \dfrac{\sum_r X_{or}d_{2r}\delta_{2r}}{X_{20}} & 0 & & 0\\[10pt]
d_{32}\delta_{32} & 0 & \cdots & d_{3m}\delta_{3m} & 0 & 0 & \dfrac{\sum_r X_{or}d_{3r}\delta_{3r}}{X_{30}} & & 0\\[6pt]
\vdots & \vdots & & \vdots & \vdots & \vdots & & \ddots & \vdots\\[4pt]
d_{m2}\delta_{m2} & d_{m3}\delta_{m3} & \cdots & 0 & 0 & 0 & 0 & & \dfrac{\sum_r X_{or}d_{mr}\delta_{mr}}{X_{mo}}
\end{array}
\right]
=
\left[
\begin{array}{c}
1-\dfrac{X_{22}}{X_{02}}\\[8pt]
1-\dfrac{X_{33}}{X_{03}}\\[8pt]
\vdots\\[6pt]
1-\dfrac{X_{mm}}{X_{om}}\\[8pt]
\hline
1-\dfrac{X_{11}}{X_{10}}\\[8pt]
1-\dfrac{X_{22}}{X_{20}}\\[8pt]
1-\dfrac{X_{33}}{X_{30}}\\[8pt]
\vdots\\[6pt]
1-\dfrac{X_{mm}}{X_{mo}}
\end{array}
\right]
\end{array}
\tag{15}
$$

The problem of cross-hauling

The fact that within a given network of interregional shipments the flow from some particular region g to some region h equals zero has a significance fundamentally different from the observation that region h imports from one region a small, from another a larger, and from some other a still larger positive amount. A zero flow is most likely to reflect a fairly persistent disadvantage of that particular delivery route, as compared with other delivery routes that compete with it. Such disadvantage will, more often than not, continue to exist — that is the shipment from the particular region g to the particular h will remain zero — even after some relatively small shifts in the magnitudes of the regional pools of demand and of supply in these two or in some other regions would bring about corresponding readjustments in the magnitudes of all non-zero (i.e., positive) flows throughout the entire system. It takes a larger change in the magnitudes of the X_{go}'s and the X_{oh}'s to start new flows where they did not exist before, or to eliminate entirely some of the existing interregional flows, than to increase or to reduce the levels of previously existing flows.

The reader familiar with the principles of linear programming, and with its conventional application to transportation problems, will recognize that a change affecting only the (positive) magnitudes of the existing flows means an adjustment of the 'solution' without, however, any shift in the original 'base', while the introduction of new, or discontinuation of the existing, flows signifies a more radical adjustment involving a change of 'base'.

In equations (6a) and (7b), the subsidiary conditions, $\delta_{i,hh}=0$, $\delta_{i,gg}=0$, serve as a convenient device for eliminating the corresponding terms under the summation signs; all other $\delta_{i,gh}$'s have been, so to say, completely neutralized by the preliminary assumption that $\delta_{i,gh}=1$, if $g \neq h$.

As long as all $\delta_{i,gh}$'s are assumed to equal 1, when $g \neq h$, the empirical application of the multiregional system described above would be based on factual information of two kinds: (a) the base year magnitudes of the regional supply and demand pools, $\bar{X}_{i,go}$, $\bar{X}_{i,oh}$ and $\bar{X}_{i,gg}$, and (b) the distances — or some other measures of the relative costs of transporting each good i — from each region g to every other region h; this latter information is incorporated in the interregional equations through the magnitudes assigned to the coefficient $d_{i,gh}$.

By setting the appropriate $\delta_{i,gh}$'s equal to zero, even when $g \neq h$, we introduce in the empirical basis of our computations a third significant and — what is particularly important — easily secured type of factual information: (c) the knowledge that, for essentially logistic reasons, good i is not being shipped at all from a particular region g to another particular region h. Large changes in the other factors can, of course, modify even a relatively stable logistic pattern. However, such changes must be very great indeed before, for example, even a single ton of bricks will be shipped, in the United States, from Illinois to Texas.

The mathematical structure of our system is such that its solution would in general contain at least some shipments of each good from every region to every other region — that is, as long as the corresponding δ_{gh}'s are not explicitly assumed to be equal to zero. Thus, whenever the available information indicates that the good in question is not actually being shipped from one particular region to another — and most likely will not be shipped in the future either — the appropriate δ_{gh} can be put equal to zero in the structural equation (5a), in all the balance equations derived from it, and consequently in the structural matrix (15) too. This will affect of course the numerical values of all the constants C_g and K_h computed through inversion of that matrix.

In Section 1 above, while discussing the problem of cross-hauling, we have observed that in an aggregate multiregional system nominally identical — and even actually identical — goods can be expected to be moving between two regions simultaneously in opposite directions. This does not mean, however, that in such a system all goods must necessarily be traded in both directions between all regions. Even in setting up an aggregate system we often know — for reasons that do not need to be explained in detail — that a particular good i can be expected to flow from region g to region h, but not from region h to region g. The simple device of setting the appropriate $\delta_{i.gh} = 1$, but the corresponding $\delta_{i.hg} = 0$, will automatically incorporate that important kind of factual information in our system of equations.

Computing procedures

The method of determining for each good i the numerical values of the interregional constants $C_{i.g}$ and $K_{i.h}$, described above, is in principle similar to the procedure used in computing the technical coefficients a_{ij} from a given interindustrial input-output matrix. In both instances we obtain a 'single point estimate' from a given set of base-year figures.

The computation of the interregional parameters does not require knowledge of the actual base-year interregional flows $\bar{X}_{i.gh}$. Once, however, the magnitudes of the $C_{i.g}$'s and $K_{i.h}$'s have been computed, they can be inserted — together with the externally determined parameters, $d_{i.gh}$ and $\delta_{i.gh}$, and with the base-year magnitudes of the total regional inputs and outputs $\bar{X}_{i.go}$, $\bar{X}_{i.oh}$ and $\bar{X}_{i.gg}$, in (5), which will then yield the 'theoretical' magnitude of the corresponding interregional flows $X_{i.gh}$.

If the actual base-year magnitudes of the interregional flows happen to be known, they can be compared with the corresponding indirectly computed 'theoretical' values. Such comparison, as shown in Section 3, permits us to test the goodness of fit of at least some of the interregional equations. On the other hand, instead of being used for testing purposes, such additional information can be directly incorporated into the analytical system, thus strengthening its empirical base. As indicated above, if the actual magnitude of the flow $X_{i.gh}$ from region g to region h happens to be known, all four figures can be inserted respectively on the right- and the left-hand side of (5). The magnitude of the corresponding coefficient $Q_{i.gh}$ can then be determined from it directly. This still leaves open the possibilities of using the method described at the beginning of this section to determine the coefficients pertaining to all those inter-regional flows on which no base-year information is available. To do so it will only be necessary to remove in equations (5) and (6) one term containing the directly computed $Q_{i.gh}$'s from under the summation sign and place them separately along with $X_{i.gg}$ and $X_{i.hh}$.

In addition to those described above, other procedures could obviously be used to determine the magnitude of the interregional coefficients $C_{i.g}$ and $K_{i.h}$.

While presented as a device for conditional projection, the multi-regional input-output system put forth here can also serve as an instrument of regional, or rather multiregional, economic planning. Not only can the magnitudes of final regional demand be prescribed, rather than projected, but the values of some of the interregional para-meters can be prescribed too. If, for example, commodity i is to be produced in region g — in which it has not been manufactured before — the corresponding column of technical input coefficients must be included in that region's internal structural matrix. In case the new industry is intended to serve only the internal demand of region g itself, the parameters $\delta_{i.gh}$ for that particular g and all h's should be set equal to zero; if on the other hand, exports to some other region are planned, the corresponding $\delta_{i.gh}$ should be set equal to 1. In either case the completed multiregional computation will reveal the effects — on the outputs and inputs of each good in every region — of the proposed introduction of the new industry i in region g.

The complexity of all kinds of theoretical schemes which can be effectively used in practical empirical analysis is as a rule strictly limited by the nature and the amount of factual information available. The multiregional input-output system presented above has been designed as an 'economy model' that can be used for projection or planning with a bare minimum of statistical data. As additional information becomes available it also will supply a flexible, but at the same time internally consistent, general equilibrium framework into which one can build in more powerful tools of partial analysis, such as linear programming.

3. Empirical Solutions

As a first step towards the empirical implementation of the multiregional input-output system described above, a few experimental computations were performed to test its interregional part. Four different estimating methods were used, called the 'Exact Solution', the 'Simple Solution', the 'Least Squares' procedure and the 'Point Estimate' procedure.

In the Exact Solution the values of the structural parameters C_g and K_h are determined through solutions of the set (15) of simultaneous linear equations as described in Section 2 above. Information on the magnitudes of the actually observed interregional shipments enter into these computations only to the extent that it helps us to decide which of the subsidiary constants δ_{gh} should be set equal to zero and which equal to 1.

Inserted into (5), together with other exogenously determined parameters d_{gh}, the C_g's and K_h's permit us to derive the values of the corresponding interregional flows. The discrepancies between these computed and the corresponding actual magnitudes of the interregional flows provide a basis for measuring the effectiveness of the estimating procedure (see below).

This method of estimating interregional flows yields total estimated exports and imports for each region which correspond exactly to the (observed) regional output, input and internal consumption figures ($\bar{X}_{go}$, $\bar{X}_{og}$ and $\bar{X}_{gg}$) used in deriving the values of the parameters C_g and K_g inserted on the right-hand side of equation (5). Thus, the resulting estimates can be said to be entirely consistent with the primary information incorporated into them, at least in the base year.

The Simple Solution is what its name indicates. Instead of containing m^2 overall — and many more subsidiary — constants as does (5a), the structural equations used in this case contain only one constant (for each good) besides the $\delta_{i.gh}$'s:

 B.S.I.E.D.

$$X_{gh} = \frac{X_{go}X_{oh}}{X_{oo}} b\delta_{gh} \qquad \begin{array}{l}(g \neq h) \\ (g=1, 2, \dots, m) \\ (h=1, 2, \dots, m)\end{array} \qquad (16)$$

The constant b is computed from the observed base year magnitudes of all total regional outputs and inputs, X_{go} and X_{oh}:

$$b = \frac{\bar{X}_{oo} - \sum\limits_{r=1}^{m}\bar{X}_{rr}}{\sum\limits_{g=1}^{m}\sum\limits_{h=1}^{m}\dfrac{\bar{X}_{go}\bar{X}_{oh}\delta_{gh}}{\bar{X}_{oo}}} \qquad (\delta_{gh}=0, \text{ when } g=h) \qquad (17)$$

With b, the exogenously determined δ_{gh}'s and the observed regional outputs inserted on its right-hand side, equations (16) yield the estimates of all the interregional flows X_{gh}.

The method by which the magnitude of the constant b is determined guarantees that the grand total of the estimated flows of good i between all regions will equal the actually observed total of all regional exports or imports, $\bar{X}_{oo} = \sum\limits_{r=1}^{m}\bar{X}_{rr}$. However, unlike in the case of the Exact Solution, the estimated total exports and total imports of each region — obtained through summation of the appropriate (estimated) interregional flows — will differ in the case of the Simple Solution from the actually observed $\bar{X}_{go}$'s and $\bar{X}_{oh}$'s. Because of that the Simple Solution may be said to yield an internally inconsistent estimate of unknown interregional flows even for the base year. Whatever 'predictive' power the Simple Solution has is due to the non-linear expression $\dfrac{X_{go}X_{oh}}{X_{oo}}$ on the right-hand side of equation (16), which it incidentally shares with the basic structural relationship (5).

Each of the two procedures described above enables us to estimate the interregional flows X_{gh} in some particular year without recourse to information on the actual magnitude of such flows in that or in any other year. In both instances we only need to know the total regional outputs $\bar{X}_{go}$, inputs $\bar{X}_{og}$, and intraregional flows $\bar{X}_{gg}$ of the year for which the estimate is being made.

The Least Squares method represents, on the other hand, a direct application of the conventional statistical curve-fitting procedure to the structural equation (5a). In addition to information concerning the values of the 'external' parameters d_{gh} and δ_{gh} and the observed base-year levels of all the regional outputs and inputs $\bar{X}_{go}$ and $\bar{X}_{oh}$ employed

in the Exact Solution, this procedure requires also base-year information on the actual magnitudes of all the interregional flows $\overline{X}_{gh}$.
Let a new auxiliary variable X_{gh}^* be defined by,

$$\overline{X}_{gh}^* \equiv \frac{\overline{X}_{go}\overline{X}_{oh}}{\overline{X}_{oo}}d_{gh}\delta_{gh}, \qquad \begin{array}{l}(\delta_{gh}=0, \text{ when } g=h)\\ (g=1,\,2,\,\dots,m)\\ (h=1,\,2,\,\dots,m)\end{array} \qquad (18)$$

The difference u_{gh} between the observed interregional flow X_{gh} and the corresponding flow computed theoretically on the basis of the structural function (5a) is then described by:

$$u_{gh} = \overline{X}_{gh}^*(C_g + K_h) - \overline{X}_{gh} \qquad (g \neq h) \qquad (19)$$

The sum of the squares of all the u_{gh} — let it be called S — can accordingly be described by:

$$S = \sum_g \sum_h u_{gh}^2 = \sum_{g=1}^{m} \sum_{h=1}^{m} [\overline{X}_{gh}^*(C_g + K_h) - \overline{X}_{gh}]^2 \qquad (g \neq h) \qquad (20)$$

To minimize this sum equate to zero its partial derivative in respect to each C_g and K_h:

$$\frac{\delta S}{\delta C_g} = 2\sum_{h=1}^{m} [C_g\overline{X}_{gh}^{*2} + K_h\overline{X}_{gh}^{*2} - \overline{X}_{gh}\overline{X}_{gh}^*] = 0 \qquad (g=1,\,2,\,\dots,m) \qquad (21)$$

$$\frac{\delta S}{\delta K_h} = 2\sum_{g=1}^{m} [K_h\overline{X}_{gh}^{*2} + C_g\overline{X}_{gh}^{*2} - \overline{X}_{gh}\overline{X}_{gh}^*] = 0 \qquad (h=1,\,2,\,\dots,m) \qquad (22)$$

Since the sum totals of the observed regional inputs and outputs, from which $\overline{X}_{gh}^*$ has been computed, balance each other for the system as a whole, one of these $2m$ 'normal' equations is redundant and one of the unknown $2m$ parameters, say K_1, can be set equal to zero. All the other C_g's and K_h's can be computed through solution of the system of $2m-1$ simultaneous equations made up of sets (21) and (22) with, say, the first equation in (21) struck out.

The 'theoretical' estimates of all the interregional flows can be finally determined from (5a). In contrast to the Exact Model, the Least Squares method does not involve the assumption that total imports and total exports of the good in question as estimated for each region must necessarily equal the observed values. The imposition of such additional conditions would make the number of estimating equations equal to the number of available observations and thus transform the Least Squares into the Exact model. Since, in fact, the estimated regional exports and imports will in this case differ from the actual, this estimate is internally inconsistent in the same sense in which the estimate based on the Simple Solution was said to be internally inconsistent.

Similarly to the Least Squares method, the Point Estimate procedure requires complete base-year information on interregional flows. Since such direct derivation of the magnitudes of all parameters Q_{gh} involves the use of as many degrees of freedom as there are such flows, it obviously precludes the possibility of any discrepancy appearing between the estimated and the observed figures in the base year itself. This is the reason why the Point Estimate procedure was not used in computations related to a single year.

Errors of estimation

The errors of estimation entered in the tables given below are computed from the absolute differences (i.e., differences irrespective of sign) between the actual and the estimated magnitudes of the variable considered in each particular instance. Thus for interregional flows the Weighted Average Percentage Error is computed as follows:

$$D(X_{gh}) = \frac{\sum\limits_{g=1}^{m} \sum\limits_{h=1}^{m} \left[\frac{|X_{gh} - \overline{X}_{gh}|}{\overline{X}_{gh}} \overline{X}_{gh} \right]}{\sum\limits_{g=1}^{m} \sum\limits_{h=1}^{m} \overline{X}_{gh}} = \frac{\sum\limits_{g=1}^{m} \sum\limits_{h=1}^{m} [|X_{gh} - \overline{X}_{gh}|]}{\overline{X}_{oo} - \sum\limits_{r=1}^{m} \overline{X}_{rr}} \qquad (g \neq h) \quad (23)$$

The corresponding formulae for the total regional exports and total regional imports are,

$$D(X_{go}) = \frac{\sum\limits_{g=1}^{m} \left| \sum\limits_{h=1}^{m} \left[\frac{X_{gh} - \overline{X}_{gh}}{\overline{X}_{gh}} \overline{X}_{gh} \right] \right|}{\sum\limits_{g=1}^{m} \sum\limits_{h=1}^{m} \overline{X}_{gh}} = \frac{\sum\limits_{g=1}^{m} \left| \sum\limits_{h=1}^{m} [X_{gh} - \overline{X}_{gh}] \right|}{\overline{X}_{oo} - \sum\limits_{r=1}^{m} \overline{X}_{rr}} \qquad (g \neq h) \quad (24)$$

$$D(X_{oh}) = \frac{\sum\limits_{h=1}^{m} \left| \sum\limits_{g=1}^{m} \left[\frac{X_{gh} - \overline{X}_{gh}}{\overline{X}_{gh}} \overline{X}_{gh} \right] \right|}{\sum\limits_{g=1}^{m} \sum\limits_{h=1}^{m} \overline{X}_{gh}} = \frac{\sum\limits_{h=1}^{m} \left| \sum\limits_{g=1}^{m} [X_{gh} - \overline{X}_{gh}] \right|}{\overline{X}_{oo} - \sum\limits_{r=1}^{m} \overline{X}_{rr}} \qquad (g \neq h) \quad (25)$$

Absolute errors are used in these formulae rather than their squares in order to avoid an undue sensitivity of the index to differences in the sizes of the individual regions. If a large area is, for example, split in two, the sum total of the absolute deviations between the actual and the predicted in-and-out flows of the two sub-areas will be of the same general order of magnitude as the corresponding differences previously computed for the combined region as a whole; the sum total of their squares would be much smaller than the sum total of the squared deviations computed for the larger region as a whole. Thus an average of the absolute deviations can be expected to be less dependent on the size distribution of the economic regions than a corresponding average of their squares.

The results

Empirical implementation of an analytical model is a slow, laborious process, particularly where the model is as complex as the interregional system described above. In presenting the results of the computations we only intend to show what kind of known, partly known and unknown data are involved in this type of analysis and what their orders of magnitude are.

Table 1 describes the results of the base-year analysis of interregional flows of four goods: bituminous coal and lignite, portland cement, soybean oil, and steel shapes (i.e., iron and steel ingots, billets, blooms, slabs, etc.). The regional breakdowns are rather rough: for coal continental United States is subdivided into 13 regions, for the other three goods into only 9 regions.

A comparison of Columns 3 and 4 of Table 1 shows that, of the two estimating procedures that do not require information on the actual interregional flows, the Exact Solution yields better estimates of these flows than the Simple Solution. The Least Squares procedure, which requires for its application full knowledge of the base year interregional flows, gives an even closer fit, but when utilized for a base year estimate it does not actually yield an estimate of unknown flows but simply smooths out their observed distribution.

Since the estimated Total Exports and Total Imports of each region are obtained through summation of the corresponding interregional flows, the errors shown in Part B of the table are smaller both for the Simple Solution and the Least Squares method. Since the Exact Solution, when it is applied to the estimation of base year interregional flows, permits no discrepancy between the actual and the indirectly computed totals, Column 3 in Table 1B contains only zeros.

Table 2 shows the errors of estimation characterizing the 'prediction', by various methods, of interregional steel shape movements in 1950, 1952 and 1958. Structural parameters in every case were computed from 1954 (base year) information.

In addition to the three methods of estimation the results of which are shown in Table 1, a fourth method based on the direct, single point estimate of parameter Q_{gh} was used for the non-base year predictions

TABLE 1

Weighted Average Errors for Base-Year Estimates, by Commodity and Method of Estimation*

A. *Interregional Flows* $(X_{gh}; g \neq h)$

Commodity (1)	No. of non-zero flows (2)	Weighted average percentage errors†		
		Exact solution (3)	Simple solution (4)	Least squares procedure (5)
Bituminous coal & lignite	25	27	55	21
Portland cement	17‡	51	94	37
Soybean oil	22	42	51	35
Steel shapes	17	14	39	8

B. *Total Exports from or Imports to a Region*

Commodity (1)	No. of regions with exports or imports (2)	Weighted average percentage errors§		
		Exact solution (3)	Simple solution (4)	Least squares procedure (5)
Exports $(\sum\limits_{h=1}^{m} X_{gh}; g \neq h)$				
Bituminous coal & lignite	8	0	15	8
Portland cement	8‡	0	40	15
Soybean oil	6	0	8	8
Steel shapes	6	0	11	6
Imports $(\sum\limits_{g=1}^{m} X_{gh}; g \neq h)$				
Bituminous coal & lignite	12	0	32	5
Portland cement	8‡	0	64	23
Soybean oil	8	0	13	13
Steel shapes	8	0	22	2

* For commodity description, regional classification, data sources, etc., see Tables 5, 6, and the Appendix. Detailed estimates for an illustrative commodity, steel shapes, are shown in Table 7.

† Computed, using equation (23).

‡ A 2 per cent near-zero flow criterion was employed in identifying 'non-zero' cement movements. For details see Table 5 and Appendix.

§ Computed using equations (24) and (25).

in Table 2. For the Exact, Simple and Least Squares methods of estimation, figures in the 1954 (base year) column of Table 2 are taken directly from Table 1; for the Point Estimate method, the base-year interregional flows satisfying the structural equations (5) must obviously be identical to the observed, i.e., the base-year 'errors' will equal zero, and zeros are therefore shown in Table 2 for the Point Estimate model in 1954.

TABLE 2

Weighted Average Errors of Estimation,* Steel Shapes,
Base Year (1954) Parameters Applied to Estimates for 1950, 1952, 1958
(In percentages)

Solution method	Year			
	1950	1952	1954†	1958
(1)	(2)	(3)	(4)	(5)
A. Interregional Movements $(X_{gh}; g \neq h)$				
Exact solution	50	43	14	47
Least squares solution	54	46	8	51
Simple model	36	25	39	69
Point estimate model	54	47	0	71
B. Total Exports from a Region $(\sum_{h=1}^{m} X_{gh}; g \neq h)$				
Exact solution	34	26	0	20
Least squares solution	40	32	6	21
Simple model	29	22	11	31
Point estimate model	37	30	0	36
C. Total Imports to a Region $(\sum_{g=1}^{m} X_{gh}; g \neq h)$				
Exact solution	23	18	0	32
Least squares solution	24	19	2	35
Simple model	25	20	22	51
Point estimate model	22	19	0	44

* Computed using equations (23)–(25). Data sources, etc., are the same as for Table 4.
† 1954 values for all but Point Estimate Model are taken from Table 1. Base-year errors for the Point Estimate Model are zero by definition.

In years other than 1954, Table 2 indicates that the Simple model performed best in two of the three years studied. The Exact model gave best results in the third year (1958), and was superior to both the Least Squares and the Point Estimate methods in all three non-base years. The Exact Solution also performed better than any of the others in 'predicting' total regional imports in every year. The Least Squares and

Point Estimate procedures, both requiring more detailed base-year information, had the highest weighted average errors of prediction.

Table 3 gives volume of base-year movements, both in terms of tons and ton-miles, for the four commodity groups. Inter- and intraregional movements have been differentiated. Average distances moved have been computed by dividing ton-miles by tons.

TABLE 3

Volume of Observed Base-Year Shipments, All Commodity Groups Tested*

Commodity (1)	Location of shipments (2)	Tons shipped (000's) (3)	Shortline ton-miles (million) (4)	Average distance moved† (miles) (5)
Portland cement	Interregional	64·5	18·8	292
	Intraregional	219·4	26·1	119
	Total	283·8	44·9	158
Steel shapes	Interregional	21·0	3·5	168
	Intraregional	50·0	3·9	78
	Total	70·9	7·5	105
Soybean oil	Interregional	8·6	5·9	688
	Intraregional	3·0	0·5	162
	Total	11·6	6·4	554
Bituminous coal and lignite‡	Interregional	66·0	20·3	307
	Intraregional	98·6	17·5	177
	Total	164·6	37·7	229

* For data sources, regional classification, etc., see Tables 5, 6, the Appendix, and footnote ‡, below. Volume figures based on Interstate Commerce Commission rail shipments have been inflated for sample coverage.

† Except for coal, the distances have been computed by dividing reported ton-miles by reported tons shipped. In the case of coal where ton-mile figures were not available, approximate straight-line distances were first measured between each producing region and each consuming state and then used to estimate the ton-miles for each reported producing-region-to-consuming-state movement. The sums of these estimated ton-miles are shown in column (4), and average distances in column (5) have been computed using the total ton-miles shown.

‡ Commodity coverage and regional classification for bituminous coal are not the same as used elsewhere in this paper. Coverage, although based upon the same data source as listed in the Appendix, is limited to industrial use only. Reported shipments have been reclassified into the same nine regions used for the other three commodity groups shown, and the interregional-intraregional breakdown is therefore comparable in all four commodity groups.

Table 4 presents volume-of-movement data for all observed region-to-region movements of steel shapes in the years covered by Table 2. Each region-to-region flow is described in terms of tons shipped and of average mileage per ton; this latter figure was obtained by dividing the total number of ton-miles moved from the specific region of origin to

TABLE 4

Volume and Average Distances Moved, Railroad Shipments of Steel Shapes, by Originating and Terminating Regions, 1950, 1952, 1954, and 1958

Regions*	1950		1952		1954		1958	
From To	Average miles	Tons (000's)	Average miles	Tons (000's)	Average miles	Tons (000's)	Average miles	Tons (000's)
(1)	(2)	(3)	(4)	(5)	(6)	(7)	(8)	(9)
A. Interregional Railroad Shipments								
NE MA	255	51	255	39	255	40	377	18
MA NE	438	179	460	117	459	120	283	189
MA ENC	200	2122	261	1561	186	641	188	391
MA SA	140	1049	195	833	175	44	153	68
ENC NE	669	47	668	42	658	20	727	15
ENC MA	142	1316	162	1227	79	718	113	488
ENC WNC	307	43	357	94	377	43	325	36
ENC SA	286	117	441	232	60	326	45	199
ENC ESC	242	18	630	23	506	4	176	76
ENC WSC	1080	39	1157	32	1076	2	655	7
ENC Pac.	2094	5	2487	42	2115	3	2219	17
SA NE	353	25	383	18	318	35	292	13
SA MA	210	155	131	112	177	57	108	36
ESC ENC	213	93	176	33	285	14	357	27
ESC SA	—	0	—	0	259	5	—	0
ESC WSC	—	0	321	21	441	7	469	34
Pac. WSC	—	0	—	0	813	18	—	0
Other†	1330	165	1274	242	—	0	771	40
Total Inter-regional	232	5425	320	4668	169	2096	211	1655
(Index, 1954=100)	(137)	(259)	(189)	(223)	(100)	(100)	(125)	(79)
B. Intraregional Railroad Shipments								
NE NE	48	65	82	51	64	67	96	49
MA MA	60	2551	69	2976	67	1832	83	1736
ENC ENC	99	5405	106	4418	79	2988	70	3202
SA SA	11	5	12	10	446	11	16	29
ESC ESC	—	0	220	30	204	21	94	9
WSC WSC	—	0	—	0	265	32	—	0
Pac. Pac.	70	51	166	91	264	46	97	56
WNC WNC	—	0	—	0	—	0	250	5
Mt. Mt.	—	0	589	33	—	0	—	0
Total Intra-regional	86	8077	94	7609	78	4998	75	5088
(Index, 1954=100)	(110)	(162)	(121)	(152)	(100)	(100)	(96)	(102)
Total Shipments	145	13502	180	12277	105		109	6742
(Index, 1954=100)	(138)	(190)	(171)	(173)			(104)	(95)

Source: U.S. Interstate Commerce Commission, 'Carload Waybill Statistics; State-to-State Distribution of Manufactures and Miscellaneous and Forwarder (C.L.) Traffic and Revenue,' various years. All average miles shown are computed by dividing reported shortline ton-miles by reported short tons moved. Tonnage figures shown have been inflated to represent total Class I railroad shipments. Individual tonnages may not add up to totals shown because of rounding.

* For regional designations and descriptions, see Table 6-B.

† Includes all interregional shipments reported as zero in the base year (1954).

the specified region of destination by the corresponding tonnage figure. An examination of these figures calls attention to the following two problems that are likely to play a considerable role in further work on empirical application of our multiregional input-output scheme.

The large variations in the average number of miles which an average ton of steel had to travel between the same two regions in different years brings up the question of regional aggregation. The largest of all the tonnages transported between two regions was shipped from the Middle Atlantic (MA) to the East North Central (ENC) states; the second largest moved in the opposite direction. The 'distance', i.e., the average mileage, travelled from the first to the second region in 1954 is only half as long as that from the second to the first. Moreover, the 'distance' — from ENC to MA — fell between 1952 and 1954 by more than 50 per cent. The grossly aggregative definition of trading regions is obviously responsible for all this. There is good reason to believe that it is also responsible, at least in part, for the high errors of estimation registered in Tables 1 and 2.

Can this phenomenon be accounted for within the framework of the multiregional input-output system presented above, or will its explanation require a change in the general form of some of its basic structural equations? Much further empirical and analytical work will be required before even a tentative answer to such a question can be found. Its theoretical implications lead directly to the important problem of the homogeneity or non-homogeneity of the system. In their present form, both the linear equations describing input-output relationships within each region and the non-linear relationships which describe the interdependence of the different regions are homogeneous (of the first degree). That means that a proportional change in the magnitude of all the independent variables of the system, i.e., the final demands, $Y_{i.g}$, for all n goods in all the m regions, would be accompanied by an equal proportional change in all regional outputs and inputs and in all interregional flows. In particular all intraregional and interregional flows will in this case fall and rise exactly in the same proportions. The disproportionality of the cyclical fluctuation reflected in Table 4 could be explained on the basis of the present homogeneous system only in terms of uneven, i.e. disproportional, fluctuations in the components of the final bill of goods.

If, on the other hand, all elements of the final bill of goods in fact move strictly in the same proportion, only replacement of at least some of the homogeneous equations in our system with corresponding non-homogeneous relationships would make it possible to explain the disproportional fluctuation observed in Table 4. In linear approximation this would require introduction in these equations of free-standing constant terms. Before resorting to this rather radical solution, it might be advisable to explore the empirical and analytical implications of the first possibility.

APPENDIX

Sources and Organization of Data used in the Empirical Computations

In the United States, regional production and consumption as well as inter-regional shipment figures are available in reasonably complete form for only one commodity, bituminous coal (including lignite), and the post World War II years for which we have data are 1946 and the coal-year 1945–46.[1] Major movements of coal by rail and water are included in these data. Coverage of truck movements is limited, but the omissions are small in the aggregate. An important omission from the data is railroad consumption of coal, an amount equal to about one-third of domestic production in the years covered. Most overseas exports have also been excluded. We have no information on actual distances moved, but we do have estimates made by James Henderson of unit coal transportation costs in the year 1947.[2] (The distance estimates shown in Table 3 are only rough approximations.) Henderson, in preparing his estimates, excluded movements of both railroad fuel and bituminous coal used for coke manufacture.

Producing-district-to-consuming-state movements of bituminous and lignite coal for the coal year 1945–46 have been aggregated to a total of thirteen regions (see Table 6–A). Total movements originating in a region, including shipments terminating within the region, have been termed regional production (X_{go}). Total movements terminating in a region, including shipments originating within the region, have been termed regional consumption (X_{oh}). Not included in any of the figures are coal used for bunker fuel, railroad fuel, coal used at coal mines, coal exported, certain amounts of coal shipped by truck, and a moderately large number of shipments whose destination is unknown. Total exclusions amount to about 40 per cent of production.

For the transportation cost term, d_{gh}, the reciprocals of Henderson's 1947 interregional unit transportation costs are used. The only complicating factor is the need to aggregate Henderson's regions 2 and 3 to give a 13-region arrangement consistent with that derived from the Bureau of Mines' coal movement data.

Of the possible $m^2 - m$, or 156 interregional flows, actual movements were reported for 55 cases in 1945–46. These included 30 relatively small movements,

[1] U.S. Bureau of Mines, 'Bituminous Coal Distribution,' Mineral Market Report, M.M.S. No. 1497 (coal year 1945–46) and No. 1592 (1946).
[2] James M. Henderson, *The Efficiency of the Coal Industry* (Cambridge: Harvard University Press, 1958). Table A-4. pp. 130–131.

TABLE 5

A. *Commodity Groups and Coverage*

Commodity name (1)	Coverage		
	Type of sample (2)	*Per cent of domestic production* (3)	*Year* (4)
Bituminous coal and lignite	Monthly dock operators' reports and producers' reports from mines with average daily production of 50 tons or more per day	59·8	April 1945– March 1946
Cement, natural and Port-land (I.C.C. No. 633)	1 per cent I.C.C. railroad waybill sample	53·9	1954
Soybean oil (I.C.C. No. 515)	1 per cent I.C.C. railroad waybill sample	89·7	1954
Steel ingots, billets, blooms, slabs, etc. (I.C.C. Nos. 575, 577)	1 per cent I.C.C. railroad waybill sample	39·5*	1950 1952 1954 1958

B. *Interregional Movements Observed*

Commodity (1)	Year (2)	No. of regions (m) (3)	Number of observations (excluding intraregional)			
			Maximum possible $(m^2 - m)$ (4)	*Zero flows* (5)	*'Near-zero' flows* (6)	*Non-zero flows* (7)
Coal	1945–46	13	156	101	30	25
Cement	1954	9	72	41	17† 14‡	14 17
Soybean oil	1954	9	72	50	0	22
Steel shapes	1950	9	72	52	0	20
	1952	9	72	46	0	26
	1954	9	72	55	0	17
	1958	9	72	48	0	24

* In 1954.

† Includes all movements equal to or less than 2½ per cent of both the exporting region's total production and the importing region's total consumption. (This was the criterion used to identify near-zero flows for all other commodity groups.)

‡ Includes all movements equal to or less than 2·0 per cent of both the exporting region's total production and the importing region's total consumption.

each of which amounted to less than 2½ per cent of both the originating region's total output and the consuming region's total consumption. In the aggregate these 30 flows totalled 1,184,000 short tons, or 0·6 per cent of total interregional movements. These small, 'near-zero' flows were excluded from further computations, leaving a total of 25 off-diagonal, non-zero flows with which to test the interregional trade models.

TABLE 6

A. Regional Classification Used for Bituminous Coal and Lignite

Regional Designation		States included
This study	Henderson†	
1	1	Pennsylvania* and Maryland*
2	2, 3	West Virginia*, Virginia*, Kentucky*, and District of Columbia
3	4	Alabama*, Tennessee*, Georgia*, North Carolina, South Carolina, Florida, Mississippi, and Louisiana
4	5	Ohio*
5	6	Illinois*, Indiana*, and Michigan*
6	7	Iowa*, Missouri*, Kansas*, Arkansas*, Oklahoma*, and Texas*
7	8	North Dakota*, South Dakota*, and Nebraska
8	9	Montana*, Wyoming*, Utah*, and Idaho
9	10	Colorado*, New Mexico*, Arizona*, California, and Nevada
10	11	Washington*, and Oregon*
11	12	Maine, Vermont, New Hampshire, Rhode Island, Connecticut, and Massachusetts
12	13	New York, New Jersey, and Delaware
13	14	Minnesota and Wisconsin

* States which produced bituminous coal or lignite in 1945. See U.S. Bureau of Mines, *Minerals Yearbook*, 1946, pp. 326–339.
† James M. Henderson, *op. cit.*, Table 11, p. 44.

B. Regional Classification Used for Cement, Soybean Oil and Steel Shapes*

Regions (Abbreviations used in this chapter)	States included
1. New England (NE)	Maine, New Hampshire, Vermont, Rhode Island, Massachusetts, Connecticut
2. Middle Atlantic (MA)	New York, New Jersey, Pennsylvania
3. East North Central (ENC)	Ohio, Indiana, Illinois, Michigan, Wisconsin
4. West North Central (WNC)	Minnesota, Iowa, Missouri, North Dakota, South Dakota, Nebraska, Kansas
5. South Atlantic (SA)	Delaware, Maryland, District of Columbia, Virginia, West Virginia, North Carolina, South Carolina, Georgia, Florida
6. East South Central (ESC)	Kentucky, Tennessee, Alabama, Mississippi
7. West South Central (WSC)	Arkansas, Louisiana, Oklahoma, Texas
8. Mountain (Mt.)	Montana, Idaho, Wyoming, Colorado, New Mexico, Arizona, Utah, Nevada
9. Pacific (Pac.)	Washington, California, Oregon

* *Census of Manufactures, 1954*, Volume I, Industry Statistics, Department of Commerce, Bureau of the Census.

Although bituminous coal is the only commodity for which reasonably complete information is available on the interregional movement, the transportation patterns of other commodities transported largely by rail may be examined using the U.S. Interstate Commerce Commission's annual 1 per cent waybill sample analysis.[1] To obtain this sample, the I.C.C. uses copies of one out of every 100 waybills issued by railroads during the course of a year. These waybills are coded by commodity classification, quantity shipped, shortline distance between the two points involved, and transportation revenue. The waybill sample is aggregated to show state-to-state movements by commodity classification. It is this body of data which forms the basis for most of our current knowledge of United States freight movements and costs of transportation. The sampling error in cases in which the number of individual shipments observed between two particular regions is very small — say, between one and four — is bound to be quite large.

From this body of data for 1954 we selected a moderately high value-per-ton, homogeneous commodity group (soybean oil); a low value-per-ton, homogeneous commodity group (hydraulic cement); and a moderately low value-per-ton, moderately homogeneous group (steel ingots, billets, blooms, bars, rods and slabs). The steel shipments in the year 1954 represented about 40 per cent of all interplant shipments (after inflating for sample coverage but without allowing for possible sample bias arising from the issuance of two or more waybills for a single movement of freight). Soybean oil and cement railroad shipments in 1954 represented about 90 and 54 per cent, respectively, of total domestic shipments. As in the case of coal, each region's 'production' and 'consumption' were set equal to total shipments originating or terminating within the region. What bias this may introduce into our calculations has not yet been investigated; whatever bias exists will of course decrease as total railroad shipments originating or terminating within the region approach total shipments made by all means of transportation.

As transportation cost constants, d_{gh}, we used for these last three commodity groups the reciprocals of weighted average rail distances between two regions. (For steel shapes these average rail distances are shown in column 6 of Table 4.) Weights used in computing regional average distances were actual sample tons shipped of the particular commodity group. The regional grouping consisted of the nine regions standard for U.S. Census data. (See Table 6-B.)

Of the $m^2 - m$, or 72, interregional flows that were possible for each of the three commodity groups, 1954 sample data showed only 22 flows for soybean oil, 17 flows for steel shapes, and 31 flows for cement. On a 'near-zero' criterion of $2\frac{1}{2}$ per cent of an exporting region's production and an importing region's consumption, none of the soybean oil or steel shapes movements fall into the near-zero category. This was not true for cement where 17 of the 31 observed flows could be classed as near-zero. For cement this reduced the number of observed movements to the point where the least squares model became over-determined; that is, the system of equations (21) and (22) contained more

[1] U.S. Interstate Commerce Commission, Bureau of Transport Economics and Statistics, 'Carload Waybill Statistics: State-to-State Distribution of Manufactures and Miscellaneous and Forwarder (C.L.) Traffic and Revenue,' Statement SS-6, each year since 1947. Excluded from the published data is information on shipments originating or terminating in Canada and Mexico and on shipments originating in states with less than three shippers.

parameters than were needed to estimate the observed movements. It later became desirable in the case of cement, therefore, to reduce the near-zero flow rejection criterion from $2\frac{1}{2}$ per cent to 2 per cent. This added three more inter-regional movements to the list of observed flows and permitted a solution to be found for the least squares model. (Alternatively, it would have been possible to reduce the number of solution equations by 1.) The effect of these three additional

TABLE 7

Estimated Parameters and Estimated and Calculated Values of Interregional Trade in Steel Shapes, 1954*

(Steel quantities in thousands of short tons)

Direction of shipment†		Value of $(C_g + K_h)$		Actual ship-ments (X_{gh})	Calculated shipments (X_{gh})		Difference (M_{gh})	
From (g)	To (h)	Exact solution	Least squares		Exact solution	Least squares	Exact solution	Least squares
(1)		(2)	(3)	(4)	(5)	(6)	(7)	(8)
NE	NE	(not estimated)		67·4	n.a.	n.a.	n.a.	n.a.
NE	MA	252	253	39·5	39·5	39·5	0	0
MA	NE	424	326	119·6	83·2	63·8	-36·4	-55·8
MA	MA	(not estimated)		1831·9	n.a.	n.a.	n.a.	n.a.
MA	ENC	87	88	641·1	632·5	641·1	-8·6	0
MA	SA	109	70	43·9	88·9	57·3	45·0	13·4
ENC	NE	392	343	20·1	83·4	72·9	63·3	52·8
ENC	MA	36	37	718·5	691·6	718·5	-26·9	0
ENC	ENC	(not estimated)		2987·8	n.a.	n.a.	n.a.	n.a.
ENC	WNC	652	652	42·6	42·6	42·6	0	0
ENC	SA	76	87	326·1	282·8	323·2	-43·3	-2·9
ENC	ESC	123	123	3·5	3·5	3·5	0	0
ENC	WSC	280	72	2·1	9·0	2·3	6·9	0·2
ENC	Pac.	253	253	3·4	3·4	3·4	0	0
WNC	WNC	(not estimated)		0	n.a.	n.a.	n.a.	n.a.
SA	NE	741	574	35·1	8·2	6·4	-26·9	-28·7
SA	MA	385	269	57·1	84·0	58·6	26·9	1·5
SA	SA	(not estimated)		11·2	n.a.	n.a.	n.a.	n.a.
ESC	ENC	266	170	14·1	22·7	14·5	8·6	0·4
ESC	SA	287	152	4·6	2·9	1·5	-1·7	-3·1
ESC	ESC	(not estimated)		21·4	n.a.	n.a.	n.a.	n.a.
ESC	WSC	492	137	7·3	0·4	0·1	-6·9	-7·2
WSC	WSC	(not estimated)		32·2	n.a.	n.a.	n.a.	n.a.
Mt.	Mt.	(not estimated)		0	n.a.	n.a.	n.a.	n.a.
Pac.	WSC	27156	26690	17·8	17·8	17·5	0	-0·3
Pac.	Pac.	(not estimated)		45·8	n.a.	n.a.	n.a.	n.a.
	Total			7094·1	2096·4	2066·7	0	-29·7

n.a. not applicable.
* Excludes all zero flows.
† For regional identification and description, see Table 6-B.
Source: Column (2) Values obtained from solving equation set (15).
  (3) Values obtained from solving equation sets (21), (22).
  (4) Same as Table 4, column 7.
  (5), (6) Calculated by inserting $C_g + K_h$ values from columns (2) and (3) into equation (5a).
  (7), (8) Equals column (5) or (6) minus column (4).

flows on the exact solution model was to decrease the calculated goodness of fit slightly.

Finally, in order to test the applicability of base year parameters to interregional movements in a second year, railroad shipments of steel shapes were compiled by regions for the years 1950, 1952, and 1958. Parameters $(C\text{'s}+K\text{'s})$ are calculated from the 17 interregional movements observed in 1954, which served as the base year. (These parameters are shown in Table 7, along with the calculated 1954 shipments derived from their use in eq. (5a).) These 1954 parameters were then used to estimate the same 17 movements in each of the other three years. In each of these three years it turned out that there were interregional flows which had not been observed in 1954 (and for which, therefore, the estimated flow in the second year had been automatically set equal to zero). These are the 'other' interregional flows shown in Table 4. There were also a few zero flows in these other years between regions which had been observed to trade with one another in 1954. (These inter-year differences may very likely arise from the one per cent coverage of the I.C.C. sample. In evaluating a model's goodness of fit in these other years, however, we have assumed that this type of estimating error arises entirely from our initial assumption that a zero flow in the base year implies absence of shipments in all other years.)

CHAPTER 8

Application of Input-Output Techniques to Urban Areas[1]

by WERNER Z. HIRSCH

1. Introduction

A demanding task faces researchers in urban economics. They must perfect tools to attack the manifold economic problems resulting from the onslaught on urban centres by peoples all over the world. About 85 per cent of the total population growth in the Soviet Union between 1940 and 1952 was claimed by metropolitan areas. For North America, the figure is 77 per cent and for Europe and Oceania, 55 per cent. For Asia, the figure is 24 per cent and for Africa, 23 per cent, while the world figure is 39 per cent [1].

Urban growth appears to be continuing at an increasingly rapid rate. For example, in the United States, the urban population in 1970 is likely to equal its total population of 1950 — about 150,000,000 people. While not all problems that result from the urban explosion are economic in nature, some of the more challenging come under this heading.

To gain better understanding and devise purposeful policies for urban areas often requires identification and measurement of more than merely immediate and direct relationships. As Walter Isard [2] stated so aptly, 'Of the general interdependence approaches which have been investigated, the (inter-) regional input-output approach is most prominent, both in terms of accomplishment and recognition.' Input-output techniques are today's most potent tools for systematic study of direct, indirect and income-induced economic changes on the urban scene. This is true in spite of the numerous conceptual and data problems that remain to be solved.

In the United States as well as in a number of other countries, urban areas are seldom single, unified, decision making units. Even in such a setting, input-output techniques can make valuable contributions to the solution of a variety of major urban problems. If this is true, and the

[1] The author would like to express his gratitude to Resources For The Future and the Social Science Research Council for their financial aid towards the preparation of this paper.

next few pages may bear out this contention, input-output techniques should prove attractive to economists working in urban areas, regardless of whether they are parts of a federated or centralized political system.

What are some of the urban problems that do, or should, attract the attention of economists? Some are based on looking at an area *in toto*; then we disregard geographic components. Others are directed mainly to issues within an area. Urban transportation and its relation to land use and real estate values is a good example of the second type of problem; the effect of foreign trade or specific central government activities on employment and income in an urban area exemplifies the first. In many instances, work on an intra-areal problem also requires information on the total area's activity levels; in that case both types of analysis are needed.

Input-output analysis is especially applicable to a study of area-wide problems and it occupies a pivotal role in regional interaction analysis.[1] With its help it appears possible to improve comprehension, tracing and, possibly, measurement of the numerous complex interrelations between local public and private policies and external forces, and to assess how they ultimately affect an urban area's health and well-being. Such a simulation model can be used to study a variety of stimuli, e.g., specific local public policies and external forces, and estimate their impact on an area's five main dimensions of health and well-being: economic growth, basic employment stability, *per capita* income, net social benefits, and amenities of life. The first three lend themselves to an input-output analysis. To the extent that benefit and amenity estimation advances, even the latter two dimensions could be studied with the aid of input-output techniques. An important issue is the effect of urban industrialization and population growth on an urban area's health and well-being.

Another issue of wide concern involves the fiscal situation of urban areas. Input-output analysis appears to promise insight into the revenue and expenditure implications of a variety of autonomous forces. Two different models will be presented.

Finally, input-output techniques can be adapted to shed light on land requirements that are likely to result from a variety of forces, such as zoning changes, central government housing legislation, or tax revisions.

In relation to these issues, input-output analysis is mainly applied to short-run changes. Yet, for many reasons urban areas require long-run projections of economic activity, population, etc., for decision making. In applying input-output techniques to the making of projections, the researcher is haunted by most of their major limiting assumptions,

[1] On this point, see [3].

especially the stability of technical production coefficients, the linearity of production functions and equality between marginal and average coefficients. Perhaps the most damaging assumption of urban area projections concerns stability of trading coefficients. This paper, however, will not discuss long-run projections by input-output techniques which has been done elsewhere [2], [4], [5].

In Section 2, the St. Louis input-output model will be presented, and in Sections 3 to 5 it will be applied to analyse the impact of various forces on major dimensions of an area's health and well-being, on net fiscal resources of urban governments, and on urban land requirements. A summary, which also looks into the future, follows in Section 6. In line with its title, the paper focuses on applications, not on methodological problems and the shortcomings of this approach, although they admittedly are numerous.

2. The St. Louis Model

Two major types of input-output models with application to urban problems have been developed — regional and interregional models. The regional models are essentially of the two-region type, showing interindustry transactions within an urban area, as well as between the area and the rest of the world. They are often referred to as 'balanced' regional models, because the local output of each product either is equal to local consumption, or is made equal to it through import and export transactions with the rest of the world. Interregional models constitute the second type. They can show the interindustry relations among several urban areas of the national economy.

The St. Louis regional input-output model is designed to give as complete a structural description as possible of the transactions occurring in the area during a given period. The model can be represented by an interindustry flow table composed of three sub-tables — a local matrix in the upper left represents local sales to local sectors; an export matrix in the upper right represents local sales to non-local sectors; and an import matrix in the lower left represents non-local sales to local sectors. Non-local activities could be broken down further into those that take place in the rest of the nation and those in foreign countries.

The St. Louis model is an open, non-dynamic equilibrium model in which, under equilibrium conditions at a given point in time, a limited number of goods and service flows are balanced. It is a gross rather than a net output table and it includes intra-sector transactions. The St. Louis model relied for its implementation mainly upon company and government records. Secondary data sources were used in connection with households and state and federal government. Household and local government sectors are treated as parts of the endogenous segment of the economy. Such an arrangement appears to be appropriate for urban areas, since the activities of households and local governments are closely related to the general level of economic activity in the area.

The St. Louis Standard Statistical Metropolitan Area, in 1954–5, consisted of five counties with a total population of 1·8 million. The area is far removed from other metropolitan areas and is surrounded by a sparsely populated and mainly agricultural hinterland. Very little labour mobility exists between the metropolitan and adjacent areas. Thus, in many respects the St. Louis Standard Statistical Metropolitan Area is a distinct, closely inter-related economic entity.

Its economy is highly diversified. It produced an output totalling $15·6 billion in 1955. Of this output, $11·6 billion was sold to the local economy, while $4·0 billion was exported. Thus, about 74 per cent of local output was produced for direct local use. Both exports and imports varied greatly from industry to industry. For instance, the products of the petroleum and coal industry imported almost 72 per cent of its inputs, whereas the medical, educational and non-profit organizations industry and the local government sector each imported less than 2 per cent.

The St. Louis model identifies 29 endogenous industry sectors, plus a final demand segment which includes federal government, state government, gross capital formation and exports. Exports are broken down into 33 export industries.

3. *Urban Health and Well-Being Impact Analysis*

In this section the application of the St. Louis input-output model to three dimensions of an area's health and well-being will be discussed.

Growth impact

Since growth can be measured in terms of total physical output, income or employment, all three will be examined in turn. At least three different formulations are possible.

Formulation 1: Changes in final demand lead to production adjustments, not only in the specific local sector, but also in all those which are directly or indirectly linked to it. The assumption is made that neither consumer expenditures nor investment expenditures for new plant equipment are affected. For implementation, the inverse matrix $(I - A)^{-1}$

is computed with the household and local government sectors as part of final demand. It is multiplied by final demand, and the product is horizontally summed to give an estimate of directly and indirectly stimulated local industry output.

Formulation 2: Allowance is made for consumer expenditure adjustments; they occur because of output changes which lead to a chain of interindustry reactions on income, output and, once more, on consumer expenditures. A linear and homogeneous income-consumption function is assumed, and implementation takes the same form as in formulation 1, except that household and local government sectors are part of the endogenous segment of the local economy.

Formulation 3: The linear income-consumption function incorporated into formulation 2 is replaced by a more realistic curvilinear income-consumption function. For this purpose income-consumption functions are empirically derived and output reactions calculated in an iterative fashion. With the help of three, four or more iterations, expression is given to the fact that a final demand change results in direct and indirect income changes which, in turn, lead to consumption changes and to a second round of production, income, and consumption changes, etc.

All three formulations are also possible in relation to total annual income. Formulation 1 is implemented by computing the inverse matrix after household and local government sectors have been moved into the final demand segment. The direct and indirect income change, per dollar of final demand, is obtained by multiplying each figure of a given row by the appropriate household coefficients and then summing the product. The direct, indirect and induced income changes, per dollar change of final demand, on the assumption of linear and homogeneous income-consumption relationships, i.e., formulation 2, are found in the households column of the inverse matrix, with households and local government in the endogenous segment. Iterations made to estimate the output of formulation 3 also produce estimates of total annual income consistent with that formulation.

Table 1 presents income multipliers which are based upon formulation 2. They vary from a low of 1·79 for the 'other transportation equipment' industry (mainly aircraft) to a high of 2·75 for the products of the petroleum and coal industry. By breaking down the total income change into its three component parts — direct, indirect and income-induced change — some interesting facts are uncovered. The share of the income-induced change varied very little among industries: it was 35 to 41 per cent in all cases but one, the leather and leather products industry, where it was 47 per cent. The share of the direct change varied

TABLE 1

*Income Multipliers in Manufacturing Industries
St. Louis Metropolitan Area, 1955*

Industry	Income Multiplier*
1. Food and kindred products	2·57
2. Textiles and apparel	2·00
3. Lumber and furniture	2·20
4. Paper and allied products	2·38
5. Printing and publishing	1·93
6. Chemicals	2·04
7. Products of petroleum and coal	2·75
8. Leather and leather products	1·97
9. Iron and steel	2·08
10. Nonferrous metals	2·37
11. Plumbing and heating supplies; fabricated structural metal products	1·97
12. Machinery (except electrical)	2·26
13. Motors and generators; radios; other electrical machinery	1·91
14. Motor vehicles	2·65
15. Other transportation equipment	1·79
16. Miscellaneous manufacturing	2·30

* Direct, indirect and income-induced income change divided by direct income change.

greatly, from 36 to 56 per cent. Likewise, the share of the indirect change varied greatly, from 7 to 25 per cent.

Finally, employment estimates can be made. Formulation 1 is implemented by using the inverse matrix, with households and local government sector parts of final demand, and recording the direct and indirect effects of a given final demand change on the production requirements of each of the area's industries. The employment change associated with these changes in production is estimated by inserting each production change into an appropriate employment-production function. Formulations 2 and 3 require employment estimates to be obtained in an iterative fashion, similar to the procedure followed in the estimation of output and income.

The analysis reveals that in 1955 St. Louis industries differed greatly in their employment impacts. With St. Louis manufacturing divided into 16 major industries, the extreme cases were the products of the petroleum and coal industry, where a $1 million change in final demand produced a mere 14 man-year change in St. Louis direct and indirect employment, and the plumbing and heating supply and structural metal products industry where a similar change in demand produced a 138 man-year change. Comparable figures for the lumber and furniture industry were 135, for the motors and generators, radios and other electrical machinery industries 133, and for the textiles and apparel industry 130.

Basic employment stability impact

The employment stability of an area depends on the overall importance of the exogenous segment industries, the nature of each of the exogenous segment industries, the relative importance of output going to the exogenous segment, and the magnitude of employment multipliers of the exogenous segment industry. While industry studies are needed for the first two elements, input-output analysis can shed light on the latter two. The final demand matrix can indicate the percentage of each local industry's total output that goes into specific final demand uses. Likewise, employment multipliers can be estimated by input-output techniques.

For example, an analysis of St. Louis industries in 1955 indicates that the motors and generators, radios and other electrical machinery industry sold mainly to unstable final demand industries, and its employment multiplier was comparatively large. This industry could be expected to produce substantial employment instability in the area. The transport equipment industry excluding motor vehicles, furnishes another interesting example. About 97 per cent of local output was shipped outside the area and demand was highly volatile. Yet the employment multiplier was the smallest of any local industry, mainly because the local aircraft industry subcontracted large portions of its work to manufacturers outside the area.

Per capita income impact

Once total income and employment impact of a change in final demand have been estimated, dividing the first by the second produces per man-year income estimates. Deflating these data by an appropriate index produces an estimate of *per capita* real income.

Again the St. Louis Metropolitan Area in 1955 may be used as an example. Differences were smaller when measured in per man-year income rather than in man-year employment. These findings are reasonable in the sense that they are consistent with the fact that wage rates tend to change less from industry to industry than do technical coefficients of labour to output. As shown in Table 2, a $1 million final demand change for the textiles and apparel industry produced only a $3,200 direct and indirect per man-year income change in St. Louis; comparable figures for motor vehicles and products of the petroleum and coal industries were $9,700 and $9,300, respectively.

TABLE 2

Direct and Indirect Income Changes per Man-year in Manufacturing Industries Resulting from $1 Million Final Demand Change St. Louis Metropolitan Area, 1955

Industry	Income changes per man-year in $s
1. Food and kindred products	6,400
2. Textiles and apparel	3,200
3. Lumber and furniture	3,700
4. Paper and allied products	4,200
5. Printing and publishing	4,900
6. Chemicals	6,000
7. Products of petroleum and coal	9,300
8. Leather and leather products	4,200
9. Iron and steel	5,600
10. Nonferrous metals	6,300
11. Plumbing and heating supplies; fabricated structural metal products	3,300
12. Machinery (except electrical)	3,700
13. Motors and generators; radios; other electric machinery	4,000
14. Motor vehicles	9,700
15. Other transportation equipment	5,100
16. Miscellaneous	5,400

Foreign trade impact

In many respects an analysis of the effect of foreign trade on an urban area is a special case of the previously discussed applications.[1]

Input-output analysis makes it possible to assess short-run area adjustments to foreign trade and to identify therein the stakes of individual regions and their specific sectors. Foreign trade has a dichotomy of area effects — a complementary effect which tends to result in income increases, and a substitution effect which causes income losses to domestic resources displaced by imports. Input-output analysis is

---

[1] For a detailed discussion, see [5].

especially relevant to an analysis of the complementary effects. It can mainly show what has occurred and not what might have been. While it cannot readily show the competitive injury suffered by the local industry as a result of foreign transactions, it can nevertheless help in stating the assumptions about injury and its local income effects more precisely.

The dichotomy of complementary and substitution effects is not limited to the direct effect. It can also shed light on indirect and income-induced effects of foreign trade, as well as on the local economic activity impact generated by national industries which export and, in turn, buy in the region. Complementary industry transactions create income, leading to a chain reaction of new consumption and investment. The income effect can be traced and estimated with the help of the area's input-output table. The corresponding substitution effect, which expresses the fact that something else could have been bought but for the transaction which took place, is important for competitive imports. But, as stated before, input-output analysis cannot be of much help in the quantification of this substitution effect.

Finally, it is possible to estimate the local economic activity generated by national industries which export and, in turn, buy in the region. The resulting local output is approximated by multiplying the ratio of national exports to total national output for each industry, by local domestic shipments to each of these national export industries. Substitution effects exist, but what their magnitude might be is a matter of mere speculation.

4. *Net Fiscal Resources Impact Analysis*

Answers to the following question will be sought in order to show the usefulness of input-output analysis for urban finance studies: 'Will a given local industrial development add to or subtract from the net fiscal resources available to the area?' In short, an attempt will be made to shed light on whether a local industrial development will permit a reduction in tax rates, while services are maintained at their existing level and the price level remains unchanged.

For this purpose a model needs to be constructed that relates local industrial development to a region's net fiscal resources status, i.e., the balance between direct, indirect and income-induced contributions made to all levels of government, and the direct, indirect and income-induced costs of public services returned by all levels of government in the area.

Two different approaches will be explored. The first relies directly on a balanced regional input-output model which splits the local government row and column, respectively, into two or more columns and rows. State government rows and columns (and possibly federal government rows and columns) could be treated in a similar fashion. The second approach relies on a two-stage model and uses area employment, output and income multipliers for estimating the tax base, as well as the activities requiring public services. Fiscal side calculations are made to produce revenue and expenditure estimates.

In addition to the assumptions common to all input-output analyses, the following will also be made:

1. The regional economy is either operating below its full employment level, or it draws on outside resources which are highly mobile and willing to migrate without bidding up factor prices inside the region.

2. To the extent that taxes are shifted, no major income effects result.

3. Local industrial development involves the instantaneous establishment of a new local industry associated with a known change in the region's final demand and technical coefficients.

4. The value of public services is measured in terms of the costs incurred by the government providing the services.

5. During the period under consideration the region's industrial structure and technology, as well as the proportion of local purchases to imports, remain relatively stable.

Modified balanced regional input-output model

It is convenient to treat the fiscal resources of local governments separately from those of state and federal governments. In order to estimate the local government net fiscal resources, the local government row is split in two. The first row represents 'local government service costs' and reflects the costs incurred by local governments in providing services to specific local beneficiaries on an industry basis. To provide this information requires major imputations. A second row represents 'local government fiscal resources', i.e., the difference between local government tax receipts from a given industry located in the area and the costs of servicing the industry, with all indirect effects neglected. Industries that pay more for the provision of local government service than they receive in turn, show a positive local government fiscal resource status, and vice versa.

It is not uncommon for local government current costs, including service charges, to exceed tax receipts in any one year. When this happens, the difference is usually made up by state and federal subsidy. With this phenomenon in mind, the local government column is also split in two. The first column reflects local industries' sales to local government. The second column, needed mainly to balance the matrix, has no entry. It is the 'state and federal subsidy' column.

Potential direct, indirect and income induced service cost changes, associated with specific industrial development programmes, can be estimated by multiplying the inverse matrix values of the 'local government service cost' row by the expected final demand. Likewise, by using the values of the 'local government fiscal resources' row of the inverse matrix, estimates of the local government net fiscal resource status can be obtained. The latter is an absolute measure of the local fiscal implication of a given industrial development policy on the area's local government fiscal position. Both figures taken together can indicate the policy's relative impact on the local government net fiscal resources.

It is possible to treat public education and all other local government services separately. In this manner, changes in the local school governments' net fiscal resources, resulting from the establishment of a new industry, can be estimated.

In the United States a very large portion of local government receipts is derived from property taxes. In 1959, these accounted for 87 per cent of total local government tax receipts and 70 per cent of all locally raised revenue. But an industry's annual output and property tax payment are often poorly correlated. For example, extended strikes can reduce sales to almost zero, without having any short-run effect on the firm's property tax obligations. With this situation in mind, the following modification can be introduced if the input-output function is linear, although not homogeneous. If there is but one observation, i.e., for the base year, a function of inputs to outputs can be created by drawing a straight line through that observation and the origin. If it is known that the input is a less-than-proportional function of output (but still linear), this information can profitably be used. Such a function is represented by inserting its slope as a coefficient in the appropriate cell in the matrix, and by stipulating the intercept as a component of final demand in the row of the input.

On the assumption that the urban area under consideration is politically powerful enough to influence the state's fiscal activities with regard to the area, the state government net fiscal resources status in the area can be estimated. State government rows and columns can be placed into the processing sector of the input-output table. One state government row can be called 'state government service costs' (with the area the immediate beneficiary), and the second row 'state government fiscal resources' (with the region the immediate beneficiary). Data for the first row can be obtained by estimating the service costs incurred by the state government in serving each of the area's main industries. The state government fiscal resource status for the area's industry is the difference between the local industry's tax payments and service cost to the state government. The state government column is split in two in approximately the same manner as the local government column. Again, these government services could be broken down into education and other services.

Two-stage model

In this approach it is also convenient to separately estimate the local government and state government net fiscal resources, respectively. A simplified version of the model is presented in Figure 1.

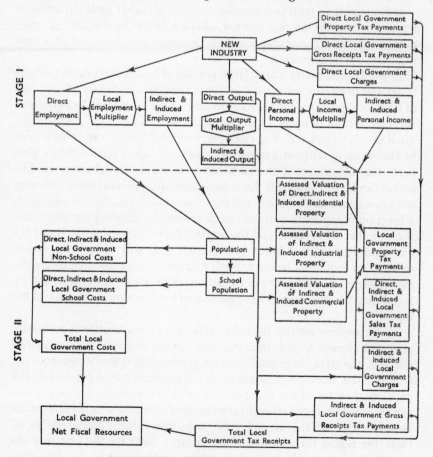

FIG. 1. Local government net fiscal resources

On the revenue side, there is little difficulty in estimating the local tax payments which can be expected from the new industry itself. Only important taxes need to be included. Local government taxes mainly take the form of property, sales, and gross receipts taxes.[1]

In most instances it is not difficult to get good estimates of the direct employment, output and income that can be expected to result from the new industry. Combining this information with local employment, output, and income multipliers of area input-output analysis produces estimates of new direct, indirect, and income-induced employment, output, and income. For example, with the aid of a housing cost coefficient, indirect and income-induced income per family can produce estimates of corresponding assessed valuation of residential property. Likewise, direct, indirect and income-induced output can be translated into assessed valuation of industrial and commercial property with the help of output-property coefficients. By applying the prevailing property tax rate to the assessed valuation estimate, an estimate can be obtained of local government property tax payments that could be expected under present tax conditions (minus those directly made by the industry).

Direct, indirect, and income-induced local government sales tax payments can be related to direct, indirect, and income-induced personal income. Indirect and income-induced local government gross receipts tax payments are more closely related to direct, indirect and induced output. Finally, indirect and income-induced local government charges are probably related to both income and output.

On the cost side, this approach makes a major simplifying assumption, with the hope that it will not affect the quality of the results in any major way. It assumes that local government services are not plant- but person-oriented. More specifically, the average person in a given region requires a relatively fixed amount of local services not only in relation to his family and home, but also in relation to his place of work and sale of goods and private services.[2]

Furthermore, costs are defined as current costs plus debt service. While local government expenditures include all funds spent by local

---

[1] In addition, there are certain charges but the property tax overshadows all other revenue sources.

[2] Thus, costs to local governments for streets and roads, for instance, will be assumed to be closely related to the number of people in the area. In many respects the number of people reflects the presence of plants. Shipping goods by truck in and out of plants is assumed to have a minor voice in the building of roads, particularly if compared to the fact that people must travel to their homes, place of work and shopping areas. This assumption may not be far wrong, particularly since many industrial establishments, especially the larger ones, furnish their own fire and police protection, rubbish collection, etc. Many even provide for their own water supply and sewage disposal.

government, costs cover only that amount that has been raised by local government.

Estimation of the direct, indirect, and income-induced local government costs associated with the new industry is perhaps best accomplished by separately considering local government non-school and school costs. The first are more closely related to the overall population increase which results from the new industry, while the second is more directly correlated with school population. (See left-hand side of Figure 1.) For example, direct, indirect and income-induced employment can be translated into the corresponding number of pupils in average daily attendance. With the aid of data on per pupil operating cost and capital outlays, total local government costs for schools can be estimated.

After adding these various total local government tax payments, and subtracting from them the total local government costs, an estimate of the final local government net fiscal resources is obtained.

State government net fiscal resources can also be estimated by taking two successive steps. First, there is need to estimate the regional impact of the new industry in terms of those who require services from the state and are tax-obligated to it. This calls for the same steps that were taken in connection with the first stage of local fiscal resources estimation. In the second stage, the region's state service requirements must be translated into state government costs and the tax base into state government tax payments. On the cost side, the steps taken in relation to local government can be duplicated in relation to state government. Thus, population estimates are made from employment estimates and, in turn, are used to estimate state non-school and school costs.

An analysis of the receipts side needs only to encompass the more important state government taxes, i.e., general sales and gross receipts taxes, individual income taxes, corporation income taxes, motor vehicle and operators' licences, property taxes, and death and gift taxes. By far the most important are sales and receipts taxes, which in 1959 accounted for about 59 per cent of state taxes.

Again, first the direct state taxes that can be expected from the new industry are estimated. Indirect and induced state sales taxes and personal income taxes can be deducted from the income estimates. Likewise, indirect and induced state gross receipts taxes and corporation income taxes can be related to output estimates. Both population and income estimates may be used to obtain indirect and income induced state gift and death tax estimates. Finally, population output and income estimates may be used to estimate indirect and induced state motor vehicle and operator licence payments and state charges.

In theory, determination of the area's federal net fiscal resources could proceed in line with the general model developed above. On the receipts side, the emphasis would be on income and output in order to estimate personal and corporation income tax payments. On the cost side, employment and population would be emphasized.

An attempt has been made to implement the two-stage model in relation to public education. Specifically, estimates have been made of the impact of industrialization on the net fiscal resources of the local school governments of the St. Louis Metropolitan Area in 1955. Industrial development was assumed to result in a $1 million final demand increase for one of the area's major industries. Such a step could have led to greatly different results, depending on the industrialization that was assumed to have taken place. For one extreme case, a $1 million final demand increase led to $1,900 improvement in the local school government's net fiscal resources; at the other extreme, a $9,300 deterioration in the net fiscal resources resulted.

5. *Urban Land Requirement Analysis*

One of the pressing urban problems is related to land requirements. The St. Louis output model can be adapted to help estimate land and even floor space requirements generated by final demand changes [6].

Figures in the transaction and technical coefficient matrices need not be in dollars and cents. They can be expressed in physical units, as long as all entries in a given row are presented in the same unit. Thus, a transaction matrix can be constructed with acreage data in a row. In some cases, it might be preferable to have three rows — floor space, parking space, and land reserve. If an industry's land requirements differ with location, separate output and acreage columns and rows can be introduced for the industry in the core city and in suburbia, respectively.

In a sense, acreage rows can be considered quasi-exogenous rows with no column counterpart. However, it is convenient to include corresponding columns and fill in zeros. For example, to the 29 × 29 processing sector transaction matrix of St. Louis, in which all figures are in dollars, three quasi-exogenous rows with all data given in acres can be added, viz. —

Row 30 — Floor space occupied by industries 1–29
Row 31 — Parking space occupied by industries 1–29, and
Row 32 — Land reserve of industries 1–29.

There are three corresponding columns, containing only zeros.

In order to get the floor space row of the technical coefficient matrix, each cell in transaction matrix row 30 is divided by the output level of the column, adjusted for inventory changes. The same is done in connection with rows 31 and 32. In this way, figures in rows 30–32 of the coefficient matrix are expressed in acres per dollar of output. Data in the inverse matrix are expressed in the same terms as those in the technical coefficient matrix. Figures in rows 30–32 state the direct and indirect acreage requirements per dollar of final demand change.

Land requirements per unit of output appear to increase over time, especially as plants move out of the core city [7]. This phenomenon can be incorporated into a dynamic model. A block diagonal matrix can be used. It will have as many submatrices as there are periods.

6. *Summary and Conclusions*

Some of the applications of urban area input-output analysis have been discussed. Although the table used here for computational purposes was constructed for a metropolitan area in the United States, the application should transcend national boundaries. The need for industrialization, and planning for industrialization, are problems common to virtually all urban areas in the world. Input-output analysis can help to disclose some of the economic implications of alternative development proposals. Thus it can facilitate decisions on whether a particular plan appears consistent with the needs, capabilities and aspirations of the area. It might also be used to elicit support for area-wide development and to persuade members of the community to take an active part in weighing alternative plans for the area.

It has been shown that area input-output analysis can be applied to provide estimates of the *per capita* personal income impact resulting from different types of industrial development. Relatively high *per capita* income effects can be interpreted to mean that the overall income effect overshadows the employment and, most likely, also the population effect. Under these circumstances, ability to afford public services tends to exceed public service needs. Consequently, an improvement in the area's net fiscal resources status is likely to result, or vice versa. Computations using the St. Louis input-output table produced results which are consistent with this hypothesis. Of the 16 principal St. Louis industries, the products of the petroleum and coal industry were found to have had the second highest *per capita* income effect and the highest positive net fiscal resources effect. At the same time, the textiles and apparel industry had the lowest *per capita* income and the lowest positive net fiscal resources effect.

Let us now briefly look ahead. The rapidity with which imaginative research on urban problems and improved urban decision making can be expected to advance throughout the world will be conditioned in a major way by the availability of a powerful framework and data for its implementation. Forward-looking work in urban economics must develop such a system of urban accounts, together with appropriate data of high quality, comparability and continuity.

The great urgency of information requirements for enlightened urban decision making points to the desirability of developing a data flow system which can use existing analytical tools and data sources. Area input-output analysis promises to be an important component of such a system. It is uniquely equipped to represent the flow account. In conjunction with a wealth account which, in terms of relative regional advantage analysis, helps to determine what portion of the national and foreign demand constitutes the area's final demand, a well articulated information flow system can result.

The input-output studies for Stockholm [6], Amsterdam [8], Kalamazoo [5] and St. Louis [4] have shown the feasibility of developing input-output tables for metropolitan areas with the aid of special surveys. They are expensive and, at best, likely to be undertaken on a piecemeal basis in a sporadic and uncoordinated manner which will make comparisons virtually impossible. For this reason it might be desirable to attempt a nation-wide approach, which will generate input-output tables mainly from centrally tabulated census data of all of a country's metropolitan areas plus the rest of the country.

The magnitude of the worldwide urban explosion, the manifold practical challenges and opportunities, and the paucity of satisfactory analytical frameworks, should convince many scholars of the prime need of efforts in this area.

REFERENCES

[1] GIBBS, J. P. and SCHNORE, L. F., 'Metropolitan Growth: An International Study,' *American Journal of Sociology*, Vol. 66, 1960, p. 164.
[2] ISARD, W., *Methods of Regional Analysis*, New York, 1960.
[3] HIRSCH, W. Z., 'Regional Accounts: Objectives and Framework,' *Proceedings of the American Statistical Association, Business and Economic Statistics Section*, 1959, p. 282.
[4] BOLLENS, J. C. (*ed.*), *Exploring the Metropolitan Community*, Berkeley, 1961, p. 369.
[5] HOCHWALD, W., *et al.*, *Local Impact of Foreign Trade*, National Planning Association, Washington, 1960, p. 89 and p. 180.

M

[6] ARTLE, R., *Studies in the Structure of the Stockholm Economy*, Stockholm, 1959.

[7] University of Pennsylvania Institute for Urban Studies, *Industrial Land and Facilities for Philadelphia*, Philadelphia, 1956, p. 41.

[8] Bureau van Statistiek der Gemeente Amsterdam, *Stedelijke Jaarrekeningen van Amsterdam, 1951 en 1953*, Amsterdam, 1960.

PART III

Input-Output Techniques and National Planning

Chapter 13

Input-Output Techniques and Regional Labour

CHAPTER 9

The Use of Statistical and Mathematical
Methods in Soviet Planning

by V. S. NEMCHINOV

1. *Introduction*

Planning, as it is carried out in socialist states, is a very complicated series of social and economic measures. Statistical and mathematical methods occupy only an auxiliary and subsidiary place — though an important one — within these measures.

Planning is inseparably linked with a regulated organization of the economy, without which it would lose its most important properties and characteristics. This organization comprises the following:

(1) The public ownership of the means of production (at least in the main sectors of the economy) — a cardinal condition making possible the implementation of public directives.

(2) The existence of an economic system in which the direction and the rate of social development are determined in the interests of the entire community (account being taken of the deliberate use of economic laws). The purposefulness of the economy is determined by a precisely-formulated social goal embodied in directives and plan-target figures.

(3) Annual and long-term plans for economic and cultural develop-ment substantiated by appropriate technical and economic calculations. These are based on the directives and plan-target figures mentioned above rather than on forecasts. Although some elements of forecasting are present in planning, account is always taken of the need for attaining the social goal expressed as a directive. Forecasting covers only the means of attaining the objectives and not the objectives themselves. This characteristic of directive planning is exemplified in the methods used for planning standards of living.

2. *Methods of Planning Consumer Welfare*

A capitalist economy is motivated by profit maximization in the production process. The motivation of a socialist economy is the attainment of an expansion of personal consumption within the shortest possible time, viz., to maximize within the plan horizon that rate of growth of final product which is determined by the optimal ratio of consumption to accumulation.

A slowing down of the attainment of this goal may result from the need to ensure defence against external aggression. Therefore a socialist society, by all means and at all times, seeks to eliminate this restriction by struggling for general and complete disarmament and for peace throughout the world. The struggle for peace is inherent in the very nature of socialist society with its maximum concern for the interests of man as a member of society and for the interests of society as a whole.

The planning of the economic development of socialist countries has its own characteristics as regards the application of statistical and mathematical methods. The targets for investment and national product are, as a rule, rigidly specified but those for living standards are more flexible, since the pattern of consumption is not prescribed for each member of society; only average consumption levels are set by the plan. In this sense the planning of material welfare does involve some elements of forecasting. Preference is given to narrowing the gap between the living standards of different social groups by ensuring a rise in the living standards of the numerically largest strata of the population.

The following example of the procedures adopted for the long-term programmes for 1970, 1975 and 1980 illustrates the method of setting planned targets of consumption. Changes in the age and sex composition of the population in each of the large economic zones of the country were calculated for urban and rural districts separately, the data of the All-Union census of population for 1959 and demographic data on birth and death rates being taken as the point of departure. Then, on the basis of well-known methods of demographic and mathematical statistics, using electronic computers, expected population totals were calculated for the bench-mark dates of the long-term programme, broken down by major economic zones, showing separately children of pre-school and school age and the adult population by two broad age-groups, viz., working and retired. These results showed that considerable differences exist in the regional rates of natural growth of the population, due to variations in the age and sex composition of the population (caused by the World War) as well as to relative differences in birth, death and fertility rates. Next, expected migration resulting from planned capital projects and future regional development was taken into account.

The Nutrition Institute of the USSR Ministry of Health has established long-term, scientifically-substantiated, nutrition standards for the

USSR as a whole and for its economic zones. Similar perspective norms have been elaborated by the State Economic Council of the USSR for the consumption of staple manufactured goods, housing (living space in square metres, etc.), communal facilities, and services (electricity, gas and water supply). Account was taken of local and national consumption patterns, as revealed in the 35 years during which household budget statistics were collected. In the post-war period more than 20,000 families of workers and employees and 25,000 families of collective farmers kept daily accounts of their purchases and consumption of goods and of their income in cash and in kind. Monthly and annual family budgets are made up from these. This information is supplemented by occasional wider surveys: in September 1958, for instance, the composition and income of 240,000 families of workers and employees were examined.

For systematizing household-budget and other sample studies, with a view to using them in setting plans for living standards, a special programme was worked out for use on electronic computers; in this the Laboratory of Economic and Mathematical Methods of the Armenian Academy of Sciences took part. On the basis of empirical data, the Institute for Research in Labour and Wages constructed a model of the formation of household demand and consumption. In this model consumption levels of various products and services (expressed both in value and physical units) vary with type of family (classified by size and composition) and family income (low, medium or high). The pattern of household consumption derived from sample data was then adjusted to be consistent with the total wage bill and with the value of retail sales. The model makes it possible to estimate the future structure of family expenditure and the likely level of consumption. In the model, the matrix of demand coefficients varies with the level of family income, and the sex and age structures of households. At present a number of research institutes are carrying out supplementary studies on income and price elasticities of consumer goods.

For a more detailed assessment of consumption standards for the long-term perspective, a linear programming model was set up. Calculations using the model are being carried out by the Institute of Electronic Controlling Devices. In the process of long-range planning the aggregate requirements of consumer goods and services were adjusted to those consistent with scientifically-substantiated norms by iteration. The model of household demand and consumption thus incorporates into a single entity data from samples, censuses, and budget inquiries.

For long-term consumption planning, the models described above (for population forecasts, the formation of household demand and consumption, and for consumption norms) are used in combination with four other models.[1] These are (a) the distribution of employees by wage; (b) the formation of incomes of households in money and also in kind; (c) a classified balance of the income and consumption of households; (d) and the inter-industry table of production and distribution.

In model (a), to compute the distribution of workers and employees according to wage rates, account was taken of the expected effect of increases in productivity on wages and salaries, of proposals for a higher minimum wage, and of possible changes in the structure of wage payments. These calculations were made at the Computing Centre of Moscow University and at the Institute of Electronic Controlling Devices on the 'M-20' computer.

Model (b) was used to predict the future distribution of workers' families according to *per capita* income, taken to characterize their material welfare. Account was taken both of money incomes (the sum of the incomes of all the working members of a family), and of total incomes, including free services and government allowances. The calculations were performed on the 'Ural-2' computer. A specific feature of this model is that it makes it possible to pass from the distribution of employees according to wage and salary to those according to family income in cash and in kind.

Model (c), which combines the model on the formation of household demand and model (b), results in accounts of household income and consumption for categories of families classified by *per capita* income. This provides a basis for determining living standards for the plan period. The consumption side of this last model, when fed into the relevant final demand column of the interindustry model, permits the calculation of the total output required to ensure the planned improvement in levels of living.

The above models are also employed for working out the implications of various measures aimed at improving levels of living such as the abolition of income taxes and the increase of benefits from public funds.

These models, already in wide use, avoid inconsistencies in planning and allow a choice between alternative ways of improving levels of living. We believe that this large-scale use of electronic computers and of mathematical models is unprecedented in the planning of levels of living.

[1] This part of the report has been prepared in collaboration with A. G. Aganbegyan, Learned Secretary of the Scientific Methodological Council of the Computation Centre of the USSR State Economic Council. (See also the proceedings of the First Scientific Conference on the Application of Mathematical Methods to Economics, reproduced in abstract in [1].)

3. *The Balance-Sheet Method in Planning*

The balance-sheet method reflects most vividly the use of statistical methods in planning. In the early years of Soviet administration the balance-sheet method was employed in planning the output and the distribution of grain and fuel. These were the first commodity balance-sheets, expressed in physical units. As planning developed, the list of goods, for which the commodity (physical-unit) balances were drawn up, grew. At present, the Soviet Government approves annually about 150 planned commodity balance-sheets expressed in physical units. The State Planning Committee of the USSR and the Planning Committee of the Union-Republics make up nearly 1,600 commodity balance-sheets. The agencies dealing with procurement and marketing draw up 10,500 balance-sheets for the distribution of the corresponding number of products.

The balance-sheets requiring the Government's approval are in aggregate commodity terms (e.g. electric power, coal, rolled steel, timber, etc.). The balance-sheets of the USSR State Planning Committee show greater detail, while those of procurement agencies include commodities subdivided according to grade, type, size, etc.

The balance-sheets for commodities and capital goods on the inflow side specify the principal sources of supply and on the outflow side the channels of distribution. Material balance-sheets constitute a most important instrument of commodity planning; the greater part of social product is planned thereby.

The latest table of interindustry transactions, based on production and distribution returns for 1959, and drawn up by the Central Statistical Administration of the USSR, is a 157 by 157 matrix (intermediate consumption) in physical units; the matrix includes columns for seven non-producing sectors, such as additions to inventories, exports and uses in the non-productive industries.[1] The table is expressed in both physical units of measurement and in constant prices. It is possible to pass from this interindustry table to another one expressed in current prices.

The commodity table required the reconciliation of aggregates of enterprise returns, data on usage of consumer-goods, as well as of standard input coefficients for fuel, power and other materials. This was necessary because the enterprise returns did not always fit the sector classification of the table.

---

[1] The system of the national-economy balance is discussed in detail in [2] and [3].

The tabulations used in the USSR are in physical quantities and in value terms, permitting a corresponding analysis of total product by the principal spheres of production, viz., the output of 'means of production', i.e. of capital goods; of the 'objects of labour', i.e. intermediate products; and of 'articles of consumption'. The elements of the tables are so grouped as to give the fund of the reimbursement of material expenditures (*c*), i.e. purchases from other branches and depreciation; the fund of the remuneration for labour (*v*); and the fund of surplus product (*m*).

Use of the material and value aspects makes it possible to analyse the structure of an economy, notably because the interindustry table, expressed in monetary terms, consists of two overlaid rectangular accounts, the common quadrant they form being the matrix of inter-industry flows from which is derived the matrix of technical coefficients. Distribution of products is traced in the horizontal rectangle while the vertical one shows production costs.

The right-hand part of the horizontal rectangle indicates the final use of product (consumption, accumulation and exports). The bottom part of the vertical rectangle sets out the resources (net product subdivided into the wage fund and the value of surplus product, imports and depreciation). The quadrant outside the two rectangles describes the processes of redistribution, e.g. wage outlays and profits in the non-productive sphere, and re-exports.

It may be noted that in the Soviet accounting system, the commodity balance-sheet is but a variant of the horizontal rectangle of the inter-industry table. The interindustry table is only part of the USSR national accounts and links the latter with the commodity tabulations. The system of national accounts, apart from the interindustry table of production and distribution, includes:

(i) A summary account of the national economy;

(ii) An account of the production, consumption and accumulation of total material product;

(iii) An account of the distribution, redistribution and final use of the national income;

(iv) An account of household monetary income and expenditure;

(v) A capital account (fixed and circulating capital) for the productive and non-productive sectors;

(vi) A summary manpower balance (viz. utilization of labour resources).

The account of material product by use (ii) breaks down final national product into the consumption and accumulation funds. The value of material costs of production is not available from this account but is derived from the interindustry tables of production and distribution, and from the summary commodity balance-sheets.

In the national income account (iii), it is possible to analyse the formation of primary incomes (i.e. those accruing in production), of secondary incomes in the process of redistribution (i.e. those accruing in the non-productive sphere), and of the final incomes of the population (the latter being subdivided by major social categories).

The household money income and expenditure account (iv) is also drawn up separately for major social categories. Expenditures are compared with the saleable fund of consumer goods (viz. retail turnover plus stock change).

The capital account (v) shows new investment and the scrapping of physical assets, and changes in the value of fixed-assets between the beginning and the end of the year, depreciation having been subtracted from the end-year value.

An interindustry table of production and distribution was already incorporated in the Soviet national accounts for 1923–4 [6].[1] Leontief's input-output analysis represents the application of a similar method to the United States census data for 1919, 1929 and 1939. In 1925 he had published a detailed review of the first Soviet national balance [7]. The concepts of total national product and of technical coefficients used by him corresponded to those already embodied in the first Soviet balance.

Leontief's merit consists in expressing the interindustry production relations mathematically, and especially in the synthesis of the balance-sheet method and linear programming. Subsequently, British economists and mathematicians (Barna [8] and Stone and Utting [9]) gave input-output analysis its present appearance, that is, an open model with four quadrants and with two open endings.

The main historical phases of development of the balance-sheet method in the USSR are as follows: in 1920, within the Central Statistical Administration of the Soviet Union, a 'Section of the Balance-Sheet of the National Economy' was created. As has just been mentioned, the first national accounts were drawn up for 1923–4 and initially appeared in a number of issues of the newspaper *Economicheskaya zhyzn* in mid-1925, and were subsequently published in a separate book [6]. The first balance-sheet incorporating financial flows and a summary account of planned aggregates was for 1937–8. The first long-term account was drawn up for 1951–5, while the latest was drawn up for 1959–65. The

[1] Further discussed in the present writer's reports to the 31st and 32nd sessions of the International Statistical Institute [4], [5].

latest interindustry table, based on enterprise returns of an economic region (the Mordvin Autonomous Soviet Socialist Republic), was worked out for 1958 and 1959. The first planned interindustry balance-sheet based on plan data for an economic region (the Karelian Autonomous Soviet Socialist Republic) was drawn up for 1961. The first inter-industry plan table for the USSR as a whole was elaborated by the Economic Research Institute and by the Computation Centre of the State Economic Council of the USSR for 1962.

The elaboration of independent interindustry tables for 1962, based on planned technical coefficients rather than on those from enterprise returns, together with tables based on actual returns, constitutes a very important phase in the development of the Soviet balance-sheet method. In a plan interindustry table, the use of statistical extrapolation is reduced to a minimum: its elaboration is based on directives and plan-targets for the coming year as well as on planned technical coefficients furnished by experts.

4. *Models in a Planned Economy*

In the USSR large-scale experimental and research work is carried on with the aim of constructing models of a planned economy. The wide use of mathematical methods in economics, particularly with the aid of computor programming, is possible only if models of the national economy are created suitable for processing. Such models define — in a statistical and mathematical form — specific economic processes or phenomena, concentrating on their major characteristics and parameters to the exclusion of detail. Each model is based on a system of equations connecting economic variables and providing the parameters relevant to the solution of given problems.

As a rule, constraints expressing existing or desirable levels or limits (for example, the limits to investments, or the available resources of raw materials) are introduced into the model as inequalities. Furthermore, each model is set up with a certain objective function in view (usually in linear form), for which an optimum must be determined. A model, usually presented in the form of matrices of economic or technical coefficients, describes the above-mentioned system of equations and inequalities.

One of the examples of an economic-mathematical model is the inter-industry table of production and distribution. Proceeding from the 1959 USSR table of production and distribution, the Computation Centre of the State Economic Council of the USSR determined the coefficients of direct and indirect inputs expressed both in monetary and physical units of measurement. Using the same table, the Institute of Electronic Controlling Devices computed planned output prices at the industry level on the basis of three proposed schemes of price formation.[1]

Moreover, the above mentioned coefficients of direct and indirect inputs were widely employed by the Economic Research Institute of the State Economic Council of the USSR in the elaboration of an interindustry table for the 1962 Plan — though in the latter case, as stated, the decisive role is played by scientifically determined technical coefficients.

At present, as a result of the organization of economic councils in administrative-economic regions and in connection with the decentralization of planning in the USSR, interindustry tables of production and distribution have been drawn up for some economic regions. For example, the Laboratory of Economic and Mathematical Methods of the USSR Academy of Sciences has elaborated pilot interindustry tables for 1958, 1959 and, using planned figures, for 1961 for some economic-administrative regions.

Recently, some economic councils and local planning bodies have themselves begun to elaborate interindustry tables (actual and planned). Such work is undertaken, for example, in the Byelorussian SSR, in the Tatar Autonomous SSR and in the Moscow region. A number of other economic regions will embark on similar studies in the near future. The Council for the Study of Productive Forces of the State Economic Council of the USSR has started the elaboration of interindustry tables for large economic zones (for example, for the Baltic economic-geographical zone comprising the Lithuanian, Latvian and Estonian union republics).

The use of mathematical programming and of electronic computers demands, as has already been noted, the elaboration of various economic-mathematical models of a planned economy. Some of the operational uses to which such models have been put cover the supply, at the national level, of steel plates, cement, gas and oil pipes, transformer steel, pulpwood, etc.; special production and transport models are used to determine the optimum location of plant. These models, elaborated by the Computation Centre of the State Economic Council of the USSR, are similar to the usual transport models, but, through the introduction of additional constraints (e.g. location of raw materials), indicate the optimal distribution of production facilities.

---

[1] See also Section 6 below. It may be observed that interindustry tables for plan-price setting are even more widely used in Hungary.

The needs of regional planning put special emphasis on the problem of drawing up a model of an economic region. Such a model must be patterned on an interindustry table. A regional model, however, differs considerably from the usual national interindustry table, by the incorporation (in the shape of wings) of a number of additional matrices.

A suggested model of an economic zone comprises the following matrices:

I. The matrix of interindustry technical coefficients involving the 'objects of labour' (i.e. intermediate products) and productive services (transport, communications, agencies supplying materials and equipment, the procurement of farm and public catering).

II. The matrix of coefficients for different kinds of fixed and working capital.

III. The matrix of capital coefficients computed from the investment content of a unit increment of output in a given industry; the type of investment is specified.

IV. The matrices of the regional and sector coefficients of interregional imports and exports. These matrices indicate the external economic resources employed by the given economic zone (indicating the zones of supply), as well as the zone's external production flows, identifying the sector of production in the region analysed and totals supplied to each zone (the USSR being divided into 17 large economic-geographical zones).

Such a regional model can be applied to the analysis of foreign trade flows, between independent states with separate currencies, for the optimal selection of the structure of foreign trade. This is already being done, for example, in Hungary. In addition, in future, the dual of the regional model should give an indication of the optimal regional rates of growth in relation to the economy as a whole, and the rates of relative efficiency (profit).

Optima from dual problems can also be arrived at for the material structure of global social product (rectangular matrix of interindustry flows and value-added) and the structure of national income by industry (rectangular matrix of final demand). Further variants on the same principle would have individual components of final demand as objective functions in the dual, e.g. distributed surplus product, household consumption, or external sales in a regional model.

A further development of the model of an economic region is the territorial model of production with a supplementary matrix of the factor-content of sectors of production identifying labour and natural resources (e.g. fuel, minerals, agricultural resources, timber, and water). In this model the matrix of resource coefficients will make it possible to calculate resource-profiles for each region and sector, e.g. the geological reserves of coking coal and iron ore furnishing the metallurgical enterprise in question (the ratios being calculated per unit of productive capacity). Similar profiles would be calculated for enterprises with respect to labour (for example, the ratio of agricultural labour per hectare of arable area), and to power (electricity consumption per unit of capacity), etc.

The problem of the optimal location of manpower and plant consists in distributing production centres rationally as a function of the location of the centres consuming their products and of the agglomerations of natural and labour resources they require. The territorial model of production on which experimental work has recently been started will make it possible to solve such complicated planning problems as those involving the optimum location of sites for new industrial and agricultural projects, and the selection of enterprises to be reconstructed.

5. *National Economic Proportions and Economic Development*

Of special importance in economic planning will be the dynamic model of socialist expanded reproduction. Experimental work on the elaboration of this model is being carried out by the Institute of Economics and by the Laboratory of Economic and Mathematical Methods of the USSR Academy of Sciences.

The theoretical bases of such a model, based on the scheme of expanded reproduction evolved by Marx and Lenin, have been described elsewhere.[1] A dynamic model of expanded reproduction is being simulated on an electronic computer to trace the variation in rates of economic development as a function of structural changes in the economy reflecting the modification of the basic proportions.

The principal task of national economic planning is to bring the essentially variable *proportions*, which characterize a given economic structure of society, into *conformity* with feasible rates of economic development. One of the cardinal national economic proportions, established by Marx and Lenin, is formulated in their thesis that — for expanded reproduction — the income of a society realized in the sphere of capital goods production, Y_1, must exceed the material costs of the

[1] The relationships between specified aggregates in the model ('proportions') are to be found in [4] and [5]. The concept of economic balance is treated in the first paper, some of the relationships having been originally specified in [10].

sphere of consumer-goods' production (C_2) by not less than the magnitude of real investments (J).

Thus, the following inequality is fundamental:

$$Y_1 - C_2 \geqslant J$$

This is the first fundamental condition of an expanding economy. Here, in the usual symbols of Marxist economics:

$$Y_1 \equiv v_1 + m_1$$

where v_1 is the fund of remuneration for labour and m_1 the fund of surplus product in the sphere of capital goods production. The main difficulty concerning this condition consists in the fact that fixed funds are included in the material cost in the form of depreciation, while in investment they are represented by their full value. In a market economy, where there is no public ownership of capital goods to serve as the material base for implementing public directives, the realization of the above condition is impeded by the multiplicity of the sources of capital finance — perhaps one-third of investments might be financed out of cost-price, another third out of the depreciation charge, and the last third out of profits — further complicated by the fact that incomes accrue both to individuals and to corporations.

No theories of marginal propensities to save and to invest can, in our view, help overcome this principal difficulty under market conditions. It should be stressed that in the above inequality the left-hand side cannot exceed the right-hand one by a large amount since, in case of considerable excess, another disproportion appears in the national economy as a result of the violation of the second condition of expanded reproduction. This second condition requires that the fund of the remuneration of labour (v) and the part of surplus produce to be consumed (pm) should not exceed the total product of the sphere of consumer goods production (P_2), that is:

$$(v + pm) \leqslant P_2$$

Since $Y_1 = v_1 + m_1$, and P_2 is closely related to C_2, an excessively large Y_1 would violate this second condition.[1]

Our historical experience fully confirms the scientific validity of the Marxist model of expanded reproduction determined by these basic conditions. Without complying with the first basic precondition of expanded reproduction, it would be impossible to ensure the constant, uninterrupted maintenance of our economic development at such high

[1] See [3], p. 273.

rates as were recorded in the USSR for the period of more than 40 years, despite the incursions into civilian outlays necessitated by the Intervention and World War II.

Another important national economic proportion which underlies the rate of economic development is the share of investment within the national income $\left(\dfrac{\mathcal{J}}{Y}\right)$. Accelerator and multiplier theories are attempts to explore the role of this proportion. Nevertheless, the viewpoint of Soviet economists on this question differs substantially from that of their western colleagues. In western theories of economic growth, decisive roles are played by the time factor (lags), the multiplier, and the accelerator. Soviet economists uphold the theory of 'economic development' and not the theory of 'economic growth'. The basic provision of the Soviet theory is that the rates and the nature of economic development depend on the initial structural proportions of the economy. The rates of development depend on what may be termed the 'structural potentials' of each preceding period.[1]

Sometimes it is essential also to take account of the increment of investment within the national income increment $\left(\dfrac{\Delta \mathcal{J}}{\Delta Y}\right)$ or the proportion of investment to national income in the base year ($\mathcal{J}_0 : Y_0$).

In a sense this approach is similar to the multiplier, but it lays emphasis not on the marginal propensity to save and to invest, but on the potential structural elements of the dynamics of a given economic system. A requirement of national economic planning consists in planning such rates of growth of investment and of national income as would correspond to the relationship of investments to national income in the base year, and to the share of the increment of investments within the national income increment during each year planned.

An even more important task of planning[2] consists in ensuring every year, firstly, that investment ($\mathcal{J}$) corresponds to the potential of expanded reproduction (M), where

$$M = v_1 + m_1 - C_2$$

and, secondly, that the physical volume of consumer-goods' production (P_2) corresponds to the value of wages plus the part of the surplus product that is to be consumed ($v + pm$).

In determining the optimum relationship between the accumulation and consumption funds, as well as between the rates of growth of

---

[1] These 'potentials' are described in [4], p. 323, and elaborated by A. I. Notkin in [11].
[2] This is further developed in [4].

national income and investment, the model of expanded reproduction can be of great assistance, readily simulated on a computer with varying structural parameters to yield the corresponding rates of development, or the other way round. This requires the calculation of coefficients of accumulation and consumption of each sector; the labour content of a unit product; and the capital intensity of an incremental unit of product. It is obvious that a change in these parameters either accelerates or decelerates the process of expanded reproduction, but what one wants to know is the rate of such acceleration or deceleration.

As has already been noted, for such a model it is particularly important to determine the proportions between the rates of growth of national income and of investment, and between the magnitude of the potential of expanded reproduction and that of the potential of the expansion of the consumption fund, in order to comply with both the first and second basic conditions of the process of expanded reproduction.

6. *Planned Prices and Economic Criteria*

Human society lives and develops as a result of its action on Nature. Society masters Nature's objects and forces and adjusts them, through collective labour, to human needs and requirements.

In the sphere of production, on the basis of a social division of labour, labour-value is created as an objective characteristic of a commodity. People begin to exchange commodities proportionally to the socially necessary labour crystallized in them, that is, proportionally to their value. Although value is created exclusively in the sphere of social production, it is used both in the productive and non-productive spheres as a result of the processes of distribution and redistribution.

Prices embody value to the extent that their sum equals total value, but individual prices of commodities may deviate from value. Price is a very complicated phenomenon. If prices are considered from the cybernetic viewpoint they contain two codes of information. On the one hand, there is the code concerning the magnitude of the social labour-value, and on the other hand, there is the code of information concerning the use value or, in other words, the social assessment of scarcity. According to the first code, prices are formed at the value level, and according to the second code they deviate from value with respect to cost of production. All the deviations, however, are limited to the surplus product.

These processes of price formation are valid for both capitalist and socialist economies. But under socialism the deviation of prices from value takes place in different conditions than under capitalism, for the process of planned price-formation is very different from the process of market price-formation.

Value embodies the socially-necessary labour inputs, viz. the total direct and indirect) inputs of labour per unit of final product in optimal economic systems. Under socialism, with a planned guidance of the economy in the light of social needs, the sum total of prices must necessarily equal total value of product in every period, notably insofar as concerns the consumption fund, constituting the final product going to households. Planned prices, unaffected by cyclical distributions, are based on the socially necessary expenditure of labour and on a rate of profit formulated for a long-term period (for example, five years).

Market prices mutually adjust themselves (are iterated) in a market. However, the iteration process of planned prices can be simulated more efficiently with electronic devices.

The socialist economy does not preclude the existence of a market; on the contrary, it presupposes its existence, but it seeks to organize the market in a balanced way on the basis of state-operated and co-operative trade. In conditions of capitalism a market replaces the plan, whereas in the conditions of socialist economy the organized market is subordinate to a plan, and, in particular, is regulated by a system of planned prices.

The system of planned prices currently in use is based on the concept of 'average value'. According to this concept the value of the surplus product is distributed among commodities proportionally to their '*cost value*'. This system of planned price formation can be expressed symbolically in the following way,[1] in which:

$$p_i = \bar{p}_i + \zeta_i, \tag{1}$$

$$\bar{p}_i = (1+\pi)\left(\omega_i + \frac{\mu_i F_i}{X_i}\right), \tag{2}$$

$$\pi \sum_i \left(\omega_i + \frac{\mu_i F_i}{X_i}\right) = \mathcal{J} + C - T, \tag{3}$$

$$\sum_i \zeta_i X_i = T, \tag{4}$$

where p_i = price of commodity i including turnover tax,
  ζ_i = rate of turnover tax on commodity i,
  $\bar{p}_i$ = price of commodity i excluding turnover tax,
  X_i = output of commodity i,

[1] These equations were formulated by the Italian economist Vincenzo Vitello as a result of his talks with Soviet economists on problems of price formation in the USSR.

F_i = aggregate of fixed assets installed for the production of commodity i,

μ_i = the rate of depreciation of F_i,

ω_i = 'cost value' excluding depreciation of commodity i,

π = profit margin on costs,

$\mathcal{J}$ = accumulation fund (gross fixed capital formation and inventory increment),

C = consumption fund,

and T = total receipts of turnover tax.

This system of equations describes more or less precisely the system of planned price-formation functioning in the USSR. Yet, it should be noted that the planned profitability rate (5 per cent of the 'cost value') amounts approximately to a mere half of the rate of profit (π), the other half of the profitability rate being realized in the above-plan profits of enterprises and not in the price of their commodities.

According to another concept of planned price formation the value of the surplus product should be distributed proportionally to the total fund of the remuneration for labour crystallized in a given commodity. In accordance with this concept, the value of the surplus product is distributed among commodities proportionally to the total fund of the remuneration of labour which is crystallized in those commodities, i.e. to cumulative labour costs.

According to a third concept of planned price formation the value of surplus product must be distributed proportionally to the fixed funds of enterprises, and not to 'cost value', since the latter does not take account of many social costs, e.g. the expenses connected with the expansion of production (ancillary investments, expenditure involved in geological exploration and prospecting, etc.).

Of particular interest, from the mathematical point of view, are the 'objectively conditioned estimations' obtained in the process of optimizing linear or curvilinear programmes. It would, however, be wrong to identify them with either planned or market prices. 'Objectively conditioned estimations' are similar to 'shadow prices' and represent coefficients which define the inter-relation between the available resources and needs of society. In our view, they can and must be employed only for the scientific substantiation of deviations of planned prices from value. They should only serve as commodity distributive indices with respect to the value of surplus product and not as indices of the real value to the economy.

Deviations of planned retail prices from value result from the effects of demand and supply, and depend in particular on supply and demand elasticities (on income and price). Retail prices, furthermore, reflect certain aspects of social policy; for instance, in the USSR the prices of alcoholic drinks and tobacco exceed their value but rents are lower than they should be on the basis of the value of dwellings. However, in the retail sector, the sum total of prices must be equal to costs.

At present, planned price formation with its variants is being simulated experimentally on electronic computers. This experiment should foster the improvement of the process of planned price formation. There is no doubt that such an improvement in the system of national-economic planning can be beneficial since it allows the introduction of optimal estimates (in the system of planned prices), and such criteria as optimal planned rates of profit.

7. Conclusion

The statistical and mathematical methods employed in the planning of the USSR national economy have been described in this paper only in general terms. It is quite natural that some characteristics or important details had to be omitted. On the other hand, in many cases stress was laid on research and experimental work in this field. Without this it would have been impossible to present a more or less complete picture of the application of statistical and mathematical methods in Soviet economic planning.

REFERENCES

[1] 'Matematicheskie metody v ekonomike' (Mathematical methods in economics: Report of a meeting on the introduction of mathematical methods in economic research and planning), *Voprosy ekonomiki*, No. 8, 1960.

[2] SOBOL, V. A., *Ocherki po voprosam balansa narodnogo khozyaistva* (Essays on the problem of the national-economy balance), Moscow, 1960.

[3] BOR, M. Z., *Voprosy metodologii planovogo balansa narodnogo khozyaistva SSSR* (Questions of the methodology of the planned balance of the USSR national economy), Moscow, 1960.

[4] NEMCHINOV, V. S., 'Some aspects of the balance-sheet method as applied in the statistics of interdependent dynamic economic systems,' *Bulletin de l'Institut international de statistique*, Vol. 37, 2, p. 313, 1960.

[5] NEMCHINOV, V. S., 'The interindustry production and distribution balance-sheet as a macro-economic model of optimal programming,' *Bulletin de l'Institut international de statistique*, Vol. 38, 2, p. 471, 1961.

[6] Central Statistical Administration of the USSR (POPOV, P. I., ed.), *Balans narodnogo khozyaistva SSSR 1923–24 goda* (The balance of the USSR national economy in 1923–24), Moscow, 1926.

188   *V. S. Nemchinov*

[7] LEONTIEF, W. W., 'Balans narodnogo khozyaistva SSSR: Metologicheskii razbor raboty Ts.S.U.' (The balance of the USSR national economy: Methodological critique of the work of the Central Statistical Administration), *Planovoe Khozyastvo*, No. 12, 1925.

[8] BARNA, T., 'The interdependence of the British economy,' *Journal of the Royal Statistical Society*, Vol. 115, p. 29, 1952.

[9] STONE, R. and UTTING, J., 'The relationship between input-output analysis and national accounting,' in *Input-Output Relations*, Leiden, 1953.

[10] NEMCHINOV, V. S., 'O proportsiyakh rasshirennogo vosproizvodstva' (On the proportions of expanded reproduction), *Voprosy ekonomiki*, No. 10, 1958.

[11] NOTKIN, A. I., 'Optimalnoe sochetanie nakopleniya i normy nakopleniya' (The optimum combination of accumulation and consumption and the accumulation rate), in *Voprosy politicheskoi ekonomii sotsializma*, Moscow, 1960.

CHAPTER 10

Collection and Organization of Data for Interindustry Study in France

by GEORGES DELANGE

1. *Introduction*

The purpose of this paper is to describe the use made of the input-output table in France and the experience that has been gained with it. No attempt is made here to review the entire work done in this field by the Department of Economic and Financial Research, Ministry of Finance, in recent years — a period during which the methods used in inter-industry transactions studies have considerably changed. Attention is here concentrated on the table in its present form, which is very close to Leontief's standard table. The theoretical bases established by him are not discussed but are implicitly accepted.

The French input-output table was from the outset intended to be integrated with the system of national accounting, which it complements and perfects. It is a tool designed for studying the past and for making short-term economic forecasts, particularly in connection with the annual budget, and medium-term forecasts in connection with the preparation of the four-year modernization and capital investment plan.

In accordance with the principles established by Leontief, the French input-output table breaks down the economic activity of the country into sectors in such a way that each product or service is produced by one sector, and that each sector produces one product or service.

The French table is nevertheless decidedly utilitarian in character, and this, as we shall see, determines the principles on which it is constructed, its division into sixty-five commodity sectors, and the methods of estimating the figures included in it. While the internal logic of the table has been fully preserved and a deliberate effort has been made to bring about consistency with the system of national accounts, the specification of products and sectors have been established quite empirically, largely with reference to the composition and state of the available statistics and the use to which the table was to be put. The arrangement and the specifications adopted were chosen with a view to providing the public authorities with the best possible guidance for short-term and long-term decisions. They were also adapted to the peculiarities of French statistics, which, despite the efforts of the National Institute of Statistics and Applied Economics (INSEE), are still very incomplete, covering neither all production nor all consumption and only in exceptional cases showing changes in stocks.[1]

In these circumstances, the input-output table — in conjunction with the system of national accounts — becomes an effective instrument for estimating, as reasonably as possible, the supply and consumption of goods and services. This makes possible, by means of cross-tabulations using the best available statistics, to arrive at probable, if not exact, estimates of certain other values. The internal agreement between the table and the system of national accounts provides a cross-check that takes on added importance when the quality of the basic statistics is poor.

To meet the problems connected with the use of the table and the structure of French statistics, those responsible for national accounting have given the French table special features which affect it as a tool for interindustry studies. In Section 2 we shall consider the use made of the table, in Section 3 the sources of data and the special features of the French table, and in Section 4 the treatment of the technical coefficients.

2. *The Use of Input-Output Tables for Short-term Forecasts*[2]

In France, short-term forecasts are made twice a year — in May, when the National Accounts Commission meets, and in October when the appropriation bill is being drafted.

These forecasts are based on figures for the preceding year and relate to the current year and the following year. They are worked out primarily on the basis of the input-output table, which is thus calculated twice a year for a period of three years — the preceding year, the current year and the following year. In this way, the input-output table relating to any one year is computed twice a year over a period of three years— four times as a forecast, and twice for the purpose of studying the past. Eventually, three years after the end of the year in question, when statistical documents are available from fiscal sources, it is possible to make a final revision of all the accounts and to prepare a definitive input-output table, again in conjunction with the tables for the national accounts.

---

[1] There has been no industrial census in recent years, and the first one since the war will be taken in 1963.

[2] The use of the table for the medium- and long-term plans, though very important, is not within the scope of this paper. On this subject, see [1] and [2].

Organizational structure

Such constant revision requires proper organization, and this is provided by the Department of Economic and Financial Research, Ministry of Finance, where the national accounts — and the input-output table as one of the key elements — are prepared. The Department is divided into the 'Foreign Trade' Section, which is responsible for collecting all import and export data for each of the products specified and for making assumptions concerning future trends; the 'Households' Section, which studies past and future consumption of households by consumption function and classifies it under the various headings of the nomenclature; the 'Government' Section, which similarly analyses the budgets of the State, local authorities and independent agencies and prepares predictions for coming years; the 'Enterprises' Section, which collects all data concerning production, turnover, producers' prices, value added, stocks, intermediate consumption and investments of enterprises, compares them with the figures provided by the sections mentioned above, and reconciles, commodity by commodity and sector by sector, the supply and consumption of goods and services; and the 'Accounts and Budgets' Division, which collects the data on goods and services recorded in the input-output tables for previous years and other data that are important for national accounting purposes, and ascertains the future trends of the aggregates needed by the sections.

As there is a perfect accounting connection with the aggregate accounts, which is effected by comparing the total value added and stocks shown in the table with the estimates made elsewhere concerning the various components of the national product, income and expenditure, two successive adjustments can be made, in relation to both the past and the future. The first of these concerns transactions in goods and services subdivided into products and sectors, and is carried out by the Enterprises Section; the other concerns the aggregate figures, and is effected by the Accounts and Budgets Division.

The data received by the Department are routed to the various sections. The forecasts at section level are co-ordinated through a series of adjustments, a stage at which the specialists compare their respective points of view in order to arrive at a balance between supply and consumption.

Preparation of tables relating to previous years

The tables for any one year are prepared about two months after the end of the year, and again a year later. When the first table is prepared, much information concerning either the last months or the whole of the year, according to the sectors involved, is not available. The immediate past must, therefore be forecast. After the data are collected, the main task of the statisticians in each section is to allocate to the various sectors the aggregate values, which are sometimes the only figures available, and to extrapolate for the whole year the figures known for eight, nine, ten or eleven months. Since the data are incomplete, the striking of a balance between the supply and consumption of a particular product or sector is often an intricate matter, so that the different sections must work together to arrive at a solution.

When the second revision is made, a year later, all the statistical data which can be expected have been received, apart from the fiscal data previously mentioned, and the work of the sections may be said to consist merely of classifying this information. The number of adjustments that must be made between the sections is, of course, at this stage much smaller.

When the final tables are eventually prepared, about three years after the end of the year in question, the fiscal data by industrial classes have become available. The Enterprises Section then breaks down the various industrial classes — in which, by contrast with the sectors, the enterprises are classified according to their main activity without separating their secondary activities — and reassembles the data in accordance with the specification of the sectors. This difficult operation, which has not yet been perfected, makes it possible to introduce further changes into the provisional tables to a degree varying according to the sector and to check the accuracy of the earlier aggregate figures for value added, stocks and investments. Until such time as this work of revision is completed, the tables are used only inside the Department.

Preparation of short-term forecast tables

Aggregate forecasts concerning transactions in goods and services are made by the Accounts and Budgets Division in collaboration with the sections. These aggregate forecasts serve as a rough 'frame' for the estimates of the various sections, which make these estimates, product by product, in each of the fields with which they are concerned.

In arriving at these latter estimates, reference is made to: research carried out by various specialists of the Department on the basis of all possible methods and more particularly of the elasticity coefficients resulting from studies of the past, due account being taken of economic conditions during the year under consideration; any public or private studies which may be available; information obtained from the technical departments and agencies of the Ministries; and the medium-term forecasts of the planning commissions.

The supply and consumption of goods and services are then compared, product by product and sector by sector. Many adjustments are made as a result of these comparisons, and the new aggregates thus arrived at are forwarded to the Accounts and Budgets Division, which then makes further adjustments by agreement with the various sections.

3. *Sources of Data and Special Features*

The Department does not carry out any special inquiry for the preparation of its input-output tables but simply uses the existing statistics. Some of these, however, are forwarded to the Department by other government departments and agencies before their final publication or in accordance with some special classification.

The main sources of information are:

(*a*) Tax information arrives too late to be used otherwise than for purposes of confirmation. This information was used to a considerable extent in preparing the 1956 table, which serves as a basis for the tables for later years. For the current work, each year, some statistical data relating to large enterprises are made available to the Department very promptly.

(*b*) The Customs Administration prepares statistics by product on a monthly basis and classifies these specially for the Department in accordance with the nomenclature used by the Department.

(*c*) Many types of statistics are regularly collected by the technical and economic departments and agencies of the Government through business and industrial organizations. These statistics relate primarily to output or deliveries, by value or by physical units, and to consumption, stocks and transport. Much of this information is published by INSEE and the Central Bureau of Industrial Statistics, after being checked and classified by them.

(*d*) The governmental sources include budgets of the State and of local governments showing government expenditure on goods and services; statistics of INSEE relating to producers' and consumers' prices; and investment statistics compiled by the Office of the Planning Commission, the Economic and Social Development Fund, and the Central Bureau of Industrial Statistics.

(*e*) Two other particularly useful sources are the surveys of consumption made by the Consumption Research and Documentation Centre

(CREDOC) and the accounting data supplied to the Department by the nationalized enterprises.

The work of the statisticians is facilitated by the existence of a considerable body of statistics by product, prepared by business and industrial associations, and of an inter-departmental nomenclature of products, from which transfers to the nomenclature of sixty-five products used by the Department can be easily effected.

The immediate future

The close relationship between the various governmental statistical organs and the Department enable the latter to keep abreast of current trends in the main economic sectors and to make plausible assumptions concerning future short-term trends. In addition, at the beginning of each year consultations are held with the various technical ministries and the Office of Foreign Relations and Foreign Trade concerning the current year and the following year. Systematic use is made of the information and the occasional studies produced by business and industrial associations, the surveys of economic conditions made three times a year by INSEE and the forecasts forwarded to the Department direct by the national enterprises.

Taken as a whole, the data thus collected provide a sufficient basis for forecasts for the current year. Since, however, they are far from complete, caution is called for in applying them to the following year, and in this connection a good deal of additional information is needed in the light of the objectives laid down when the four-year plans are prepared. Hence, while the forecasts for the current year are forecasts in the true sense, the forecasts for the following year are based in part on the objectives of the Government. These forecasts serve to show the factors that stimulate or retard economic development, and they make it possible to decide what steps must be taken to achieve the objectives considered desirable and feasible.

Special features

As already mentioned, the special features of the French table[1] are due primarily to the use which is made of the table and to the composition and state of French statistics.

The latter consideration has caused us to adopt a special approach to products and sectors. Broadly speaking, the one-to-one relationship between a product and a sector has been respected only where the

---

[1] For further details, see [3].

product has been involved in transactions. In other words, the unity of the enterprise, the basic economic cell, has been broken where products of different kinds were turned out by the enterprise, but has been respected where the enterprise produced commodities for its own consumption. For instance, where a motor vehicle works also manufactures agricultural tractors, the enterprise is divided into two parts, one part being included in the motor vehicle manufacturing sector, and the other in the machinery and mechanical equipment sector. On the other hand, a foundry which forms part of the enterprise has not been separated from the enterprise and is included in each of the sectors mentioned above to the extent that it serves them. In this way, the vertical economic integration of each enterprise has been respected.

The reason for adopting this procedure is the practical impossibility of knowing what an enterprise produces for its own consumption. It has the disadvantage that enterprises which are differently integrated are lumped together in one sector, and entails the risk of neglecting the technical processes of production in order to concentrate on relationships which are not so well defined and are susceptible to change.

As an extension of this principle, and for the same reasons, secondary products are removed from the sector only if their value exceeds the value of such products consumed by the sector in question. If their value is less, they are merely deducted from the consumption figure. Fictitious transfers which would be shown under a strict procedure have been confined to the very rare cases where complete statistics exist, as, for instance, for scrap iron.

Even more unusual is the way in which the French table deals with foreign trade, trading activities, unallocated inputs and outputs, and transport; for the sake of brevity, transport will not be discussed here.

Foreign trade

Unlike Leontief's model, the French table does not show 'foreign trade' as a sector; imports and exports of a product are included in the supply and consumption of that product.

We consider this procedure necessary because we know very little about the total quantity of imported products used by a particular sector. As a result, the square table indicates only technical relationships which are assumed to be comparatively constant for the purpose of projections, while the problems of international competition are dealt with outside the table, the trends of such competition requiring an entirely separate treatment.

The procedure has not been supplemented, as in some foreign tables, by allocating imported products to the sectors which consume them, since we feel that the market as a whole is the only important reality.

Trading activities

The approach adopted in the French table is rather different in form, but very close in substance, to that of the 1939 United States table constructed by Leontief. The only output of trading enterprises consists of trading mark ups, which are the difference between the values of products at consumers' prices and at producers' prices. On the other hand, they consume the products they need for their activities (excluding the products in which they trade).

In order that the value of output at producers' prices — which are fairly easily obtainable from French business and industrial statistics — may be clearly seen, trading profits by product have not been included in the square table but have been shown outside it as a supplementary supply of the product.

This method retains all the advantages of Leontief's model. Transactions are shown at real prices, and it is particularly easy to project household consumption by product, as is not the case if the trading services purchased by households are separated from the purchase of the product as such.

Unallocated inputs and outputs

One original feature of the French table is that there is no heading for 'unallocated inputs and outputs'. This is not due, of course, to any particular precision in the French operations, but simply to a desire to make the preparation of projections easier. Faced with a heading 'unallocated inputs and outputs', the person making a forecast is helpless. It seems better to us that the statistician should decide, before the table is constructed, to allocate to the best of his ability the products and transactions about which little is known.

4. *Technical Coefficients*

The peculiarities of the French table affect the very concept of technical coefficients, because, as the result of retaining the vertical integration of enterprises, the transaction coefficients deduced from the table must be regarded more as economic coefficients linking together sectors of production than as purely technical coefficients. In practice, however, vertical integrations appear to be comparatively stable. At least in the short or medium term, the observed variations in the coefficients result only to a very small degree from changes in the structure of enterprises.

Leaving aside variations in imports and trading mark ups, which are not included in the body of the French table and are thus regarded explicitly as variables which are independent of production, the changes in technical coefficients which have been observed since 1956 are due to four main causes: (*a*) Substitution of certain products for others (e.g. refined petroleum products substituted for solid mineral fuels, and synthetic textile materials substituted for natural textiles); (*b*) Savings in materials or power (e.g. the constant reduction in the amount of electricity required to manufacture a ton of aluminium); (*c*) Changes in the relative proportion of commodities produced by a sector (e.g. the increase in the relative proportion of special steels in iron and steel production); and (*d*) Improvement in quality (e.g. rubber products, machine tools).

Changes in the output structure and in the quality of products are more difficult to interpret. Thus, changes in the output structure of a sector, such as iron and steel manufacturing, directly affect the inputs of that sector. Although requirements of iron ore are in a general way related to the total output in tons of pig-iron and steel, those requirements cannot be linked to the volume-index of iron and steel output without qualification, since the latter is affected by the increase in output of highly priced products like special steels.

It is even more apparent that there is no relationship between this volume index and the iron and steel industry's consumption of manganese ore or metals such as nickel, chromium and molybdenum. Similarly, it is difficult to determine variations in the input of iron and steel products used by the different sectors because of the substitutions which are made between the various iron and steel products.

The difficulties thus observed in analysing sectors which produce a variety of products are also encountered where there is a change in the quality of products. In such cases, it is difficult to separate variation in volume from variation in price. If, for instance, the market price of tyres remains unchanged but the mileage for which they can run increases, one cannot but take the view that the real price decreases and that the variation in quality must be recorded as a variation in volume. The technical coefficients relating to the use of tyres by the various sectors will then remain constant. As, however, the consumption of raw materials by the rubber manufacturing industry will decrease in relation to a given volume, the technical coefficients of that industry cannot be regarded as constant.

As it appears, therefore, that technical coefficients cannot be assumed to be constant, even in the short term, the variations in these coefficients are taken into account when the forecast tables are prepared.

Finally, mention must be made of the special case of agriculture, where no relationship can be established between output inputs for any one year, since climatic influences are too great. In addition, so far as the medium term is concerned, the broad range of outputs of agriculture and the rapid changes in agricultural techniques in France make it inevitable that the very concept of technical coefficients must be abandoned here.

5. Conclusion

The input-output table must, therefore, be used with great caution, particularly where substitution phenomena are of importance (for example, electricity). In such cases, it is necessary to resort to studies of aggregate or semi-aggregate elasticity, which are based on principles very far removed from those underlying the construction of the table.

The 1956 input-output table, on which our work is based, is still in need of improvement and refinement. It is a compromise between what the table should be according to a logical and homogeneous system, what it can be in the light of the statistics available, and what it must be to meet our requirements.

Because of the inadequacy of the statistical sources in France, many of the figures in the table have only a guidance value. We feel that any improvement in economic forecasts based on the system of national accounting and the input-output table depends more on an improvement in the basic statistics than on any refinement which might be introduced into our accounting methods. The input-output table has played and will play an important part in the improvement of statistical data because, since it is a means for achieving consistency, it clearly shows those major statistical shortcomings which should be eliminated first.

REFERENCES

[1] U.N. Economic and Social Council, *Evaluation of long-term economic projections*, 1960 (mimeo).

[2] Political and Economic Planning, *Economic Planning in France*, London, 1961.

[3] MINISTÈRE DE FINANCE, *Compte de la Nation*, Vol. 2, Annex A, Part 3, Paris, 1960.

CHAPTER 11

The Input-Output Model in a Developing Economy: Egypt

by GAMAL E. ELEISH

1. *Introduction*

The first input-output table constructed in Egypt is for 1954. The original table contains 83 productive sectors. Table 1 is an aggregated version distinguishing 33 sectors, and Table 2 shows further aggregation into 7 sectors. Similar tables were constructed for 1959.[1]

Final demand is divided into six categories, a distinction being made between government and private investment. Private education and medical services are included as a productive sector, but the corresponding public services are entered as part of government consumption, since it could be argued that government policy in these fields is not determined through a set of technical coefficients.

The original table shows a detailed breakdown of primary factor inputs but Table 1 shows value added in the aggregate. Transactions were valued at producers' prices except that imports were valued c.i.f. and exports f.o.b. Trade and transport margins were included in separate sectors of the table. Transactions are shown gross, that is, inclusive of transactions within the sector.

Perhaps the most important characteristic of the table is that inputs of domestic origin are separated from imports in each cell. This is necessary in a developing economy, like Egypt, because of its heavy dependence on imports.

One alternative is to distinguish between competitive and non-competitive imports, and to show the latter as a separate row in the table, while competitive imports are combined with domestic inputs.

[1] At the time of writing, the 1959 tables were not fully processed and therefore this paper makes use mainly of the 1954 tables. The original work and the calculations for this paper were carried out in the Input-Output Unit of the National Planning Committee. I wish to acknowledge the interest and the help of Dr I. H. Abdel Rahman, then Under Secretary of the Ministry of Planning, Dr N. Dief, Assistant Under Secretary, Dr Shazly, and Mr Tore Thonstad, of Oslo University.

TABLE 2

Summary Table of Input-Output Relations, Egypt, 1954
(in ten thousand Egyptian Pounds)

From \ To	INDUSTRIES							Capital formation (private sector)	Change in stocks	Household consumption	Government consumption	Capital formation (government)	Exports	Total final demand	Gross production
	1	2	3	4	5	6	7								
1. Agriculture	4748	—	20579	—	—	—	9	—	2762	11361	305	—	317	14745	40081
2. Electricity & petroleum	282	210	918	612	26	123	479	—	4	719	359	—	85	1167	3817
3. Industry & mines	1122	1002	19079	334	22	1786	1135	930	1343	29991	2291	145	10676	42691	67169
4. Transport & communications	110	156	685	166	82	138	2915	—	—	3200	528	—	638	4365	8617
5. Suez Canal	—	—	—	2	—	—	—	—	—	—	—	—	3141	3141	3143
6. Construction	2	6	4	13	—	—	300	4317	—	—	234	2254	—	6805	7131
7. Services	14873	440	7722	690	204	880	2866	710	—	21677	1261	33	4100	27781	55456
Imports	1650	535	4352	734	46	1023	731	2460	20	4896	728	106	—	8211	17288
Value added	17293	1468	13825	6066	2763	3182	47021	—	—	3872	9922	—	—	13794	105411
Total	40081	3817	67169	8617	3143	7131	55456	8418	1443	75716	15628	2538	18957	122699	308113

We were against this[1] as the import matrix is an essential tool in the calculation of savings which arise from a policy of import substitution such as the one which has been adopted in Egypt. Furthermore, the combination of competitive imports with domestic inputs would have led to complications in some of the calculations based on the table.

In this paper we are concerned with the applicability and utilization of the input-output model in a developing economy. In Section 2 we show that significant interdependence exists among the different sectors of the economy. In Section 3 we discuss the applicability of the input-output model in developing economies by examining the stability of the technical coefficients in such economies. Starting with the assumption that the substitution of imports by domestically produced goods will play a dominant role in the pattern of industrialization in Egypt, we develop an argument which emphasizes that this will affect the stability of the technical coefficients. We try to show that the coefficients will be subject to more frequent changes than in more developed economies. We also emphasize that in developing economies the projection of future technical coefficients is of paramount importance for a better utilization of the input-output tables. In Section 4 we deal with the utilization of the input-output model in Egypt. The method of computations which we followed was by no means new, but it illustrates the usefulness of the input-output model in planning.

2. The Interdependence of the Egyptian Economy

The usefulness of constructing input-output tables for developed economies has more or less ceased to be a topic of argument. This, however, is not always the case as far as developing economies are concerned. The usefulness of tables for these economies has been a subject of lengthy discussions and doubts were raised by a number of economists, particularly those who attempted to construct tables for some of the highly underdeveloped countries of Africa and those who are engaged in planning activities in some Asiatic countries.

Their argument is based on the idea that in these countries there is a drastic lack of statistics, particularly of that type which is necessary for the construction of an input-output table. Other accounting systems, like the national income accounts, were favoured on the ground that they require less effort and serve better the needs of these economies (which were sometimes naïvely stated). In the case of Egypt, however, it could

[1] In a table prepared for Professor R. Frisch we distinguished, however, between competitive and non-competitive imports.

be safely said that the data necessary for an input-output table were dispersed rather than scarce. Our main task was the finding, verification and processing of data; but this did not exclude the fact that we were confronted, as it is naturally expected, with a number of contradictory statements due, in most cases, to the adoption of different definitions by the various statistical authorities.

But the most serious criticism is the one which rests upon the argument that in these economies there is hardly any significant interdependence between the different sectors, with the result that, after exerting great effort to construct an input-output table, one ends with a productive matrix which is practically empty except for some insignificant transactions. The table which was prepared for the Gold Coast has been quoted [1] as an example of this lack of interdependence, that only three of the 30 elements included in the productive matrix contained figures of any statistical significance. It was also shown that the productive sectors received inputs worth £4·2 m., out of a total domestic production of £59·7 m. The case of Tanganyika was by no means less depressing: Peacock found that the lack of interdependence is a grave one and illustrated his point by showing that it was possible to fill no more than 23 cells of the interflow matrix out of a total of 306. Moreover, deliveries from domestic production to intermediate consumption were only £8·3 m. as compared to £181·6 m. delivered to final demand. Cyprus is another example which may be referred to. The two tables prepared by Simous Vassiliou [2] show insignificant structural relationship among the productive sectors. A point of great importance, to which Vassiliou calls attention, is the fact that the 14 per cent increase in output which occurred between 1954 and 1957 had no significant effect on the structural relationship between the productive sectors, nor did it reduce their reliance on imports.

On the other hand, experience in Latin American countries shows that the construction of input-output models is not impossible as far as the basic statistical data are concerned. The experience of ECLA in Columbia, shows, however, that there is heavy reliance on imports for both intermediate and final demand; nevertheless it was found that the input-output model provided an unique tool for calculating the effects of an import-substitution policy. But it may be argued that those economies, though not developed, are not of the type which may be described as highly underdeveloped, the latter being characterized by lack of interdependence among the productive sectors.

Although the lack of reliable statistics is certainly a stumbling block for the construction of input-output tables in underdeveloped countries yet this should not be a hindrance and the model should not be stamped on this account as a useless tool of analysis. In fact, the postponement of constructing such tables may lead to the postponement of a serious review of the gaps in the data and their processing. Admittedly, the lack of interdependence in the highly underdeveloped economies makes the rewards for the effort spent on the construction of input-output tables extremely small. It is this lack of interdependence rather than the lack of statistics which presents the most serious argument against the construction of input-output tables in underdeveloped countries. However, at this point instead of making general statements we should be careful to distinguish between developing and highly underdeveloped economies.

When constructing the input-output table for Egypt we were very much aware of these arguments. Our doubt as to the possibility of constructing the table, as well as to its usefulness, was not related to the lack of the necessary data but rather to the amount of interdependence which exists in the economy. However, these fears were apparently unfounded. It is clear that a substantial interdependence exists among the different productive sectors of the Egyptian economy, despite its heavy reliance on imports. Out of the 1056 cells included in the productive matrix of the aggregated table for 1954, 542 (or about 50 per cent) contained entries from domestic production. These figures represent a sharply contrasted picture to that given for the countries mentioned above. In the case of Italy [3], however, out of 462 cells in the interflow matrix (excluding the row for construction) of the aggregated 22 × 22 table for 1950, 340 cells (73 per cent) contained entries. This is a higher percentage than that for Egypt and it could be taken as an indication of the higher level of development of Italy.[1]

The extent of interdependence in the Egyptian economy could be further illustrated by the fact that in 1954 deliveries from domestic production to intermediate consumption were £E 847 m. as against £E 1,007 m. delivered to final demand. This is in sharp contrast with the figures given for Tanganyika.

3. The Stability of Input Coefficients

The examination of the degree of stability of the technical coefficients in developing countries is of paramount importance as this would indicate the reliability of the input-output table for purposes of projection. The technical coefficients in the interflow matrix are expressed in

---

[1] However, this is only a rough comparison because the level of aggregation in the two tables is not the same; the Italian table is of the order of 22 × 22, whereas the Egyptian table to which we referred is of the order of 33 × 33.

value terms and are therefore bound to be sensitive to changes in relative prices. The coefficients would also change if the economy adopts a new technology or if a change occurs in the scale of production.

In order to predict the frequency and nature of these changes one should examine closely the structure of the Egyptian economy as well as the path of development likely to be taken. For a long time Egypt depended on imports for its supply of goods which need capital intensive investments for their production. Before 1952 these types of commodities were imported to satisfy consumption needs, but then Egypt started an extensive industrialization programme (as well as programmes designed for the development of the other sectors of the economy) and there has been a shift from consumer to capital goods. This in itself made reliance on imports more prominent than before: the import content in the type of investment included in the national plan is 47 per cent but it is only 15 per cent for household consumption, 12 per cent for government consumption and 7 per cent for exports. For this reason we found it essential to show separately in our table inputs from imports and those from domestic production.

Before 1952 Egypt was mainly an agrarian economy with a small industrial sector. The country then embarked on a large development programme, which was increased in magnitude in 1960. These programmes aimed at a balanced development of all sectors of the economy. However, the achievement of a faster rate of growth meant that a larger investment had to be poured into the industrial sector. For a country with a small industrial sector this means that any new production from that sector will be a substitute for a commodity which was previously imported (or an increase in the output of a commodity which was already being produced but in quantities insufficient to meet demand). This in fact has happened. Leaving aside the investments in the High Dam and the other sectors whose output could not be imported — electricity for instance — the bulk of the investment allocated to the industrial sector aimed at the production of the type of goods which was previously imported. Here we are not concerned with examining the wisdom of this policy of import substitution, its effect on the balance of payments, or whether this policy will result in the long run in a net savings in imports or not. All that we are concerned with at the moment is to state the fact that this trend of import substitution has been a decisive element in forming the industrial policy of the country. It is my opinion, if we accept the argument that a faster rate of growth in Egypt necessitates a faster growth of the industrial sector, that this trend is inevitable simply because a larger number of the newly produced commodities are likely to be substitutes for imports. Import substitution is not merely a deliberate policy but rather a consequence of industrialization. This trend, in my opinion, will be the main characteristic of the industrialization of Egypt for some years to come.

In the light of this statement we may proceed with the examination of the stability of the technical coefficients of the input-output table for Egypt, to see how the table could be effectively used under such conditions. To be able to do that, we will examine the factors mentioned above which affect the technical coefficients.

Technological change

In a developed economy technological change may be regarded as a continuous attempt to increase the amount of output per unit of input or to reduce the amount of inputs per unit of output. To achieve this, substitution plays a prominent role. There may be substitution of capital for labour, or capital for materials, or material for material, and such changes will be reflected in the input structure of the productive sectors. The frequency of such changes has been the subject of extensive examination in developed economies, like the United States, and it was found that input-output tables need not be subject to extensive revision except perhaps every ten years.

This, however, is not the case in an economy like Egypt. If economic development is pursued as it is intended, the technical structure of the economy is bound to change rapidly. In fact the introduction of most new industries in Egypt, which had fewer major ones before, should be looked upon as a positive step in that direction. Here we are assuming that the types of new industries installed are those using the most advanced techniques available in the more developed economies. The wisdom of this step, as well as the reasons for it, are not of interest here; but it is important to emphasize that the introduction of these techniques will mean major changes in the technical structure of the economy. If we accept the argument that the results of these investments will be in the direction of replacing imports by locally produced goods, then we have to examine separately the effects on the technical coefficients of replacing competitive imports and those of replacing non-competitive imports.

Substitution for competitive imports

A competitive import is a commodity which is also obtained from local production, whatever the magnitude of the latter; local production may only supply a very minor part of demand yet the production of the commodity in question could be increased whenever it is found possible and desirable to do so. Now substitution for a competitive import will have a variety of repercussions on the technical coefficients, the magnitude and type of which will depend on a variety of factors such as the magnitude of substitution, the distribution of the new production over the purchasing sectors as well as the technology utilized in the new production.

The straightforward effect of any such substitution would be expressed in a higher input coefficient from local production and a lower import coefficient. The simplest form of change of this type will occur if the new production is distributed along the row in the same proportions. That is to say, if we are substituting for 40 per cent of agricultural imports, then all deliveries of agricultural imports to all the purchasing sectors, including the final demand sectors, will be reduced by 40 per cent. In this case the correction of the coefficients along the row will not require elaborate changes. Along the columns it will be also an easy task once we know the magnitude of the substitution and its distribution.

But this is not always the case since substitution for a certain competitive import may be limited to a particular brand of this commodity which goes entirely to final demand or to particular sectors. If all the new production is substituted for imports which were purchased by the final demand sectors, this will not require the introduction of any changes in the technical coefficients of the productive sectors. But if the new production is substituted for imports purchased by particular sectors, this obviously will necessitate a change in the input coefficients of these sectors.

In all the above cases, however, we assumed that substitution for competitive imports will be through an investment based on the techniques already utilized. Consequently we anticipated no changes in the coefficients of the industries which are increasing their production except by the portion of the increase of the delivery from local production from the sector itself. But this is not always the case as the substitution of a certain import may be accompanied by the introduction of new technology, and in fact in a developing economy there is a strong leaning towards the introduction of the latest techniques which are available in the more developed economies. If this is the case, then substitution of competitive imports will entail certain modifications in the input structure of the particular industry, the magnitude of which depends upon the deviation of the new technique from that which is already being utilized, as well as on its importance. The new technology may utilize less labour or different types of inputs in different proportions.

The frequency of changes in the technical coefficients will be closely tied to the rate of industrialization. How can these changes be embodied in the solution so that the table could be effectively used for projecting the future production levels required to meet a final bill of goods?

This could be done in different ways, the first of which is to restrict the coefficients in the interflow matrix to only one type which would combine inputs from domestic production and from competitive imports. Only non-competitive imports should be excluded and grouped in one row of inputs. These coefficients (i.e. of domestic and competitive imports) are the ones to be inverted instead of the coefficients of inputs from domestic production, as is normally the case. This means that in solving for the levels of production required to meet a final bill of goods, our production targets will be overestimated because we allowed the inputs from imports to have indirect effects which they do not actually have. This may be a correct procedure in an economy with insignificant reliance on imports or if we are substituting all competitive imports by domestic production. However, this is not generally the case and something should be done to correct this overestimation. We may regard imports which are not going to be substituted as final demand and then, by utilizing the same inverse of the matrix, we can calculate the direct and indirect import requirements necessary for the production of these goods. This should be deducted from gross production obtained from our solution.

This is more or less a satisfactory method if the substitution of competitive imports does not entail the introduction of a new technology or a different distribution of the new production. However, another method of solution may be offered to deal with those last points. Provided that the magnitude of substitution, the distribution of new production along the purchasing sectors and the new technology, if any, are known, we can incorporate their effects on the technical coefficients from domestic production and consider that these will be the coefficients in the year for which the production level will be calculated. Then we proceed as usual by utilizing the inverse of the new coefficients. In this case we do not need another set of calculations as in the first case, because inputs from imports were not included in the inverted matrix. Imports could later be calculated simply by multiplying the required production from each sector by the import coefficient.

Substitution for non-competitive imports

For our purpose a non-competitive import is an import which has no similar form of domestic production. This may be due to the fact that it is impossible, except with too high cost, to produce it, or that the state of development did not so far allow for its production. It may be concluded therefore that the number of such imports is inversely related to the state of economic development in the country and that the faster the rate of development the faster the rate at which non-competitive imports become competitive in the sense that each commodity will be produced domestically. The substitution of such imports would mean the installation of an entirely new activity in the economy and with it a new technology would be introduced. Motor cars, for instance, were until recently a non-competitive import in Egypt, but as new motor factories are under construction such import will become a competitive one. Now let us examine how this substitution will affect the technical coefficients.

As is the case with competitive imports, a shift in the input coefficients from imports to domestic production will occur. But unlike the competitive imports, the non-competitive imports could not be fitted into the old matrix as that industry did not exist before. This necessitates the insertion of a new row to show deliveries from the new industry, and of a column to show its purchases from other sectors of the economy (as the introduction of such industry will entail a claim on domestic resources as well as on imports).

In such a case it would be necessary to introduce, as explained before, the necessary changes in the technical coefficients before utilizing the table for projection. The important point to emphasize here is that the substitution of non-competitive imports will affect the technical coefficients and the frequency of the changes in these coefficients will be tied to the rate of substitution which in itself is tied to the rate of development.

The stability of relative prices

The second factor which affects the technical coefficients is the change in relative prices. If it is assumed that prices move in the same general direction, with a minimum of relative changes, changes in technical coefficients would be negligible. This assumption was made to fit the case of a developed economy with minimum reliance on foreign trade to satisfy the need of its productive sectors.

These arguments are only partly satisfactory in a developing economy. The mere fact that we express the coefficients in value terms makes us concerned about changes in prices in general and in these economies in particular. It is difficult in an economy where movements in prices accompany changes in technology to separate the effect of each on the technical coefficients.

Now let us examine the frequency of these changes in the light of our statement, that Egypt relies to a sizeable degree on imports and that import substitution will play a dominant role in economic development. The technical coefficients, expressed in value terms, will not only depend on the stability of relative prices of the domestically produced commodities but also on the stability of import prices. These prices, as it is known, are subject to world supply and demand and also other exogenous factors, and therefore their stability depends a great deal on movements in these factors. Moreover a country like Egypt with limited supply of hard currencies may decide or be obliged to change the suppliers of its imports, a step which often entails drastic revision of the previous cost structure of the productive sectors. The frequency of such moves could not be predicted a long time ahead as they are subject to economic as well as political considerations. The point to emphasize here, however, is that these changes do happen and that their frequency is very likely to be higher than in developed countries.

As import substitution takes place, the relative prices of inputs will most likely be subject to change, the frequency and magnitude of which depends on the role of import substitution. It is not always the case that inputs from the new domestic production will have the same prices as those of the old inputs from imports. In fact the contrary is more frequently the case. The point to emphasize here, however, is that the frequency of these changes in a developing economy is more than in an already developed economy with less reliance on imports and with minor amounts of substitution among the inputs.

From the above we can see that the likelihood of changes in relative prices is greater in a developing economy than in a developed one. In dealing with this problem the technical coefficients will have to be adjusted to take into consideration not only the changes in technology, but also the anticipated changes in relative prices (which are likely to happen more frequently than assumed). This is very difficult, but it is of paramount importance if a realistic picture is to be drawn from the input-output table.

Economies of scale

The third factor which affects the technical coefficients is that an increase in the scale of production may bring about a change in the input coefficients. The general assumption in the input-output model is that there is a proportional relation between the inputs and the outputs of a sector. This, however, is not always true, in which case different coefficients, which may be called marginal coefficients, should be utilized.

The occurrence of non-proportionality in a developed economy depends of course on the type of industry and its production function; until better information is collected, one may be contented with the assumption of proportionality between the inputs and the level of production. However, we should like to emphasize that the occurrence of non-proportionality may be frequent in a country like Egypt. An argument in support of this view runs as follows. Industries may be established below their optimum size because of limitation of markets or other reasons. The expansion of these industries at a later stage may bring about a change in the input coefficients of the type we have mentioned. Similarly the substitution of competitive imports by local products would entail the expansion of the industries concerned which may have already been operating at a size below the optimum.

The way to deal with this problem is not in itself difficult, but only adds to the complication of the solution as it requires additional information on marginal coefficients. These latter take more effort to determine than the average coefficients and we may have to rely to a greater extent on technical experts and to a lesser extent on historical data. Having determined these coefficients, the iterative method of solution would be the best to utilize. The procedure would be to examine after each round the level of production and then utilize for the different levels of production the appropriate marginal coefficient.

4. *The Utilization of the Input-Output Table*

This section describes some of the uses of the input-output table in connection with the annual national budget for 1960–1.[1] The starting point of the estimates is a projection of changes in final demand between 1959–60 and 1960–1. Changes in investment were projected in great detail, distinguishing 25 categories, in conformity with the first version of the Five-Year Plan. An attempt was also made to distinguish 4 categories of exports.

The forecasts of final demand are shown in Table 3 analysed according to sectors of origin. The table shows investment in a summary form; full details of the investment forecast are shown in Table 4.

An important aspect of planning is to calculate not only direct import requirements, as shown in Tables 3 and 4, but also indirect requirements which arise through the interdependence of producing sectors. This calculation was based on the 1954 model.

[1] In the short time since its construction, the table was used for other purposes also, notably by Professor Frisch during his visits to the National Planning Committee.

TABLE 3

Projected Deliveries to Final Demand in Fiscal Year 1960/1

(in million £E)

Deliveries from	House-hold consumption	Govern-ment consumption	Exports	Total fixed investment	Total final demand*
Agriculture	136·3	4·0	6·1	1·0	147·4
Mining and quarrying	—	0·1	6·4	—	6·5
Electricity	4·3	0·6	—	—	4·9
Metals	—	0·1	—	—	0·1
Metal products	0·8	3·3	0·7	—	4·8
Cement	—	—	2·8	—	2·8
Petroleum refining	7·9	3·1	1·9	—	12·9
Machinery	2·6	2·3	—	26·3	31·2
Basic chemicals	10·2	1·7	—	—	11·9
Other chemicals	1·6	0·6	—	—	2·2
Construction	—	3·8	—	138·4	142·2
Meat products	69·0	2·1	—	—	71·1
Dairy products	57·9	2·4	—	—	60·3
Grain milling	51·4	1·2	4·0	—	56·6
Bakery products	84·8	2·5	—	—	87·3
Sugar	22·5	0·3	—	—	22·8
Oils and fats	12·0	0·4	—	—	12·4
Other food products	14·4	1·0	3·3	—	18·7
Spinning and weaving	80·3	4·2	25·4	—	109·9
Processing of cotton	—	—	103·9	—	103·9
Clothing	17·9	3·5	—	—	21·4
Paper and paper products	2·0	1·4	—	—	3·4
Tobacco	40·8	0·2	—	—	41·0
Wood and furniture	7·1	—	—	—	7·1
Fertilizers	—	—	—	—	—
Other industries	15·8	0·6	8·7	—	25·1
Transport and communications	44·1	3·5	13·0	—	60·6
Suez Canal	—	—	46·5	—	46·5
Education	7·6	—	—	—	7·6
Medical services	13·9	—	—	—	13·9
Trade and finance	85·1	6·2	21·0	8·3	120·6
Banking and insurance	0·9	—	0·6	—	1·5
Other services	205·2	2·7	3·0	—	210·9
Total from domestic sectors	996·4	51·8	247·3	174·0	1469·5
Imports	56·6	14·2	—	124·0	194·8
Value added	19·0	154·7	—	—	173·7
Total	1072·0	220·7	247·3	298·0	1828·0

* Excluding changes in inventories.

TABLE 4
Required Deliveries for Projected Investment for 1960/1
(in million £E)

Type of Investment	Total	Deliveries from:				Total deliveries from domestic sectors	Imports
		Construction	Domestic production of equipment	Agriculture	Trade and finance		
Vertical investment in agriculture	12·3	5·6	1·9	0·4	0·6	8·5	3·8
Horizontal investment in agriculture	29·7	18·7	3·9	0·6	1·3	24·5	5·2
Irrigation and drainage	25·9	19·9	—	—	—	19·9	6·0
High Dam	9·0	1·4	—	—	—	1·4	7·6
Mining and quarrying	3·2	0·5	0·8	—	0·3	1·6	1·6
Electricity	13·5	3·0	2·0	—	0·7	5·7	7·8
Metals	6·7	2·0	0·2	—	—	2·2	4·5
Metal products	0·9	0·3	0·1	—	—	0·4	0·5
Petroleum refining	14·8	1·1	3·9	—	1·2	6·2	8·6
Chemical and pharmaceutical	13·1	3·0	1·3	—	0·4	4·7	8·4
Machinery	12·5	2·6	2·4	—	0·8	5·8	6·7
Rural industries	1·0	0·3	0·4	—	0·1	0·8	0·2
Food, beverages and tobacco	4·8	2·2	0·9	—	0·3	3·4	1·4
Textiles and clothing	9·8	1·7	1·7	—	0·5	3·9	5·9
Paper and printing	3·8	1·5	0·5	—	0·1	2·1	1·7
Wood and furniture	0·5	0·1	0·1	—	—	0·2	0·3
Non-metal industries	0·3	0·1	0·1	—	—	0·2	0·1
Other industries	3·0	0·7	—	—	—	0·7	2·3
Education	2·0	0·6	0·5	—	0·2	1·3	0·7
Medical services	3·4	—	—	—	—	—	3·4
Transport and communications	56·4	25·1	5·1	—	1·6	31·8	24·6
Suez Canal	14·9	6·8	—	—	—	6·8	8·1
Housing	28·0	22·3	—	—	—	22·3	5·7
Public utilities	14·6	9·3	—	—	0·2	9·3	5·3
Services	13·9	9·6	0·5	—	—	10·3	3·6
Total	298·0	138·4	26·3	1·0	8·3	174·0	124·0

Writing $X = (x_i)$ for the vector of outputs,

$Y = (y_i)$ for the vector of final demand, and

$A = (a_{ij})$ for the matrix of technical coefficients based on domestic inputs, the solution of the input-output model is given by

$$X = (I - A)^{-1} Y. \tag{1}$$

Writing $M = (m_j)$ for the vector of import coefficients, import requirements can be calculated from

$$MX = M(I - A)^{-1} Y = M^* Y \tag{2}$$

where $M^* = M(I - A)^{-1}$ is a new vector, calculated from the inverse of the matrix of technical coefficients and the import coefficients.[1]

This formula enables us to calculate total (direct and indirect) import requirements per unit of final demand originating in different sectors. M gives direct imports (obtained from Table 1), M^* total imports, and indirect imports are obtained as the difference. The results for 1954 are shown in Table 5.

As can be seen, import requirements are relatively large in heavy industry (like metals, metal products, cement, machinery and paper) and small in light industry and in agriculture. There is also the familiar fact that indirect import requirements are sometimes larger than direct ones.

The coefficients in Table 5 can be applied to any pattern of final demand. As an illustration the import content of four categories of demand was calculated, making use of the demand estimates in the 1959 table (in terms of 1954 prices). As shown in Table 6, the total import content of investment is estimated at 47 per cent but of household consumption at 15 per cent only. Most of the import content of investment consists of direct imports while in the case of household consumption indirect import requirements exceed direct ones.

The coefficients shown in Table 5 can now be applied to the projections given in Tables 3 and 4. The results of the calculation, direct and indirect import requirements forecast for different categories of final demand, are shown in Table 7. Imports (including indirect requirements) are lowest for exports and government consumption, and highest for investment. As expected, those categories of investment which used construction activity rather than plant and machinery, have lower

---

[1] We could make full use of the entries in the input-output table and distinguish imports according to commodity classes. In that case, M and M^* would be matrices instead of vectors. $(M = (m_{ij}).)$

TABLE 5

*Direct and Indirect Import Requirements Per Unit of
Final Demand from each Productive Sector*

Sector	Direct imports	Indirect imports	Total
Agriculture	0·041	0·018	0·059
Mining and quarrying	0·068	0·029	0·097
Electricity	0·158	0·043	0·201
Metals	0·225	0·062	0·287
Metal products	0·221	0·071	0·292
Cement	0·131	0·063	0·194
Petroleum refining	0·132	0·051	0·183
Machinery	0·166	0·097	0·263
Basic chemicals	0·076	0·048	0·124
Other chemicals	0·146	0·047	0·193
Construction	0·143	0·067	0·210
Meat products	0·026	0·050	0·076
Dairy products	0·028	0·054	0·082
Grain milling	0·027	0·057	0·084
Bakery products	0·064	0·065	0·129
Sugar	0·032	0·034	0·066
Oils and fats	0·052	0·019	0·071
Other food products	0·080	0·063	0·143
Spinning and weaving	0·055	0·072	0·127
Processing of cotton	0·006	0·060	0·066
Clothing	0·049	0·095	0·144
Paper and paper products	0·236	0·090	0·326
Tobacco	0·059	0·078	0·137
Wood and furniture	0·186	0·064	0·250
Fertilizers	0·075	0·026	0·101
Other industries	0·162	0·068	0·230
Transport and communications	0·085	0·027	0·112
Suez Canal	0·015	0·007	0·022
Education	0·034	0·027	0·061
Medical services	0·143	0·052	0·195
Trade and finance	0·017	0·020	0·037
Banking and insurance	0·012	0·026	0·038
Other services	0·006	0·106	0·112

coefficients. An exception is the High Dam which has a large import content.[1]

In these calculations imports are treated as a primary factor input. We can perform similar calculations for other primary inputs, like

[1] It should be noted that the calculations are based not on complete investment projects but only on the stage of projects likely to be carried out in 1960–1. The High Dam, in particular, will be constructed over a number of years.

TABLE 6

Direct and Indirect Imports Per Unit of Final Demand

	Direct imports	Indirect imports	Total
Fixed investment	0·327	0·138	0·465
Household consumption	0·053	0·094	0·147
Government consumption	0·075	0·040	0·115
Exports	0·000	0·074	0·074

household income,[1] and this is shown in Table 8. If we write $H = (h_j)$ for the vector of household income coefficients, household incomes per unit of final demand are given by $H(I - A)^{-1}$.

By calculations similar to those performed for exports, we calculated the income-generating effect of different categories of final demand for 1960–1, as shown in Table 9. Direct value added represents domestic services and the income of government employees. The income-generating effect of different categories of final demand varies, of course, inversely with their import content.

Lastly, the changes forecast are analysed in Table 10. The calculations show that of an increase of £E 181 m. in final demand, £E 84 m. would be spent on imports. This exercise has also brought to light an interesting inconsistency in the assumptions, resulting in a forecast of £E 77 m. in household income but only £E 42 m. in consumption. Clearly the assumptions need revision in further work. It is possible that the increase in imports required for consumption has been under-estimated. It would also be preferable to assume that agricultural output is determined not by demand but by capacity. Alternatively, if the forecasts were correct, a drastic increase in taxes would be required to close the gap between household income and consumption.

5. *Conclusion*

Research based on input-output and similar techniques is only at its beginning in Egypt but it is obvious from the above description of a few applications that it is already proving itself useful in planning the economic development of the country.

To sum up, we argued that the lack of interdependence, which is often quoted as an objection to the construction of input-output tables in underdeveloped countries, is not valid as far as Egypt is concerned.

[1] Equal to wages, salaries and distributed profits. The difference between value added and household income consists of undistributed profits and indirect taxes

B.S.I.E.D.

TABLE 7

Direct and Indirect Import Requirements as Percentage of Categories of Final Demand, 1960/1

	Direct imports	Direct and indirect imports
Household consumption	5	14
Government consumption	6	10
Total exports	—	7
Total investment in fixed capital	42	54
Exports		
Cotton	—	7
Yarn and cloth	—	13
Suez Canal	—	2
Other exports	—	10
Investments in		
Vertical investment in agriculture	31	45
Horizontal investment in agriculture	18	34
Irrigation and drainage	23	39
High dam	85	88
Mining and quarrying	50	59
Electricity	58	67
Metals	67	75
Metal products	56	67
Petroleum refining	58	67
Chemical and pharmaceutical	64	72
Machinery	54	63
Rural industries	20	40
Food, beverages and tobacco	29	44
Textiles and clothing	60	68
Paper and printing	45	57
Wood and furniture	60	80
Non-metal industries	33	67
Other industries	77	80
Education	35	50
Medical services	100	100
Transport and communications	44	55
Suez Canal	54	64
Housing	20	37
Public utilities	36	50
Services	26	42
Total investment in construction	—	21
Total investment in domestically produced machinery and equipment	—	26

On the other hand, we questioned the stability of the technical coefficients and came to the conclusion that owing to the present structure of the Egyptian economy and its future development, the frequency of changes in the coefficients are likely to be greater than in a developed economy.

TABLE 8

Direct and Indirect Household Income* Per Unit of Final Demand from each Productive Sector

Sector	Household income per unit of production	Indirect household income per unit of final demand	Direct and indirect household income per unit of final demand
Agriculture	0·406	0·402	0·808
Mining and quarrying	0·236	0·197	0·433
Electricity	0·214	0·143	0·357
Metals	0·301	0·174	0·475
Metal products	0·360	0·194	0·554
Cement	0·256	0·222	0·478
Petroleum refining	0·127	0·288	0·415
Machinery	0·304	0·293	0·597
Basic chemicals	0·297	0·291	0·588
Other chemicals	0·254	0·279	0·533
Construction	0·374	0·217	0·591
Meat products	0·109	0·674	0·783
Dairy products	0·265	0·550	0·815
Grain milling	0·051	0·726	0·7⁻
Bakery products	0·166	0·576	
Sugar	0·060	0·349	·9
Oils and fats	0·563	0·119	·682
Other food products	0·075	0·523	0·598
Spinning and weaving	0·164	0·514	0·678
Processing of cotton	0·018	0·77⁻	0·789
Clothing	0·215		0·643
Paper and paper products	0·152	·ⅰ	0·533
Tobacco	0·060	·379	0·439
Wood and furniture	0·455	0·187	0·642
Fertilizers	0·499	0·168	0·667
Other industries	0·⁻	0·262	0·623
Transport and communications		0·113	0·807
Suez Canal	·03	0·078	0·581
Education	0·675	0·186	0·861
Medical services	0·316	0·290	0·606
Trade and finance	0·288	0·164	0·452
Banking and insurance	0·417	0·170	0·587
Other services	0·790	0·032	0·822

* Wages, salaries and distributed profits.

TABLE 9

Direct and Indirect Value Added and Household Income as Percentage of Categories of Final Demand, 1960/1

	Value added directly created by final demand	Direct and indirect value added created by final demand	Direct household income created by final demand	Direct and indirect household income created by final demand
Household consumption	2	86	2	68
Government consumption	70	90	67	82
Total exports	—	93	—	69
Total investment in fixed capital	—	46	—	34
Exports				
Cotton	—	93	—	79
Yarn and cloth	—	87	—	68
Suez Canal	—	98	—	58
Other exports	—	90	—	61
Investments in				
Vertical investment in agriculture	—	55	—	41
Horizontal investment in agriculture	—	66	—	49
Irrigation and drainage	—	61	—	46
High Dam	—	12	—	9
Mining and quarrying	—	41	—	28
Electricity	—	33	—	24
Metals	—	25	—	19
Metal products	—	33	—	22
Petroleum refining	—	33	—	24
Chemical and pharmaceutical	—	28	—	21
Machinery	—	37	—	26
Rural industries	—	60	—	60
Food, beverages and tobacco	—	56	—	42
Textiles and clothing	—	32	—	22
Paper and printing	—	44	—	32
Wood and furniture	—	20	—	20
Non-metal industries	—	33	—	33
Other industries	—	20	—	13
Education	—	50	—	35
Medical services	—	—	—	—
Transport and communications	—	45	—	33
Suez Canal	—	36	—	27
Housing	—	63	—	47
Public utilities	—	50	—	38
Services	—	58	—	44
Total investment in construction	—	79	—	59
Total investment in domestically produced machinery and equipment	—	74	—	60

TABLE 10

A Rough National Budget for 1960/1 showing Changes in Imports,
Value Added and Household Income for Given Changes in Final Demand

(in million £E)

	Changes in total final demand	Changes in imports required	Changes in total value added required	Changes in household income created
Private consumption	42·4	6·1	36·3	28·8
Government consumption	17·2	1·7	15·5	14·1
Exports of cotton	−2·4	−0·2	−2·2	−1·9
Exports of yarn and cloth	8·3	1·1	7·2	5·6
Suez Canal	1·0	—	1·0	0·6
Other exports	6·7	0·7	6·0	4·1
Investment in construction	40·4	8·5	31·9	23·9
Investment in domestically produced equipment	2·1	0·6	1·5	1·3
Imported equipment	65·1	65·1	—	—
TOTAL	180·8	83·6	97·2	76·5

We attempted to show how in a country with a minor industrial sector and an over-populated agricultural sector a faster rate of growth would require a faster rate of development of the industrial sector. This being the case we attempted to show that industrialization for some years will take the shape of substituting domestic production for imports. In the light of this statement we attempted to examine the stability of the technical coefficients. To do that we considered the most important factors which generally cause changes in these coefficients and we found that the future pattern of development and its magnitude will affect the coefficients in that it will introduce drastic changes in the technical structure of the productive sectors. Relative prices were also shown as likely to be affected by the anticipated pattern of development more frequently than is the case in an already developed economy. We also came to the conclusion that the effects of economies of scale may occur more frequently than in a developed economy. Although this is so, the usefulness of the input-output table for long-term projections is not by any means questioned. We only indicated the fact that certain considerations should always be made when the table is utilized for such projections. Adjustments of the technical coefficients to a future situation should always be attempted as an effective way to deal with these problems.

REFERENCES

[1] PEACOCK, A. T. and DOSSER, D. M., 'Input-Output Analysis in an Underdeveloped Country,' *The Review of Economic Studies*, Vol. 25, 1957, p. 21.

[2] VASSILIOU, S., *Input-Output Analysis for the Economy of Cyprus*, Centers for International Studies and Middle Eastern Studies. Harvard University, 1958–9, (mimeo.).

[3] CHENERY, H. B., CLARK, P. G. and CAO-PINNA, V., *The Structure and Growth of the Italian Economy*, Rome, 1953.

ADDENDUM TO MR ELEISH'S PAPER

by A. R. ABDEL MEGUID

The economists of the Planning Commission and of the Planning Institute of Egypt have elaborated an overall system of interdependence, and cooperated with economists and engineers in each sector and in some plants to measure and to produce practical policy decisions relevant to their activity within the general framework of an overall equilibrium.

Our experience in attempting to base input coefficients upon technology rather than money flow transactions has shown that input coefficients based on technology are essential for proper planning on both national and plant level but that it is not possible to incorporate them in an input-output table of workable dimensions. Let me elaborate by giving an example for the petroleum sector.

In almost any country the petroleum sector is characterized by varying input specifications, numerous process alternatives, and joint production. In the overall model for Egypt, these characteristics were kept hidden through the aggregation of different types of output under the heading 'Refined Petroleum Products', as well as through the aggregation of different types of inputs (mainly the different types of crude oil obtained from local or foreign sources). In the meantime the numerous process alternatives were no longer apparent, as the technical coefficients included in the table hide the fact that one of these alternatives has been chosen. In fact in the petroleum sector, no less than 648 different groups of technical coefficients are actually used in producing 9 types of refined petroleum products.[1] These processes have been grouped together to produce the coefficients appearing in the petroleum sector in an input-output table. Such coefficients, to use a chemical terminology, are in the nature of a compound in which each component loses its characteristics completely. The economist need not be unduly perturbed about such loss. This is analogous, in fact, to the justifiable use of *per capita* income, for instance, as an indicator to the state of economic development, in spite of the existence of inequal distribution of income. The sociologist would take the argument further by qualifying the *per capita* concept with the pattern of distribution. In the same way, the petroleum engineer takes the technical coefficients appearing in the table, and proceeds to qualify them according to types of products, and decompose them according to the technology prevailing in each refinery hitherto grouped together.

On the relative merits of an activity analysis and a conventional input-output model, we found the conventional input-output model a useful leaning post for launching many types of analysis on firm level. The general equilibrium picture obtained in the input-output model serves the purpose of pinpointing the position of the plant or the sector, and its dependence upon, and interdependence with, the rest of the economy. Let me again give an example for the petroleum sector. In Egypt, the activities of this sector, both extraction and refining, are controlled by the General Petroleum Authority. They decide, among other things, the course which should be followed to satisfy the demand for petroleum products. Local production is neither quantitatively nor qualitatively sufficient. The demand and supply equations for crude and refined petroleum may be summarized in the following 5 equalities and inequalities:

Demand for local crude = Capacity of refineries designed for local types < Supply of local crude.
Demand for imported crude = Capacity of refineries designed for imported types.
Aggregate capacity of local refineries < Aggregate demand for refined products.
Demand for imported refined petroleum products > 0.

In determining the levels of these equalities and inequalities, the Authority faces various problems concerned with the decision to import

---

[1] The treatment of the petroleum sector in this memorandum is based on a study prepared by the Operation Research Group in the National Planning Institute (Drs Salah Hamed, Salib Rafael and M. Desouky).

crude and/or refined petroleum, the allocation of various types to each refinery, and the geographical distribution of the finished product. The first step was to determine the size of total demand for petroleum products, which is a function of aggregate economic activity, petroleum being an input for almost all sectors of the economy. This was done with the aid of an input-output table. Total intermediate consumption of each of the petroleum products was calculated (assuming constant fuel input coefficients) in the light of increased production forecast from normal trends, as well as planned expansion according to the National Plan for Development.

The second step was to consider those cells of the input-output table which either affect or are affected by our decisions, and to investigate them through disaggregation or further technical data. The following input-output model gives an example:

SELLING SECTORS		BUYING SECTORS					
	...	Crude oil production	Refined petroleum production	Imports (negative exports)	Exports	...	Total output
⋮							
Crude oil		—	A_4	A_2	A_1		A'
Refined petroleum production			—	A_3			A''
⋮							

The decision to export local crude A_1 implies a decision to import foreign crude A_2; hence we have two cells. Further, the more local crude is exported, the less is available for use in the local refineries A_4; thus we have one more cell to consider. Finally, the importation of crude to be refined locally A_2 is an alternative to the importation of petroleum products A_3, and so on. The consequences of these decisions on total cost, labour input, transport, etc., were worked out from the input-output table. Making use of constant technical coefficients and constant prices, the reaction of a change in any one of the cells was calculated for all sectors affected directly or indirectly. Until this stage, the input-output table was utilized; the solution is, however, complex and requires linear programming as the interdependence is closely knitted and the six variables shown above embrace many complications. For instance, as shown in Table 11, there are five local sources of crude oil of varying quality. The local crude goes to five of the local refineries; the sixth refinery cannot technically handle local crude. Again, the six refineries have different characteristics which are reflected in the amount of crude intake. For example, refinery 1 can handle a maximum of 1,380,000 tons of local crude coming from source 1. If this refinery is allotted crude from source 3, its maximum input capacity would be increased to 1,449,000 tons.

Furthermore, production yields of the different refineries vary according to the type of local or foreign oil used as input. From a certain type of crude the yield is 0·962 in refinery 1, but only 0·871 in refinery 4. Waste or losses, a very important element in petroleum refining, vary from 0·006 to 0·033.

With the use of the model, two optimum solutions were worked out, one giving the minimum use of foreign currency, and the other minimum total costs.

Input-output tables are applied not only to industry but also to the services sector. In commercial banking the traditional financial analysis of the balance sheets of clients applying for loans is being replaced by the analysis of technical coefficients. Credit facilities supplied by the bank are invariably granted for the purpose of providing the working capital of the firm, i.e. for the purchase of inputs and payment of wages. The firm is asked to supply the bank with enough information to work out its technical coefficients. These are then compared with the average for the sector. We believe this throws a great deal of light on the firm's productivity and technical efficiency. These two factors are uppermost in a country which has a national development plan; the profitability criterion based on balance sheet analysis necessarily plays a secondary role.

Again in the services sector, it was suggested that the administration of import licensing be based essentially on the import coefficients appearing in the input-output table. This will help the allocation of available foreign exchange not only according to sector but also according to the type of imported goods required within the framework of centrally planned targets of production. Further, such system will ensure the consistency, or point out the contradictions, of the targets since for most developing countries foreign exchange is the scarcest input.

CHAPTER 12

Some Applications of Input-Output Techniques to the Analysis of the Structure and Development of Israel's Economy

by MICHAEL BRUNO

---

1. *Introduction*

The following survey discusses some of the uses of input-output techniques in the analysis of the structure of the Israeli economy and of its future development. The present phase of input-output work in Israel started in 1959 as part of the Bank of Israel's project on long-term development forecasting.[1] An analytical framework was needed by which the consistency of long-term sector plans with each other and with over-all policy objectives and factor limitations (such as a reduction in the foreign currency inflow and maintenance of full-employment growth) could be checked. At the same time this tool was supposed to serve as a means of forecasting production and investment by sector and their respective contribution to the balance of payments. An input-output model was considered the most suitable tool for this purpose, especially in view of the importance of impending changes in the composition of demand between broad final demand categories (increasing exports relative to domestic consumption) as well as between sectors of production (increasing manufacturing relative to agriculture and housing, and some branches of manufacturing more than others).

Input-output work proceeded on two different levels. On the one hand work on the construction of a detailed table for 1958 was started at the beginning of 1959. This table, consisting in its most detailed internally consistent form of 297 commodities and 164 sectors of production, was completed in February 1961 and has subsequently been used in the analysis of the structure of the economy and its development in 1958–60.

[1] Input-output techniques of more limited scope have first been introduced in the pioneering work of Dr A. L. Gaathon [1], [2]. The present project has been the product of team-work by economists in the Research Department of the Bank of Israel, including M. Merhav, H. Francuz, and J. Rafiah. Z. Sussman participated in the 1959 work on development programming. Most valuable contribution and active guidance throughout has been given by Professor H. B. Chenery.

Simultaneously with this long-term project a more modest 20×20 sector model was constructed, in the second half of 1959, for purposes of the analysis of development alternatives in 1958–64, to serve as a basis of government discussions of long-term development plans.

In the following sections we shall briefly indicate a few aspects of both of these tables. Section 2 discusses an empirical 'test' of the production forecast based on the summary input-output model. Section 3 describes some of the applications of the more detailed model, in which greater emphasis has been put on a detailed analysis of primary factor use.

2. A Test of the 1958–64 Forecast by Comparison with Actual Sector Developments in 1958–60

The use of an input-output table for forecasting is by now familiar from the experience of a number of countries, such as Italy [3], and in Israel the usual procedure was followed — beginning with the estimation of a provisional final bill of goods for the projection year (1964), using information on expenditure elasticities (for private consumption), on development plans (for fixed investments), on government budgets (for public consumption) and on foreign market trends (for exports). The inverse of the table is then used for the estimation of implied production levels. Next, using supplementary estimates of per unit primary factor requirements (imports, capital and labour), the various equilibrium conditions are checked: the balance of payments and the related savings-investment equilibrium, and the labour-employment equilibrium condition.

The main emphasis in Israel was put on the balance of payments problem, mainly because this was considered the effective limit to growth in the long run. The existing import surplus of $300–350 million, amounting to 50 per cent of annual import requirements, will have to be reduced gradually while imports continue to grow at a rate only slightly lower than that of GNP. At the same time Israel's past staple export commodity — citrus — is declining in profitability, with growing competition and limited markets, and exports of manufactures have to take its place. Because of the highly unrealistic official exchange rate at that time, alternative, higher, shadow prices had to be used in working out alternative export forecasts.[1] A similar device was used in estimating import substitution. Here, rather than adjusting input

---

[1] For the use of input-output techniques in calculating the cost of foreign exchange see also Section 3 of this paper.

coefficients in the matrix for the projection year, an approximation method was used, by bringing in a separate final demand vector for import substitutes. The latter was based on existing blueprints for import substitution projects which again take into account a shadow price for foreign exchange.[1]

The 20-sector input-output table which was constructed for this purpose was of a very provisional nature. At the time when it was prepared none of the sources of information, which were later used for the detailed table, could be utilized, and the provisional table had to be based on partial data, mostly commodity totals with no breakdown by destination. The main emphasis was put on speed, at the expense of accuracy, so that it could be used for the analysis of long-term development alternatives, which had to be completed by the end of 1959. The table thus had to be prepared within 2 months.

The essence of the analysis consisted of a series of rounds of successive approximations, not only in order to arrive at one feasible solution but to suggest a range or 'area of choice' as between various policy alternatives (such as foreign borrowing, the exchange rate affecting the supply of exports and import substitutes, and the savings rate). In the course of the analysis, and in order to facilitate the process of successive solutions, the input-output model was reduced to an aggregate model in terms of main final uses and direct and indirect factor requirements, and resort to the original input-output table was made only for working out the detailed output levels of the finally suggested policy solution.[2]

This short description was only intended to form the background for a discussion of an attempt to test the 1958–64 forecast by comparison with actual developments in the economy during 1958–60. Although the forecast was prepared in the second half of 1959, no information on actual developments in 1959 was available at the time and the analysis was based on 1958 and previous years. This justifies the inclusion of 1959 in this comparison. One could, of course, argue that a forecast prepared for a later year (1964), in which the greatest emphasis is put on an impending structural change, does not necessarily imply a corresponding gradual change over the intervening years. Nonetheless it seems of interest to spell out the forecast in terms of annual growth rates and to compare these with actual developments for the period for which

---

[1] Ideally, of course, the analysis should be formulated in mathematical programming terms, in which case the shadow price for foreign exchange should itself be an outcome of the analysis. Although in practice this was not possible, the rationale of this idea was followed here. See also [4].

[2] Details of the input-output model and the provisional 1964 forecast are described in two internal summary memoranda [5], [6] and of the aggregate model used for the analysis of development alternatives in [4].

data exist.[1] It thus gives an indication how far the assumptions as to the final bill of goods were realistic and, once discrepancies in the latter are allowed for, how far the provisional and seemingly unreliable input-output table was an adequate tool for forecasting. The outcome of this experiment might thus be of great help when the long-term forecast is modified and the tools used for it are improved.

For a more complete test of the forecast a number of additional investigations ought to be made, into, for instance, investment requirements or labour inputs. We shall here confine ourselves to one particular but central aspect of such a forecast, namely the prediction of production levels by sector and the relation which the estimate of the final bill of goods has to the latter. The results of this exercise are summarized in Tables 1 and 2 below.

Table 1 compares the forecast of the national accounts with actual growth over the last two years and over the past period 1955–8, all in terms of real annual growth rates. The main feature of the 1964 forecast, as compared to past development, has been a suggested shift from consumption and investment (mainly housing) to exports. A slightly lower

TABLE 1

National Accounts 1958–60: Comparison with Forecast to 1964

	Average annual rates of increase (%)		
	Actual 1955–58*	*Forecast 1958–64*	*Actual 1958–60†*
Private Consumption	8·7	7·4	9·6 (7·9)
Public Consumption	7·2	5·9	8·4 (8·4)
Fixed Investment	9·2	4·2	4·0 (–0·9)
Exports	14·4	18·6	27·6 (26·1)
Total Uses	9·1	7·9	9·9 (8·2)
Imports	8·5	7·6	10·4 (15·0)
GNP	9·3	8·4	10·2 (8·0)
Population	4·6	3·5	3·1 (3·1)

* For absolute figures in 1958 see Table 3.
† Figures in brackets refer to changes from 1959 to 1960.

[1] Reference to a period of only two years is also justifiable on account of the high rates of growth and rapid structural changes: from 1958 to 1960 GNP grew by 20 per cent, output in manufacturing increased by 30 per cent and manufacturing exports almost doubled, all in real terms.

rate of increase in GNP was assumed. The figures for 1958–60 bear out the fact that the great export drive did in fact bear fruit even more than was expected,[1] and investment also followed the pattern more or less as predicted. Both private and public consumption, however, increased at a considerably higher rate than assumed; similarly for GNP and imports. In the latter of the two years, 1960, the change in composition of final uses (and correspondingly GNP) seems to have been closer to the predicted long-term trend.

The aggregates, however, give only one side of the story. We have accordingly estimated the actual final bill of goods in 1959 and 1960 by type of final use and by 20 sectors of origin (according to the classification of the provisional input-output table), and compared these with the projected final bill, after interpolation of the latter to 1960. The main discrepancies between the two sets of final bills can be summed up as follows:[2]

(*a*) The overall higher level of private consumption[3] has brought about a correspondingly higher level of demand for the output of most sectors of the economy. This was most marked, however, in agriculture where a considerable fall in relative prices accompanied a higher growth rate (in real terms) than might have been expected from expenditure elasticities.

(*b*) Surprisingly enough, although one might expect export forecasts to be generally unreliable, the higher increase in exports is almost wholly explained in terms of two sectors: diamond polishing (in which the import component is very high — some 80 per cent — thus explaining part of the higher increase in imports) and in services, where invisible exports increased by 31 per cent on the average (mainly tourism) as compared with an assumed 9 per cent. Most other exports increased more or less as expected.

We can now turn to the analysis of discrepancies in the production forecast using the following procedure. By feeding the actual increase in the final bill of goods from 1958 to 1960 into the inverse of the original 20×20 table (modified as before to take into account predicted import substitution), we arrive at an evaluation of what predicted production levels in 1960 would have been if the final bill of goods had been estimated correctly. The remaining discrepancy between the revised 'forecast' and actual sector growth rates, can thus be regarded as a

---

[1] Although the price in terms of real resources yet remains to be determined. See next section for an investigation of this point.

[2] For greater detail see [7], Ch. 6.

[3] In public consumption the discrepancy consists mostly of wages and salaries.

measure of the inaccuracy of the input-output matrix itself (including the assumption on import substitution). Table 2 gives the results.

A comparison of columns 2 and 3 shows the change in the composition of output predicted on the basis of input-output analysis. The most important change forecast was the shift of emphasis from agriculture and construction (mainly housing) to manufacturing, and that within manu-

TABLE 2

Comparison of the Production Forecast
with Actual Development, 1958–1960

	1958 sector weights in GNP (%)	Average Annual Rates of Increase (%)				Share of final use in 1958 output (%)
		1955–58*	1958–64 forecast	1958–64 'forecast' corrected for actual final bill	Actual 1958–60†	
	(1)	(2)	(3)	(4)	(5)	(6)
Agriculture‡	13	13	7·6	10·5	9·8 (4·8)	66
Mining and Manufacturing	21	11	13·0	13·9	14·1 (11·6)	60
Mining	*0·5*	*30*	*20·3*	*21·7*	*20·0 (7·7)*	*24*
Foodstuffs	*3*	*10*	*6·7*	*10·4*	*10·4 (5·6)*	*83*
Textiles, Wood and Paper	*8*	*10*	*13·0*	*14·3*	*14·0 (12·0)*	*58*
Chemicals and Fuel	*2*	*11*	*18·3*	*14·6*	*16·0 (16·9)*	*43*
Non-Metallic Minerals	*1·5*	*13*	*6·7*	*7·4*	*7·5 (1·0)*	*14*
Diamonds	*0·5*	*14*	*10·0*	*30·0*	*30·0 (22·7)*	*100*
Base Metals	*0·5*	*12*	*21·8*	*26·9*	*26·2 (25·5)*	*1*
Machinery and Metal Products	*5*	*12*	*14·5*	*10·7*	*14·0 (13·5)*	*60*
Construction	7	6	2·8	5·4	5·7 (−2·1)	100
Power	1	11	10·4	10·7	15·8 (17·5)	39
Water	1	9	8·9	8·7	4·6 (5·3)	31
Transportation‡	8	9	9·9	8·6	11·2 (9·2)	66
Services and Trade	49	10	7·3	8·6	11·5 (10·7)	85
Total GNP	100	9	8·4	10·2	10·2 (8·0)	

* Manufacturing: 1956–58 only.
† Figures in brackets refer to changes from 1959 to 1960.
‡ In the original forecast there were 5 sub-sectors in Agriculture and 3 in Transportation. These have here been aggregated.

facturing the growth of individual sectors would greatly diverge from the mean (and from the rate experienced in the past). This was mainly because of a greater orientation to foreign markets and because of the assumed concentration of import substitution in particular sectors (such as chemicals, basic metals and machinery).

In reality (column 5) the growth of agriculture slowed down but not as much as was expected. An excessively high rate of growth in 1959 (17 per cent) was accompanied by a considerable worsening of the terms of trade of the sector and a fall in incomes (which was predicted, in the event of over-production). The result was a much lower rate of growth (5 per cent) in 1960, more in line with long-term requirements. The fact that the correction for final demand (column 4) gives a higher figure than was obtained in practice, shows that there was negative import substitution in this sector (fodder and grains had to be imported because of the drought).

The most remarkable results are the figures for manufacturing, which is also the most important sector for development considerations. The only sub-sector for which there is a considerable discrepancy between forecast and actual events is diamond polishing (as mentioned above), which is a 100 per cent export-oriented sector and input-output technique has thus no role to play in the prediction of its output level. Otherwise the divergent growth rates in manufacturing have been estimated quite successfully. In most subsectors, whatever discrepancies there are, can be explained in terms of errors in the final bill of goods (cf. columns 3 and 4) rather than in input coefficients.[1]

The results are particularly encouraging when industries are considered in which intermediate demand plays an important role (e.g. mining, chemicals, non-metallic minerals and base metals). Also to be noted is the fact that more 'naïve' methods of projection — e.g. by relating the output of a sector directly to its final demand component (the figures do not appear here) or by a regression of output on total GNP — would on the whole give worse results than the input-output method, especially when subsectors are considered.

Although the two are relatively small sectors, we have here reproduced the figures for power and water, and this for a special reason. Both sectors give good examples where simplified input-output analysis is liable to produce wrong results. The input coefficients of electricity are apparently positive functions of time, because of changing technology,

---

[1] Except for metal products, as more import substitution of final equipment was predicted than has so far actually taken place. On the other hand inputs of spare parts and repairs had been underestimated, as more detailed input-output work later bore out.

and thus a time-trend correction would have to be brought into the calculations. As for the water supply, irrigation requirements are little if at all connected with the level of output, and are more a function of climate, area of cultivation, etc. In Israel an additional important factor is the recent introduction of administrative measures of economy in the use of water, which is one of the country's scarcest resources. For both water and power, the correction for actual final demand (column 5) does not, for these reasons, produce better results.

Final demand explains only part of the considerable under-estimate of services, but so little is known about this important sector that there is not much one can say, except that more detailed input-output studies revealed much higher input coefficients from this sector.

To add a word on imports: a successful attempt has been made to explain the increase in imports in terms of the changed composition of output. Although part of the discrepancy is due to unrealized import substitution, most of it disappears when the new production and demand estimates are taken.[1]

To sum up this part of our discussion: although this piece of analysis can hardly pass as a complete 'test' of the adequacy of this particular exercise in input-output forecasting, the results have on the whole been quite reassuring, especially if we remember the quality of the matrix on which this early experiment had been based. I also believe that the results can be of great help in improving the design of similar future forecasts in Israel.

3. *Some Applications of the Detailed Input-Output Table for 1958*[2]

In this section we shall survey some of the uses of a much more detailed input-output table for 1958 whose construction was completed in February 1961. Apart from its eventual use for projections of a kind mentioned in the last section, it has been employed for the analysis of the structure of the economy in the base year 1958 and as an aid in the analysis of developments during 1958–60.

Construction of the detailed table

The table was constructed from individual input-structure tables for each sector, supplemented by check totals of production and imports for each commodity. The main data came from a detailed survey in 4000 manufacturing plants carried out in 1958 jointly with the Central

---

[1] This has only been done with the more detailed table. See next section.
[2] The detailed input-output table and some of its additional applications are discussed more extensively in [7].

Bureau of Statistics. Construction, Agriculture and Transportation were defined on an activity basis and data were based partly on direct information (as in most transportation branches) and partly on engineering data (as in construction). For imports a separate research project was conducted into the allocation of imports by destination (from the customs card-file). In addition information was collected on the price mark-ups of some 300 commodities.

All this information was fed into 'resources and uses' tables for each of the 300 commodities, leaving discrepancies between the two sides (where independent estimates were available) as 'errors and omissions'. The total of discrepancies, I£ 8 million, does not give a true measure of the accuracy of the table as a whole since for quite broad sectors, such as services and trade, no reliable independent estimates from different sources could be obtained.

To give an example of the difficulties encountered in research of this kind, when basic statistics in some of the main fields of economic activity are missing or are unreliable, one might note that the first 5 months were spent on working out a rough substitute for a non-existing commodity classification; without a classified list of raw materials and commodities the detailed industry survey would have been of little use. In practice this was done by modification of the Standard International Trade Classification into a six-digit classification and by relating the latter to industrial branches of origin.[1]

Table 3 gives the data of the detailed input-output table for 1958 in summary form, aggregated into 6 productive sectors, 4 categories of final use and 9 primary factors. The table indicates for each box the number of rows and columns in which the initial data were tabulated and checked for internal consistency. The most detailed internally consistent table consists of 297 commodities (rows) allocated among 164 sectors of destination (columns) for both domestic production and imports, with corresponding tax, subsidy, transportation and trade mark-ups for each commodity. The latter was aggregated into a square 77 × 77 table from which most of the calculations have been made. The table is in producer prices (and c.i.f. imports) with each of the mark-ups aggregated into one separate input in each column. The original data, however, incorporate the corresponding figures in purchaser prices with specific mark-ups indicated for each box in the table. Thus the analysis can be made of import requirements by commodity, including, for

---

[1] One particular difficulty in the translation into Hebrew was the problem of different terms used for raw materials by different producers. The reason is that Israel is a country of immigrants, and people often stick to the different terms which were used in their respective countries of origin.

TABLE 3

Summary Input-Output Table, 1958
(I£ million, current producer prices)

Sales from	No. of sectors in detailed table	Sector code in 77 table	*Purchases by* 1	2	3	4	5	6	Total intermediate	C+G (3)	I_1 (1)	I_2 (2)	X (1)	Total use
			27	108	9	2	12	7	164					
			1–11	12–61	62–66	67–68	69–74	75–77						
1. Agriculture	45	1–11	105	147	0	0	—	—	252	297	102	6	109	766
2. Mining and Manufacturing	221	12–61	99	492	193	6	53	87	930	818	70	29	169	2,016
3. Construction	9	62–66	—	—	0	—	—	5	5	40	517	—	—	562
4. Water and Power	2	67–68	39	24	0	21	1	5	90	25	—	-2	—	113
5. Transportation	13	69–74	24	42	35	3	12	137	253	146	9	3	108	519
6. Services and Trade	7	75–77	17	163	48	15	50	247	540	716	24	-1	85	1,364
7. Total Intermediate	297		284	868	276	45	116	481	2,070	2,042	722	35	471	5,340
Unallocated Stocks				-19					-19			19		
M — Imports*	297		54	392	14	14	78	92	644	193	167	21		1,025
T_1^e — Taxes on Imports	297		21	85	6	0	4	2	118	33	14	3		168
T_1 — Taxes on Domestic Production	297		10	31	31	3	54	67	196	225	3	3		427
S_1 — Subsidies on Domestic Production	297		-18	-24	0	-8	-2	0	-52	-36	0	0	-56	-144
S_2 — Subsidies on Imports for Exports	297		-2	-13					-15					-15
W_1 — Wages and Salaries	297		91	358	157	26	140	260	1,032	522				1,554
W_2 — Imputed Wages (Self-Employed)	1		122	106	31	—	42	108	409					409
P — Profits and Interest	1		163	165	43	-1	46	340	756	222			9	987
D — Depreciation	1		41	67	4	34	41	14	200	88				288
Total Input			766	2,016	562	113	519	1,364	5,340	3,289	906	81	424	10,040

C — Private Consumption (total — 2601) I_1 — Fixed Investment;   X — Exports
G — Public Consumption (total — 688) I_2 — Change in Stocks (including 8 million Errors and Omissions)
* Valued c.i.f. at the official exchange rate, $1 = I£ 1.80.

instance, the effective exchange rate at which this particular commodity was sold to the consuming sector (direct and indirect).

Analysis of developments in 1958–60

In March-May 1961 an attempt was made to use the detailed table as an aid in the analysis of the development of the economy during 1958–60. This was done with several aims in mind. First, the analysis of the determinants of growth of various sectors and of imports can be done with much greater accuracy and insight with the aid of a model in which the interdependence of sectors is taken into account, quite apart from the fact that the table can serve, at least for a number of sectors, as a check on the internal consistency of relatively weak statistical data obtained from various sources; this kind of analysis, on a current basis, is required for the Bank of Israel's annual reports on economic development [8]. Secondly, trying out the model on a past period gives a good indication of the relative accuracy of the basic table and of its main weaknesses, as has been illustrated for the provisional model in Section 2. Last and by no means least, this analysis makes it easier to bring up to date the coefficients where technological changes can be detected; most important in Israel, and presumably also in other developing countries, is the problem of import substitution.

We shall give two illustrations of the work done.[1]

Detailed (77 sector) final bills of goods were constructed for 1959 and 1960[2] and the inverse of the table was used in order to compute implied production levels. After comparison with production estimates obtained from independent sources, adjustments were made; in a great number of cases the actual production estimates, rather than those worked out by means of the inverse, had to be corrected. As a result, direct and indirect shares of the final uses in production by sector were obtained, for each of the three years 1958 to 1960, and for the increments between these years.[3]

Table 4 opposite gives the aggregate result of the calculation for manufacturing. The figures show quite clearly the role of exports in the growth of this sector over the period.

In another analysis an attempt was made to explain the divergent growth of imports and GNP in 1959 and 1960. For that purpose we estimated

---

[1] For more detail see [7] and [8].

[2] This was later aggregated into 20 commodity groups for the analysis described in Section 2.

[3] Suppose Y_i are the elements of the increase in a final use vector in a certain year, and r_{ij} are the elements of the inverse, then the part of the increase in output attributed to this final use is estimated as $y_i = \sum_j r_{ij} Y_j$. Adjustments had to be introduced to take account of import substitution and other discrepancies.

TABLE 4

*Direct and Indirect Output of Manufacturing
by Final Destination, 1958–60**

(I£ million and %, 1958 prices)

	Exports	Fixed investment	Consumption†	Total
1958	291	367	1,353	2,011
	14	*18*	*68*	*100*
Increase 1958–59	140	56	138	334
	42	*17*	*41*	*100*
Increase 1959–60	142	19	107	268
	53	*7*	*40*	*100*
1960	573	442	1,598	2,613
	22	*17*	*61*	*100*

* Figures in italics refer to percentages.
† Including changes in stocks and errors and omissions.

imports for intermediate use by projecting the 1958 import matrix (using a 42 × 42 table) to 1959 and to 1960, and compared the results with actual imports.[1] The results can be used for a check on the import matrix and detection of import substitution. In addition, they give an explanation of actual development, which could not easily be done by other means.

TABLE 5

Growth of Imports 1958–60, Projected and Actual

	1958	1959		1960	
		Projection	Actual	Projection	Actual
Absolute values (in I£ m.)					
Direct Imports for final use (incl. stocks)	382		343		396
Imports for intermediate use	644	749	762	861	855
Total Imports	1,026		1,105		1,251
Rates of Increase (%)					
Direct Imports			−10·2		15·5
Intermediate Imports		16·3	18·3	13·3	12·2
Total Imports			7·7		13·2
GNP			12·6		8·0

[1] Actual intermediate imports were estimated by subtracting, for each commodity, direct imports for final use from total imports.

As seen from Table 5: (*a*) In both years intermediate imports increased more than GNP, and nearly all of the discrepancy is explained in terms of the change in the composition of output. (*b*) The main difference in development thus turns out to be a considerable fall in direct imports for final use in 1959 (half of it due to stocks, the rest due partly to import substitution of agricultural consumer goods and partly to a fall in imported equipment). In 1960 imports of both final consumer goods and equipment increased considerably. (*c*) If we assume the difference between predicted and actual intermediate imports to be due entirely to import substitution, there appears to have been negative intermediate import substitution of I£ 13 million in 1959 and positive substitution of I£ 6 million in 1960. A more detailed independent investigation by commodity confirms these results. Most of the negative import substitution in 1959 was due to the increase in imported fodder at the expense of domestic production[1] which was not matched by positive substitution in industry.[2]

Analysis of direct and indirect factor use

A particular feature of the more detailed input-output table, as compared to the provisional 20 × 20 table, is not only greater accuracy and considerable commodity and sector detail but also greater stress on detailed estimates of primary factor inputs.

Table 6 gives estimates of direct and indirect primary factor use in 1958 for the main national accounting aggregates.[3, 4]

Taxes are divided into taxes on domestic production and taxes on imports. The latter is of particular importance in view of the fact that the effective exchange rate for imports (i.e. the price in I£ per dollar at which imports are sold, including all taxes but excluding trade and other mark-ups) was in 1958 some 30 per cent higher than the official rate, a substitute for the actual devaluation of the Israeli Pound. The input-output table can be used not only for the estimation of the effective rate for imports by sector of destination but by means of the inverse matrix

[1] See Section 2, above.
[2] The input-output analysis was carried out on a 42-commodity basis. Independent information on import substitution by commodity was collected from various industries and compared with input-output results.
[3] The Capital Stock estimates are mainly based on Gaathon [9] and a distinction is made between inventories, imported equipment, other equipment and structures.
[4] Denoting the elements of the direct primary factor matrix by f_{ij} and those of the final demand matrix by D_{ij}, we have for the matrix of direct and indirect primary factor use

$$b_{ij} = \sum_{k, s} f_{ik} r_{ks} D_{sj}$$

where r_{ks} are the elements of the inverse.

TABLE 6

Direct and Indirect Factor Use in the National Accounting Aggregates, 1958

(£1 million and percentages)

Purchases from	Sales to					
	Private consump-tion	Public consump-tion	Gross capital formation	Change in stocks	Exports	Total resource
Labour remuneration	949	437	395	14	167	1962
	36	*64*	*43*	*18*	*39*	*42*
Capital remuneration	690	37	111	24	123	985
	26	*5*	*12*	*31*	*29*	*21*
Depreciation	193	15	38	3	41	290
	7	*2*	*4*	*4*	*10*	*6*
Taxes on Domestic	305	18	49	3	16	391
Products	*12*	*3*	*5*	*4*	*4*	*8*
Taxes on Imports	142	23	50	5	23	243
	6	*3*	*6*	*6*	*5*	*5*
Subsidies on Domestic	− 76	− 1	− 6	− 2	− 100	− 185
Products	*− 3*	—	*− 1*	*− 3*	*− 24*	*− 4*
Subsidies on Imports	—	—	—	—	− 15	− 15
					− 4	—
Gross National	2203	529	637	47	255	3671
Product	*85*	*77*	*70*	*61*	*60*	*78*
Imports*	398	157	270	30	170	1025
	15	*23*	*30*	*39*	*40*	*22*
Total Use	2601	686	907	77	425	4696
	100	*100*	*100*	*100*	*100*	*100*
Labour (millions of man days)	89	40	35	2	15	181
Capital Stock (excl. dwellings, incl. inventories)	3290	358	1038	57	819	5562
Effective Exchange Rate† I£ per $	2·30	2·06	2·13	2·10	1·84	2·21
Average Wage Rate, I£ per day	10·7	10·9	11·4		11·1	10·9
Rate of Profit on Capital %	14·9		10·7		15·0	14·1
Capital/Labour Ratio	37·1	8·4	30·0		54·6	30·9
Capital/Output Ratio	1·27	0·52	1·14		1·93	1·18

* Valued at the official rate $1 = I£ 1.80.
† Official rate corrected by taxes on imports.
Note: Figures in italics are percentages.

the effective rate for direct and indirect imports in different final demand categories can be worked out. Table 6 gives this measure for the main categories of final use in 1958 and clearly the same calculation can be made for any breakdown of final use. The estimate gives an indication of the extent of tax or subsidy which is levied throughout the economy on the scarce factor foreign exchange. E.g., if we were to consider $1 = I£ 2.50 to represent the more or less real (accounting) rate of exchange for future development programmes as viewed in 1958, then clearly both exports and investment were highly subsidized, relative to private consumption. The indirect effective rate also gives an indication for economic policy of the first impact on prices which devaluation might have.[1]

An estimate of the wage component by commodity is important for the analysis of the likely effect of alternative wage policies on relative prices. An interesting fact borne out by the data in Table 6 is that for broad final demand categories the average direct and indirect wage rate varies only little. When direct wages in individual sectors are considered, the amount of variation is quite considerable, in spite of the egalitarian economy of Israel, varying from I£ 6–7 per day in some agricultural sectors to I£ 15–20 per day in some services.

Another application of the estimates of indirect factor use is the comparison of degrees of capital intensity by final demand category. Table 6 suggests that in Israel exports are by far the most capital intensive of the final uses. This stands to reason if we remember that both citrus and shipping — two important export industries — are relatively capital intensive. Diamond polishing is, on the other hand, very labour intensive. Over-all capital intensity was to be expected but not to that extent.[2] In Israel it is usually argued that our comparative advantage lies in promoting exports of skilled and highly skilled labour, which is a relatively cheap factor. It is quite likely that if the analysis is carried out for later years, in which manufacturing (and in particular diamonds, clothing, etc.) takes an increasingly large share, the capital-labour ratio will have become lower. One would also have to analyse the ratios underlying the production of import substitutes. The fact that the capital-output ratio in exports was so much higher than in other final uses is mainly because exports at the $1 = 1.80 rate were highly undervalued; at a $1 = 2.50 rate, for instance, the capital-output ratio in 1958 would become 1.93 instead of 1.39.

Analysis of profitability to the economy and the cost of foreign exchange earned

The points mentioned automatically lead to another, less orthodox, application of input-output analysis in Israel. This is the problem of

[1] At the time of writing, in February 1962, devaluation has at last taken place, raising the official rate to $1 = I£ 3.00.
[2] One is invariably reminded of the famous Leontief 'parodox' for the United States [10].

analysing comparative advantage or profitability to the economy of producing different arrays of commodities when the correct price of foreign exchange is unknown. The disadvantage of the usual profit calculation for open economies, in which there are considerable distortions in the pricing of foreign exchange, is that the price of foreign exchange components has to be taken as given arbitrarily, and these loom large in any such calculation. Alternatively one could impute a price to capital (equal, say, to the interest on marginal foreign borrowing), both on the imported and the domestic components of the latter, leaving all foreign trade components in dollar terms, and all domestic production components in I£ terms, and then calculating the cost of foreign exchange earned (in case of exports) or the cost of foreign exchange saved (in case of import substitutes).[1]

A system of this kind for the analysis of specific development projects has been in use for some time in Israel, long before over-all input-output techniques have been applied. It seems to me, however, that input-output provides a way of both rationalizing and generalizing this approach from the individual commodity to the evaluation of the performance of larger sectors. Since one can calculate direct and indirect capital requirements, with a breakdown into imported and domestic components, and since one can also compute other import components, given the ratio of prices of exports to their corresponding domestic counterparts one can work out the I£ price of a dollar earned by a sector. This is the kind of analysis that has to be applied to the development of exports between 1958 and 1960 in order to assess the real price paid by the economy for this tremendous export drive.

Table 7 gives the aggregated results of the calculation for exports of agricultural commodities (mainly citrus), diamonds and other manufactured goods for 1958 and 1960. Columns (1) and (2) of the table present estimated net value added (i.e. export receipts after deduction of the total import component and the imputed foreign exchange element of capital costs), and columns (3) and (4) indicate the cost in terms of domestic resources per unit of net foreign exchange earned. The rising price of foreign exchange reflects mainly the fall in the foreign prices of

---

[1] Suppose the production of a sector in value terms consists of X_1 pounds' worth of domestic consumption goods and X_s dollars' worth of exports, and that direct and indirect real production costs throughout the economy are C_1 (I£) + C_s ($). C_s would include all direct and indirect imports (including part of replacement and imputed interest on capital), and similarly for C_1. The cost per dollar earned is then defined as:

$$\frac{C_1 - X_1}{X_s - C_s} \frac{\text{I£}}{\$}$$

A similar definition applies for import substitutes.

Israel's exports, and partly (for the total figure) the change in composition of exports; manufactures, with an increasing share, have on the whole been relatively unprofitable.

TABLE 7

The Cost of Foreign Exchange Earned by Exports, 1958–60

	Net export earnings		Cost per net dollar earned		
	1958	*1960*	*1958*	*Movement 1960*	*1958–60*
	(Million dollars)		I£	I£	I£
	(1)	(2)	(3)	(4)	(5)
Agriculture	40	37	1.57	2.25	Negative
Polished Diamonds	8	12	1.73	1.78	1.80
Manufactures (excluding diamonds)	20	34	3.58	3.87	4.28
Total*	110	153	2.04	2.35	2.81

* Including tourist services and shipping, which do not appear separately in the table.

Even more illuminating, perhaps, are the figures in the last column of Table 7. Here we have calculated the cost of the *increase* in exports between 1958 and 1960. Clearly, the tremendous spurt in exports was achieved at a high price in terms of domestic resources. In agriculture physical exports increased but prices fell and with them net earnings declined; this explains the negative figure for the exchange cost. In manufacturing (excluding diamonds) the doubling of exports in real terms was achieved at an implicit exchange rate that was more than double the official rate (1.80 I£/$). What matters for planning purposes, clearly, is not the average price in a specific base year but rather some estimate of future marginal revenue. If it is correct to assume that Israel's export prices will continue to fall in the future, as a result of rapid expansion and stronger competition in foreign markets, then this kind of calculation no doubt gives an indication of the magnitude of the foreign exchange pricing problem and of the required effort in terms of domestic resources.[1]

REFERENCES

[1] GAATHON (GRUENBAUM), A. L., *National Income and Outlay in Palestine, 1936*, Jerusalem, 1941.
[2] GAATHON (GRUENBAUM), A. L., *Survey of Israel's Economy, 1951*, Jerusalem, 1959.

[1] The analysis to which this Section refers was originally carried out in much greater sector detail, and even that would probably not be detailed enough for planning purposes. For a more thorough discussion of the estimation procedure and implications of the analysis see [7], Chapter IV–8 and Chapter V–4.

[3] CHENERY, H. B., CLARK, P. G. and CAO-PINNA, V., *The Structure and Growth of the Italian Economy*, Rome, 1953.

[4] CHENERY, H. B. and BRUNO, M., 'Development Alternatives in an Open Economy: The Case of Israel,' *Economic Journal*, Vol. 72, p. 79, 1962.

[5] BRUNO, M., *Construction of the Preliminary Input-Output Model*, Bank of Israel, 1959 (mimeo.).

[6] CHENERY, H. B., BRUNO, M. and SUSSMAN, Z., 'Alternatives for Development Policy in Israel,' Bank of Israel, 1959 (mimeo.).

[7] BRUNO, M., *Interdependence, Resource Use and Structural Change in Israel*, Special Studies No. 2, Bank of Israel, Jerusalem, 1962.

[8] BANK OF ISRAEL, *Annual Report, 1960*, Jerusalem, 1961.

[9] GAATHON, A. L., *Capital Stock, Employment and Output in Israel, 1950–9*, Special Studies No. 1, Bank of Israel, Jerusalem, 1961.

[10] LEONTIEF, W., 'Factor Proportions and the Structure of American Trade,' *Review of Economics and Statistics*, 1956, p. 386.

COMMENTS ON PAPERS BY MR BRUNO AND MR ELEISH

by A. GHOSH

There is some difference of opinion as to the use of input-output techniques for forecasting. But there is general agreement that, as an extension on a sectoral level of a double-entry type of national accounts, input-output approach is of great use in giving a comprehensive and consistent view of the economy in all its details, of the type needed for policy purposes.

The second point of broad agreement is that, for mobilization of resources for a particular objective, input-output technique gives an approximate but useful preliminary blue-print which may be used as a tool of planning.

The papers from both Israel and Egypt confirm these points rather well. I am not sure whether the results of the experiment in prediction carried out in Israel will be generally acceptable; but even in a country where the economic structure is undergoing rapid change, as in Israel or Egypt, the use of input-output models to study alternative strategies of planning is clearly brought out.

The degree of interdependence demonstrated for an underdeveloped economy seems to me to be generally a function of the classification system, except in a very primitive economy where little actual exchange takes place. (But even there technical interdependence between commodities rather than between establishments exists.)

In the projection exercise tried out in Israel the sectors where intermediate product is important (such as mining, chemicals, non-metallic minerals, or base metals) come out rather well as regards forecasts of three years growth. However, not much confidence can be placed on a comparison of these rates as year-to-year variation seems to be very high; in mining, for instance, the actual annual growth rate during 1958–60 was 20·0 per cent, against a forecast of 21·7 per cent, but the actual rate in 1959–60 was only 7·7 per cent. By and large, however, the experiment gave similar results as one carried out in the United Kingdom [1].

In all the papers the problems associated with imports have been elaborated in detail. It seems to me that in a forecasting model import-coefficients are better left out if rapid changes are taking place. Instead, one may decide on a level of imports exogenously and then study the domestic production that would be required to support a final demand programme. An alternative but less efficient way would be to use import coefficients to find the import requirements of a given level of final demand. In the latter case import coefficients have to be changed taking into account the particular import policy which is being adopted.

Apart from the direct use of the matrix multiplier in projecting changes in the level of outputs resulting from changes in final demand, there are certain structural properties of the economy which the matrix multiplier describes very effectively. Many such descriptions of structural properties based on the multiplier may be formulated, of which the Israel experiment has provided some — e.g. factor uses by categories of final demand.

These analyses of the structural properties of future systems depend, however, on the stability of the coefficient matrix. Even if the matrix is subject to error, such studies certainly give us a lot of information without which the general repercussions of a development plan cannot be grasped.

I shall now present some specific forms of the model which may be of use in these countries.

It has often been seen that industries tend to form groups, or islands of interdependence. In such cases it can be assumed that the amount available for absorption outside the block to which a given industry belongs is dictated by supply consideration. On this view, an industry's production level depends on final demand and on the demand expected within its block and is then raised by an appropriate small percentage to allow for intermediate demand outside that block. Thus if industries r and s are in different blocks, the amount of r's production absorbed by s depends on r's output level rather than on the output level that s desires to achieve. The availability of r's product to all s-type industries is represented in this method by a certain proportion of r's output.

Written in terms of partitioned matrices we have:

$$\frac{X_r}{X_s} = \left(\begin{array}{c|c} a_{rr} & a_{rs} \\ \hline a_{sr} & a_{ss} \end{array}\right)\left(\frac{X_r}{X_s}\right) + \left(\frac{F_r}{F_s}\right)$$

where X_r and X_s are the vectors of total outputs, and F_r and F_s the vectors of final demand in the two groups.

On the partial approach suggested here $a_{rs}X_s$ is replaced by $\hat{a}_rX_r$ and $a_{sr}X_r$ is replaced by $\hat{a}_sX_s$ where $\hat{a}_r$ is a diagonal matrix whose elements express the proportion of the output of one of the r-type industries available for s-type industries and where $\hat{a}_s$ has a corresponding meaning.

On this basis we have:

$$\frac{X_r}{X_s} = \left(\begin{array}{c|c} a_{rr}+\hat{a}_r & 0 \\ \hline 0 & a_{ss}+\hat{a}_s \end{array}\right)\left(\frac{X_r}{X_s}\right) + \left(\frac{F_r}{F_s}\right)$$

Hence $\qquad\qquad X_r = (1 - a_{rr} - \hat{a}_r)^{-1}F_r$

and $\qquad\qquad X_s = (1 - a_{ss} - \hat{a}_s)^{-1}F_s$

This approach should enable us often to isolate sectors for which data are lacking or the coefficients are suspected to be unstable. It also enables us to work on smaller matrices with equal effectiveness.

The idea originally used by Leontief of considering the household sector as an industry, which transforms fixed amounts of final outputs into labour, may seem too rigid; but there is every reason to think that the daily needs of the household for non-durable consumer's goods and services move in a simple relation with gross national income, while demand for durable consumer's goods and asset formation in general are largely determined by long-term factors. We may, therefore, set up the model as stated below.

Let x represent the matrix of intermediate products, x_n the augmented matrix whose last column consists of final user's purchases of non-durable commodities and whose last row consists of factor costs. Then we rewrite the open model of the traditional type by taking away the final user's purchases of non-durable goods from final demand and putting it into the inter-industrial augmented matrix as

$$X_n \cdot i + F_n = X_n$$

where F_n consists of final demand for capital goods by industrial sectors, durable consumer's goods by private and public bodies, and the net balance of trade; and X_n represents the output vector of the augmented matrix, i being the unit vector. We thus have

$$a_n X_n + F_n = X_n$$

or
$$X_n = (1 - a_n)^{-1} F_n$$

where a_n is the augmented matrix including in the last column consumption coefficients for non-durable goods purchased by final users, F_n is the reduced vector of final demand not containing the non-durable goods.

It is suggested that this approach will reduce work on the final demand vector without too much loss of accuracy. It will also bring out the implications of a final demand vector more fully by including the repercussion on final demands of a particular bill of goods.

REFERENCE

[1] Ghosh, A., *Experiments with input-output models*, ch. 4, Cambridge, 1963.

CHAPTER 13

Construction and Use of Input-Output Tables in Latin American Countries

by MANUEL BALBOA

---

1. Introduction

Input-output research in Latin America, promoted by the Economic Commission for Latin America, began in 1954 in Colombia, and by 1961 extended to Argentina, Bolivia, Brazil, Ecuador, Mexico and Peru. Summary particulars of the available tables[1] are given in Table 1.

The tables relate to the whole economy and are consistent with the social accounts of the countries concerned, except that the earlier table for Colombia is limited to the manufacturing sector only, and those for Brazil for some states and they show the inputs of raw materials into manufacturing industries only.[2]

The tables for Argentina, Bolivia, Colombia and Peru have been used by the Economic Commission for Latin America (ECLA) in its country studies and its programming for the region.

The number of producing sectors varies greatly from country to country, depending mainly on the number of manufacturing sectors distinguished, which in its turn depends on the availability of statistics. The classification is not identical. Thus, Argentina distinguishes crop farming from livestock farming, while Colombia (1956) includes forestry with crop farming, fishing with livestock farming, and adds coffee as a third agricultural sector; and one of the Colombian manufacturing sectors is coffee processing. Bolivia distinguishes petroleum from other mining industries, and food from non-food manufacturing. In the twenty-sector table for Peru construction is not included among the producing sectors. The classification of the service sectors also varies: Argentina includes communications with transport but Bolivia does not; Argentina and Colombia take housing as a separate sector but not the other countries.

---

[1] The table for Mexico is unpublished but an account of it was given in [12].
[2] The table for Peru does not estimate the input of 'other sectors'. A summary three-sector table is, however, consistent with the social accounts.

TABLE 1

Input-Output Tables in Latin America

Country	Year	Prepared by	No. of sectors					Final demand sectors	Valuation
			Agr.	Min.	Mfg.	Other	Tot.		
Argentina	1946	Nat. income unit &	2	1	15	5	20	4	} purchasers' price
	1950	ECLA experts					23	4	mixed
	1953	Central Bank			200		200	—	
Bolivia	1958	Nat. Planning Board ECLA/BTAO/FAO	1	2	2	5	10	5	producers' price
Brazil									
Fed. Dis. of Rio	1952								
Minas Gerais	1953								
R. Grande do Sul	1953				} 17				mixed
Pernambuco	1953								
Bahia	1953								
Colombia	1953	ECLA	—	—	16	1	17	4	mixed
	1956	Nat. Dept. of Planning ECLA/BTAO/FAO	3	1	21	10	35	5	producers' price
Ecuador	1955	Nat. Planning Board & ECLA	1	—	1	1	3	3	mixed
Mexico	1950	Bank of Mexico	4	2	19	7	32	6	producers' price
Peru	1955	ECLA	1	1	17	—	19	3	mixed
	1950–1957 (annual)	Bank of Peru	1	1	1	4	7	3	mixed

Note: For a fuller description of the tables, see Argentina [1], [2] and [4] , ; Bolivia [5] and [6]; Brazil [7]; Colombia [8], [9] and [10] Ecuador [11]; Mexico [12]; and Peru [13] and [14].

Final demand in standard input-output tables consists of personal consumption; government consumption; fixed investment; exports; and inventory changes (including residual errors). In the Argentinian table personal and government consumption are taken together, the Peru (1955) table shows exports, consumption and investment, while the Colombia (1953) table shows exports, capital goods, durable consumer goods and non-durable consumer goods.

The valuation of transactions is in some tables at producer's prices, in other tables in purchaser's prices; and there are mixed systems where output is valued at producer's and input at purchaser's prices.

A distinguishing feature of Latin American tables is that in each row domestic and imported goods are shown separately; only in the table for Mexico are imports aggregated in a single row as in the earlier Leontief tables. It is one of the fundamental aims of research to make a thorough analysis of imports because of their special importance in connection with development programmes and balance-of-payments problems.

The next section describes some of the statistical problems arising in Latin America; Section 3 the uses of input-output tables in analysing the economic structure; Section 4 the uses of input-output models for economic programming; and Section 5 particular Latin American problems.

2. *Statistical Problems*

The Latin American tables are usually compiled by column, though that for Mexico was compiled by both column and row, adjustments being made for discrepancies. Among sectors of final demand, it is relatively easy to compile the export column, and the capital formation column is easy inasmuch as a large proportion of capital formation consists of imported goods and of public investment. Consumption and inventory changes are usually residual estimates.

Statistics are best for manufacturing industry; in Argentina, for instance, industrial censuses were taken since 1935. Difficulty arises, however, where small-scale or handicraft industries, which are outside the scope of industrial censuses, are important.

The 1946 industrial census in Argentina supplied a certain amount of information from which input coefficients could be calculated for small establishments, defined as units employing fewer than 5 workers. In Table 2 these coefficients are compared by major economic sectors with those for larger establishments. The figures suggest that the input coefficients for raw materials in small-scale industry are smaller than

R

those for large-scale industry. In some cases the differences may be understated, since in the larger establishments inputs of services and certain goods that are not usually recorded in the industrial statistics are probably relatively greater than in small-scale production. In any case, the relative differences in the table are seldom very big; only in 4 of the 12 sectors do they exceed 10 per cent. For inputs of fuel and electricity, however, the gap is much wider.

TABLE 2

Argentina: Inputs and Value Added in Large and Small-scale Industry, 1946

Sector		Coefficients per mille			
		Raw materials	Fuels and lubricants	Electric energy	Value added
Foodstuffs and beverages	A	620·2	21·3	5·6	352·9
	B	486·3	35·0	7·9	470·8
Clothing	A	578·6	1·3	2·6	417·5
	B	516·2	0·1	1·6	482·1
Wood	A	407·6	5·3	6·2	580·8
	B	456·0	3·8	6·8	533·4
Paper and board	A	504·7	30·8	21·3	443·2
	B	511·2	4·8	4·3	479·8
Printing and publishing	A	366·2	2·0	9·9	621·9
	B	346·3	4·4	7·4	641·9
Chemicals	A	467·3	24·0	9·0	499·7
	B	505·3	13·8	3·3	477·5
Leather	A	587·9	5·0	5·0	402·0
	B	560·3	0·7	1·0	438·1
Stone, glass and pottery	A	260·3	127·5	16·8	595·4
	B	271·6	67·1	4·4	656·9
Metal products, excluding machinery	A	431·8	26·0	11·4	530·8
	B	367·2	16·1	5·6	611·1
Vehicles and machinery (non-electrical)	A	367·7	18·1	9·5	604·6
	B	219·9	22·3	5·9	751·9
Electrical machinery and appliances	A	396·2	10·7	11·5	581·6
	B	385·6	3·0	8·5	602·9
Miscellaneous	A	333·0	23·5	22·4	621·0
	B	328·5	26·5	20·3	624·7

Note: A. Establishments employing 5 persons or more.
B. Establishments employing less than 5 persons.

The 1950 industrial census for Argentina distinguished about 200 trades, giving output and input data. In the initial stages of construction of the input-output table this information was fully used but eventually manufacturing was aggregated in 15 sectors. In Argentina handicraft industries are relatively unimportant, but in Peru a large part of industrial activity is not covered by official statistics. Estimates for small-scale industry in Peru were made with reference to consumption of raw materials or numbers employed. The statistics cover 120,000 persons employed in industry with a gross output of 10 billion soles; 400,000 persons are not covered by statistics with an estimated output of 6 billion soles. There were, however, big differences between sectors: in the tobacco and fuel industries, for instance, all activity was covered by industrial statistics but in the food, furniture, leather and engineering industries only about one-half of the estimated output, and in clothing only 20 per cent.

Estimates of the output of small-scale industry were made in Colombia for 1956. Input-output tables were prepared both including and excluding small-scale activities.

Data for other sectors are generally weak. In agriculture a well-known problem is production for own consumption or for a limited market. Information on private building activity is also poor. Little is known about distributive margins or about stocks.

In Bolivia, for instance, agricultural output was estimated on the basis of area cultivated and average yields, and reproduction and mortality rates for livestock. A statistical analysis was then made for each product. In the transport sector, separate analyses were made for the railways, urban road transport, rural road transport, and air transport, making use of the accounts of railway and air companies and of some road transport companies. Distributive margins on various groups of commodities were determined mainly from an analysis of accounts of enterprises. Fairly full information was available in respect of financial services. For the construction sector, government accounts provided some information but private building was estimated indirectly, for instance from the consumption of building materials.

In general, countries which estimate national income from the output side rather than from the income side appear to have an advantage in introducing input-output research. The input-output table in Bolivia, for instance, served to check the consistency of product and income estimates. On the other hand, in Argentina input-output work led to a revision of national income estimates made by the traditional method. In all countries, even where the number of sectors was small, input-output estimates helped to improve estimates of national product, national income and their components.

3. *The Use of Input-Output Tables in Analysing Economic Structure*[1]

Input-output tables have been used for the analysis of the economic structure of Argentina, Bolivia, Colombia, Mexico and Peru. But the most detailed work has been done in Argentina and this section is confined to that country.

On the basis of the 23-sector table, indices of the sales and total inputs of the producer sectors were determined for each row and column. An experiment in triangulation of the inter-sectoral table was also carried out.

A comparison with similar indices calculated by Chenery and Watanabe [15] for the United States, Italy, Japan and Norway led to the conclusion that for some sectors coefficients of total inputs in relation to the value of production are similar, although cases do exist in which significant differences can be observed; that the total coefficient of intermediate sales in relation to the total flows of goods is virtually identical with the average coefficient for the other countries referred to (0·45 and 0·43), except Norway; that coefficients of total input in relation to the total value of production are, therefore, very similar (0·47 and 0·45); and that an experiment in triangulation showed that 95 per cent of the whole body of transactions was situated below the main diagonal, a proportion resembling that for the above-mentioned countries. It must be borne in mind, however, that these comparisons are of a global and superficial character, since the tables of transactions differ in respect of sectoral classification, the grouping of activities in sectors, and the system of valuation.

Intermediate import component in final demand for domestic goods and services

A valuable use of the input-output model in the study of the structure of the Argentina economy was in analysing the utilization of imports. If the inverse of the Leontief matrix of the domestic input coefficients (23×23) is pre-multiplied by the matrix of the coefficients of the inputs of imported goods (18×23), a new matrix of 18×23 is obtained. The elements in each row in the product-matrix measure the content of intermediate imports per unit of each of the sectors of final demand for each class of imports. Consequently, the sum of the columns of the

---

[1] For further details, see [2].

product-matrix is the total content, direct and indirect, of intermediate imports in each of the 23 sectors of final demand for domestic goods. If from these coefficients there are subtracted those representing direct imports in each sector, the coefficient of the indirect content of intermediate imports is obtained. This procedure brings out the points that for a number of sectors of final demand the indirect content of intermediate imports is relatively large, and may be as much as or greater than the direct content; that exports have a content of 4 per cent in value of intermediate imports; and that the total content of intermediate and final imports is 6 per cent in consumption, 15 per cent in fixed investment, and 4 per cent in exports.

Imports, factor cost and other final demand components

The content of primary resources, in terms of the payments concerned, was determined for each of the sectors of final demand. It was shown that for an average total coefficient of 8 per cent of imports in final demand, there was a marked dispersion for the various types of goods composing it, ranging from 1·5 per cent to 40 per cent per monetary unit of final demand. It is interesting to note that the wages and salaries coefficient was almost the same for consumption as for exports, but was much higher for gross capital formation, which also had a higher import coefficient.

Final destination of sectoral resources

An analysis was made of the final destination of resources by means of the content of the gross sectoral product and of imports in final demand, using an aggregated 12-sector matrix. This showed that 80 per cent of the product of the agricultural sector is used for consumption, and 20 per cent for exports; 60 per cent of the industrial product is used for consumption, 35 per cent for capital formation and 5 per cent for exports; for services, 80 per cent of the product is used for consumption, 13 per cent for capital formation and 7 per cent for exports.

In round figures, 55 per cent of total imports are absorbed by consumption, despite the low unit coefficient of imports in this aggregate; 40 per cent are for capital formation, and barely 5 per cent for exports.

A rough comparison of these results with those obtained from similar studies for European countries gives a quantitative idea of the differences in the productive structure of the Argentine economy. Whereas Argentine exports absorb 20 per cent of the agricultural product, the percentage is much lower for Western Germany, France, Italy and the United Kingdom. On the other hand, the exports of Norway, Sweden and the Netherlands contain a larger percentage of primary products than those of Argentina. A comparison with Australia shows that in Argentina there is a larger service component in exports and a smaller import component.

Response of the various economic sectors and of imports to changes in final demand

A calculation was made to determine the changes in production that take place in each of the 23 producing sectors and in imported intermediate and final goods as the result of changes in each of the final demand components. In making this analysis, account was taken of the differences in consumption elasticities of the goods included.

The conclusions reached included one of particular interest for the study of the Argentine economy: an increase of 10 per cent in consumption would increase total imports by 6 per cent, whereas a change of the same amount in investment, an item with a higher import content, would cause an increase of only 4 per cent, and a 10 per cent increase in exports would lead to an increase of only 0·4 per cent in imports. Lastly, an increase of 10 per cent in total final demand would lead to an increase of 11 per cent in imports.

It should be remembered that these calculations exclude the additional requirements of productive capacity in each sector, and that it was assumed that demand for imported goods for personal consumption would be maintained at the same proportion of total consumption as for the period 1950–5.

4. The use of input-output models in economic programming[1]

The tables for Argentina, Bolivia, Colombia (1953), Ecuador, Peru and Mexico were transformed into input-output models and applied to determine future production and import requirements for intermediate use. The projections were for the following years:

	Base year	Projection for
Argentina	1950	1962, 1967
Bolivia	1958	1966, 1971
Colombia	1953	1960
Ecuador	1955	1965
Mexico	1950–5	1965
Peru	1955	1965

[1] In addition to references given in Table 1, see also [3].

In the Bolivian table for 1958 the sector classification was designed partly to illustrate the implications of the country's development programme: petroleum, energy and transport are separate sectors.

The characteristics of ECLA's projections for Argentina, Colombia and Peru are described in the paragraphs below. In general, the starting point of the method used consists of one or more alternative projections of the national product, imports, and components of final demand. The model is used to determine the sectoral production and import implications of these projections. Final demand is determined separately and the model provides information on those imports only which are used in the producer sectors.

Final demand is projected for each main component. Personal consumption is estimated by means of coefficients of elasticity deduced from statistical analysis for each country, in some cases supplemented by drawing on the experience of similar economies. Government consumption is estimated by industry, usually according to the proportion recorded for the base year. Gross investment is determined taking account of output-capital ratios, the aims of public investment, estimates of replacement needs and some other factors. Sectoral analysis of investment by industry presents no great problem in view of the high degree of aggregation of the model, and is partly determined by the distribution for the base year. Exports are projected by groups of items in accordance with studies of the world market and demand in the purchasing countries.

Final demand is classified according to domestic or foreign origin, and two sets of projections are made, respectively without and with import substitution. The projections without import substitution assume that there is no change in the input coefficients or in the ratio of domestic to imported goods for particular categories of final demand. The model thus provides information on the additional imports needed on the given hypothesis.

The alternative projections determine production needs assuming that given imports for intermediate or final destination are replaced by domestic production, according to either preliminary judgments or specific studies. This type of projection is usually made by various methods of successive approximations. One method is to modify the coefficients of inputs of domestic goods for the base year by allowing for substitutions, thus establishing a new model of coefficients which is applied to final demand. A second method is to apply the model for the base year to the total of imports to be substituted so as to determine the additional resources required. A third method is to apply the model of coefficients of total inputs to final demand, deducing the projections of imports that would result from effecting given substitutions.

It is usual when making such projections to introduce modifications of a structural nature into the matrix of input coefficients to take account of changes that the inputs might be expected to undergo as a result of new activities or alterations in production processes. In practice these modifications have been confined to the most obvious cases, or to those that were known at the time the model was applied.

Argentina

The input-output model was used in programming analyses for the purpose of determining the targets to be set for national production and intermediate imports if certain specific projections of final demand up to 1962 and 1967 were to be met.

The final demand aggregates were projected by industry. Two types of projection were made: without import substitution, and with import substitution and other structural changes.

The first step was to determine production levels for 23 sectors, and intermediate import requirements for categories of goods broken down by 18 sectors of origin and 23 sectors of intermediate destination. This was done by inverting the matrix of domestically-produced input coefficients.

Secondly, changes were made in these coefficients and in the supply of domestically-produced finished goods for final demand, with a view to determining the implications of alternative import substitution programmes. During the same stage, structural modifications were made in the coefficients for the agricultural sector after new inputs had been introduced into it. A new set of production and import projections was thus obtained at an aggregation level of 12 sectors.

The input-output model was applied to the studies of the Argentine economy before the investigations of sectoral and specific activities were completed. As a result, it was difficult to foresee the other structural changes that were liable to be produced by the import substitution programmes.

The projections at the aggregation levels of 23 and 12 sectors were insufficient for the requirements of a programming analysis of the Argentine economy. These sectors include key activities which remain undifferentiated, such as the capital goods, chemicals, metallurgical and paper industries, transport and energy. The programming analysis was extended by projections and specific studies of most of the economic sectors (agriculture, industry, energy, transport). Those relating to import substitution levels were particularly detailed.

In some cases, the projections of the 23 and 12 sector models formed a base or point of reference for further progress in these studies, while in others the projections of production and the relevant inputs were carried out by independent methods. In short, the various studies gave rise to a group of production and import projections, which partly constituted a disaggregation of the projections of the 23 and 12 sectors, and partly consisted of estimates that were independent of the input-output model.

An attempt was made to check the consistency of the highly aggregated projections of the 12 sectors and the more detailed projections of the individual studies. In the case of the agricultural sector they were easy to compare, and the sum of the projections by products was found to be surprisingly close to the results of the global projections in the model. In others, the comparison was merely an approximate one owing to the high aggregation level of the model. There were cases, however, in which it was easily demonstrable that the import substitution programme implied a new input structure, for instance in the metallurgical industries.

TABLE 3

Argentina: Relation between Projections Excluding and Allowing for Import Substitution, 1962

Origin of goods and services	Percentage difference	
	Total	Intermediate goods
I. *Domestic production*	5	10
1. Agriculture	—	1
2. Quarries and mines	50	52
3. Foodstuffs, beverages and tobacco	—	2
4. Textiles, clothing and leather	—	1
5. Timber and building materials	7	9
6. Paper and printing	12	17
7. Chemicals and rubber	11	31
8. Fuel, electricity and water	10	15
9. Metals and metal products	31	56
10. Vehicles and machinery	19	5
11. Construction	—	—
12. Miscellaneous services	2	5
II. *Imports*	- 31	
Intermediate goods	- 32	
Capital goods	- 36	
Consumer goods	—	

Some idea of the scale and nature of the new activities that might originate from an import substitution programme is given by the estimates for the expansion of production and decline of imports that may be obtained from a comparison of the two types of projections, as shown in Table 3. It was found that the import substitution programme involves an increase of only 5 per cent in total production up to 1962, whereas total imports would drop 30 per cent below their theoretical level. The effects of substitution are particularly strong in mining, metal products, vehicles and machinery.

Colombia

The input-output analysis was mainly used in projecting industrial production and intermediate import requirements in 1960 on the basis of various economic development hypotheses expressed in terms of the corresponding final demand projections.

Two kinds of projections were prepared: excluding and permitting import substitution. The magnitudes of the additional changes in sectoral production that would result from programmes aiming at the

TABLE 4

Colombia: Relation between Projections of Intermediate Production, Excluding and Allowing for Import Substitution, Hypothesis B, 1960

Origin of goods and services	Percentage difference
I. *Intermediate domestic production*	17
1. Non-manufacturing sectors	6
2. Foodstuffs	8
3. Beverages	18
4. Tobacco and tobacco products	—
5. Textiles	18
6. Footwear and clothing	25
7. Wood and cork	11
8. Wooden furniture	—
9. Pulp and paper	163
10. Printing, etc.	10
11. Leather and leather goods	6
12. Rubber	78
13. Chemicals	88
14. Petroleum derivatives and coal	1018
15. Cement, pottery, glass, etc.	50
16. Metals and engineering	214
17. Other industries	78
II. *Intermediate imports*	– 64

substitution of domestically-produced for imported intermediate goods are shown in Table 4.

The projection of output excluding import substitution was formulated by inverting the matrix of coefficients of domestically-produced inputs. In their turn, the additional domestic production requirements entailed by specific substitution programmes were calculated by means of the same model.

It was stressed by ECLA that the model was not sufficiently accurate, since it was observed that when the second set of projections was formulated, sectors which had nothing to do with the substitution postulated appeared as having undergone modification. Attention was then drawn to the need to work with models comprising a larger number of sectors and breaking down activities by more homogeneous groups.

Peru

An input-output model was constructed on the basis of the coefficients for inputs of domestic goods in relation to production values. Inputs in the agricultural sector were modified in such a way as to make allowances for structural changes and import substitution.

The model was applied to projections of final demand up to 1965, formulated in accordance with specific hypotheses on the growth of income and exports and with technical studies on the probable development of domestic industry to supply the necessary goods for satisfying final demand.

Production and import requirements were established under the terms of the hypotheses including and excluding import substitution. The import substitution programmes, in their general technical and economic aspects, were analysed separately, according to specific studies of each activity. Some idea of the possible implications of the new activities or additional production required by the import substitution programme for intermediate goods in relation to 1965 production levels may be obtained from Table 5, according to which the chemicals, metallurgical, metal-transforming, paper and beverages industries would be considerably affected by substitution.

The application of the inter-sectoral model was effected at three levels: first, at a very high aggregation level; second, in relation to the table of 20 sectors, including import substitution programmes; and third, in relation to specific activities and even products.

The analysis of the specific activities was made to agree as far as possible with the 20-sector model. The input-output technique was used to show the interrelations between each activity, and a link was maintained with the model for the purpose of the successive comparisons required in the course of the programming analysis.

TABLE 5

Peru: Relation between Projections of Intermediate Production, Excluding and Allowing for Import Substitution, 1965

Origin of goods and services	Percentage difference
I. *Intermediate domestic production*	6
Agriculture	1
Extractive industries	1
Foodstuffs	1
Beverages	37
Textiles	1
Footwear and clothing	8
Timber	1
Furniture, etc.	—
Paper	28
Printing, publishing, etc.	8
Leather	—
Rubber	2
Chemicals	85
Petroleum and coal derivatives	3
Cement, glass, china and earthenware, etc.	12
Basic metal industries	25
Engineering	61
Other industries	4
Services	5
II. *Intermediate imports*	− 20

5. *Some problems in applying the models in Latin America*

The hypothesis implied in an input-output model is that each economic sector, either in isolation or as a part of the whole economy, provides a group of goods from a given structure of inputs. It is current practice to make the additional hypothesis that inputs are proportionate to the levels of production. As a result of aggregation, the input coefficients are weighted averages of the separate coefficients for each of the goods included in the sector.

As regards countries with a low level of income or in the process of development, it is maintained that these hypotheses are more limiting for various reasons, including the predominance of an agricultural sector with a heterogeneous structure whose input coefficients may be subject to sharp change; the strong influence of external factors, which affect levels of production and lead to changes in input coefficients; the permanent or temporary substitution of domestic products for imports; the existence of an active process of technological transformation and the addition of new activities; the existence of smaller inter-sectoral transactions in the producer sectors.

The brief experience of Latin American countries provides some basis for commenting on the above points, even if the experience is too limited to permit definitive observations to be made.

Agricultural activities in the Latin American tables are generally grouped together in one or two broad sectors. The input coefficients here do not represent a particular period, since in the absence of adequate statistics they are estimated on the basis of normal conditions. Usually those branches of production that depend essentially on external demand are kept separate (e.g. coffee in the Colombian table, petroleum and mining in the Bolivian table). In the models for Argentina and Peru the input coefficients in the agricultural sector were adjusted for substitutions and technological change.

Quite apart from the sectoral projections of the model, all the country programming studies include an analysis of specific activities in the commodity production, energy and transport sectors, with special attention to substitution industries. The aim of this analysis is to ensure consistency between particular activities and products and the higher level of aggregation involved in the input-output model. This makes it possible, for example, to give due weight to the level of factor utilization in particular activities.

One of the primary aims of input-output analysis in Latin America is to determine import requirements, with a view to assessing specific development possibilities in the light of domestic conditions for industrial development and balance of payments prospects. Consequently, import inputs are analysed in the matrix for all sectors of origin and destination and at the level of activities and products.

It is true, of course, that in the present models the input coefficients for a particular period may be affected by import substitutions of a non-permanent nature; this is often the case in the construction industry, where certain supplies are greatly affected by changes in relative prices and import controls.

As indicated, the input-output model is used mainly as an instrument for effecting a certain breakdown of macroeconomic projections. The study is continued within the framework of these sectoral projections, at the level of specific activities and of products. The end result is a set of production and import goals and factor requirements which, if put together in a table comparable with that for the base year, will indicate the structural changes deriving from the development process.

With respect to intermediate transactions, it should be noted that the Argentine table shows that these constituted over 40 per cent of the total flow of goods; the proportion would be considerably less in Bolivia, and is currently estimated as 24 per cent. In Bolivia *per capita* income is approximately one-seventh of that in Argentina; however, an accelerated rate of economic development in Bolivia may raise this proportion within the next ten years from 24 per cent to something approaching 30 per cent. In Mexico and India, where *per capita* income is lower than in Argentina, the coefficient appears to be in the neighbourhood of 30 per cent.

Furthermore, as regards productive structures it is interesting to note that a preliminary comparison has been made of the input coefficients for the large-scale sectors of manufacturing industry in Peru (that is, excluding small establishments and artisan activity) with those of the same activities in Argentina. The result seems to indicate a certain similarity in the two structures at a given level of aggregation.[1]

In countries with a low income level, there is the problem of the influence that may be exerted on the model by the different structures and degrees of development of large-scale manufacturing industry, on the one hand, and of small-scale industry and handicrafts, on the other. During the process of development, the former of course expands more than the latter, and in the long run at its expense.

The application of the model in the alternative 'allowing for import substitution' adds to the problems arising from the conventional hypotheses of the model other problems that are particularly important in countries in process of development. From the practical standpoint these problems may be summed up as the changes that have to be introduced into the model, either in the average coefficients or through the inclusion of new activities in the light of changes entailed by the substitution process. This is a matter of practical, as well as theoretical, concern, as substitutions are usually of great relative significance and often relate to one part of the activities of the sector. Experience in Colombia and Argentina demonstrated that the model for the base year operated with respect to certain sectors or particular applications with significant errors in the case of import substitution. In some cases this was due to the high level of aggregation, in others to a change in the structure of inputs. The question of determining import costs and inputs is closely bound up with this problem.

---

[1] For further details, see [3].

In the construction of the tables, the aggregation of activities by sectors has depended mainly upon the method of presentation and classification of the statistical data available. There has been no opportunity for specific studies of aggregation criteria. Every attempt has been made to establish the largest possible number of manufacturing sectors, but the statistics available, as well as the time and resources that could be devoted to these ends, have constituted limiting factors. In some countries, no doubt, the number of sectors in the input-output tables might be increased and some research on aggregation criteria conducted.

To sum up, the shortage of statistical data has sometimes limited the possibilities of extending the tables to the economy as a whole or to a larger number of sectors. There is evidence that countries estimating their national accounts aggregates on the basis of the determination of production and inputs can extend the research to the compilation of inter-sectoral tables, if they have at their disposal industrial statistics registering input figures by products. The tables, even at a high level of aggregation and for countries where few statistics are available, have made it possible to check the estimates of the main economic aggregates in the national accounts.

The distinguishing feature of input-output analysis in the Latin American countries is the detailed treatment accorded to imports. The models have been used to determine production and import requirements by sector, in relation to specific development targets expressed in terms of projections of final demand. These sectoral projections have been used during preliminary phases of the work to evaluate the prospects of attaining specific development objectives, and at a later stage of the analysis have constituted the frame of reference or the basis ensuring consistency for a set of development targets at the level of activities and products.

REFERENCES

ARGENTINA

[1] Naciones Unidas, Comisión Económica para América Latina, *Análisis y proyecciones del desarrollo económico: V. El desarrollo económico de la Argentina*, 1959.

[2] BALBOA, M., 'Some Applications of the Input-Output Model to the Argentine Economy', *Economic Bulletin for Latin America*, ECLA, Vol. V, No. 1, 1960.

[3] BALBOA, M., *Comparación de la estructura intersectorial de la producción de Argentina y de Perú*. Paper presented at the Regional Conference of the International Association for Research in Income and Wealth, Rio de Janeiro, 1959.

[4] Banco Central de la República Argentina, *Transacciones de bienes intermedios del sector manufacturero argentino, año 1953*, Suplemento del Boletín Estadístico No. 9, septiembre 1961.

BOLIVIA

[5] República de Bolivia, *Desarrollo Económico y Social*, 1962–71, 1961.
[6] Junta Nacional de Planeamiento de Bolivia, *Revista de Planeamiento*, marzo 1961.

BRASIL

[7] ANDRADE, L. C. DE, 'Relaçoes Interindustriaes,' *Revista Brasileira de Economia*, Vol. VI, 1960, Nos. 1 and 2, pag. 18–29.

COLOMBIA

[8] United Nations, Economic Commission for Latin America, *Analyses and projections of economic development: II. The economic development of Colombia*, 1957.
[9] VUSKOVIĆ, P., 'The input-output model', *Economic Bulletin for Latin America*, ECLA, Vol. 1, No. 2, 1951.
[10] Departmento de Planeación y Servicios Técnicos, Colombia, *Cuadro de insumo-producto, 1956*. (To be published).

ECUADOR

[11] Junta Nacional de Planificación y Coordinación Económica, *Bases y directivas para programar el desarrollo económico de Ecuador, 1958*.

MEXICO

[12] EKKER, M. H., *Algunas experiencias con la utilización de la disciplina insumo-producto en la proyección económica*. Paper presented at the Regional Conference of the International Association for Research in Income and Wealth, Rio de Janeiro, 1959.

PERU

[13] United Nations, Economic Commission for Latin America, *Analyses and Projections of Economic Development: VI. The Industrial Development of Peru*, 1959.
[14] Banco Central de Reserva del Perú, *Renta Nacional del Perú* (annual from 1957).

OTHER REFERENCES

[15] CHENERY, H. B. and WATANABE, I., *International Comparisons of the Structure of Production*, Econometrica, Vol. 26, 1958, p. 598.

PART IV

Problems of Estimation and Statistics

CHAPTER 14

The Labour Coefficient and the Size of Establishment in Two Japanese Industries[1]

by RYUTARO KOMIYA and TADAO UCHIDA

1. Introduction

In the ordinary application of input-output technique a sector is defined to consist of all establishments which belong to an industry. The rationale of this definition is that the establishments included in the same industry are supposed to produce similar outputs and hence have similar input coefficients.

It is generally observed, however, that rarely does an establishment with five employees produce the same products, or have the same input structure, as an establishment with over a thousand employees, even when they are classified in the same three- or four-digit industry. There seems to exist, particularly in Japan, a considerable difference in input coefficients between large- and small-scale establishments in an industry because of what is called the 'dual structure' of the Japanese economy. The term 'dual structure' refers to the fact that methods of production, capital intensity, managerial organization, working conditions, wage rates and so on, differ very much between firms or plants of different size. Large-scale firms or plants use modern techniques of production and hence are more productive and can pay higher wage-rates than small-scale ones. For example, in 1958 the average annual wage and salary per employee paid by manufacturing establishments with 5 to 29 employees was only 43·6 per cent and by establishments with 30 to 99 employees only 54·7 per cent of that paid by establishments with over 500 employees. For the two industries studied below (textiles and non-electric machinery) details are given in Table 1.[2]

---

[1] The study was undertaken as a part of a research programme supported by the Tokyo Centre for Economic Research. The authors wish to acknowledge the coopera-tion of the Research and Statistics Division, Ministry of International Trade and Industry, in regard to the use of the Census of Manufactures I.B.M. cards, and Mr Kei Mori, of Keio University, who directed the machine computation.

[2] In the postwar years, the wage-differentials had widened year by year until 1958. It seems that the trend has recently been reversed owing primarily to the labour shortage in some of the low-wage sectors.

These wage differentials might be considered as a measure of the extent to which technological and institutional conditions differ between large- and small-scale establishments. Why there exist such vast differences in wage-rates and in technological and institutional conditions, is an interesting as well as a difficult question. However, we will not be concerned with such a question in this paper which is a descriptive rather than an analytical one. Whatever the explanation may be, if there exists a large technological difference among establishments of different size, in some applications of input-output technique they must be classified not only according to product but also according to size.

TABLE 1

*Average Annual Wages and Salaries in Cash per Worker
by Size Classes, 1958*

(In percentages of Wages and Salaries for Establishments with more than
1,000 employees)

Size class	Number of employees per establishment	Textiles (CM 20)	Non-electric machinery (CM 34)
1.	4–9	56·1	51·3
2.	10–19	60·2	55·1
3.	20–29	63·3	58·7
4.	30–49	65·5	61·2
5.	50–99	68·1	65·2
6.	100–199	70·3	72·2
7.	200–299	75·8	78·6
8.	300–499	85·3	92·5
9.	500–999	90·6	94·9
10.	1,000 and over	100·0	100·0

Source: Ministry of International Trade and Industry, *The Census of Manufactures for 1958.*

The purpose of the present study is to examine the pattern of the difference in one input-coefficient, namely the labour coefficient, among establishments within two Japanese manufacturing industries.[1] In other words, we wish to see to what extent establishments in an industry are heterogeneous with respect to the use of labour input. The labour input is singled out because more reliable data on it than on other inputs are available from the Census of Manufactures, and also because it is very often the largest single item in the total cost of production. The two

[1] For an attempt to examine the pattern of the difference in input-output coefficients within an industry, see [1].

industries, Textile Mill Products and Non-electric Machinery (Industries No. 20 and No. 34 in the Census of Manufactures[1] respectively) are chosen, partly because the size-distributions of establishments are more or less balanced in most of the three-digit industries within these two industries, and partly because they are two typical industries within the manufacturing sector characterized by the 'dual structure', namely the existence of large- and small-scale plants producing side by side the same or related products. Two empirical studies for the purpose are reported in Sections 2 and 3 respectively.

2. *The Effects of Industry and Size*

For the first study all establishments included in CM 20 and CM 34 in the Census of Manufactures, some 15,000 and 35,000 respectively, are classified in two ways: by three-digit industry (indicated by subscript i in the following) and by size (indicated by subscript j). Thus each establishment belongs to a particular i-j subgroup. The appendix gives the list of the three-digit industries and the size-classification; Table 6 in the appendix shows the number of establishments included in each i-j subgroup.

Let us write

X_{ijk} for the total value of shipments in 1958 by the kth establishment in the i-j subgroup, and

L_{ijk} for the number of persons, including the owner and members of his family, in the same establishment.

X and L here are to represent 'output' and 'labour input' respectively.

Linear homogeneous labour-output relationships were fitted by the least squares method at four different levels. First, for each i-j subgroup, we fitted

$$L_{ijk} = \alpha_{ij} X_{ijk} + \epsilon^1_{ijk}, \tag{1}$$

where α_{ij} $(i=1, \dots I, ; j=1, \dots , \mathcal{J})$ is the labour coefficient for the i-j subgroup and ϵ^1_{ijk} is the 'true' error for the kth observation in the subgroup. Secondly for each i-group, we fitted

$$L_{ijk} = \alpha_{i.} X_{ijk} + \epsilon^2_{ijk}, \tag{2}$$

and thirdly for each j-group, we fitted

$$L_{ijk} = \alpha_{.j} X_{ijk} + \epsilon^3_{ijk}, \tag{3}$$

---

[1] Indicated in the following as CM 20 and CM 34.

where $\alpha_{i\cdot}$ $(i=1, \ldots, I)$ or $\alpha_{\cdot j}$ $(j=1, \ldots, \mathcal{J})$ is the labour coefficient for the ith industry or for the jth size-class when it is assumed that the same labour coefficient applies to all establishments in the ith industry or in the jth size-class. Finally, a single equation

$$L_{ijk}=\alpha X_{ijk}+\epsilon_{ijk}^4, \tag{4}$$

was fitted to all observations within the two-digit industry under study. These α's are estimated as $(\sum L_{ijk}X_{ijk})/(\sum X_{ijk})^2$ and are naturally different from the usual input coefficients, which are simply $\sum L_{ijk}/\sum X_{ijk}$. ϵ_{ijk} in each case represents an error term corresponding to the regression model in question.

We then tested whether the difference in the estimates for α_{ij}'s (to be written as a_{ij}) is significant or not among size-classes which belong to the same three-digit industry, applying the F-test. In the same way, we also tested the significance of the difference in α_{ij} among industrial groups which belong to the same size-class. Then the difference among $\alpha_{i\cdot}$ or among $\alpha_{\cdot j}$ was tested in a similar way.

Some of the results of the computation and the tests are given in Table 2. Column (1) gives the estimate for $\alpha_{i\cdot}$ (for each three-digit industry) or $\alpha_{\cdot j}$ (for each size-class); the unit is 'number of workers (man-years) per million yen'. Columns (2) and (3) are respectively the correlation coefficient and the sum of squares of unexplained errors (in millions of square man-years) for the regression in question. Column (4) is the of sum of squares of errors when a separate regression line for each i-j subgroup within the three-digit industry or size-class is fitted. Columns (5)–(7) give the data for the F-test[1] to see whether the a_{ij}'s within each industry or each size-class differ significantly.

The results of the computation show that the difference in the labour coefficients among different size-classes is highly significant within each of the 17 three-digit industries. Although the correlation coefficient is fairly high in most cases in Part A of the table, extremely large F-ratios show that there is an important difference between small- and large-scale establishments.

On the other hand, according to Part B of Table 1, a_{ij}'s for the subgroups within the same size-classes are also quite significantly different from each other in most cases. The F-ratio in this case, however, is generally smaller than in Part A. In fact in one case, CM 34–7, the F-ratio is not significant even at the 5 per cent level.[2] Also the correlation

---

[1] $F = \dfrac{(SSE - SSE')}{n_1} \Big/ \dfrac{SSE'}{n_2}.$

[2] Other F-ratios are all significant at 1 per cent level.

coefficients for the size-class regression are considerably lower than those for the industry regression.

TABLE 2

Summary of the Results of the Study Based upon the Census I.B.M. Cards

	a (1)	R^2 (2)	*SSE* (3)	*SSE'* (4)	*F-ratio* (5)	*Degrees of freedom* n_1 (6)	n_2 (7)
A. Regression for Each Industry							
CM 201	0·867	0·91	1·1	1·0	15·9	8	1,087
202	0·425	0·81	38·4	37·6	10·3	9	4,149
203	0·440	0·50	16·5	14·6	235·4	9	16,966
204	0·536	0·73	2·2	1·5	236·9	9	4,455
205	0·224	0·57	12·4	9·1	182·3	9	4,455
206	0·711	0·85	0·7	0·7	81·3	9	525
207	0·960	0·89	0·4	0·3	72·5	9	918
209	0·390	0·64	1·2	1·2	10·0	7	2,251
341	0·337	0·74	6·0	4·5	45·0	9	1,280
342	0·587	0·82	1·1	0·8	39·1	9	1,035
343	0·456	0·89	1·7	1·4	16·0	9	767
344	0·418	0·73	5·9	3·3	188·3	9	2,209
345	0·721	0·92	1·6	1·5	17·5	9	1,951
346	0·450	0·90	1·4	1·1	81·9	9	2,572
347	0·334	0·76	11·9	11·0	23·6	9	2,660
348	0·408	0·89	3·9	3·2	35·3	9	1,285
349	0·584	0·82	4·6	4·4	6·9	9	1,721
B. Regression for Each Size-Class							
CM 20–1	0·636	0·33	0·4	0·4	98·9	7	14,626
20–2	0·432	0·41	1·2	1·2	94·5	7	10,284
20–3	0·438	0·49	1·3	1·1	73·4	7	3,848
20–4	0·395	0·51	2·3	2·0	58·7	7	2,786
20–5	0·392	0·54	4·4	3·9	31·5	7	1,748
20–6	0·489	0·68	5·9	5·0	20·8	7	778
20–7	0·494	0·74	5·6	4·6	9·5	7	285
20–8	0·472	0·78	8·4	7·2	5·3	7	218
20–9	0·413	0·83	22·4	15·5	13·2	6	175
20–10	0·348	0·73	34·0	25·2	4·2	5	59
34–1	1·143	0·61	0·1	0·1	24·9	8	5,387
34–2	0·872	0·62	0·4	0·3	62·3	8	4,699
34–3	0·815	0·65	0·4	0·4	19·1	8	1,987
34–4	0·659	0·57	0·9	0·8	22·1	8	1,605
34–5	0·584	0·67	1·9	1·7	15·8	8	1,057
34–6	0·587	0·75	2·3	2·2	2·6	8	448
34–7	0·446	0·70	2·7	2·3	3·1	8	143
34–8	0·389	0·61	5·1	2·7	8·3	8	76
34–9	0·395	0·78	6·3	4·2	3·1	8	47
34–10	0·394	0·80	25·0	16·5	2·1	8	31

For the industry as a whole, the part of the total variance in L_{ijk} explained by the regression, namely R^2, is given in Table 3.

TABLE 3

The Squared Correlation Coefficient* of Each Regression Model for the Industry as a Whole

	CM 20	CM 34
Regression equation (1), with α_{ij}	$R^2 = 0.780$	$R^2 = 0.838$
Regression equation (2), with α_i.	0.756	0.803
Regression equation (3), with $\alpha_{.j}$	0.713	0.766
Regression equation (4), with α	0.702	0.757

* Not adjusted for the degrees of freedom.

The differences in R^2 between equations (1) and (2), and between (1) and (3), are highly significant. Also, the differences in R^2 between (2) and (4), and between (3) and (4) are both highly significant, indicating that α_i.'s (or $\alpha_{.j}$'s), of which the estimates are given in Table 1, are different from each other.

The difference between regressions (3) and (4), although highly significant (F-ratios are 147·6 and 64·5 for CM 20 and CM 34 respectively), is much smaller than others: in other words, the additional reduction in the sum of squares of errors is relatively small when, instead of fitting a single equation to the whole industry, separate regression lines are fitted for different size-classes. The reduction is much greater when the difference in the labour coefficient among three-digit industries is taken into account, while the size-class differences are ignored. When Columns (3) and (4) of Table 2 are compared, it is seen that the failure of equation (3) to reduce the sum of squares of errors much is largely confined to groups of establishments with more than 300 employees (size-classes 8, 9 and 10).[1]

[1] It may be mentioned here that apparently the assumption of homoscedasticity is not valid for the regression equations (2) and (4), since according to Part B of Table 1 the estimated variance — Column (3) divided by Column (4) — is greater for large establishments than for small establishments. If this is the case, some of the above F-tests concerning equations (2) and (4) would, strictly speaking, not be valid. In cross-section studies, to avoid this kind of heteroscedasticity, the regression of the ratios of the variables in question is frequently preferred to the regression of the variables themselves. See [2].

However, in the present case, this procedure was not followed since in this section we wish to compare between the four regression models the errors in the absolute magnitude rather than in ratio form. For practical purposes of input-output analysis, very often what matters is not the errors in terms of the labour-output ratio but the errors in absolute amount of labour. The F-tests in this circumstance, although not quite valid, still indicate approximately to what extent a_i.'s or $a_{.j}$'s differ from each other.

The ratio regressions will be dealt with in the next section.

3. The Stability of the Labour-Output Ratio

The above results show that a two-digit industry is composed of heterogeneous units of production: the labour coefficient clearly differs between size-classes as well as between three-digit industries. We now wish to examine to what extent the ordinary labour-output ratio — not the regression coefficient considered above — differs between size-groups as well as between industries. We are also interested in the degree of stability over time of the labour coefficient since the Japanese economy in recent years was characterized by a very rapid economic growth and technological change.

For this purpose we set up an experimental design type, analysis of variance model. From the Census of Manufactures tabulation for each of the four years, 1955–8,[1] the labour coefficient Y_{ij} for each i-j sub-group is computed as

$$Y_{ij} = \sum_k L_{ijk} / \sum_k X_{ijk}$$

where L_{ijk} and X_{ijk} are labour input and output respectively, as defined earlier. Since we are dealing with four years, a new subscript $t\,(=1, \ldots, 4)$ is necessary in addition to subscripts i and j used in the preceeding section (see Appendix). Thus, Y_{ijt} is the average labour coefficient of establishments in the ith three-digit industry with size j, in year t, and the basic regression equation for our analysis of variance model is written as:

$$Y_{ijt} = \mu + \alpha_i + \beta_j + \gamma_t + \xi_{ij} + \eta_{it} + \omega_{jt} + \epsilon_{ijt} \qquad (5)$$

where the variables are defined as follows:

μ: the general mean.
α_i: the effect of the ith three-digit industry.
β_j: the effect of the jth size-class.
γ_t: the effect of the tth year.
ξ_{ij}: the interaction effect of the ith industry and the jth size.
η_{it}: the interaction effect of the ith industry and the tth year.
ω_{jt}: the interaction effect of the jth size and the tth year.
ϵ_{ijt}: an error term.

The model, which may be characterized as a three-way factorial

---

[1] These four years are chosen because for earlier years the Census classification is considerably different and also because reliable price deflators are available only since 1955.

experiment model with one observation in each cell, is estimated with the usual statistical technique.[1]

The estimates a_i, b_j, c_t and m for the regression coefficients α_t, β_j, γ_t and μ in equation (5), are entered in Table 4 and the analysis of variance table is shown in Table 5. The result may be summarized as follows.

First, the analysis of variance shows that the difference in the labour coefficient can be explained primarily by the three main effects. The interaction effects are much less significant than the main effects. The industry-time interaction effect for CM 20, that is the differential effect of technological change over time among industries, seems somewhat significant, but in other cases the interaction effects seem unimportant. This is an interesting result. It was found in the previous section that the labour coefficient differs from one i-j subgroup to another, but now the coefficient of each i-j subgroup in a particular year is shown to be explained by three additive terms representing respectively the industry, the size, and the time effects.

Second, the analysis of variance table shows that among the main effects the scale effect is far more significant than the others. Of the total variance (unadjusted for the degrees of freedom) of the labour coefficient among subgroups of establishments, about 57·5 per cent and 62·8 per cent in CM 20 and CM 34 respectively are explained by the

TABLE 4

Estimates of the Regression Coefficients in the Variance Analysis Model

Subscript	CM 20			CM 34		
	a_i	b_j	c_t	a_i	b_j	c_t
1	0·136	0·717	0·116	0·123	1·104	0·048
2	−0·194	0·346	0·008	−0·045	0·629	−0·098
3	−0·081	0·146	−0·034	0·016	0·334	−0·075
4	−0·127	0·019	−0·090	0·145	0·094	0·125
5	0·063	−0·101		0·144	−0·128	
6	0·057	−0·134		−0·057	−0·317	
7	0·341	−0·226		−0·229	−0·265	
8	−0·196	−0·248		−0·191	−0·382	
9		−0·256		0·095	−0·541	
10		−0·263			−0·529	
	$m=0{\cdot}939$			$m=1{\cdot}314$		

[1] An iterative computational device was used to fill the cells where the observation is missing.

TABLE 5

Analysis of Variance

	Sum of Squares	Degrees of Freedom	Mean Square	F-ratio
CM 20				
I (industry) effect	962	7	137·4	135·46
J (size) effect	2,978	9	330·9	326·34
T (time) effect	182	3	60·6	59·74
IJ interaction	812	63	12·9	12·71
IT interaction	61	21	2·9	2·89
JT interaction	38	27	1·4	1·40
errors	150	148	1·0	
Total	5,183	278		
CM 34				
I (industry) effect	640	8	80·1	5·97
J (size) effect	9,505	9	1,056·1	78·79
T (time) effect	299	3	99·6	7·43
IJ interaction	1,418	72	19·7	1·47
IT interaction	311	24	13·0	1·15
JT interaction	416	27	15·4	0·97
errors	2,547	190	13·4	
Total	15,136	333		

difference in their sizes.[1] Indeed, the difference in the labour coefficient differs quite considerably between small- and large-scale establishments. Adding the values of b_1 and b_{10} to the value of m, on the average the labour coefficient of the smallest size-group is seen to be about 2·45 times in CM 20 and 3·08 times in CM 34 greater than that of the largest size-group.[2]

[1] This result is not directly comparable with the earlier result that the values for R^2 for the regression equations (3) in the preceeding section differ only a little from the values for equation (4) (see Table 3) because the total variance to be explained is entirely different between the two sections. In the preceeding section the amount of the labour input of individual establishments was the dependent variable, whereas in the present section the labour input coefficient of each subgroup of establishments is being analysed.

[2] The differentials in the labour coefficient estimated in this way are considerably larger than the ones computed in Section 2 above (see Part B of Table 2). In fact, the values of the regression coefficients a's estimated in Section 2 are generally much smaller than the usual labour-input ratios, and this is particularly so for smaller establishments for which the labour-output coefficient is from 1·5 to 2·5 times as large as the regression coefficient.

Third, the change in the labour coefficient from year to year is also considerable. For CM 20, the labour coefficient declined from 1·05 to 0·85 worker per million yen in three years: a change of 24 per cent. This is a sort of a pure average time shift for the industry as a whole, in the sense that the effects of the changes in the product-mix and size-mix have been eliminated. On the other hand, for CM 34 the change over time is not systematic. The industry's average labour coefficient declined from 1·36 in 1955 to 1·12 in 1956, but then increased slightly to 1·24 in 1957 and jumped to 1·44 in 1958. This could perhaps be explained by a wide cyclical fluctuation in this industry during the period. 1955–6 were years of a sustained investment upsurge in the Japanese economy, and the machinery industries experienced an unprecedented boom until mid-1957. The depression which followed the worsening of the balance of payments and monetary tightening in May 1957 hit the machinery industries more than any other industry. Since the Census labour input data used in this study are not adjusted for changes in working hours, and also since Japanese firms do not generally adjust the volume of employment to the volume of production readily, the statistics tend to give a lower labour coefficient during a boom and a higher one in a depression.

4. *Conclusion*

Many factors affect the input coefficients of individual establishments or a group of establishments. In this paper we have examined statistically the effects on the labour coefficient of three factors — that of the product (that is, of the three digit industry to which the establishment belongs), that of size, and that of time. Our results show that the size of the establishment is one of the most important factors which cause the difference in the labour coefficient among establishments: the coefficient for smaller establishment is markedly larger than the one for larger establishment. This suggests that, as far as the Japanese economy is concerned, there is a need to define the sectors of input-output analysis not only on the basis of major products but also on that of the size of individual units of production, particularly in those applications of input-output technique which deal with employment and income generation.

REFERENCES

[1] PHILLIPS, A., 'The Variation of Technical Coefficients in the Antifriction Bearing Industry,' *Econometrica*, Vol. 23, p. 432, 1955.

[2] KUH, E. and MEYER, J., 'Correlation and Regression Estimates When the Data are Ratios,' *Econometrica*, Vol. 23, 1955, p. 400.

APPENDIX

The Census Industry and Size Classifications Used in the Present Study

(i) Industry Classification

CM 20 Textile Mill Products (Except Apparel and Other Finished Products Made from Fabrics)

CM 201	Silk Reeling
CM 202	Yarn and Thread
CM 203	Woven Fabric
CM 204	Knitting
CM 205	Dyeing and Finishing Textiles
CM 206	Ropes and Nets
CM 207	Miscellaneous Textile Goods
CM 209	Miscellaneous Textiles

CM 34 Machinery (Except Electrical)

CM 341 Boilers, Engines and Turbines

CM 342 Agricultural Machinery and Equipment (Except Agricultural Hand Tools)

CM 343 Construction and Mining Machinery and Equipment (Including Construction, Agriculture, and Transportation Tractors)

CM 344 Metal Working Machinery

CM 345 Textile Machinery

CM 346 Special Industrial Machinery (Except Metal Working Machinery)

CM 347 General Industrial Machinery and Equipment

CM 348 Office and Store Machines and Devices and Service-Industry and Household Machines

CM 349 Miscellaneous Machinery and Parts

(ii) Size Classification

Size-Class	Number of Persons Engaged
1	4–9
2	10–19
3	20–29
4	30–49
5	50–99
6	100–199
7	200–299
8	300–499
9	500–999
10	1,000 and over

TABLE 6

The Number of Establishments in the Census of Manufactures for 1958

CM 20

Size-Class	201	202	203	204	205	206	207	209	Total
1	175	2,063	7,354	1,776	1,694	191	459	1,002	14,714
2	346	835	5,095	1,550	1,379	147	265	677	10,294
3	176	300	1,874	541	564	73	88	245	3,861
4	138	254	1,389	334	412	49	60	177	2,813
5	61	217	879	187	227	39	34	117	1,761
6	92	139	298	53	120	22	15	48	787
7	77	70	63	15	49	10	4	5	293
8	30	97	45	6	34	4	2	8	226
9	3	128	16	5	22	4	4	—	182
10	—	59	1	1	2	1	1	—	65
Total	1,098	4,162	17,014	4,468	4,503	540	932	2,279	34,956

CM 34

Size-Class	341	342	343	344	345	346	347	348	349	Total
1	506	417	233	811	741	936	760	394	664	5,462
2	386	304	250	716	591	827	790	348	503	4,715
3	159	119	115	246	212	363	384	180	224	2,002
4	112	96	85	214	204	242	336	164	166	1,619
5	83	55	53	141	128	161	242	107	104	1,074
6	28	29	27	58	51	58	105	59	43	458
7	7	20	6	17	15	12	37	25	13	152
8	14	8	5	9	14	5	15	7	8	85
9	12	2	3	10	5	2	8	8	6	56
10	6	1	3	7	3	2	9	4	5	40
Total	1,313	1,051	780	2,229	1,964	2,608	2,686	1,296	1,736	15,663

CHAPTER 15

Incremental Flow Coefficients for a Dynamic Input-Output Model with Changing Technology

by ANNE P. CARTER

---

1. *Methods of Approach*

This paper reports some findings of the Harvard Economic Research Project on the treatment of technological change within the context of dynamic input-output analysis. The general theoretical formulation of the problem is the following.[1]

Let us begin with the Leontief dynamic open model

$$(I - A)X(t) - B\dot{X}(t) = Y(t) \tag{1}$$

where X and Y are output and final demand vectors, and A and B are matrices of flow and capital coefficients, respectively. (1) can be approximated by a difference equation[2]

$$(I - A)X(t) - B(X(t) - X(t-1)) = Y(t). \tag{1a}$$

B is operationally defined to represent 'marginal' or 'incremental' coefficients, that is, capital coefficients for techniques currently being introduced, presumably the newest or 'best practice' techniques for each industry.[3] This interpretation of the B matrix is rationalized by the assumption that expansions of capacity are not bound by commitments to older technological patterns, and hence that new capital will reflect the most advantageous techniques available. In the dynamic model with 'fixed technology', however, the A matrix is assumed constant, presumably representing an average of coefficients for all techniques in use in an industry at a given time.

These interpretations of the A and B matrices are clearly asymmetrical. If new techniques are being introduced with investment, these new techniques will presumably be reflected in the average flow coefficients too. The linkage of changes in the flow matrix to investment constitutes

---

[1] See [1], [2], [3], [4], [5].
[2] There are, of course, many possible difference equation formulations which may be said to 'approximate' the differential equation (1), and these have different dynamic properties. (See, for example, [6].)
[3] See, for example, [7].

our key point of departure in introducing technological change into the dynamic input-output model. If we distinguish a matrix, A', of incremental or 'best practice' flow coefficients, and a matrix $A(t-1)$ of average flow coefficients in the previous year, then A, the average flow coefficients at time t, can be replaced by a capacity-weighted average of A' and $A(t-1)$ as follows:

Let $Z_{1j}(t)$ [1] represent the proportion of the total capacity existing at time t, that was installed between $t-1$ and t. Then an input coefficient $a_{ij}(t)$ can be expressed as a capacity-weighted average of the initial value of the input coefficient $a_{ij}(t-1)$ and the 'incremental' input coefficient, a'_{ij}, thus:

$$a_{ij}(t) = a'_{ij}Z_{1j}(t) + a_{ij}(t-1)(1 - Z_{1j}(t)). \qquad (2)$$

$Z_{1j}(t)$ constitutes the link between changes in flow coefficients and growth in the capacity of the system. If a simple accelerator theory of growth is used, then we can write: [2]

$$Z_{1j}(t) = \frac{X_j(t) - X_j(t-1)}{X_j(t)}. \qquad (3)$$

(2) and (3) can be substituted in (1) to give a new system with changing input structure:

$$X_i(t) - \sum_j a'_{ij}X_j(t) - \sum_j b_{ij}(X_j(t) - X_j(t-1))$$
$$= Y_i(t) + \sum_j (a_{ij}(t-1) - a'_{ij})X_j(t-1) \qquad (4)$$

or, in matrix notation,

$$(I - A')X(t) - B(X(t) - X(t-1)) = Y(t) + (A(t-1) - A')X(t-1). \qquad (4a)$$

[1] The subscript 1 in $Z_{1j}(t)$ does not denote a specific value of 1, but is used to distinguish the variable Z_1 from a second variable, Z_2, which is introduced later.

[2] Where available techniques are changing, some replacement of old capacity will be economically warranted. New capacity over and above net industrial expansion can be introduced explicitly through an 'autonomous replacement' factor $C_j(t)$, the proportion of current capacity replaced. Then (3) should be rewritten

$$\hat{Z}_{1j}(t) = \frac{X_j(t) - X_j(t-1)}{X_j(t)} + C_j(t) \qquad (3a)$$

The portion $\hat{Z}_{1j}(t)$ represented by $C_j(t)$ differs from the rest in that old capacity will be retired at the same rate $C_j(t)$ that this portion of new capacity is added. If a^r_{ij} represents an input coefficient characterizing retired capacity, then (2) can be rewritten:

$$a_{ij}(t) = a'_{ij}Z_{1j}(t) + \left(\frac{a_{ij}(t-1) - a^r_{ij}C_j(t)}{(1 - C_j(t))}\right)(1 - Z_{1j}(t)). \qquad (2c)$$

Presumably a^r_{ij} represents technology which is inferior to that characterized by the average, $a_{ij}(t-1)$. However, both a^r_{ij}, the coefficients characterizing scrapped capacities, and $C_j(t)$, the capacities scrapped, are very difficult to estimate with data currently available. As an approximation it is assumed that $a^r_{ij} = a_{ij}(t-1)$, so that (2c) becomes equivalent to (2).

This elaboration of the dynamic input-output model to allow for changes in input structure with new investment brings with it important new problems of empirical implementation. The key parameters governing the operation of the system are now B and A', characterizing the *incremental* rather than the average technologies in each industry. Difficulties in obtaining appropriate incremental capital coefficients have been discussed in detail elsewhere [8]. Essentially parallel problems are involved in the determination of incremental as opposed to average flow coefficients. Average flow coefficients have traditionally been estimated by computing input-output ratios in a single observed input-output flow table. No such straightforward expedient is available for estimating incremental flow or capital coefficients. To determine the coefficients characterizing new technology one can refer, industry by industry, to engineering estimates or to performance records of new establishments. However, such information is not readily available for many sectors. Where some sample information on the technical characteristics of new capacity is available, it is still difficult to ensure that it will be representative of the actual expansions of individual establishments which will take place with the growth of the industry.

Alternatively, one can turn to indirect statistical procedures, inferring what the incremental coefficients must have been in a given period from observed changes in average coefficients with a given volume of new capacity. Under appropriate circumstances these incremental coefficients can be projected for future expansions characterized by new technology. In this second approach we estimate the coefficients by 'running the model in reverse', that is, by treating the ultimate unknowns of the model as given, and the parameters of the model as unknown. Equation (2) supplies the prototype relationship from which a'_{ij} may be estimated. Known values of $a_{ij}(t-1)$, $a_{ij}(t)$ and $Z_{1j}(t)$ for a given base period are substituted into (2) and the equations are solved for the (unknown) parameters of a'_{ij}. Assuming that 'best practice' technology remains reasonably stable, one can then use the estimates of a'_{ij} in the dynamic model (4) to predict values of $X_i(t)$ for periods other than the base period.[1]

---

[1] The estimation of a'_{ij} (i.e., of A') in this way is analogous to the derivation of flow coefficients from the input-output ratios of a given flow table in the static analysis. The same sorts of problems as to the stability and/or representativeness of technical parameters which are raised with respect to the 'fixed coefficients' in the static analysis can be raised with respect to indirectly derived 'incremental coefficients'. Since the dynamic model with changing technology (i.e., (4a), or even (2)) is more complicated than the static model, the generation of implicit coefficients may well be open to more serious question. Considerably more information — a minimum of two flow tables, a set of capital coefficients, and a vector of capital expenditures over the period spanned by the two flow tables — is required for deriving a set of incremental flow coefficients in

T

The remainder of this paper is concerned with exploring and comparing these two approaches to estimating incremental flow coefficients. In this pilot study[1,2] both approaches are applied to labour and electric energy inputs in two industries, *Tin Cans and Other Tinware* (SIC 3411), and *Ball and Roller Bearings* (SIC 3593).

The topics discussed include (1) the use of input coefficients of new plants as estimates of incremental coefficients representing expansions of new and older plants; (2) the derivation of incremental coefficients for expansions of older plants indirectly from cross-section data; and (3) the use of estimates based on new plants and individual expansions of older plants to predict changes in industry-wide coefficients, and comparison of these estimates with estimates of incremental coefficients derived from time series for the industry as a whole.

In all but Sections 6 and 7 of this chapter, incremental or 'best practice' coefficients are evaluated as predictors of changes in the distribution of technical coefficients for individual establishments in each industry. When 'best practice' coefficients are derived indirectly, in Section 4, they are, similarly, inferred from observed changes in the coefficients of individual establishments. Strictly speaking the same relationships and/or parameters will not necessarily be appropriate for predicting changes in the cross section of an industry's coefficients and in time series of coefficients for the industry as a whole. The analysis of changes in the cross section is useful, however, for evaluating the assumption that the same incremental coefficients can be used to represent all expansions of capacity in a given industry at a given time. If the conclusions of Sections 6 and 7 are borne out in other industries, intra-industry cross sections may also provide a much needed supplementary source of data from which to derive incremental industry coefficients for an interindustry dynamic model such as (4).

In Section 2, 'best practice' coefficients are estimated for each industry by averaging performance records of new plants. These parameters are used in Section 3 to predict changes in the input coefficient distributions of the respective industries. In Section 4, indirect estimates of 'best practice' coefficients are made by substituting known values of $Z_{1j}(t)$,

this way. On the other hand the use of engineering data or of records of new plant performance as a basis for estimates of 'best practice' parameters may well prove more satisfactory than the use of such materials in estimating average coefficients since the technical universe to be represented is smaller and more homogeneous.

[1] The present study is part of a broader programme to explore the estimation of incremental labour and electricity coefficients by alternative standardized methods in a large number of manufacturing industries for the period 1951–8.

[2] The author wishes to thank the staff of the Bureau of the Census — in particular Messrs. H. Grieves, M. Conklin, O. O. Gretton and J. Gottsegen — and also Mr Morris Goldman for generous cooperation in making available special tabulations.

$a_{ij}(t)$, and $a_{ij}(t-1)$ for individual plants in relationships resembling (2). In Section 5, these estimated incremental coefficients are compared with those based on new plants. Then the relationships using indirectly derived input coefficients are used to explain changes in the cross section of input coefficients over time, and these predictions are compared with those based on extrapolation and other simple traditional methods. In Section 6, estimates of 'best practice' coefficients based on new plants and those inferred from changes in the cross section are used to predict changes in the total industry coefficients over time. Finally, in Section 7, 'best practice' coefficients are estimated indirectly from given total industry time series of input-output ratios and of $Z_{1j}(t)$. These estimates of 'best practice' coefficients are compared with the estimates based on cross sections. Perhaps surprisingly, estimates of incremental coefficients based on industry time series are found not to differ greatly from those derived from cross-section data.

2. New Plant Performance Records as Estimates of 'Best Practice' Technology

Records of new plant performance provide a direct and straightforward source of data for estimating incremental technical coefficients. In the United States, however, new plants constitute only a very small — almost a negligible — portion of new capacity in most industries; in many industries there have been no new plants built within the past ten years. Hence the information can provide estimates for, at best, a fraction of industries. Even when such information is available, it will not necessarily represent the techniques adopted in expansions of existing establishments. It is therefore important to investigate how well the technical coefficients of new plants represent those of expansions of older establishments in view of the importance of the latter.

The two pilot study industries, Tin Cans and Ball and Roller Bearings, were represented by a fair sample, five and four, respectively, of new plants during the interval studied.[1] Labour and electricity coefficients for each plant were derived by taking input-output ratios beginning two years after the construction of the plant,[2] and averaging them for the two or three subsequent years. Incremental coefficients for the industry were estimated as output-weighted means of the four or five individual

---

[1] This was a major reason for choosing these industries for the pilot study.

[2] In the first two years of a plant's operation, coefficients seemed to exhibit some irregularity as compared with later years. This is probably due to starting-up problems, to the fact that the plant may have operated only a portion of the first year, and to the difficulty of distinguishing labour involved in installation from production workers.

plants' coefficients[1] and are presented in Table 1. Capital coefficients, estimated from the same source, are also presented in the table.

TABLE 1

Incremental Labour, Electricity and Capital Coefficients Based on New Plant Records, Two Industries, 1951–8

Coefficient (per unit of output)*	Tin Cans	Ball and Roller Bearings
Labour	$0.0435 \pm \sqrt{0.0001}$	$0.1302 \pm \sqrt{0.0043}$
Electricity	$0.3345 \pm \sqrt{0.0165}$	$0.9640 \pm \sqrt{0.1142}$
Capital†	0.29	0.3117

* Output is measured in 1951 dollars for Tin Cans and in 1947 dollars for Ball and Roller Bearings, labour in production worker manhours, electricity in thousands of kilowatt-hours, and capital in actual dollar cost of plant.

† Capital coefficient for Tin Cans represents expenditure on equipment only. Care was taken to use this coefficient with corresponding expenditures on equipment only.

3. *Average New Plant Coefficients as Estimates Applicable to Expansions of Older Plants*

The degree to which the average new plant coefficient a^N represents capacity expansion in older plants can be measured in terms of how well it can predict changes in the latter's coefficients following capital

[1] The amount of variation among new plant input-output ratios within industries can be surveyed for those industries represented by two or more new establishments. The table below gives the percentage range of variation for selected input coefficients.

Relative Range of Labour, Electricity and Capital Coefficients for New Plants.*

Coefficient (per unit of output)	Number of industries	Relative range for individual industries†		
		Minimum	Maximum	Average
Labour	55	0.04 (2)	4.29 (6)	0.98
Electricity	54	0.02 (2)	3.60 (2)	1.25
Capital	55	0.08 (2)	3.32 (4)	1.37

* Coefficients for 1957 or 1958, for plants constructed in 1955–6. Figures in brackets refer to number of plants on which calculations are based.

† (Highest coefficient – Lowest coefficient) ÷ Mean coefficient.

expenditures. To test this, we restate (2) as a hypothesis describing individual plant behaviour

$$a_t^i = a^N Z_{1t}^i + a_{t-1}^i (1 - Z_{1t}^i) \qquad (2a)$$

(For convenience, the subscripts i and j are dropped when dealing with a single industry at a time.)

The superscript i denotes an individual plant,

$\qquad\qquad a_t^i$ represents an input coefficient of an individual plant for year t, measured by the ratio of its input of labour (or electricity) in year t to its output in year t,

$\qquad\qquad a_{t-1}^i$ represents the input coefficient for year $t-1$,

and $\qquad\qquad Z_{1t}^i$ represents gross new capacity in year t.

For each plant Z_{1t}^i is measured by $\dfrac{E_{t-1}^i}{O_t^i} \cdot \dfrac{1}{K}$, where E_{t-1}^i measures expenditure on new plant and equipment during year $t-1$, O_t^i measures the plant's output in year t (thus assuming that capital purchased in year $t-1$ becomes effective capacity for the first time in year t) and K is the industry's capital coefficient, an estimate of total capital expenditure requirements per unit increase in capacity.[1]

Using the relevant value of a^N based on new plant experience, we estimate a_t^i, given a_{t-1}^i and Z_{1t}^i.

Superficial evidence suggests that there may be variations in a_t^i, superimposed on those explained in (2a), due to variations in the utilization of capacity. Allowance for this is introduced by adding a term $A_2^i Z_{2t}^i$ to the right side of (2a), where A_2^i is a constant and Z_{2t}^i represents the relative amount of last year's output which is unutilized capacity this year.[2]

Allowance for the partial utilization of older capacity in individual plants can be made by estimating A_2^i by least squares from time series for *individual plants*, given a^i, a_{t-1}^i, a^N, Z_{1t}^i and Z_{2t}^i. The efficiency of a^N as

---

[1] In computations involving individual plants of the Tin Can Industry, a capital coefficient for equipment only and capital expenditures on equipment only are used, on the theory that building construction requirements are subject to much greater variability among plants than equipment requirements. Later experimental computations in Ball and Roller Bearings showed that total capital expenditures did as well as equipment expenditures alone, and total capital expenditures, with a corresponding capital coefficient, are used in Ball and Roller Bearings.

[2] It is assumed that all new capacity (purchased in $t-1$ and becoming effective in year t) is fully utilized at t, but that older capacity is subject to fluctuation in rate of utilization. For such older capacity, the relation

$$L_{t-1}^i = M_{t-1}^i + N_{t-1}^i O_{t-1}^i \qquad (5)$$

representative of new technology can then be appraised with partial utilizations taken into account. Values of a_t^i, called a_{tp}^i, are predicted for all values of t on the basis of A_2^i, a^N, a_{t-1}^i, Z_{1t}^i and Z_{2t}^i. The closeness with which a_t^i is approximated measures the suitability of a^N as an estimate of new technology.

Alternatively, a single value of A_2, representing a weighted average A_2^i for *all plants*, can be obtained by combining information for all plants in the least squares estimate. Thus another version of (11) is

$$a_t^i = a^N Z_{1t}^i + A_2 Z_{2t}^i + a_{t-1}^i (1 - Z_{1t}^i). \tag{12}$$

or
$$\frac{L_{t-1}^i}{O_{t-1}^i} = a_{t-1}^i = \frac{M_{t-1}^i}{O_{t-1}^i} + N_{t-1}^i \tag{5a}$$

is assumed, where L_{t-1}^i =labour (or electricity) input in year $t-1$ and M_{t-1}^i and N_{t-1}^i are technical constants characteristic of the installed capacity in year $t-1$.

At time t the output of this portion of older capacity will be $O_t^i(1 - Z_{1t}^i)$, and the input coefficient characterizing old capacity in year t will be

$$\hat{a}_{t-1}^i = \frac{M_{t-1}^i}{O_t^i(1 - Z_{1t}^i)} + N_{t-1}^i. \tag{6}$$

Substituting $\hat{a}_{t-1}^i$ for a_{t-1}^i in (2a), we have

$$a_t^i = a^N Z_{1t}^i + \left(\frac{M_{t-1}^i}{O_t^i(1 - Z_{1t}^i)} + N_{t-1}^i \right) (1 - Z_{1t}^i). \tag{7}$$

But from (5a)

$$N_{t-1}^i = a_{t-1}^i - \frac{M_{t-1}^i}{O_{t-1}^i}.$$

Substituting for N_{t-1}^i in (7) we get

$$a_t^i = a^N Z_{1t}^i + a_{t-1}^i (1 - Z_{1t}^i) + \frac{M_{t-1}^i}{O_{t-1}^i} \left(\frac{O_{t-1}^i - (1 - Z_{1t}^i) O_t^i}{O_t^i} \right). \tag{8}$$

For convenience, we rename

$$\frac{O_{t-1}^i - (1 - Z_{1t}^i) O_t^i}{O_t^i} = Z_{2t}^i \tag{9}$$

and
$$\frac{M_{t-1}^i}{O_{t-1}^i} = A_2^i \tag{10}$$

and rewrite (8)

$$a_t^i = a^N Z_{t1}^i + A_2^i Z_{2t}^i + a_{t-1}^i (1 - Z_{1t}^i). \tag{11}$$

The three alternative versions of equation $(2a)$ — i.e., $(2a)$, (11) and (12) — were used to predict the coefficients in the two industries. The results are summarized in Table 2.

In the Tin Can Industry, there were 99 expanding establishments (85 for electricity inputs) with coefficients given for 1951 and 1954, and investment summed over the interval 1951–3, inclusive. For the Ball and Roller Bearings Industry a sample of 32 plants was covered, with annual information for 1951–8. Thus, for the Tin Can Industry the coefficients for only one year, i.e., 1954, were predicted for each of the 99 plants. In the Ball and Roller Bearings Industry, coefficients for each plant for each year 1952 to 1958 were predicted.[1]

Examination of Table 2 suggests that, on the average, new plant coefficients, when used in version $(2a)$, result in an understatement of actual input coefficients for individual older plants. When the second constant, A_2, is introduced, however, there is a tendency for predicted values to overstate the actual coefficients. Differences among the various estimates are small in comparison with the residual variance and there seems to be little basis here for advocating the use of the more complicated equations (11) and (12), rather than the simpler $(2a)$.

4. *Estimates of Incremental Coefficients Inferred from Data for Older Establishments*

In this section incremental coefficients are inferred statistically from observed changes in the input-output ratios of a large sample of older establishments and their plant and equipment expenditures. Several alternative but essentially similar procedures are employed. Given observations of inputs and outputs of individual establishments at two or more points of time and their expenditures on new plant and equipment over the relevant interval, each procedure asks the question: What must the input coefficients characterizing newly added or modified capacity have been in order to produce the observed changes in average input-output ratios? This means recomputing the relationships $(2a)$ and (12) of the previous section, but this time treating *both* a^N and A_2 as parameters to be estimated from cross-section data.

a^N is renamed A_1 when it is inferred from information on expansion of existing establishments rather than based directly on new plant coefficients. $(2a)$ and (12) are restated, in terms of A_1:

$$a_t^i = A_1 Z_{1t}^i + a_{t-1}^i (1 - Z_{1t}^i) \tag{2b}$$

[1] Since Tin Can plants furnished input and output information for only two terminal years, it was not possible to estimate separate values of A_2^i for each plant and estimates based on (11) had to be omitted from the table.

TABLE 2

Predictions, Using New-Plant Coefficients, of Labour and Electricity Coefficients in Older Establishments, Two Industries, 1952–8

Prediction by equation No.	Ball and Roller Bearings						Tin Cans					
	Labour			Electricity			Labour			Electricity		
	Predicted coefficient	Residual variance	A_2	Predicted coefficient	Residual variance	A_2	Predicted coefficient	Residual variance	A_2	Predicted coefficient	Residual variance	A_2
(2a)	0·1721	0·0008	—	0·8360	0·0388	—	0·0672	0·0005	—	0·2558	0·0039	—
(11)	0·1847	0·0010	0·0306	0·8819	0·0216	0·0691	—	—	—	—	—	—
(12)	0·1859	0·0007	0·0419	0·8923	0·0345	0·1929	0·0700	0·0003	0·0065	0·0265	0·0038	0·0017
Actual co-efficient	0·1817			0·8609			0·0710			0·2732		

and $$a_t^i = A_1 Z_{1t}^i + A_2 Z_{2t}^i + a_{t-1}^i(1 - Z_{1t}^i) \tag{12a}$$

As noted above, for the Tin Can Industry coefficients for two terminal years, 1951 and 1954, and expenditure on new equipment over the interval 1951–3 were available. Here the interval was treated as a single 'year' and least squares estimates of A_1, and A_1 and A_2 together, were derived over the cross section.

For the Ball and Roller Bearings Industry, continuous series of annual capital expenditure, inputs, and outputs were available over the period 1951–8. For this group of plants it was possible to experiment by estimating slightly different versions of A_1 and A_2 as follows:

(i) — Separate values of A_1^i, and A_1^i and A_2^i together, were derived from the time series for each individual plant, over the period 1951–8.

(ii) — Common values of A_1, and A_1 and A_2 together, were assumed for all plants, and all year-to-year changes in all plants were combined into a single population.

(iii) — 1958 and 1951 coefficients were viewed as end links in a 'chained' relationship. The individual annual relationships between a_t^i and a_{t-1}^i were solved simultaneously so as to express the change in each plant's coefficients between 1951 and 1958 as a function of Z_{1t}^i's, or of Z_{1t}^i's and Z_{2t}^i's together, in the intervening years 1952–8, thus:

$$a_{58}^i = a_{51}^i(1 - Z_{152}^i)(1 - Z_{153}^i)\ldots(1 - Z_{158}^i)$$
$$+ A_1[1 - (1 - Z_{152}^i)(1 - Z_{153}^i)\ldots(1 - Z_{158}^i)] \tag{13}$$

and $$a_{58}^i = a_{51}^i(1 - Z_{152}^i)\ldots(1 - Z_{158}^i) + A_1[\ldots\ldots]$$
$$+ A_2[Z_{252}^i(1 - Z_{158}^i)\ldots(1 - Z_{153}^i)$$
$$+ Z_{253}^i(1 - Z_{158}^i)\ldots(1 - Z_{154}^i) + \ldots + Z_{256}^i(1 - Z_{158}^i)(1 - Z_{157}^i)$$
$$+ Z_{257}^i(1 - Z_{158}^i) + Z_{258}^i]. \tag{14}$$

The various estimates of A_1 and A_2 just described are presented in Table 3. The variance in the last column of the table measures squared differences between actual coefficients and those estimated by the relationship in question.

The formulae differ primarily in regard to whether an allowance for capacity utilization is introduced (with A_2) and whether different incremental coefficients are estimated for each plant. Allowance for differences in capacity utilization, $A_2 Z_{2t}^i$, appears to contribute substantially to the explanation of changes in the coefficient cross sections in some cases, particularly lines (2), (8) and (13). On the other hand, the net reduction in residual variance with the addition of the second

Table 3

Estimates of Incremental Labour and Electricity Coefficients Inferred from Information on Older Establishments, Ball and Roller Bearings Industry, 1951–8, and Tin Can Industry, 1951–4

Coefficient	t	$t-1$	Relationship	A_1	A_2	Predicted a_t	Actual a_t	Residual variance
(1) Tin Can, Labour	1954	1951	2b	0·0768	—	0·0732	0·0710	0·0002
(2) Tin Can, Labour	1954	1951	12a	0·0574	0·0182	0·0697	0·0710	0·0002
(3) Tin Can, Electricity	1954	1951	2b	0·4180	—	0·2724	0·2732	0·0035
(4) Tin Can, Electricity	1954	1951	12a	0·5018	−0·0302	0·2890	0·2732 ·	0·0039
(5) BRB, Labour	1952–8	1951–7	2b	0·1782*	—	0·1845	0·1817	0·0008
(6) BRB, Labour	1952–8	1951–7	12a	0·1339*	0·0210*	0·1855	0·1817	0·0006
(7) BRB, Labour	1952–8	1951–7	2b	0·1786	—	0·1855	0·1817	0·0008
(8) BRB, Labour	1952–8	1951–7	12a	0·1289	0·0426	0·1850	0·1817	0·0007
(9) BRB, Labour	1958	1951	13	0·1584	—	0·1637	0·1599	0·0011
(10) BRB, Labour	1958	1951	14	0·1603	−0·0014	0·1637	0·1599	0·0013
(11) BRB, Electricity	1952–8	1951–7	2b	1·1164*	—	0·8630	0·8609	0·0201
(12) BRB, Electricity	1952–8	1951–7	2b	1·1148	—	0·8720	0·8609	0·0361
(13) BRB, Electricity	1952–8	1951–7	12a	0·7124	0·3413	0·8796	0·8609	0·0353
(14) BRB, Electricity	1958	1951	13	1·0201	—	0·9493	0·9340	0·1430

* Means of estimates for individual plants.

constant, A_2, is very small in each case. For statistical reasons, estimates of A_1 tend to vary inversely with A_2. Since there appears to be some problem of multicollinearity, estimates of A_1 are apt to be misleading if interpreted as incremental coefficients when they are estimated jointly with A_2.[1]

Allowance for different incremental parameters for each plant rather than a single coefficient for all plants reduces residual variance appreciably in the case of the Ball and Roller Bearings Industry's electricity coefficients, but not in the case of the labour coefficients.

5. *Comparison of Indirectly Inferred Incremental Coefficients with New Plant Coefficients*

Estimates of 'best practice' coefficients based on new plants and those obtained indirectly from changes in older plants can be compared by inspection of Tables 1 and 3. In general, it appears that new plant coefficients are lower than those derived indirectly. This may be interpreted as a tendency for new plant coefficients to exaggerate the technological change embodied in expansions of older plants.[2] In both industries average labour coefficients tend to be falling; estimated incremental coefficients based on new plants are lower than those based on partial expansions. The same is true for electricity coefficients in the Tin Can Industry. In the Ball and Roller Bearings Industry electricity inputs are rising, and new plant coefficients are higher than the average coefficients for older plants. In this situation, however, the indirectly derived incremental coefficients still tend to be slightly higher than the new plant coefficients.[3]

The tendency of new plant coefficients to overstate change seems reasonable. Older plants are presumably committed to some features of older technology and hence are more limited in their choices of alternatives in installing new capacity. New capacity in older plants seems to be characterized by a sort of 'compromise' technology.

[1] Intuitively this can be characterized as follows: A_2 is an estimate of the average 'fixed' component of a^i_{t-1}, and A_1 represents the incremental coefficient. It is shown below that plants with high initial coefficients tend to have high incremental coefficients as well. Thus there will be some 'competition' between A_1 and A_2 as to which will 'represent' the plant's rank in the industrial size-distribution of coefficients.

[2] This comment refers to the predictions which do not involve the second constant A_2. Where the second constant is introduced, it tends to compensate for low values of a^N.

[3] This exception may be attributed to sampling, since the two estimates are moderately close, the number of new plants small, and the variance of new plant coefficients fairly large.

On the other hand, residual variance $(a_{tp}^i - a_t^i)^2$ is of the same order of magnitude for both the indirect and the new plant estimates of incremental coefficients. This is due in part to the general method of predicting a_{tp}^i. Where new capacity in each plant is small relative to remaining older capacity, the term $A_1 Z_{1t}^i$, or $a^N Z_{1t}^i$, contributes relatively little to the prediction of a_t^i. However, when Z_{1t}^i is large, the relative magnitudes of A_1 and a^N will appear more important. The bulk of the variance arises, apparently regardless of the kind of incremental coefficient estimate, from two major sources: deficiencies in the basic formulation of the hypothesis and long-term structural differences among plants.

First, obviously it is an oversimplification to assume that all innovation is the result of capital expenditure, or that each year's capital expenditure exerts its full influence in the following year. Some experimental computations were performed to see whether variance was reduced by changing the assumed time relation between investment and coefficient changes, but no appreciable improvement resulted. It may well be that the lag between equipment expenditure and its technical consequences is quite variable. Coefficient changes resulting from the scrappage of obsolete capacity in the replacement process have been treated under the assumption that discarded (or idle) capacity is characterized by the average coefficient of the plant at $t - 1$. Actually one would expect the oldest, least-efficient capacity to be discarded first. It is possible to think of other sources of variation in coefficients in addition to investment. These will be apt to contribute to errors in prediction of coefficients regardless of the estimated value of a^N or A_1.

Second, where there are persistent differences among coefficients for individual plants, errors are introduced by assuming a common incremental technology for all of them. Even in supposedly homogeneous industries such as these two, the differences among plant coefficients are surprisingly large, as shown in Table 4 for 1951. Moreover, the differences tend to persist over time, despite sizeable equipment expenditures by many of the establishments. Thus, for the sample of Tin Can plants the average labour coefficient dropped from 0·0747 in 1951 to 0·0710 in 1954, and the average value of Z_{1t}^i over the interval is 0·1867; nevertheless the rank correlation coefficient for labour coefficients in 1951 and 1954 is 0·9315. For the sample of Ball and Roller Bearings plants, the average labour coefficient dropped from 0·1980 to 0·1609 between 1951 and 1958 and the average value of Z_{1t}^i is 0·2557; the rank correlation coefficient is 0·8246. It would appear that factors other than vintage of installed equipment — such as specific product characteristics, degree of integration, and size of plant — have an

TABLE 4

Frequency Distributions of Labour and Electricity Coefficients,
Two Industries, 1951

Labour coefficients	No. of establishments	Electricity coefficients	No. of establishments
BALL AND ROLLER BEARINGS			
0·00–	9	0·00–	7
0·16–	5	0·40–	5
0·19–	5	0·60–	9
0·22–	7	0·80–	5
over 0·25	5	over 1·0	5
Average 0·1980		Average 0·7036	
Standard deviation		Standard deviation	
0·0608		0·3497	
TIN CANS			
0·00–	7	0·00–	6
0·03–	12	0·09–	6
0·04–	13	0·13–	10
0·05–	18	0·17–	15
0·06–	7	0·21–	10
0·07–	10	0·25–	11
0·08–	8	0·29–	5
0·09–	11	0·33–	10
0·12–	5	0·37–	4
over 0·15	8	over 0·41	7
Average 0·0747		Average 0·2438	
Standard deviation		Standard deviation	
0·0453		0·1203	

important bearing on input coefficients, and one which tends to persist even while technological advances are being made within the individual plants.

It is undoubtedly an oversimplification to assume that the same incremental coefficients apply to plants with persistently higher and to those with persistently lower average input coefficients. For while, in a qualitative sense, the same sorts of technological changes may be introduced in all of an industry's plants, the 'best practice' input coefficients themselves will tend to be different for plants making different qualities of products, or starting at different stages in the vertical productive sequence. The lumping together of heterogeneous plants in the estimation of common values of A_1 and A_2 accounts for more of the residual variance in predicting changes in electricity than in labour coefficients.[1]

When a common value of A_1 is estimated for all plants, it represents an average incremental coefficient for many persistently heterogeneous establishments. This should be borne in mind not only because it bears on the size of residual variance, but also because it accounts for differences in estimates based on cross-section data and those, to be described below, based on time series for each industry as a whole.

Before proceeding to the problem of predicting changes in the total industry coefficients, we predict changes in individual plant coefficients using the incremental coefficients derived above, and compare them with predictions based on other simple common methods.

In the Tin Can Industry, the information required in equations $(2b)$ and $(12a)$ was available for the period 1954–6 for a sample of eleven sizeable expansions of existing plants. For these plants 1956 labour and electricity coefficients (called a_{56p}^i) were predicted from 1954 coefficients and given values of Z_{1t}^i and Z_{2t}^i, using equation $(12a)$ with A_1 and A_2 taken from Table 3. The residual variance of this prediction is compared with that of two common-place alternative methods of prediction, namely the use of a_{54}^i and the mean of a_{56}^i, as estimates of a_{56}^i. The comparison is presented in Table 5.

TABLE 5

Sums of Squared Deviations of 1956 Labour and Electricity Coefficients from their Respective Means and from Various Predicted Values, Tin Can Industry

Sum of squared deviations	Labour coefficient analysis	Electricity coefficient analysis
$\sum_i (a_{56}^i - \bar{a}_{56})^2$	$6 \cdot 560 \times 10^{-3}$	$0 \cdot 188100$
$\sum_i (a_{56}^i - a_{54}^i)^2$	$1 \cdot 516 \times 10^{-3}$	$0 \cdot 092352$
$\sum_i (a_{56}^i - a_{56p}^i)^2$	$0 \cdot 834 \times 10^{-3}$	$0 \cdot 086917$

[1] For the 'chained' version of estimation, some of the error arising from the assumption of a common incremental coefficient for heterogeneous plants is eliminated by stratifying plants into groups according to initial coefficient size, and computing separate incremental coefficients for each subgroup. Thus, plants in the Ball and Roller Bearings sample were arranged in order of labour input coefficient size in 1951, and divided into two groups of equal size, one including those with lower and the other those with higher initial coefficients. A_1 and A_2 were estimated separately for each of these groups in accordance with equation (14). A similar procedure was followed for the Tin Can Industry, but because of the larger number of plants represented in the sample, the plants were divided into three groups instead of two.

The results suggest a reduction in coefficient variance when plants are stratified into more homogeneous coefficient groups. Unfortunately this sort of stratification does not distinguish between initial coefficient differences due to vintage of installed plant and equipment and differences due to other factors.

The results indicate that, in this particular instance, the method of equation (12a) has considerable advantage over the other methods. Presumably this advantage would be of similar magnitude for other variants of our method considered in Table 3, and possibly even for those considered in Table 2. On the other hand, one must remember that the 'straw man' alternatives in Table 5 are fairly crude, and that the sample of eleven plants available for the test may not be representative. Furthermore, these plants expanded considerably during the period. One would expect the advantages of equation (12a) over the simpler alternatives to be clearest for large expansions; thus, when Z_{1t}^i is zero (i.e., for the case of no expansion at all) our theory would lead us to expect that $a_{54}^i = a_{56}^i$ would give perfect predictions.

Data on Ball and Roller Bearings plants were not adequate to permit predictions beyond the period for which the incremental coefficients were estimated. Instead, residual variances of actual from estimated flow coefficients $(a_t^i - a_{tp}^i)^2$ for 1958 only are compared with predictions based on a_{57}^i, a_{51}^i, $\bar{a}_{51-8}^i$ and a linear time trend for each plant. The results are shown in Table 6.[1]

TABLE 6

Means of Squared Deviations of 1958 Labour and Electricity Coefficients from Various Predicted Values, Ball and Roller Bearings Industry

Variance basis	Mean of squared deviations		Line
	Labour	Electricity	
A. Labour Coefficients			
(2b) $a_{58}^i = A_1 Z_{158}^i + a_{57}^i(1 - \mathcal{Z}_{158}^i)$	0·0005	0·0236	(1)
$a_{58}^i = a_{57}^i$	0·0004	0·0067	(2)
$a_{58}^i = \bar{a}_{51-8}^i$	0·0010	0·0209	(3)
$a_{58}^i = C^i + D^i t$ (time trend)	0·0004	0·0093	(4)
(13)' $a_{58}^i = A_1 \mathcal{Z}_1^i + a_{51}^i(1 - \mathcal{Z}_1^i)$	0·0011	0·1430	(5)
$a_{58}^i = a_{51}^i$	0·0029	0·1077	(6)

[1] $\mathcal{Z}_1^i = 1 - (1 - Z_{152}^i) \ldots (1 - Z_{158}^i)$ is the chained version of Z_{1t}^i; cf. equation (13) above.

It appears that our method does not do as well as assuming that 1957 coefficients will prevail in 1958, nor as well as the simple time trend. On the other hand, the advantage of the 'chained' formulation over the others lies in the fact that it uses information on coefficients in two terminal years only. Thus it can be used with continuous investment series even if there is no coefficient information available for the intermediate years. Where 1958 coefficients are predicted from 1951 coefficients only, *assuming no knowledge of coefficients for intermediate years* (lines (5) and (6)), our method does appreciably better for labour coefficients than the only alternative method which was tried, $a^i_{58} = a^i_{51}$. One must after all bear in mind that a^i_{58} was known in the estimation of A_1 in line (5) (and also in the time trend, (4)). Further evidence is presented below on the advantage of our method in the prediction of coefficients over relatively long intervals. Considerable work remains to be done concerning the length of the period over which it is reasonable to assume constant incremental coefficients.

6. *The Analysis of Changes in Total Industry Coefficients*

The central objective of this study has been the clarification of alternative methods for estimating 'best practice' coefficients for a dynamic input-output model. Ultimately, then, the various estimates are to be judged not on how well they explain changes in individual plant coefficients, but on how useful they are in explaining changes in average coefficients for the industry as a whole.

One way of assessing their value in the total industry context is to use the various estimates of a^N and A_1 given in Tables 1 and 3 to explain time series of industry coefficients in the two industries. Output, expenditure on plant and equipment, and labour inputs are published by the Bureau of the Census annually for 1951–8. Three different equations were used to predict industry labour-coefficient changes over this period: (2b), (12a) and (13), adjusted to an industry basis (by dropping superscripts).

Alternative values of A_1 (or a^N) and A_2 were taken from Tables 1 and 3 and substituted in (2b) and (12a). The third equation (13), i.e., the 'chained' version, uses the estimate in line 9 of Table 3 for predicting changes in Ball and Roller Bearings coefficients from 1951 to 1958. Cross-section information on Tin Cans was not sufficient to provide estimates of A_1 for the 'chained' relationship, and hence the third computation was not performed for the Tin Can time series. Versions involving A_2 were dropped for Ball and Roller Bearings.

Actual and predicted industry labour coefficients derived by these various methods are presented in Tables 7 and 8.

TABLE 7

Actual and Predicted Industry Labour Coefficients,
Ball and Roller Bearings Industry, 1951–8

Year	Coefficients predicted by equation			Actual coefficients
	(2a) $a^N = 0.1302$	(2b) $A_1 = 0.1786$	(13) $A_1 = 0.1584$	
1952	0.1883	0.1962	—	0.2042
1953	0.1913	0.1997	—	0.1956
1954	0.1873	0.1934	—	0.1823
1955	0.1756	0.1818	—	0.1712
1956	0.1660	0.1722	—	0.1776
1957	0.1690	0.1778	—	0.1780
1958	0.1696	0.1781	0.1712	0.1555
Residual variance	0.0001	0.0001	—	—
Variance about mean	—	—	—	0.0002
$Var(a_t - a_{t-1})$	—	—	—	0.0001

The results indicate that the various methods predict the time series of labour coefficients fairly closely. This is not surprising in view of the fact that each year's labour coefficients are derived in part from observed values of a_{t-1}. In both industries our method does about as well as assuming that each year's coefficient will be the same as that of the year before. The fact that predictive errors do not vary greatly with the assumed value of A_1 or a^N is due in large part to the fact that values of Z_{1t} are small (ranging from 0.1261 to 0.1825 for Ball and Roller Bearings and from 0.0662 to 0.1117 for Tin Cans) over the period studied. The particular estimate of A_1 will affect the predicted industry coefficient values much more when the prediction interval chosen is longer, or the annual rate of capital expenditure higher.

The potential differences in coefficient prediction that occur with higher investment levels are indicated in Table 9, which presents the results of predicting 1958 coefficients, given 1951 coefficients and capital

U

TABLE 8

Actual and Predicted Industry Labour Coefficients
Tin Can Industry, 1951–8

Year	Coefficients predicted by equation			Actual coefficients
	(2a) $a^N = 0\cdot0435$	(2b) $A_1 = 0\cdot0768$	(12a) $A_1 = 0\cdot0574$ $A_2 = 0\cdot0182$	
1952	0·0975	0·1005	0·1011	0·1065
1953	0·1021	0·1044	0·1033	0·1040
1954	0·1000	0·1022	0·1016	0·1009
1955	0·0945	0·0982	0·0968	0·0936
1956	0·0891	0·0921	0·0910	0·0911
1957	0·0864	0·0897	0·0905	0·0939
1958	0·0899	0·0926	0·0917	0·0874
Residual variance	0·00002	0·00001	0·00001	—
Variance about mean	—	—	—	0·00004
$\mathrm{Var}(a_t - a_{t-1})$	—	—	—	0·00002

expenditures over the interval 1951–7. The methods used are the same as those in Tables 7 and 8, but single combined values of

$$Z_{1(51-8)} = \frac{\sum\limits_{51}^{57} \text{Capital Expenditures}}{\text{Output 1958}} \cdot \frac{1}{K}$$

and $$Z_{2(51-8)} = \frac{\text{Output 1951} - (1 - Z_1)\,\text{Output 1958}}{\text{Output 1958}}$$

are used. The 'chained' prediction in Table 7 is already a prediction of 1958 from 1951, and it is repeated in Table 9 for purposes of comparison.

With these longer-range predictions, the differences among the various estimated values, derived by variants of our general method, become greater. However, the advantage of using our method, as opposed to assuming that $a_t = a_{t-1}$ (in this case that $a_{58} = a_{51}$), is also much greater, which stands to reason since the diffusion of new technology is cumulative.

In the Tin Can Industry example, the indirectly estimated A_1 predicts the 1958 coefficient more closely than the new plant coefficient,

TABLE 9

Prediction of 1958 Industry Labour Coefficients,
from 1951 Coefficients and Capital Expenditures of 1951–7,
Two Industries

Estimate by equation	A_1 or a^N	A_2	a_{1951}	a_{1958} Predicted	a_{1958} Actual
TIN CANS					
(2a)	0·0435	—		0·0692	
(2b)	0·0768	—	} 0·1028 {	0·0881	} 0·0874
(12a)	0·0574	0·0182		0·0849	
BALL AND ROLLER BEARINGS					
(2a)	0·1302	—		0·1696	
(2b)	0·1786	—	} 0·1997 {	0·1781	} 0·1555
(13)	0·1584	—		0·1712	

a^N. In the Ball and Roller Bearings Industry the indirectly derived A_1 has only a slight advantage over a^N in predicting a_{58}.[1] On the other hand, A_1 predicts a_{57} almost exactly. The 'chained' formulation seems to do best in the Ball and Roller Bearings Industry, but the evidence does not give sufficient basis for firm conclusions as to its relative superiority.

7. Estimates of Incremental Coefficients Inferred from Industry Time Series

Where sufficiently long industry time-series of the relevant variables are available, it is possible to estimate the required incremental co-efficients from aggregate industry data without using individual plant information. The methodology is identical with that used in Section 4, but industry total coefficients and investment are used instead of individual plant observations. Thus:

$$A_1^t = \frac{\sum_t (a_t - a_{t-1})(1 - Z_{1t})(Z_{1t})}{\sum_t (Z_{1t})^2} , \qquad (15)$$

where A_1^t represents A_1 estimated from industry total time series, adds

[1] In the Ball and Roller Bearings example capital expenditures over the period were sufficient to replace the entire capacity of the industry with best practice technology, i.e. the Z_{1t} of (2) was greater than one. Thus the predicted value of a_{58} is equal to the value of A_1 or a^N.

still a third class of least squares estimates to those estimates of incremental coefficients already discussed, namely a^N and A_1. Similarly sets of A_1^t and A_2^t together can be estimated by least squares from the observed industry time series of a_t, a_{t-1}, Z_{1t} and Z_{2t}.[1]

Unfortunately, available time series for our two industries covered only 1951–8, and then only for the labour input. In any event, the length of the time series to be used in this context cannot generally be extended beyond ten years because of the assumption of a constant incremental coefficient.

Estimates based on time series will of necessity draw upon a relatively small number of observations and thus be subject to considerable instability. Nevertheless, they can be extremely useful as further checks on the plausibility of the cross-section estimates, or even directly as parameters. Indeed, one may argue that industry parameters based on time series are preferable to cross-sectional ones since they are to be used primarily in predicting industry time series variables [9].

Table 10 gives estimates of A_1^t, and of A_1^t and A_2^t. Comparison with Table 3 shows that the estimates of A_1^t and A_1 without allowance for

TABLE 10

Estimates of Incremental Labour Coefficients Based on Total Industry Time Series Compared with Estimates Based on Cross Section Data, Two Industries, 1951–8

Estimated by equation	A_1^t	A_2^t	A_1	A_2	Residual variance
BALL AND ROLLER BEARINGS					
(2b)	0·1468	—	0·1786	—	0·0001
(12a)	0·1431	0·0031	0·1289	0·0426	0·0001
(2b)*	0·1894	—	0·1786	—	0·000003
(12a)*	0·1834	0·0003	0·1289	0·0426	0·000002
TIN CANS					
(2b)	0·0738	—	0·0768	—	0·00001
(12a)	0·0178	0·0711	0·0574	0·0128	0·000004

* Data for 32 plants aggregated.

[1] The normal equations of A_1^t and A_2^t together are:

$$\sum_t Z_{1t}(a_t - a_{t-1})(1 - Z_{1t}) - A_1^t\sum_t (Z_{1t})^2 - A_2^t\sum_t Z_{1t}Z_{2t} = 0$$

and

$$\sum_t Z_{2t}(a_t - a_{t-1})(1 - Z_{1t}) - A_1^t\sum_t Z_{1t}Z_{2t} - A_2^t\sum_t (Z_{2t})^2 = 0.$$

capacity utilization (without A_2^t and A_2) are almost identical for Tin Cans, but differ by roughly 20 per cent for Ball and Roller Bearings. Comparisons of A_1 and A_1^t in the two-parameter relationship indicate greater similarity for Ball and Roller Bearings. On the other hand, the cross-section and time-series based estimates differ markedly for the two-parameter relationships in Tin Cans. Unfortunately, estimates of A_1^t and A_2^t together are subject to the problems of multicollinearity mentioned in Section 4 above. Since, furthermore, the values of A_1^t and A_2^t are estimates of two parameters based on seven observations, it is not reasonable to consider this discrepancy as being too serious.

The Ball and Roller Bearings estimate of A_1^t is appreciably lower than the corresponding A_1. This may be due, in part, to sampling variation (the sample covers only 31 per cent of the plants in the industry in 1954); to weighting implicit in the aggregation process; and to other aspects of statistical procedure. To appraise the importance of the first two factors, the 32 individual plant time series for Ball and Roller Bearings were aggregated into 'industry' variables as follows:

$$a_t = \frac{\sum_i a_t^i O_t^i}{\sum_i O_t^i} \quad , \tag{16}$$

$$a_{t-1} = \frac{\sum_i a_t^i {}_1 O_{t-1}^i}{\sum_i O_{t-1}^i} \quad , \tag{17}$$

$$Z_{1t} = \frac{\sum_i Z_{1t}^i O_t^i}{\sum_i O_t^i} \quad , \tag{18}$$

$$Z_{2t} = \left[\sum_i O_{t-1}^i - \sum_i O_t^i \left(1 - \frac{\sum_i Z_{1t}^i O_t^i}{\sum_i O_t^i} \right) \right] \frac{1}{\sum_i O_t^i} \quad . \tag{19}$$

Estimates of A_1^t and A_2^t were derived from the resulting time series for the aggregate 32-plant 'industry'. They are included in Table 10. At least in this particular case, the parameters based on the cross section and on the 32-plant aggregated time series agree fairly well. This suggests that a good part of the original discrepancy between A_1^t and A_1 was due to sampling and aggregation weighting.

The remaining discrepancies between the cross section and aggregate time series estimates in Table 10 are presumably explained by differences in the statistical scatters characterizing the different data.[1] Interplant differences are sizeable in these industries, and the cross-section estimates are designed to give 'best compromise' estimates of A_1 and A_2. In the aggregated series it is not interplant scatter, but intertemporal scatter which influences the estimates. There is nothing in the statistical procedures used which would guarantee similar estimates, especially when one or both of the scatters are large.

One can argue that the general shapes of the intertemporal scatters in different time periods will be more likely to resemble each other than to resemble that of the cross section, and hence that time series estimates will generally provide more successful time series projections. From this point of view, industry time series estimates should, if possible, be used for estimating input-output parameters. This consideration must be balanced against the fact that only a very limited number of time series observations can be used for this purpose, particularly if they are to yield constants to be used for projecting still further ahead.

At any rate, at least for the two industries studied, the alternative estimates are very similar and the cross-section parameters explain changes in the time series almost as well as those based directly on industry time series. The generality of these conclusions remains to be investigated.

8. *Summary*

To allow for changes in flow coefficients with industrial growth, it is necessary to distinguish between the average technical coefficients of an industry reflecting existing capacity and incremental coefficients characterizing those portions of capacity which are being added in the course of current growth and replacement. This study is concerned with the problem of deriving incremental technical coefficients which best represent the varied combination of new plants and expansions of existing plants which contribute to an industry's growth.

Three general types of estimates were made:

1. 'New Plant Coefficients' — estimates derived by averaging performance records of new plants,
2. 'Cross-section Coefficients' — estimates inferred statistically from

---

[1] The above procedure, i.e., aggregation of the sample data to industry form, was not followed for Tin Cans because sample observations for only two years were available. However, the sample for this industry constituted a somewhat larger proportion, 44 per cent, of the industry.

observed changes in coefficients of older establishments and the capital expenditures accompanying the changes, and

3. 'Industry Time Series Coefficients' — estimates inferred statistically from observed changes in input coefficients for the industry as a whole, and its total expenditures on new plant and equipment.

These three types of estimates were compared as predictors both of changes in input coefficients of individual plants, and of input coefficients for the industry as a whole. In general, predictions of changes in individual establishment coefficients using new plant coefficients tend to overstate actual change, but residual variance is not very much lower when cross-section coefficients are used.

Again, in the prediction of changes in total industry coefficients there appears to be some small advantage in using the estimates derived from the cross section of plants rather than the new plant coefficients. Parameters derived from industry time series closely resemble those based on cross sections for the Tin Can Industry. The discrepancy between the cross-section and the time series estimate in the Ball and Roller Bearings Industry was reduced substantially by adjusting for differences in the sample of plants covered.

Because relevant data are scarce, it will not always be possible to choose among these alternative methods in each industry. Since the various estimates appear to be in substantial agreement, it seems reasonable to view them as supplementary in the context of deriving an incremental coefficient matrix for dynamic general equilibrium analysis.

The conclusions of this pilot study must await confirmation by other investigations for a larger sample of industries.

REFERENCES

[1] CARTER, A. P., *et al.*, 'Technological change,' in Harvard Economic Research Project, *Report on Research for 1953*.

[2] CARTER, A. P., *et al.*, 'Technological change', in Harvard Economic Research Project, *Report on Research for 1954*.

[3] CARTER, A. P., *et al.*, 'Technological change', in Harvard Economic Research Project, *Report on Research for 1955*.

[4] CARTER, A. P., *et al.*, 'Technological change', in Harvard Economic Research Project, *Report on Research for 1956-7*.

[5] CARTER, A. P., *et al.*, 'Technological change', in Harvard Economic Research Project *Report on Research for 1958-9*.

[6] WURTELE, Z. S., 'A Note on Some Stability Properties of Leontief's Dynamic Models,' *Econometrica*, Vol. 27, 1959, p. 4.

302   *Anne P. Carter*

[7] GROSSE, R. N., 'The Structure of Capital' in Leontief *et al.*, *Studies in the Structure of the American Economy*, Oxford University Press, 1953.
[8] CARTER, A. P., 'Capital coefficients as economic parameters,' in National Bureau of Economic Research, *Studies in Income and Wealth*, Vol. 19, 1957.
[9] KUH, E., 'The Validity of Cross-Sectionally Estimated Behavior Equations in Time Series Applications,' *Econometrica*, vol. 27, 1959, p. 197.

CHAPTER 16

Changes in Input-Output Coefficients

by PER SEVALDSON

1. *Introduction*

The question of the tenability of an assumption of stable coefficients has been the subject of innumerable discussions since Leontief first presented his input-output model. I feel that a considerable part of the discussions has been restricted to more or less emphatic statements of belief or disbelief, and even the more temperate discussions have to some extent been characterized by a certain lack of thoroughness, by a lack of systematically investigated evidence, and by a tendency to temporarily shifting positions in the face of apparently unfavourable evidence.

As far as I can see, available time series data (scarce as they be) demonstrate beyond contradiction that input-output coefficients, defined as the relation between the volume of each specific type of input and the total output of some arbitrarily defined sector of production, do in general vary over time. The question is, however, if they vary in such a way as to invalidate the input-output model.

In the following I will discuss the meaning of stability in relation to the input-output model. I will indicate the investigations to be made in order to ascertain the implications of the stability requirements and discuss the types of empirical testing required to ascertain whether the necessary stability exists. Finally, in Section 4, I will discuss the results of some very simple partial investigations of stability in individual production sectors.

2. *The Meaning of Stability*

In the usual notation the open input-output model may be written as

$$(I - A)X = Y, \tag{1}$$

and its solution as

$$X = (I - A)^{-1}Y, \text{ where} \tag{2}$$

$X=(x_i)$ is the vector of production volumes $(i=1, 2, \ldots, n)$,

$Y=(y_i)$ is the vector of volumes of final deliveries $(i=1, 2, \ldots, n)$,

$A=(a_{ij})=\dfrac{(x_{ij})}{(x_j)}$ is the matrix of units of intermediate products absorbed by a production sector per unit of production $(i, j=1, 2, \ldots, n)$, and

I is a unit matrix of the same order as A.

A general formulation of a closed model is obtained by adding a set of relationships of the general form

$$Y = F(X) \tag{3}$$

to the above system, where $F(X)$ is a set of relationships (other than (1) above) giving the y's as functions of the x's.

Denoting observed values by a bar, we have for the open model the identity

$$\bar{X} = (I - \bar{A})^{-1} \bar{Y} \tag{4}$$

if $\bar{A}$ is the matrix of input-output coefficient derived from the same set of observations as $\bar{X}$ and $\bar{Y}$. If we now have a matrix, A, of coefficients derived in some way (and representing an estimate of the structural coefficients in our input-output model) we obtain for every $\bar{Y}$ an X.

$$X = (I - A)^{-1} \bar{Y} \tag{5}$$

where X is our model estimate. Subtracting we have the vector of errors in model estimates:

$$u = \bar{X} - X = [(I - \bar{A})^{-1} - (I - A)^{-1}] \bar{Y}. \tag{6}$$

For the closed model we get:

$$\bar{X} = (I - \bar{A})^{-1}(F(\bar{X}) + w) \tag{7}$$

$$X = (I - A)^{-1}(F(X)) \tag{8}$$

where w is an error term:

$$w = \bar{Y} - F(\bar{X}). \tag{9}$$

It is obvious from (7) and (8) that the difference $u = \bar{X} - X$ in the case of the closed model must be a relatively complicated function, depending on $\bar{A}$, A, w and the coefficients of F, whereas in the case of the open model it is a relatively simple function of $\bar{A}$, A and $\bar{Y}$.

Now we may define another set of deviations, k_{ij}, where

$$(k_{ij}) = k = \bar{A} - A \quad (i, j = 1, 2, \ldots, n) \tag{10}$$

Then u will be a function of k, A and $\overline{Y}$ in the case of the open model and of k, A, w and the coefficients of F in the case of the closed model. Evaluation of the input-output model must be based on an evaluation by some standard of the error sector u, whereas the 'stability of the input-output coefficients' is described by the individual k_{ij}'s. When we set out to study variations in input-output coefficients we must therefore bear in mind that it is the effects on u of possible coefficient variations which are relevant for an evaluation of the model.

It might be argued that the proper way to study stability would therefore be to obtain observations of u, and to study their distribution directly. However, not all observed differences between $\overline{X}$ and X are necessarily relevant, and if we believe that the causes of variations are to be found in the dispositions of decision makers in the various production units in the economy, we must go back to study the k_{ij}'s as generators of u.

The requirement for stability in input-output coefficients could then be stated in this way: The distribution of the k_{ij}'s must not be such as to cause a distribution of u which leads to a rejection of the model for relevant values of Y in an open model, and for relevant forms of F and distributions of w in a closed model.

It is important to note that this requirement only refers to the stability of input coefficients for intermediate goods. No restriction is imposed on the input coefficients for primary factors of production. Substitutions, between labour and capital for instance, do not affect the validity of the input-output model as long as they do not affect the required amounts of intermediate goods per unit of product.[1]

3. *Types of Differences*

When studying variations in input coefficients for intermediate goods (the $\bar{a}_{ij}$'s), we must, in my opinion, distinguish several types of variation. We must then try to determine the scope of each type of variation and to decide how each type influences the criteria upon which the evaluation of the model will depend (the distribution of u). Let us assume that we can break down each k_{ij} into the following components:

$$k_{ij} = {}_1k_{ij}(t) + {}_2k_{ij}(x_j) + {}_3k_{ij}(Z) + {}_4k_{ij}(X) + {}_5k_{ij}(O) + {}_6k_{ij} \qquad (11)$$

where ${}_1k_{ij}(t)$ is a trend factor; ${}_2k_{ij}(x_j)$ is a function of the level of production in the receiving sector; ${}_3k_{ij}(Z)$ is a function of a vector Z of

---

[1] A model combining constant coefficients of utilization of intermediate goods with substitutability between labour and capital in the production functions has been presented by Leif Johansen in [1].

variables which are exogenous to the model; $_4k_{ij}(X)$ is a function of other variables of the model (e.g. $_4k_{ij}(X) = F(p_1(X), p_2(X) \ldots)$, where F is a function of the prices $p_1, p_2 \ldots$ and the prices are functions of the quantities produced, X); $_5k_{ij}(O)$ is a term representing errors of observation; and $_6k_{ij}$ is a residual term. We shall discuss each component in turn.

(i) $_1k_{ij}(t)$ need not concern us as long as the model is considered to be a system of relationships between inputs and outputs at alternative, simultaneous levels of output. Only when we want to apply the model to periods other than that to which the estimated coefficients pertain, does this item assume importance; we must try to determine the extent of trend-bound coefficient variations and the need for, and possibility of, identifying the trends. If the trend function can be identified, then $A(=a_{ij})$ can be redefined in such a way that the trend element is eliminated from k_{ij}.

If the trend element cannot be eliminated, the importance of the trend may be reduced if estimates of A are computed at sufficiently short intervals. Again, it must be remembered that it is not the effects of $_1k_{ij}(t)$ on individual k_{ij}'s which is of importance, but the total effect in u.

The main causes of trends in input coefficients are technological changes. Let us define as a technological change a change in coefficients depending on time and possibly on the utilization of fixed capital (and thus indirectly on the level of production) but in no other way, directly or indirectly, on other variables of the model within the domain of changes that we choose to consider for these variables.[1] By admitting a dependency on the utilization of fixed capital, we allow for the fact that introduction of new techniques may be dependent on the availability of specialized capital equipment, and consequently may be profitable only for extensions of capacity or for the replacement of worn out equipment. In that case we would see a gradual introduction of new techniques; the same would also be the case if the new technique made necessary a re-education of technical or administrative staff. The other extreme would be an abrupt industry-wide switch from one method of production to another.

---

[1] An input coefficient may, for instance, depend on the level of production but may nevertheless be considered to be constant over a range of, say, 20 per cent variation in production. We would consider a change over time caused by a more than 20 per cent change in production prior to the period of analysis as a technological change in the coefficient only if the changes encountered in the problem to which the model is applied cannot exceed 20 per cent. We must also allow for the fact that over a sufficiently wide range of prices all choices of techniques will depend on prices, so that technological change is an irreversible process only within a certain 'domain' of relative prices.

The timing and extent of both types of technological change may or may not depend on the level of production and they may or may not be predictable over shorter or longer periods. It must be a main problem in the investigation of coefficient variations to determine the extent to which input-output coefficients are subject to technological change, how far these changes are autonomously predictable, and the degree to which they depend on the level of production. If the introduction of new techniques depends on both time and the level of production, we may be unable to separate $_1k_{ij}(t)$ from $_2k_{ij}(x_j)$ in the decomposition of k_{ij}, but may have to operate with some function of the type $_{12}k_{ij}(t, x_j)$. But even in this case it may be possible to take technological changes into account in the definition of the coefficients.[1]

(ii) The assumption that input coefficients are independent of the level of production (i.e. that inputs are proportional to output) has often been criticized. The alternative assumption of linear dependency, which would probably be a satisfactory approximation in all practical problems, implies no theoretical problems. However, for all direct materials the assumption of direct proportionality appears to be the most plausible one, and even for indirect materials it is not necessarily untrue that requirements vary in step with production; this will depend both on the conditions in individual establishments and on the distribution of production between establishments.

The data requirements for estimation of linear functions are much more difficult to meet than those for the estimation of proportional coefficients. Not only are at least two observations required for the linear functions, as against a minimum of one for the proportional coefficient, but these two observations must be sufficiently far apart to eliminate the effects of stochastic influences. It would therefore be of great value if the extent and nature of cases where the proportionality assumption is untenable could be ascertained.

A somewhat different problem is presented if the utilization of a certain technique is restricted by capacity limitations, so that production in excess of a specific amount must be made with changed coefficients. Such a situation can be handled computationally, but again the problem of identifying coefficients and capacity figures is probably quite formidable.

(iii) The distinction between $_3k_{ij}(Z)$ and $_4k_{ij}(X)$ will depend on the total scope of the analyses to which the model is applied. The typical

---

[1] Research with the purpose of identifying trend functions of the type $_{12}k_{ij}(t,x_j)$ has been carried out by Anne Carter. See Chapter 15 above and references at the end of that chapter, on p. 301.

relationship for these two items is the dependency of coefficients on relative prices. In some cases these may be considered to be exogenously given, in other cases as depending on the endogenous variables. Another example is the availability of inputs: if the output of some commodities is limited by capacity, in which case alternative techniques must be applied in the consuming industries, this is a case of variations of the class $_4k_{ij}(X)$; but it is a case of the class $_3k_{ij}(Z)$ if the restrictions on availabilities are exogenously determined.

The problems of identifying relationships are much the same in the two cases, but the manner in which the model can be adjusted is of course much simpler when the arguments of the relationships are exogenously given, provided that they are known at the time when the model estimates are computed. The problems of these types of changes are therefore best treated in the next sub-section.

(iv) In considering $_4k_{ij}(X)$, the dominating problems are the problems of 'substitution' and 'product-mix changes'. If we think of production as a process of combining a given set of technically specified inputs for the creation of an output, and if we consider the effects of changes in the combination of inputs for the production of a constant amount of output, measured for instance in constant price values, there is clearly a continuous range of possible effects between those changes which do not at all affect the technical characteristics of output and those which lead to a fundamental change in it.

The Leontief approach to production theory may be interpreted as resting on the assumption that important changes in input combinations are associated with important changes in output characteristics. Then, if we classify outputs in main groups according to technical characteristics, the input combination required for the production of each group of outputs will be given. Demand for the intermediate use of each output can then be deduced if we assume that demand for the final use of each group of outputs can be determined. Since the technical classification of inputs and outputs of intermediate goods are in a certain sense interdependent, the crucial question is whether the assumption of a determinate final demand (or final demand function) for each group of outputs is tenable.

An example will illustrate this. We may assume that different input combinations are required for producing chemical pulp from coniferous timber than from broadleaf tree timber. Accordingly we may distinguish the output of 'coniferous pulp' from that of 'broadleaf pulp'. We might even carry the distinction further to the output of paper produced from these two types of pulp. Here we may encounter two types of difficulties:

one is that if the two types of pulp are mixed in varying proportions we have to operate with a continuous range of corresponding types of paper, and the other is that we have to establish final demand for each type of paper.

Thus, in principle, problems of coefficient changes due to input substitutions can be converted to problems of product mix and specification in the demand for final goods, but the less the output characterization is affected by a particular change in input combination, the more difficult it is to establish separate final demands for each product-type. The problem to be investigated therefore is to what extent possibilities for changes in input-coefficients may be treated as changes in product mix, in which case they can be disposed of by alterations in sector specification without violating the requirement for a final demand specification in identifiable units.

When considering this problem a little further, we observe that it is closely related to the effects of variations in relative prices. Again there are two extreme cases, with a continuous range of variations between them. At one extreme we have the case where output characteristics are unaffected by a change in input composition. This is the pure case of substitution, when the cheapest input combination will be chosen under varying input prices irrespective of conditions on the demand side. At the other extreme we have the case where the output characteristics are totally altered by a change in input composition. This is an extremum of the product mix case, when changes in input prices may be reflected in product prices which may affect demand, and thus influence the choice between alternative input combinations. The choice between alternative input combinations is determined by conditions of demand as well as by costs of production. Over a certain range of relative prices, not only one but all or any number of product types may be simultaneously in demand. But if the product types are interdependent in demand, there may exist price ratios where only one type is actually demanded in the market. If the product types are alternatives in demand, the range of relative prices over which simultaneously more than one type is in demand will be narrower the stronger the interdependency in demand; and in the limiting case, where the product types are perfect substitutes (i.e. identical from the point of view of demand) this range will be contracted to a single point, and we are back in the case of pure substitution. We thus see that both the question of substitution and that of product mix are closely related to relative prices and cross-elasticities of demand. We also see that in those cases where the range of relative prices over which simultaneous demand can exist, including the switchover point for perfect substitutes, is not within the domain of relative prices over which the model is to apply, the problem of substitution need not concern us. This fact enables us to dispose of a great number of irrelevant substitution possibilities, like producing ships from gold plate.

The problem of product mix is of course the problem which the Leontief model is particularly able to tackle, namely through the specification of production sectors, whereas the problem of substitution falls into the group of variations that may cause systematic errors in forecasts, and which cannot be solved within the framework of a simple Leontief model if prices are assumed to depend on the endogenous variables of the model. Substitutions brought about by price movements assumed to be exogenous to the model may of course be taken into account if the price movements can be forecast.

If substitution in response to changes in endogenously determined prices is important, the simple quantitative input-output model will, at least in part, have to be given up but it may be replaced by a model of the linear-programming type. The main complication implied, apart from the problems of estimating alternative input coefficients, would be the necessity for some sort of preference function. It should be realized that the relationship between $(_4k_{ij}(X))$ and u is of particular importance because even if the individual items $_4k_{ij}(X)$ are small they will all be under the influence of the same arguments (X), and the combined effect in u of many small but systematically influenced $_4k_{ij}(X)$'s may be serious. It will, therefore, be necessary to determine the extent and scope of substitutions in input-output models, and to test experimentally the effects of substitutions on model forecasts.

(v) The existence of observation errors $_5k_{ij}(O)$ introduces a spurious variability in input-output coefficients. Experience from Norwegian data indicates that, when coefficient estimates are based on annual reports of production and raw material consumption, there are two or three main sources of error: some establishments report sales and purchases instead of production and actual usage; the difficulty of reducing time series of reported value figures to comparable units where quantity figures are missing or where reported quantities are in heterogeneous units; and the fact that some establishments in some years give faulty reports. It is almost impossible to discover minor inexactitudes, but careful study of individual returns may enable us to draw conclusions on the extent of major errors.

To sum up, an examination of observed coefficient variations, following the principles outlined above, will leave us with three types of variation:

(1) Variations which can be eliminated through a reformulation of the model, for instance by introducing trends, by revising sector specification, or by introducing linear functions.
(2) Variations which cannot be eliminated through reformulations of the model, and which are functionally related to the endogenous variables of the model.
(3) Variations which cannot be eliminated and which are not related to the endogenous variables of the model.

Since the implications of each type of variation for the evaluation of the model are presumably entirely different, it is important to determine the extent and scope of each type separately.

4. *Empirical Studies*

In the Central Bureau of Statistics of Norway an elaborate investigation was made of the nature and causes of variations in input coefficients. For these studies we have had at our disposal the returns from individual establishments for the annual census of production, reporting quantities and values of all important inputs and outputs in manufacturing establishments. Two studies are briefly described here, for the cork industry and for the mechanical woodpulp industry.

The cork industry

The first study is that of the coefficients for the principal material, cork, and for labour in the 13 establishments which produced cork products in the period 1949 to 1954. This is a relatively small and homogeneous industry, with a relatively simple production process. Its products are: expanded cork for insulation (about 50 per cent of output), bottle cork (20–30 per cent), floaters for fishing nets (10–15 per cent), life belts and other cork products. There appears to have been no important substitute for the main input, cork.

A summary description of the statistical material is given in Table 1, where individual establishments have been designated by letters *a* to *m*. Each of the first five establishments had an output of more than 600,000 Kr. in 1950 and each of the others less than 400,000 Kr. In the annual census the establishments are asked to report quantities and values of all commodities produced, of all raw materials used, as well as hours worked and wages and salaries paid. However, as appears from the

x

TABLE 1
Basic Data for the Cork Industry, 1949–1954

Establishment code	Number of years included	Number of years (excl. 1950) with quantity data for:		Percentage of production deflated on the basis of quantity data					Percentage distribution of production in 1950		
		Cork input	Labour input	1949	1951	1952	1953	1954	Bottle cork	Expanded cork	Other products
a	6	5	5	67	94	89	85	76	60	—	40
b	6	0	5	25	73	74	64	69	25	—	75
c	6	5	5	92	96	89	95	93	—	95	5
d	6	5	5	100	100	100	100	100	—	85	15
e	6	5	5	94	92	93	96	100	—	85	15
f	6	4	5	100	100	100	100	100	100	—	—
g	6	0	5	100	100	100	100	100	100	—	—
h	6	2	5	100	100	100	100	100	95	—	5
i	5	2	4	—	100	100	0	0	—	—	100
j	4	3	3	—	0	—	100	—	—	—	100
k	3	0	2	0	—	0	—	—	—	—	100
l	6	5	5	100	100	100	100	100	—	100	—
m	3	2	2	100	100	—	—	100	—	100	—
All									21	50	29

TABLE 2

Cork Industry: Coefficients Based on Values in Current Kroner

CORK INPUT

Establishment code	1949	1950	1951	1952	1953	1954	Average	Standard deviation
a	41·1	54·7	57·3	64·1	52·6	56·4	54·4	6·9
b	53·2	52·4	58·7	53·7	57·6	69·5	57·5	5·8
c	42·3	47·6	42·3	41·4	36·8	53·0	43·9	5·2
d	42·7	50·9	64·7	58·1	56·4	56·8	54·9	6·8
e	37·6	9·5*	26·7*	43·3	56·4	63·1	50·1	8·3
f	54·1	48·1	62·7	57·9	68·2	65·1	59·4	6·8
g	37·8	47·6	43·2	40·0	59·1	45·1	45·5	6·9
h	41·0	47·3	69·8	71·8	60·0	67·6	59·6	11·7
i	—	65·4	58·9	57·5	56·2	61·5	59·9	3·3
j	—	32·6	20·5	31·1	20·8	—	26·3	5·6
k	54·0	57·2	60·6	—	—	—	57·3	2·7
l	50·0	45·8	53·6	61·8	64·7	74·8	58·5	9·8
m	24·4*	58·9*	76·9*	—	—	—	—	—
Weighted Averages	44·0	51·4	57·4	54·7	51·7	57·5	52·8	4·6

LABOUR INPUT

Establishment code	1949	1950	1951	1952	1953	1954	Average	Standard deviation
a	25·8	28·4	25·6	16·9	17·8	18·1	22·1	4·5
b	13·3	15·4	14·1	15·1	14·4	11·3	13·9	1·4
c	17·8	18·7	17·2	20·6	17·4	16·5	18·0	1·3
d	16·9	16·7	19·9	18·3	17·3	18·1	17·9	1·1
e	21·1	16·5	19·3	15·7	18·0	18·2	18·1	1·8
f	28·2	24·3	21·8	21·2	22·7	17·1	22·6	3·4
g	32·7	28·0	27·2	—†	28·7	25·6	28·4	2·4
h	23·9	23·3	19·1	18·8	19·5	16·7	20·2	2·4
i	—	28·4	31·8	27·7	28·9	29·3	29·2	1·4
j	—	27·4	32·2	16·9	16·4	—	23·2	6·8
k	16·7	17·2	14·1	—	—	—	16·0	1·4
l	16·1	16·9	11·9	24·0	14·7	12·6	16·0	4·0
m	16·7	19·3	16·8	—	—	—	17·6	1·2
Weighted Averages	19·2	19·8	18·1	18·4	18·1	17·1	18·5	0·9

* Presumed faulty figures, excluded from calculations. † Wage figure lacking.

TABLE 3

Price Indexes (Unit Values) Derived from Establishment Returns

	1949	1950	1951	1952	1953	1954
Products						
Bottle corks	93	100	125	184	174	178
	97	100	105	145	139	157
	87	100	137	157	148	181
	85	100	138	154	148	180
	104	100	116	129	131	126
Expanded cork	107	100	118	116	123	127
	99	100	117	129	129	132
	102	100	94	124	124	133
	100	100	101	127	120	120
Inputs						
Cork and cork wood	91	100	123	148	134	152
	88	100	123	119	144	160
	100	100	125	167	175	207
	94	100	108	106	108	142
	92	100	122	190	181	192
	98	100	163	167	196	232
Labour, men	100	100	110	125	135	140
	97	100	113	—	148	150
	—	100	116	130	139	136
	89	100	108	122	130	133
	97	100	115	133	145	139
	96	100	113	130	128	145
	99	100	121	121	137	146
	68	100	119	132	136	145
	93	100	110	125	128	149
	81	100	102	109	124	138

table, not all the establishments gave all quantity figures for all the years.

The value coefficients in current kroner are given in Table 2. For items where both quantity and value figures are available a deflation to constant prices is possible on the basis of unit values. An examination of the variations in levels and trends of the unit values in Table 3 suggests, however, that these are not necessarily reflections of price movements alone, but may imply quality changes as well. In order to deflate the figures for items for which quantities are not reported, we had to construct price indexes on the basis of computed unit values for similar

TABLE 4

Cork Industry: Coefficients Based on Values in 1950 kroner

CORK INPUT

Establishment code	1949	1950	1951	1952	1953	1954	Average	Standard deviation
a	44·4	54·7	56·8	55·4	49·3	51·9	52·1	5·1
b	56·7	52·4	58·4	56·4	55·9	66·9	57·8	24
c	47·9	47·6	46·0	45·1	41·6	46·8	45·8	4·4
d	47·9	50·9	49·3	48·2	51·9	49·3	49·6	1·2
e	42·9	9·5*	22·0*	45·9	47·1	47·2	45·8	1·7
f	52·5	48·1	53·1	54·5	51·6	50·8	51·8	2·0
g	35·8	47·6	45·7	42·3	59·8	50·4	46·9	7·4
h	62·9	47·3	47·7	50·0	53·9	53·4	52·5	5·3
i	—	65·4	48·9	68·2	41·9	48·4	54·6	10·3
j	—	32·6	20·7	23·6	23·9	—	25·2	4·5
k	61·9	57·2	61·9	—	—	—	60·3	2·2
l	49·3	45·8	50·3	47·8	47·7	47·9	48·1	1·4
m	32·4*	58·9*	90·2*	—	—	—	—	—
Weighted Averages	49·6	51·3	51·7	51·8	49·9	51·7	51·0	0·9

LABOUR INPUT

Establishment code	1949	1950	1951	1952	1953	1954	Average	Standard deviation
a	24·2	28·4	25·4	21·8	20·8	20·8	23·6	2·8
b	14·4	15·4	17·1	18·7	16·4	13·6	15·9	1·7
c	18·4	18·7	17·9	18·4	16·7	14·5	17·4	1·5
d	18·5	16·7	17·1	18·2	16·8	16·2	17·3	0·8
e	25·9	16·5	19·1	18·7	17·2	14·5	18·7	3·6
f	25·9	24·3	25·1	25·0	24·0	21·0	24·2	1·6
g	28·9	28·0	32·8	35·0	29·0	30·9	30·8	2·5
h	25·5	23·3	19·7	17·3	17·9	14·9	19·8	3·6
i	—	28·4	24·2	24·4	22·6	27·2	25·4	2·1
j	—	27·4	27·5	11·7	11·5	—	19·5	7·9
k	18·3	17·2	17·8	—	—	—	17·8	0·5
l	15·9	16·9	12·6	24·8	14·0	11·9	16·0	4·3
m	19·0	19·3	19·8	—	—	—	19·4	0·6
Weighted Averages	20·2	19·9	19·8	20·6	18·3	16·6	19·2	1·4

* Presumed faulty figures, excluded from calculations.

items; the extent to which this was necessary appears from Table 1. The deflated coefficients are shown in Table 4.

The input coefficients for cork for establishment e in 1950 and 1951, and all the coefficients for cork for establishment m, were judged to be based on faulty returns and were excluded from subsequent calculations. One establishment in some of the years produced a product which was not made of cork; this part of its production was excluded from the calculation of input coefficients for cork, but not for labour.

The input coefficient for cork and corkwood

The six-year averages for the constant-price coefficient for cork, shown in Table 4, vary from 46 to 61 per cent, with the exception of establishment j, which had an average of only 25 per cent; the product of j was different from those of the others.

In order to find out if the product is decisive for the average coefficients, we grouped establishments (excluding j) according to product type. The simple average of coefficients for establishments producing mainly bottle corks is $50 \cdot 8 \pm 2 \cdot 3$ per cent, expanded cork $47 \cdot 3 \pm 1 \cdot 6$ per cent, and other products $57 \cdot 6 \pm 2 \cdot 3$ per cent (4 establishments in each group). The results suggest that the coefficient is moderately influenced by the type of product.

The standard deviations for the constant-price coefficients vary from $1 \cdot 4$ to $10 \cdot 3$. In all but two cases the standard deviation for the constant-price coefficient is less than for the current-price coefficient. (Compare Tables 2 and 4.) The difference is greater for those establishments where the deflation has been based on directly reported quantities than for those where imputed unit values from other establishments have been used. Also, the absolute value of the standard deviation is less for the former class. A simple average of the standard deviations for those establishments where quantities of cork input are missing for at least two years is $5 \cdot 94$ but for the rest only $2 \cdot 47$. The reason for this may be that deflation by the use of imputed unit values has not been entirely successful, that the establishments not reporting quantities have even in other respects given inaccurate data or that these establishments are operating in a more haphazard manner than the others.

In order to decide whether there was any indication that variations in coefficients were governed by some common outside cause, such as variations in prices, we made the following computations:

Let:

$$a_{ij} = \text{cork input coefficient for establishment } i \text{ in year } j.$$

$A_i = \dfrac{\sum_j a_{ij}}{n_i} =$ average cork input coefficient for establishment i

over the number of years, n_i, covered by reports from this establishment.

$$\sigma_i^2 = \frac{\sum_j (a_{ij} - A_i)^2}{n_i} \; .$$

$$\delta_{ij} = \frac{a_{ij} - A_i}{\sigma_i} \; .$$

$N_j =$ number of establishments covered in year j.

Then we have

$$\delta = \sum_i \sum_j \delta_{ij} \frac{1}{\sum_i n_i} = 0$$

$$\sigma_\delta^2 = \sum_i \sum_j \delta_{ij}^2 \frac{1}{\sum_i n_i} = 1 \; .$$

The standard deviation of the sum $\sum_i \delta_{ij}$ must then be $\sqrt{N_j}$ and computing $\dfrac{\sum_i \delta_{ij}}{\sqrt{N_j}}$ we get:

Year	1949	1950	1951	1952	1953	1954
$\dfrac{\sum_i \delta_{ij}}{\sqrt{N_j}}$	$-0{\cdot}832$	$-0{\cdot}560$	$0{\cdot}762$	$0{\cdot}060$	$-0{\cdot}175$	$0{\cdot}781$

In no year was the deviation of this sum from zero more than 83 per cent of the standard deviation, which must be taken as a clear indication that there was no common cause of the deviations.

We have also examined whether the variation of the coefficient for individual establishments depends on variations in the level of production. For each establishment the coefficient for each year was plotted against the production level of the establishment in the same year, but no indication of correlation was found, with the possible exception of one establishment.

As appears from Table 4, the majority of deviations from the six-year averages are relatively small, more than half of them being less than 2 percentage points, and four-fifths of them less than 5 points. The deviations of more than 5 points have been examined and grouped according to the apparently most plausible explanation. Excluding faulty figures, there are 13 such deviations: 5 of these were ascribed to the reporting of sales and purchases instead of production and consump-

tion by one of the establishments, 4 to deflation difficulties, 1 to technological change, and the remaining 3 partly to inexact reporting and partly
to deflation difficulties. If this interpretation is correct, the apparent
variations in the coefficients are primarily the effects of imperfect
observation techniques.

Turning now to averages for all establishments, 'the industry', the
overall average is 48·7 ± 1·55 per cent, including all deflated values of
inputs and of outputs for each year. Excluding other than cork products
and the presumed faulty figures changes the average to 51·0 and the
standard deviation to 0·90, as shown in Table 4. The figures used in
these calculation were derived by deflating the reported figures from
each establishment by individual unit-value indexes. If instead we used
the average unit values for the entire group of establishments, the results
would be slightly modified, giving an average coefficient of 52·0 and a
standard deviation of 1·29. The latter procedure, which is presumably
less exact and which gives the greater standard deviation, is the one
which would normally be employed in computing average coefficients
for an industry.

The year-to-year variations in average coefficients for the industry
could not be explained by changes in product composition or in the
distribution of production between establishments. Nor is there any
indication of correlation between changes in production and these
coefficients. It will be seen from Table 4 that the standard deviation for
the average industry coefficient is less than that for any single
establishment.

To sum up, the volume coefficients are more stable than current value
coefficients. Variations over time in the observed individual volume
input-coefficients are probably mainly caused by inexact reporting by
the establishment and by deflation errors. Differences in coefficients
between the establishments seem partly to be caused by differences in
product mix. When the average coefficient for the industry is computed
for each year, some of the errors cancel, and some are excluded if
presumed faulty returns are omitted. The remaining variations over
time in the industry coefficient must be ascribed to variations in coefficients for individual establishments. Changes in level of production,
in product composition, or in the distribution of production between
enterprises had no appreciable influence on the industry coefficient.

The labour coefficient

As shown by Table 4, the six-year average varies from 16 to 25 per
cent, except that in one case it is as high as 31. When establishments are

grouped according to main product, for establishments producing mainly bottle cork the average is 24·6 ± 4·0 per cent, for expanded cork 17·8 ± 1·2 per cent, and for other cork 19·7 ± 3·6 per cent.

The standard deviations for individual establishments vary from 0·5 to 7·9 and only for 4 out of the 13 establishments is the standard deviation less for the constant-price than for the current-price coefficients (the latter being shown in Table 2).

However, if we plot for each establishment the constant-price coefficient against an index of production and fit a negatively inclined line to the points, we find that the standard deviation from the line is less than the standard deviation from the average for 9 of the 13 establishments, and for only 2 is the opposite true. A still closer fit would be obtained if we introduced an increase in productivity in the coefficients for 8 or 9 of the establishments in 1953 and 1954 and for one in 1952. The standard deviations from individually fitted, not positively inclined, lines are not greater than 2·1 percentage points for any of the establishments, except *j*, where obviously an important technical change occurred in 1952.

One may also ask whether the average coefficient for an establishment was related to its average level of production. Apparently this is not the case: Figure 1 shows relatively high labour coefficients in some of the small establishments, but there are also small establishments with low coefficients; the existence of a general tendency can hardly be inferred.

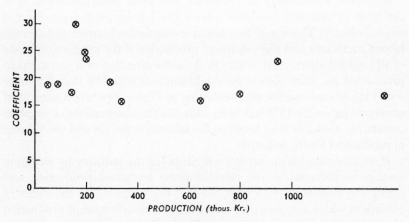

Fig. 1. Cork industry: Average production and average labour coefficient by establishment

It is more difficult to judge whether there is a central tendency for the individual establishments. The figures shown in Table 5 are inconclusive.

TABLE 5

Regression of Labour Coefficient on Volume of Production* by Establishment

Main product	Range of variations in production in % of average production	Regression coefficient
Bottle cork	10	0†
Expanded cork	18	0†
Other	54	0†
Expanded cork	18	0†
Other	34	0·05
Expanded cork	25	0·10
Other	17	0·15
Expanded cork	102	0·16
Expanded cork	74	0·29
Bottle cork	44	0·31
Bottle cork	33	0·35
Bottle cork	36	0·35
Other	12	0·38

* 1950 = 100.

† The arithmetic mean gives a better fit than any negatively inclined regression line.

Since the relationship is important for some establishments, it is desirable to examine how this affects the labour coefficients for the whole industry. There may be a negative correlation between the average labour coefficient and the volume of production if the production levels of all establishments tend to vary in the same direction or if variations in production are more violent for establishments with low than for those with high labour coefficients. According to Figure 2 (where a somewhat uncertain figure for 1939 has been added to the observations) a negative correlation seems to exist between the labour coefficient and the volume of production for the industry.

If we compute labour input coefficients for the industry by weighing average coefficients for the establishments by actual production and taking the average in each year, we find the variations in the industry coefficient which are caused by changes in the distribution of production between establishments, as shown in Table 6 below.

The standard deviation of the actual observations is 1·38 and of the computed values 1·41. Apparently there is no correlation, and all the variation in the coefficient for the industry must be due to changes in coefficients for the establishments, presumably mainly caused by product variations but also by productivity increases.

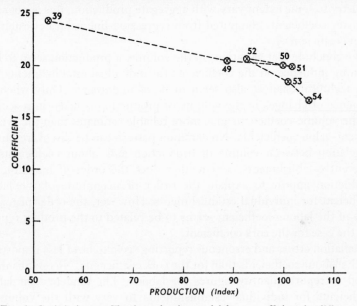

Fig. 2. Cork industry: Total production and labour coefficient in different years

TABLE 6

Labour Input Coefficients for the Cork Industry

Year	1949	1950	1951	1952	1953	1954
Actual	20·2	19·9	19·8	20·6	18·3	16·6
Obtained by 'standard computation'	19·1	19·2	19·2	19·4	19·6	19·2
Obtained by using regression-line values for individual establishments	19·8	20·1	19·3	19·2	18·2	17·3

Average coefficients were also computed and are also shown in Table 6 by taking the values of points on the regression lines corresponding to the reported production in each year for each establishment. The standard deviation of the actual values about the regression line values is 0·7 as against a standard deviation of 1·4 about the mean. The largest deviations are in 1952 and in 1954. An examination of the results for individual establishments indicates that these discrepancies would disappear if correction could be made for productivity increases in 1953 and 1954. (It is remarkable that, while the actual coefficients for the industry to some extent vary with aggregate production, this is not so for industry coefficients computed from regression-line values of establishment coefficients.)

We conclude that variations in the volume of production seem to have a strong influence on the coefficients for individual establishments, and that technical changes also seem to be of importance. Only when the influence of changes in the volume of production is taken into account do the volume-coefficients give more reliable estimates than the average current-value coefficients. No common pattern can be discovered in the correlation between volume of production and labour coefficients for different establishments, and neither does the order of magnitude of production appear to explain the order of magnitude of the labour coefficient for individual establishments. However, the order of magnitude of the labour coefficient seems to be related to the product type, as was the case for the cork coefficient.

Deflation errors and erroneous reporting seem to be of less importance for the labour coefficients than for the cork coefficients. No establishment failed to report quantity figures for labour. The tendency for labour coefficients for individual establishments to vary with the volume of production is to some extent reflected in the figures for the industry as a whole. Changes in product mix and in the distribution between establishments have no apparent influence on coefficients in the observation period.

Technological change in the mechanical woodpulp industry

The second study to be described is on the mechanical woodpulp industry. This industry also has a relatively simple production process, with one dominating raw material, lumber, which is ground to pulp. Only the coefficient for the use of lumber is discussed here. The coefficients were computed in physical units, in cubic metres of lumber per ton of pulp, for each of the years 1949 to 1956 for all establishments in the census. Altogether 48 establishments were covered, but only 38 reported production in all the years, as seen from Table 7.[1]

Five establishments (Nos. 44 to 48) were found to produce pulp of broadleaf-tree timber, which is qualitatively different from the product

---

[1] The value coefficients would be about 0·2 times the physical unit coefficient.

TABLE 7

Mechanical Woodpulp Industry:
Cubic Metres of Timber per Ton of Product (Dry Weight)

Establishment code§	1949	1950	1951	1952	1953	1954	1955	1956	Average high	low	Aver- age σ
Large est. 1	2·74	2·74	2·58	2·53	2·53	2·56	2·64	2·60	2·81	2·66	0·08
2	2·80	2·66	2·75	2·79	2·76 | 2·58	2·61	2·56		2·75	2·58	0·04
3	2·80	2·80	2·57	2·80	2·80	2·80	2·80	2·80	2·77	—	0·08
4	2·44	2·42	2·55	2·49	2·45	2·48	2·47	2·37	—	2·46	0·05
5	2·80	2·80	2·77	2·81	2·80 | 2·70	2·70	2·70		2·80	2·70	0·01
6	2·80	2·76	2·76	2·76	2·50	2·76	2·76	2·76	2·73	—	0·09
7	2·84	2·76	2·77	2·76	2·76 | 2·47	2·56	2·56		2·78	2·53	0·04
8	2·80	2·76	2·76	2·76	2·76 | 2·57	2·56	2·60		2·77	2·58	0·02
9	2·53	2·80	2·80	2·80	2·80	2·80 | 2·67	2·60		2·76	2·64	0·09
10	2.85	2·65	2·65	2·65	2·70	2·70	2·70	2·70	2·70	—	0·06
11	2·68	2·60	2·64	2·70	2·60 | 2·51	2·44	2·46		2·64	2·47	0·04
Medium est. 12	(2·89)	(2·95)	(2·76)	(2·80)	(5·09)	(1·87)	(2·06)	(2·68)	(2·89)	—	(0·91)
12*	2·85	2·85	2·85	2·85 | 2·55	2·55	2·55	2·55		2·85	2·55	—
13	2·79	2·58	2·80	2·80	2·80	2·80	2·80	2·80	2·77	—	0·07
14	(2·80)	(3·25)	(2·46)	(3·08)	(2·67)	(3·03)	(2·63)	(2·60)	(2·82)	—	(0·26)
14*	2·80	2·80	2·80	2·80	2·80	2·80	2·80	2·80	2·80	—	—
15	2·80	2·65	2·73	2·72	2·80	2·80	2·80	2·80	2·76	—	0·05
16	2·69	2·67	2·70	2·76	2·77	2·80	2·65	2·70	2·72	—	0·05
17	—	2·64	2·67	2·74 | 2·60	2·55	2·60	2·44		2·68	2·55	0·06
18	2·60	2·60	2·80	2·75	2·60	2·60	2·60	2·60	—	2·64	0·08
19	2·70	2·60	2·60	2·60	2·60	2·75	2·80	2·80	1·68	—	0·09
20	—	—	—	2·74	2·60	2·55	2·54	2·46	—	2·58	0·09
Small est. 21	2·80	2·79	2·81	2·80	2·80	2·80	2·66	2·79	2·78	—	0·05
22	2·97	2·65	2·82	2·80 | 2·65	2·65	2·69	—		2·81	2·66	0·08
23	2·99	2·92	2·97	3·01	2·79	2·80	2·80	2·66	2·87	—	0·12
24	2·80	2·80	2·79	2·79	2·80	2·77	2·80	2·80	2·79	—	0·01
25	2·80	2·80	2·80	(3·50)	(2·70)	2·80	2·74	2·77	(2·86)	—	(0·24)
25*	2·80	2·80	2·80	2·80	2·80	2·80	2·74	2·77	2·79	—	0·02
26	2·80	2·65	2·96	3·00	2·97	2·80	2·80	2·90	2·86	—	0·11
27	2·81	2·81	2·79	2·80	2·79	2·76	2·71	2·85	2·79	—	0·04
28	2·80	2·80	2·81	2·81	2·80	2·80	2·80 | 2·51		2·80	2·51	0·00
29	—	2·74	2·80 | 2·60	2·60	2·60	2·60	2·56		2·77	2·59	0·02
30	3·00	2·80	2·80	2·80	2·80	—	—	—	2·84	—	0·08
31	—	2·83†	2·83†	2·81	2·80	2·80	2·84	2·87	2·83	—	0·02
32	2·78	2·72 | 2·60	2·60	2·60	2·60	2·60	2·60		2·75	2·60	0·01
33	2·60	2·60	2·60	2·60	2·60	2·60	2·60	2·60	—	2·60	0·00
34	2·68	2·57	2·69	2·62	2·71	2·62	—	2·58	—	2·64	0·05
35	2·22	2·43	2·72	2·51	2·67	2·36	2·40	2·45	—	2·47	0·15
36	2·80	2·64	2·70	2·70	2·70	2·70	2·70	2·70	2·71	—	0·04
37	2·60	2·80	2·80	2·80	2·80	—	—	—	2·77	—	0·08
38	2·79	2·74	2·75	2·74	2·70 | 2·55	2·60	2·44		2·74	2·53	0·05
39	2·80	2·80 | 2·57	2·50	2·51	2·48	2·51	2·52		2·80	2·52	0·02
40	2·82	2·82	2·82	2·82 | 2·68	2·05	2·32	2·89		2·82	2·49	0·23
41	2·80	2·80	2·80	2·80	2·80	2·80	2·80	2·80	2·80	—	0·00
42	—	—	—	2·49	3·01	2·02	2·30	2·59	—	2·48	0·33
43	2·80	2·80	2·80	2·80	2·80	2·80 | 2·36	2·40		2·80	2·38	0·00
Weighted Average	2·75	2·71	2·70	2·72	2·71	2·63	2·62	2·62	2·78‡	2·56‡	
Broadleaf 44	3·14	3·16	3·23	—	—	—	—	—	3·18	—	0·04
45	3·16	3·00	2·93	3·07	3·16	3·03	3·20	2·82	3·04	—	0·12
46	4·00	3·70	3·43	—	—	—	—	—	3·71	—	0·23
47	3·26	3·20	3·29	4·09	2·57	2·66	3·08	3·37	3·19	—	0·44
48	2·86	3·36	3·12	3·03	3·00	2·99	2·79	2·76	2·99	—	0·18

Note: Figures in brackets are believed to be faulty.
* Corrected for presumably faulty figures.
† Average 1950–51. Production in 1950 was negligible.   ‡ Unweighted.
§ Large establishments: output 20,000–45,000 tons in 1956; small establishments: under 10,000 tons.

of the other establishments; they were excluded from the subsequent analysis.

The study indicates the existence of several levels for the coefficient. Twenty of the establishments have relatively high coefficients throughout the period, 7 have low coefficients throughout, and 16 change from high to low during the period; the approximate points of change have been indicated by vertical bars in the table. For each establishment the averages of high and low coefficients have been separately computed, and standard deviations around these averages have been calculated and, where necessary, an average taken. For only 8 of the 43 establishments are the standard deviations over 0·1. Of these none is a large establishment, 2 are medium-sized and the rest are small. The largest standard deviation, 0·91, was found in the medium-sized group: the establishment No. 12 underwent a major reconstruction in the year 1953 and we have evidence that they reported sales and purchases instead of production and usage. The other establishment in the medium-sized group (No. 14) with a large standard deviation, 0·26, shows a regular cyclical pattern in the coefficient; the weighted average for the entire period is 2·80. We take this as an indication that even in this case the variation is due to a reporting of sales and purchases instead of production and usage. Of the remaining 6 large standard deviations, 1 is definitely known to be due to a single case of erroneous reporting; the rest may well be due to reporting of sales and purchases, but we have no positive evidence of this. The variations in coefficients for the establishments concerned have, even in combination, very little influence on the coefficient for the industry.

In the following computations we substitute average coefficients for observations which we definitely believe to be based on erroneous reporting.

The unweighted average of all the establishment averages of high coefficients is 2·78 ± 0·05 and of low coefficients 2·56 ± 0·08. The scatter of (adjusted) individual observations about these two 'normals' is, however, considerable. A frequency distribution of the individual observations is presented in Figure 3.

Let us make the assumption that there are two techniques in operation, the 'old' one with a typical coefficient of 2·85 and the 'new' one with a typical coefficient of 2·45. All establishments are using either one or the other, or a mixture of the two. There will then be a given percentage of old technique associated with each coefficient, coefficients of 2·85 and above giving percentage 100, coefficients of 2·45 and below giving percentage 0, and intermediate coefficients giving intermediate percen-

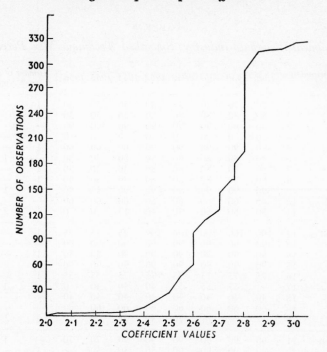

FIG. 3. Mechanical woodpulp industry: cumulative frequency distribution of observed timber coefficients*

tages. Finding the mixture corresponding to each (adjusted) observation, and adjusting these figures so as to obtain a monotonous downward trend for each establishment, we obtain the figures shown in Table 8. Assuming that these figures represent technological development in each establishment, we compute the corresponding percentage for the technology mix in the industry, and compare the corresponding coefficient with the actual industry average. The results are shown in Table 9.

The standard deviation of the adjusted coefficients about their average is 0·049, and the standard deviation of the adjusted coefficients about the corresponding 'technological-mix coefficients' is 0·013; in other words changes in 'technological mix' explain more than two-thirds of the variations in the industry coefficient. The only deviation of more than 0·01 occurs in 1950: we know that the industry bought timber in excess of use in 1949 and reduced stocks in 1950. Hence the tendency to report purchases instead of use would explain much of the discrepancy in 1950.

* Cubic metres of timber per ton of woodpulp (dryweight).

TABLE 8

Mechanical Woodpulp Industry: Smoothed 'Technique Mix' Percentages

Establishment code	1949	1950	1951	1952	1953	1954	1955	1956	Large*	Small	Total
Large est. 1	70	70	30	30	30	30	30	30	1	—	1
2	80	80	80	80	80	30	30	30	1	—	1
3	90	90	90	90	90	90	90	90	—	—	—
4	0	0	0	0	0	0	0	0	—	—	—
5	90	90	90	90	90	60	60	60	1	—	1
6	90	80	80	80	80	80	80	80	—	1	1
7	80	80	80	80	80	30	30	30	1	—	1
8	80	80	80	80	80	30	30	30	1	—	1
9	90	90	90	90	90	90	55	40	1	1	2
10	60	60	60	60	60	60	60	60	—	—	—
11	50	50	50	50	40	15	0	0	1	2	3
Medium est. 12	100	100	100	100	100	25	25	25	1	—	1
13	90	90	90	90	90	90	90	90	—	—	—
14	90	90	90	90	90	90	50	50	1	—	1
15	90	90	90	90	90	90	90	90	—	—	—
16	75	75	75	75	75	75	55	55	1	—	1
17	—	55	55	55	40	40	40	0	1	1	2
18	40	40	40	40	40	40	40	40	—	—	—
19	60	60	60	60	60	60	60	60	—	—	—
20	—	—	—	70	40	25	20	0	2	2	4
Small est. 21	90	90	90	90	90	90	70	70	—	1	1
22	90	90	90	90	50	50	50	—	1	—	1
23	100	100	100	100	90	90	90	50	1	1	2
24	90	90	90	90	90	90	90	90	—	—	—
25	90	90	90	90	90	90	80	80	—	1	1
26	100	100	100	100	100	100	100	100	—	—	—
27	90	90	90	90	85	85	85	85	—	1	1
28	90	90	90	90	90	90	90	15	1	—	1
29	—	80	80	40	40	40	40	30	1	1	2
30	100	90	90	90	90	—	—	—	—	1	1
31	—	95	95	90	90	90	90	90	—	1	1
32	80	70	40	40	40	40	40	40	1	1	2
33	40	40	40	40	40	40	40	40	—	—	—
34	50	50	50	50	50	50	50	50	—	—	—
35	0	0	0	0	0	0	0	0	—	—	—
36	60	60	60	60	60	60	60	60	—	—	—
37	90	90	90	90	90	90	—	—	—	—	—
38	85	75	75	75	75	30	30	0	2	1	3
39	90	90	30	15	15	15	15	15	1	1	2
40	90	90	90	90	10	10	10	10	1	—	1
41	90	90	90	90	90	90	90	90	—	—	—
42	—	—	—	10	10	10	10	10	—	—	—
43	90	90	90	90	90	90	0	0	1	—	1

* 20 percentage points and more.

We have thus been able to explain nearly all the variations in a physical coefficient as the result of erroneous reporting and technological change.

TABLE 9

Average Input Coefficients for Timber

Year	Index of production	Unadjusted average coefficient	Adjusted average coefficient	Average computed on the basis of 'technological mix' percentages
1949	100	2·75	2·75	2·74
1950	118	2·71	2·70	2·73
1951	123	2·70	2·71	2·72
1952	115	2·72	2·71	2·71
1953	118	2·71	2·71	2·70
1954	142	2·63	2·63	2·66
1955	140	2·62	2·62	2·63
1956	145	2·62	2·62	2·62

5. *Conclusion*

It was argued in this chapter that the input-output model must be evaluated on the basis of errors in estimates of production levels (the vector u) whereas the extent and causes of variations can best be studied by examining individual input coefficients. It was assumed that the deviations of input coefficients from expected values (k_{ij}) can be broken down into several, additive components. Some of these components can be taken into account through a reformulation of the model which, though it does not make it theoretically more complicated, adds to data requirements; some by more precise observation techniques; and some by a more detailed sector specification.

The empirical study of two Norwegian industries gives some indication of the scope and character of input coefficient variations. In the case of the cork industry it was found that (*a*) volume coefficients for the principal raw material were more stable than value coefficients; (*b*) variations over time were mainly due to observation errors; (*c*) variations between establishments were partly due to differences in product-mix; (*d*) the average coefficient for the group of establishments was more stable than individual establishment coefficients; (*e*) as regards the labour coefficient, variations in the volume of output had a strong influence on it; (*f*) technological change also had a strong influence; (*g*) but observation errors were less important than for the raw material coefficient.

In the case of the mechanical woodpulp industry it was found for the principal raw material coefficient that (*h*) while some establishments had consistently high or consistently low coefficients, there was also a number which changed from high to low coefficients during the period of observation, suggesting that the industry was undergoing technological change; and (*i*) if a few obviously faulty entries are corrected, and if observations are smoothed out in accordance with the hypothesis of unidirectional technological change in each establishment, nearly all the variation in the average industry coefficient over the time is explained.

REFERENCE

[1] JOHANSEN, L., *A multisectoral study of economic growth*, Amsterdam, 1960.

COMMENTS ON MR SEVALDSON'S PAPER

by TSUNEHIKO WATANABE

Effect of changes in input-output coefficients

There are at least two types of considerations regarding the stability of the input-output coefficient. The first concerns the possible over-all effects or disturbances on the solution of the input-output model due to the instability of the coefficients, while the second concerns characterizing the elements of variations in the coefficients, if they are varying. These two types of considerations are highly interdependent as the input-output model itself.

The first type of investigation may be helpful for practical use of the model, especially for the purpose of prediction, as Sevaldson described briefly at the beginning of his paper. Since his discussion of this problem is rather sketchy, it may be useful to add to it.

By using the author's notation, we can easily derive the following relation,

$$u = \bar{X} - X = (I - A)^{-1} k \bar{X}. \tag{1}$$

If we impose the condition that $e'K = 0'$, where e' and $0'$ are row vectors $(1, \ldots, 1)$, and $(0, \ldots, 0)$ respectively, the above relation can be rewritten as:

$$e'(I - A)u = e'k\bar{X} = 0. \tag{2}$$

Therefore, $\sum_j v_j u_j = 0$, the sum of changes due to the difference (i.e. k), is always zero under the weighting system v_j's $(j = 1, \ldots, n)$. This derivation can be interpreted as indicating that over-estimation and under-estimation of the solution level have to appear simultaneously under the condition of $e'k = 0'$, and also this statement would be a sufficient approximation for the case of $e'k \neq 0'$ unless changes are drastic, which may not happen frequently during the period considered.

A more detailed evaluation of u_j $(j = 1, \ldots, n)$ may be done in the following way. By using the same notation, the relation,

$$X = [I + (I - \bar{A})^{-1}k]^{-1}\bar{X} \tag{3}$$

is already known to us [1]. In ordinary circumstances, it will be safe to assume that the norm of the matrix $[I + (I - \bar{A})^{-1}k]^{-1}$ is sufficiently small to expand this matrix into the following series:

$$X = [I - (I - \bar{A})^{-1}k + [(I - \bar{A})^{-1}k]^2 \ldots]\bar{X}$$

$$= [I - \bar{B}k + (\bar{B}k)^2 \ldots]\bar{X}, \quad \text{where } \bar{B} = (I - \bar{A})^{-1} \tag{4}$$

Therefore,

$$u = [-\bar{B}k + (\bar{B}k)^2 \ldots]\bar{X} \tag{5}$$

This derivation implies that, as a first order approximation, the numerical value of $\bar{B}k\bar{X}$ will be a sufficient indicator of the size of u. Furthermore, if $k\bar{X} = 0$ (where 0 is $n \times 1$ matrix), there will be no errors due to changes in the original input-output coefficients. The last proposition may give us the useful criterion that if the changes in the input-output coefficients of any specified row are in both negative and positive directions, then the over-all errors would be rather small.

When a high-speed electronic computer is available, however, the direct evaluation of u based on the equations (1) or (3) is most informative and advisable.

Technological changes

The second type of consideration, which is much emphasized by Sevaldson, will give economists a more intensive and most interesting problem. The following discussion, therefore, concerns only this topic. More specifically, the scope of this discussion will be restricted mainly to the characterization of the technological changes, which may be the author's main object in his paper.

The notion of technological changes, which was initially formulated by Hicks for the case in which there are two factors of production, will be generalized into the case in which there are more than two factors of production. The production function $X = \phi(v_1 \ldots, v_n, \tau)$ specifies the maximum quantity of X, the output that can be produced, by using factors of production in quantities $v_1 \ldots, v_n$ under the state of technology

τ, and is assumed to satisfy all neo-classical schools' framework for the theory of production. Following the analogy of consumer's theory, we can define the substitution term of $S_{i\tau}$ of factor i with respect to τ by

$$S_{i\tau} = \frac{1}{v_i} \frac{\delta v_i}{\delta \tau} + \phi_\tau \quad (i = 1, \ldots, n). \tag{6}$$

Using this term $S_{i\tau}$, the technological change will be called

$$\begin{cases} i - \text{saving} \\ i - \text{neutral} \qquad \text{if } S_{i\tau} \gtreqless 0 \\ i - \text{dissaving} \end{cases}$$

For example, in the case of the Cobb-Douglas production function, it is easily shown that

$$S_{i\tau} = -\frac{\alpha_i'(\tau)}{\alpha_i(\tau)} \quad (i = 1, \ldots, n). \tag{7}$$

Furthermore, the relation of $\sum r_i S_{i\tau} = 0$, where r_i is the relative share of the ith input to total cost, will be proved easily [2]. Combining this relation with the definition of $S_{i\tau}$, the amount of technological change, ϕ_τ, will be characterized.

Statistical measurements of $S_{i\tau}$ and ϕ_τ will need one more qualification, however, if the prices of factors of production are varied. Since the definition of the term $S_{i\tau}$ was based on the *ceteribus paribus* assumption about changes in prices, i.e. the notion of the partial derivative was used to define $S_{i\tau}$, the partial derivative has to be re-defined by the total derivative. Then, after price changes, $S_{i\tau}$ will be re-defined as follows:

$$S_{i\tau} = \frac{1}{v_i} \frac{\Delta v_i}{\Delta \tau} - \frac{1}{v_i} \sum_j \frac{\delta v_i}{\delta w_j} \frac{\Delta w_j}{\Delta \tau} + \phi_\tau \tag{8}$$

where

$$\Delta v_i = \sum_j \frac{\delta v_i}{\delta w_j} \Delta w_j + \frac{\delta v_i}{\delta \tau} \Delta \tau,$$

and w_j is the price of the jth factor.

The above generalization of a Hicksian classification of technological changes implies that (1) it is impossible for a technological change to be i-saving (or i-dissaving) for all factors i; and (2) it is rather misleading to identify a technological change in a quantitative term without knowing the price situation.

This kind of formulation of a technological change is sufficiently compatible with the author's discussion, although his statements are rather scattered. Thus, we can discuss his empirical results from the viewpoint of the above stated formulation of a technological change.

Before discussing the two empirical studies, I have to express my appreciation of the data collection by the Central Bureau of Statistics of Norway because it reflects patience and time-consuming effort. The data themselves deserve merit, and so does the author's careful procedure of investigation.

Empirical studies

The author's conclusion with regard to the main input coefficient for the cork industry will be interpreted as, say, that the coefficients would be considerably stable over time under a proper reporting system and a suitable adjustment of the product-mix. Although he did emphasize this stability in volume coefficients, compared with value coefficients, there appeared to be no decisive differences between the two coefficients, because the reduction in the standard deviation may not be significant in a sample of this size. Thus in general we may be able to apply the above conclusion for both types of coefficients. This would imply that there is no conclusive evidence concerning the choice between two hypotheses on input-output coefficients, Leontief's or Klein's.

First, with regard to the difference between the stability of volume coefficients and that of value coefficients, the following test may give us the better alternative, if there is a sufficient number of samples and if there is also enough independent fluctuation in relative prices. That is, for value coefficients,

$$\log (P_i X_{ij}) = \beta_0 + \beta_1 \log (P_j X_j) + \epsilon \tag{9}$$

and for volume coefficients

$$\log (P_i X_{ij}) = \delta_0 + \delta_1 \log (P_j X_j) + \delta_2 \log \frac{P_i}{P_j} + \eta \tag{10}$$

where P_i and P_j are the prices of input and output. The constancy of the value coefficients can be tested by the criterion, $\beta_1 = 1$, while the criterion for the volume coefficients should be $\delta_1 = \delta_2 = 1$. If these two criteria are satisfied by the data, we can state that equations (9) and (10) correspond to the Cobb-Douglas and the Leontief production function respectively.[1]

---

[1] All assumptions which are ordinarily used in the neo-classical theory of production and the integrability condition have to be taken for granted in order to get the production function from the above two equations.

Secondly, the testing of the remaining input coefficients for the cork industry would be desirable in view of the statement which I made in the previous section, even though the remaining coefficients are ̄aggregated into one. This test will provide a reasonable basis to judge the nature of constancy.

The conclusion which the author derived with regard to the labour coefficient in the cork industry seemed to be very reasonable. The interpretation of this conclusion, however, may need some qualification. First, in the usual application of the input-output technique, which is mostly based on the open model, the variation in the labour coefficients will not disturb the production matrix. Furthermore, if the value-added ratio, which covers direct capital and labour costs, is stable, changes in the labour coefficients will be handled rather easily.

Second, since substitution between capital and labour is indicated by the author's analyses, a further test which would provide the classification of a technological change seems to be important and could be made either by using the formulation stated in the previous section, or another type of production function such as that with a constant elasticity of substitution.

This statement would be applicable to the case of the mechanical woodpulp industry. Although the relation between the 'new' technique and the 'old' one may well be due to the introduction of timber-saving technique, as the author pointed out, it will still be advisable to identify this element more explicitly in relation to other input changes.

In conclusion I must emphasize the necessity of this type of research in order to promote the practical application of input-output techniques.

[1] Evans, W. D., 'The Effect of Structural Matrix Errors on Interindustry Relations Estimates,' *Econometrica*, Vol. 22, 1954, p. 461.

[2] Uzawa, H. and Watanabe, T., *A Note on the Classification of Technical Inventions*, Technical Report No. 85, Applied Mathematics and Statistics Laboratories, Stanford University, 1960.

CHAPTER 17

Problems of Standardization of Input-Output Statistics: a Debate

by V. CAO-PINNA *and* B. ROELANTS DU VIVIER, W. I. ABRAHAM *and*
M. HOFFENBERG, M. R. GOLDMAN, O. AUKRUST,
Z. KENESSEY *and* A. NOVAK

A SUGGESTED APPROACH TO STANDARDIZATION

by VERA CAO-PINNA *and* B. ROELANTS DU VIVIER

Macro-economic data on national accounts now available in nearly all countries represent a substantial advance since the beginning of the present century. This advance is, however, still restricted in scope since national accounts statistics do not make it possible to analyse deeply enough the economic structure.

It is obviously no longer necessary today to dwell on the value of studying the relationships between industries since nearly all industrialized and developing countries have input-output tables, depicting the more-or-less detailed interindustry relations of their economy. It seems that, although a number of economists have made a contribution in this field since Leontief's first efforts, the possibilities of this method have not yet been exploited to the full. For example, the most promising line open to input-output analysis, namely bringing to light differences which exist between countries in respect of means of production and their cost, has not yet been fully followed up since each country has concentrated on internal studies, totally disregarding the data of its neighbours and competitors, relying upon data based solely on national nomenclatures.

The present anarchic state of the applications of input-output, which makes it impossible to draw comparisons, calls in the first place for the adoption of a common language. In order to achieve this a certain number of definitions and conventions relating to the compilation and consolidation of national tables must be established by common agreement. For the sake of international comparability, in our opinion a manual could be prepared to enable countries to establish input-output tables which would be comparable with each other and would make it possible: (*a*) to study technological changes in major sectors of the national economy; (*b*) to assess the true impact of public intervention in the national productive system; (*c*) to compare the degree of dependence of each sector of the national economy with that existing in other parts of the world; and (*d*) to make international comparisons between the structures of national economies, or at least between some basic industries such as iron and steel, fuel and power, or transport.

The input-output manual, which would be designed solely for this form of accounting, according to our view should comprise: (*a*) a set of definitions; (*b*) rules for aggregation; (*c*) the conventions relating to general questions, especially the breakdown of final demand and added value; and (*d*) criteria for compiling the internal section of the tables.

In the following paragraphs we attempt to put forward a few suggestions with the aim of having a wide international discussion and, above all, more exhaustive work along these lines.

The necessary types of tables

In view of the aims to be achieved it seems necessary to contemplate three types of table, industries being progressively aggregated: (1) National tables compiled on the basic principle that the output of each branch should be as homogeneous as possible. (2) Consolidated national tables designed to give each country a serviceable instrument as a basis for policy decisions. (3) Consolidated tables which will enable international policy decisions to be taken. We take the view that each of these tables should have more lines than columns.

The basic national table, which in practice should include some 100 to 200 sectors, should make it possible to show the maximum number of homogeneous industries without however disclosing information on individual firms which is a danger in small industrial countries and in countries which are not highly industrialized.

A main requirement in these tables is to do away with 'omnibus' headings such as 'Industries not elsewhere specified' or 'Miscellaneous Services'. Also, much more detail than hitherto should be provided for the tertiary sector.

The following are some guiding principles which could be adopted in compiling these tables: (*a*) industries producing raw materials should be kept distinct from those producing manufactured products; (*b*) industries producing consumer goods could be distinguished from those mainly concerned with capital goods; (*c*) industries which are marked by technological changes, or which may be directly affected by them, could so far as possible be shown separately; (*d*) public activities could be shown separately from those of the private sector; (*e*) there would also be great advantage in separating private building into ordinary dwellings and luxury building.

Tables showing between 100 and 200 sectors, as contemplated above, cannot easily be incorporated in the national accounts. It seems appropriate that there should be available as a basis for national policy decisions more consolidated tables as well, which, in the light of experience in various countries, might comprise 50 to 70 sectors. In these tables, the purpose of which would be to have a close link to traditional national accounts, it may be important to lay stress on some industries which, though not of general importance, make a substantial contribution to the national product of a given country. These tables would be essentially inward looking. Hence it has been thought valuable, for certain wider purposes, to compile tables which are even more condensed.

The object of these more consolidated tables, with a view to international policy decisions, is to make it possible to analyse the degree of dependence or competitiveness of an industry in one country compared with similar industries in other countries. These tables, which might include about 25 sectors, could also have more rows than columns. Horizontal tables will make it possible to give details of the sales of some aggregated industries without at the same time showing the purchases of specific industries. Consolidation could be effected in such a way as to distinguish the 'international' from the 'national' industries; the 'international' industries would be those whose level of production largely depends on supply or demand in other countries. Although the tables might be very different in an industrialized country and in a country which is a producer of raw materials, there would be some similarity of pattern between industrialized countries to whom they would, therefore, be of unquestionable value.

Proposals concerning the breakdown of final demand

With a few exceptions input-output tables are characterized by a surprising uniformity as regards the condensation of the final demand accounts into five or six columns. The result is that the 'exogenous' section of input-output tables provides very little information additional to that shown in the traditional system of social accounts and that the tables do not provide an adequate statistical basis for forecasting the future evolution of the structure of final demand.

We think, therefore, that the time has come to recognize that final demand, just as intermediate demand, originates in a complex of fairly heterogeneous forms of activity — whose needs are largely governed by endogenous factors — and to stop treating it as if it were a complex of final products delivered by the productive sectors according to productive and export capacities and not according to the economic laws which determine the evolution of a large proportion of final demand. For this reason we submit some proposals relating to the (minimum) degree of disaggregation of the final demand accounts.

For households, we propose to adopt the occupational classification currently used in France, in which the various social categories are grouped according to the professional status of the family head.[1] The reason why we prefer a breakdown of private consumption based on the social and occupational class of the family head, rather than on the basis of income, is the increasing need for identifying the various sources of savings.

The need for a more detailed functional breakdown of public expenditure is justified by the growing importance of public services, both in developing economies and in industrialized countries. A rough outline of the desirable breakdown which might be considered for extending (and for improving the quality of) the information on the structure of public expenditure is as follows: (1) Public expenditures should first be classified into two: *consumption accounts* and *capital accounts*. (2) Each category of accounts should then be broken down according to the following *public functions*: education and culture; public health and social welfare; defence, police and justice; and general administration and other public services. (3) *A standardized list of capital goods* purchased by public authorities (other than land and buildings) should be established in order to distinguish between those goods which might properly be regarded as investments, and the consumer goods ordinarily used in each of the four groups of public functions indicated above.

The reason why we propose to break down, *by major category of investors*, this fundamental account of final demand is also based on the usefulness of distinguishing between public and private investment and, among the latter, between the various categories of enterprises.

Taking realistically into account the present state of input-output work in most countries, we shall not go so far as to propose the compilation of a matrix of capital coefficients. Nevertheless, we think that the consolidated account of gross (fixed) capital formation should be broken down at least into the following six categories of investors: (1) Public

---

[1] E.g., farmers, farm labourers, etc.

authorities, (2) Farmers, (3) Major industries (to be defined), (4) Other industries, (5) Transport services, (6) Commerce and other services.

The conceptual and practical difficulties usually arising in compiling net changes in inventories, and in establishing a projection for such flow, suggest the advisability of limiting our proposals to that of introducing, whenever possible, a distinction only between the variations in the real value of inventories held by: (*a*) *producers* (materials in process and products stocked) and that held by (*b*) *traders*.

It is superfluous to mention the usefulness of breaking down the structure of imports and exports, by *geographical*, or *monetary areas*. This operation should not raise any problem in most countries, since the only real difficulty encountered in establishing the foreign trade accounts consists in the reconciliation of foreign trade statistics with the classification used in input-output accounting.

Proposals concerning the breakdown of value added

The poverty of the information available on the remuneration of capital and of entrepreneurial work in each sector is the main reason for recommending to extend the disaggregation of the final demand accounts to the *value added* row shown at the bottom of the interindustry matrix.

The breakdown of wages and salaries by sector (and, possibly, by category of workers) should not raise any serious problem since such information is available or could be easily collected in every country. On the contrary, it seems reasonable to expect that the collection of basic data required for isolating the other elements of value added (particularly the self-financing of investments and interest paid on borrowed capital) will be seriously handicapped by the ambiguity of the balance sheets of large companies and by the secrecy attached to the financial records of enterprises.

To solve this problem at the macro-economic level, we do not see — for the time being — any other possibility except that of organizing some sample surveys aiming at collecting (possibly on the basis of uniform criteria to be studied in advance) the basic data necessary to set up systematic evaluations of the *stock of fixed assets* in existence and in use in each sector.

The organization by the national statistical services of periodical evaluations of national wealth, by major categories of assets and by using sectors, would make it possible not only to break down by sector the aggregate production function, but would also enable us to calculate the values of *the real capital consumption*, in relation to the size, nature and age of the equiment available in each sector.

We venture to propose the following breakdown of value added: (1) wages; (2) salaries and compensation for managerial work; (3) social security contributions (paid by employers and by workers); (4) general expenditure; (5) inventory profits or losses; (6) *actual* capital consumption estimated in relation to the real value of capital stock; (7) residual elements, possibly broken down into: self-financing of new and replacement investment; interest paid on borrowed capital; and distributed profits and earnings retained by employers or independent workers.

Some other problems

Being impossible to embark here on a complete discussion of the many problems relating to the accounting of interindustry transactions, we shall next confine ourselves to some criticisms of the conventions hitherto accepted in many countries to solve certain practical problems concerning the compilation of this fundamental section of input-output tables.

First, as regards the obvious definition of 'competitive' and 'non-competitive' imports, we desire to question the value of this distinction in countries where imports of 'competitive' raw materials and 'competitive' intermediate products represent a relatively high percentage of the total resources of such products. While recognizing the practical difficulties involved by the attempts to eliminate the (purely apparent) distinction between the treatment of the two groups of imports we, nevertheless, think that it would be preferable to establish a separate set of estimates about the present and the *prospective* distribution of 'competitive' imports, by *sector of origin* and by *sector of destination*, rather than to make oneself content with the lack of any information either on the present distribution of such flows or on the expected changes in the proportions between domestic and imported inputs.

This leads us to recommend that all possible effort be made in order to arrive at the compilation of *two separate matrices*: one showing the allocation of domestic flows and the other showing the allocation of imports ('competitive' or 'non-competitive') originating in the corresponding foreign industries. In this context, it is worth remembering that these efforts would be greatly facilitated by the compilation of rectangular tables, with more rows than columns.

Now turning to the treatment of transport costs, trade margins and indirect taxes, one should mention that since this problem is closely related to the evaluation of either interindustry transactions or final demand, it is convenient to express first an opinion about the choice of the price system to be used for describing in monetary terms the structure of a national economy. That is, the choice between evaluation of individual flows at *producers' prices* (factor cost in the case of domestic products and c.i.f. prices in the case of imported products) or at *purchasers' prices*, that is at the prices paid by various users (industries, households, exporters, etc.). Since in our opinion it is only the second type of evaluation which raises problems worth attention, we will concentrate solely upon the compilation of tables expressed at *purchasers' prices*.

The compilation of tables in which all transactions are expressed at producers' prices does not, in fact, present any difficulty: since transportation costs, trade margins, taxes and duties paid on the inputs (both intermediate and final) purchased from other sectors are regarded as fractions of the output of the Transportation, Commerce and the Government sectors, respectively; and are treated like any other element of the cost of the producing sector, or of the expenditure of the final sectors.

It is, however, to be noted that the distribution, by sector of use, of the output of the above three sectors implies the availability of direct information either on the total value of transport services and commerce purchased by each sector, or on the amount of taxes and duties levied on the inputs delivered by other domestic, or foreign sectors.

Now, it often happens that such information is incomplete and that recourse to empirical estimates (which necessarily has to be based on the detailed structure of intermediate and final accounts) becomes unavoidable. In this case, which so far as we know is the most frequent, we do not see the reason why these estimates could not be used for establishing, in addition to the table expressed at producers' prices, a second table expressing all transactions at the purchasers' prices paid by the users of the various commodity groups.

The main advantage of this second version of the table is that it gives a full description of the *actual costs* paid for each category of inputs used by either the intermediate or the final sectors. Such a table, however, presents the disadvantage of being affected by the duplication relating to the values of transportation and trade services which are already accounted for in the purchasers' value of each commodity flow. The device of avoiding double accounting for such costs, by deducting them from the market value of each commodity group, or by registering them in the external section of the table below the interindustry matrix (as it can be done in the case of indirect taxes) cannot be, in fact, used in the mathematical solution of the model.

Unless one refrains from calculating through the model the direct and indirect effects of the demand for transport and distribution of the various commodities, such costs must be counted twice: either on the *column side*, as a fraction of the market value of individual purchases, or on the *row side* as a fraction of the market value of the output of each producing sector.

In tables where all transactions are expressed at purchasers' prices, the output of any sector i is in effect envisaged as the combination of two activities: one of production (X_i) and one of distribution of the products which are delivered to the other intermediate or final sectors (D_i).

Consequently, the technical coefficients a_{ji} of any sector i have to be calculated as follows:

$$a_{ji} = \frac{x_{ji}}{X_i + D_i} \quad \text{(for domestic inputs)}$$

$$_m a_{ji} = \frac{m_{ji}}{X_i + D_i} \quad \text{(for imported inputs)}$$

$(j = 1, 2, \ldots, n)$, and the *duplication* relating to transport and trade margins will also be represented in the matrix a_{ij} by a particular type of technical coefficient, calculated as:

$$\hat{a}_{ji} = \frac{D_i}{X_i + D_i}$$

Nevertheless, although the results of the solution are in no way affected by this mode of calculating the technical coefficients, it is obvious that if a table expressed at *producers' prices* is available, it is better to use this table for the solution of the model, especially for projection purposes. It must in fact be recognized that the detailed breakdown of transportation costs and trade margins adds elements of instability to the system of technical coefficients: which it is always better to avoid as far as possible.

There is in fact no reason why, once the problem has been solved on the basis of a matrix of coefficients related to the output values expressed at producers' prices, a second table should not then be set up at purchasers' prices, especially if information on prospective changes in the relative importance of the demand for the various transport and trade services is available.

In the light of the advantage of disposing of both types of tables, we venture to suggest that an effort be made, as far as possible, to establish two series of tables: the first of which could be used for input-output analysis, while the second one would be mainly designed for purposes of publication, since the latter is, in our view, the only one which can rightly be regarded as a real system of input-output accounts.

SOME PROBLEMS OF STANDARDIZATION

by WILLIAM I. ABRAHAM *and* MARVIN HOFFENBERG

The Background

To support or not to support — to be enthusiastic about or indifferent to — international standards for input-output statistics depends somewhat on one's conception of input-output. To some, input-output tables serve mainly to provide further detail in elaborating income and product accounts; any theoretical conflict between the needs of final product estimates and the requirements for technologically-based coefficients is resolved in favour of the former. To others, input-output tables are the raw data for econometric models of differing degrees of complexity; the emphasis is on technological structure, and the tables are oriented to implement a model, social accounting criteria being given less weight. In both cases, however, the data are merely descriptive, since some theory is necessary for converting interindustry flows into input-output relations.

There are three cogent reasons for standardizing: to create a common language among statisticians of different countries; to ease the problem of formulating and implementing models involving more than one country; and, to enforce higher standards of performance. The three reasons are of course interdependent.

An input-output model is a voracious consumer of data, obviously more so than final product estimates. A significant part of any country's economic statistics is processed in implementing and interpreting the model. 'Re-processed' is perhaps a more appropriate term, since it is doubtful whether current government statistics anywhere provide adequate and proper data to support the technologically-oriented models. The difficulties in understanding and using input-output in any country are many; they are greater still between countries. The adoption of conventional rules — and all rules are arbitrary to some degree — would facilitate the use of any table by both nationals and foreigners.

An outstanding characteristic of input-output analysis is an empirical orientation. Two developments necessarily follow from this. First, a way of structuring the economy is made operationally meaningful; the empty boxes are filled. Secondly, the data are used for problem-solving, usually through mathematical models. There is a continuous chain of empirical work ranging from data collection to model implementation and interpretation. Some important part of this chain must be subjected to standardization, and it is natural to single out the input-output table. Standardization then means a selection of agreed rules for compiling conceptually consistent tables. We go further and recommend that this be done within the framework of the U.N. System of National Accounts (SNA) [1].

The relationship of such an arrangement of data to the open model input-output table is fairly obvious. The input-output table, going beyond the consolidated production account of the nation, presents the production accounts of individual industries without cancelling out intermediate production. The payments for ultimate inputs, i.e. for factors of production, as shown for individual industries in the input-output table, agree with total national income or some variant as given in the nation's production or income account and with national income by industrial origin in the usual supporting table. Final, as distinct from intermediate, production in the input-output table corresponds to the consumption expenditure of the household and government sectors, the gross domestic investment of the nation in the capital account, and exports and imports in the rest-of-the-world account.

The ease of handling interindustry flows in the context of the national accounts is highly convenient. The fact that both are concerned essentially with real flows of production and income suggests at once that there is no reason why this should not be so. In a number of European and other countries, work on input-output and national income has long been pursued together. Apart from the obvious advantages to compilers and most users resulting from an integrated approach, this provides analysts whose concern is primarily with interindustry relations with a set of norms which is widely known and has gained acceptance. This is not to argue that a system of accounts (such as the United Nations') is not subject to modification as further experience is gained; nor does more formal integration imply that experimentation with input-output models conforming to other specifications need be hampered in any way. But to the extent that there are no cogent reasons for departing from accepted practice — as in drawing the production boundary and in defining the net output of different kinds of economic activity, the payments to primary inputs and the components of final demand — there is more to be said for conforming than for differing. On matters which do not normally come within the purview of the national accounts and for which alternative treatments are available, e.g., the valuation basis for recording intermediate inputs and the treatment of imports, decisions will naturally have to be made without appeal to the national accounts. Once a clear concensus has emerged on these issues the way should be open for achieving a greater measure of international comparability, with incidental benefits to international studies which are as yet unable to take full advantage of the material available in interindustry investigations.

Limits to standardization

The one overriding constraint is that efforts to standardize should not sterilize creative activity in either model formulation or implementation. Standardization is good, it is useful, but not at any price. Experience with input-output tables has shown that all alternative forms of classification — establishment, commodity, activity, process — have their uses; that different sectoring is needed for different problems; that the alternative ways of handling flows (e.g. imports) may depend on the accuracy with which projections can be made as much as on logic. We are advocating standards for presenting compatible national matrices, which may be derived from other, and different, matrices.

If analysts had ample resources, if computation presented no problems, and if supporting data for national tables were readily available, there would be little need for standardization other than for spreading the best practices. Given the actual situation, one may conjecture that a centralized reference collection of input-output data, including auxiliary data requirements, could be as important as standardization. It would seem worth having such a depository and systematically publishing in standard format and terminology the supporting data mentioned.

There exists another scattered body of data which, if properly collated, could make a significant contribution to our understanding of interindustry relationships and of capital requirements. We have in mind the economic and engineering-type data resulting from the technical aid programmes of the various nations, from the surveys of national and international agencies, from the innumerable engineering surveys and studies conducted in many parts of the world, and from planning and programming bodies. If these could be centralized and reprocessed in input-output form so as to be articulated with existing tables, we could materially advance our understanding of alternative technologies and even, perhaps, of technological change.

The publication programme should include more than industry

reports and auxiliary data on prices, employment, productivity, etc. We would also recommend publication of specialized matrices for secondary product transfers, by-products, imports, and capital coefficients, as well as for capital flows. These special matrices would be used to transform the standardized matrix to other forms.

For many analytical problems the major role of the matrix is as a classificatory device to bring matrix and non-matrix data into a conceptually consistent form. We should not overlook the fact that the collection and classification of these data may result in statistical aberrations reflecting inconsistencies. Efforts should be made to bring analytical studies relating to consumption expenditure projections, import elasticities, price elasticities of all kinds, and so on to the attention of workers in input-output analysis. No juggling with interindustry flows for one year will give us much of this information so necessary for our work.

Some basic characteristics of a standardized matrix

The alternative forms of the tables used for the endogenous sectors are square, rectangular, and triangular. The square table is the classical one containing the same row vectors as column ones. The rectangular adds information since the row vectors are commodity flows within industry and the column vectors are industry only. The triangular matrix is a hierarchal arrangement of industries so as to have zero flows to the right of the principal diagonal.

The choice of form turns on computational ease and publication. Experimentation with graph theory has indicated some interesting possibilities of triangularizing the matrix in the United States. The advantage of this form is computational since it eliminates the need for matrix inversion. But it may not be feasible to suggest that this form be standardized.

The choice is in part between square and rectangular tables. The latter has the advantage of including more information. It permits, if specific solutions are computed by iteration, the periodic checking of supply and demand by commodity, which has proved useful in problems dealing with import substitutions. A rectangular matrix, however, cannot be inverted. For standardization we may specify a square matrix and an auxiliary product-flow matrix.

We do not want to discuss how big a matrix should be as this depends on one's statistical conscience and computational facilities. We recommend a given sectoring which is statistically feasible and not beyond the capabilities of desk calculators. There should be no upper limit on size provided large matrices permit consolidation to a standard classification.

Classification of sectors

For the classification of activities into sectors the U.N. International Standard Industrial Classification of All Economic Activities (ISIC) provides a logical starting point. This implies the acceptance of the establishment as the basic unit for classification. The establishment as the basic unit has been criticized because of the heterogeneity of commodities produced as primary and secondary products. Such heterogeneity is a factor in the instability of input ratios.

A sector may be defined as (*a*) a commodity or group of commodities; (*b*) a group of establishments having in common certain characteristics (such as production of similar commodities, use of the same principal raw materials, or possession of similar types of equipment); (*c*) an activity (such as the activity of providing new residential construction); or (*d*) a defined process (such as sand casting of metals). Matrices have been constructed with each of the above as the sector definition and our proposed classification incorporates all these to some degree.

There is much merit in the choice of the establishment as the basic unit. Many current statistical programmes are set up on an establishment reporting basis, and the establishment is a basic action unit in the economy. Moreover, some degree of stability through time in input relationships is to be expected at this level of aggregation, since the establishment usually represents a collection of specialized equipment and specialized human experience within which rapid substitution possibilities are limited. Alternative units greatly increase the work of constructing a table and also involve the preparation of complicated transformation tables to utilize the auxiliary data necessary for implementing models.

The gross output concept

The row distributions should cover, for the most general case, receipts for: (*a*) commodities shipped by establishments in the industry; (*b*) primary products of the industry produced elsewhere; (*c*) miscellaneous receipts (such as for scrap); (*d*) competitive imports at c.i.f. value; (*e*) additions to inventories of finished products of the industry, wherever held; and (*f*) inventory depletions of finished products of the industry held elsewhere. The total of these, however, is not the production base used to calculate the input ratios. This base is obtained by deducting inventory depletions and competitive imports.

Output is defined as gross since intra-sector shipments as well as shipments to other sectors are included. (In other words, it covers all shipments outside the establishment.) In some analytical applications it has been customary to net out the intra-industry shipments. The gross measure is desirable in standardized general-purpose tables since output net of intra-industry shipments is necessarily a function of the classification system used, while gross output remains constant and additive except for secondary product adjustments. There is a proportional relationship between both the flows and direct coefficients (excluding the principal diagonal) in the two tables. However the principal diagonal of the net output inverse differs in interpretation from that of the gross since it is a measure of the feedback upon the industry, while that of the gross output inverse is not.

The handling of secondary production

In the ISIC the establishment is classified according to its main products. However, it often also produces commodities characteristic of other industries. The division between primary and secondary production depends on the level of aggregation — the greater the aggregation, the fewer the secondary products.

The alternative ways of handling secondary product flows include the following:

1. A commodity, activity or process type classification may be used, but we have already dismissed this by accepting the ISIC.

2. Industries may be combined so that almost all secondary products become primary in the more aggregative classification scheme. This would, however, introduce other problems because of the increased heterogeneity of production in the new classification system.

3. Products may be charged directly to the user from the industry where they are produced, ignoring the distinction between primary and secondary products. Under this method, industries would be purchasing similar inputs from more than one industry. Not only would it be difficult, or impossible, to make the multiple allocations, but the industry input coefficients would diminish in significance.

4. Secondary products may be charged as negative outputs of the industry where they are primary and as negative inputs into the sector where they are produced. This is equivalent to passing a product matrix through an establishment one. This alternative complicates the interpretation of both output and input.

5. All products may be charged through the industry to which they are primary while still retaining the establishment classification as the basis for cost-structure analysis. These fictitious flows, termed 'secondary

product transfers', are added to the receiving industry's output and outlays and are pooled with its products for allocation. This transfer procedure has specific defects: it automatically builds into any structural relationships derived from the flow table the ratios between primary and secondary production existing in the base period and, in addition, there is some circularity involved, since an industry may 'sell' a secondary product to an industry that it buys from. The demand for the primary product carries back into the production of its supplying industry, which in turn buys from its suppliers, including purchases of secondary products from the first industry.

Given our frame of reference and taking into account costs and benefits, we suggest the last approach as the best compromise. This solution, however, calls for an accompanying transfer matrix showing the origin and destination of secondary product transfers if the flow matrix is to be aggregated further.

The problem of unallocated production

An unallocated 'industry' — row and column — is composed of residual estimates obtained by deducting the sums of specific estimates from known control totals. These residuals possess the characteristics of accounting residuals in other kinds of social accounts. The unallocated portions of the input-output table are a heterogeneous collection of unknown physical flows and errors in pricing transactions between sectors. They reflect also errors of judgment in determining inputs and allocations between final and intermediate product, as well as discrepancies and inconsistencies in the basic data used.

There is a formal condition in an input-output matrix confined to current account flows that for each endogenous sector there be equality between input and output. (For final product sectors the equality condition is for the aggregate of such flows, not for individual sectors.) A discrepancy between row and column totals of the unallocated sector is a measure of the inequality between the estimated income and product accounts.

The unallocated sector raises problems because analysts do not know what to do about these flows; the unallocated sector influences, in different ways, any analysis. One can consider the unallocated sector as part of the autonomous demand; this means that its level and composition must be stipulated either as product or income every time the matrix is used. If an unallocated sector remains in the endogenous part of the matrix it is included as an equation of equal rank with other sectors. In price problems the changes in unit factor costs of this sector or its indirect effects are usually dampening ones, if not outright absurd. Leaving such a sector in the matrix is in effect weighting into the input coefficients of other sectors the unallocated sector's costs through the relative importance of the given sector's unallocated input. Perhaps the best practice is to eliminate the unknowns in some rational way.

The valuation of production

The need for reconciling the complete set of sector accounts requires that the basic data be assembled in terms of both producer's and purchaser's values, with all spread items between them (such as trade margins, transport costs, warehousing and storage costs, and excise taxes) specifically identified. Later, however, one or the other system of valuation must be adopted for analytical applications. This will also govern the form in which summary data are presented.

In an input-output table commodities are allocated directly from industry of origin to industry of destination. No commodities are charged through distributive sectors. To do so, as for example to have households buy commodities from trade, would introduce such heterogeneity into the matrix as to make it useless for studying structural implications. In concept then, each industry pays the distributive sectors for services, either in bringing needed commodities to it or in taking its output to the users, depending on whether producer's or purchaser's values are used.

For presentation and analytical uses, producer's values are preferred. In a purchaser's value table, all distribution costs for a sector's output will appear in its input structure — a fictitious secondary product transfer — and again distributed through its output. Input ratios will thus be based on an output total which includes distribution costs for the sector's production. But these costs in turn will depend on the output distribution itself, which may be quite variable from year to year. Hence, estimates based on purchaser's values may introduce a source of instability in input structure. In a producer's value table, on the other hand, explicit account can be taken of differential trade or other margins by type of consumer.

Whichever system of valuation is adopted, the output of the trade and other distributive sectors is defined as gross margins. The national accounts are published at purchaser's value and consequently, for general use of the input-output matrix, it is necessary to publish detailed commodity factors for each specific distributive cost in order to translate demands at purchaser's value into demands at producer's value.

The flow of services

Most of the industry groups in the services division as defined in the ISIC provide only final services, and the services of dwellings are by their very nature final. In principle, there is no reason why these industries should be handled differently from other industries. In practice the rows and columns are sometimes left blank except for factor payments; consistency then requires that the intermediate inputs needed for producing the services be treated as final output. If, for example, for private expenditure on medical services the figure at the intersection of the appropriate row and column covers only the factor costs incurred, then the other costs — food for hospital kitchens and all the rest — should be included with final expenditure on comparable items. This means that in any analysis of the implications of a change in demand for medical services these costs will have to be treated as elements of the demand.

Presumably the fact that intermediate costs are negligible in relation to factor payments for most of these services is behind the decision to leave the columns blank; and since the rows are necessarily empty, all output being final product, it becomes possible and convenient to lump together services of this kind.

Own-account construction in the ISIC is part of the enterprise's output, not of the construction industry's. This view is shared by SNA, where the value added is defined to cover the cost incurred in construction work carried out by the unit's own employees. Here we suggest a departure, namely that construction be defined to include all own-account construction as well as contract work. This means, of course, a redefinition of the affected industry's cost of materials as well as value added.

Turning to government activity, an industry 'public administration and defence' may seem strange on first sight. It is a residual category after all other productive activities of government which can appropriately be assigned to industry groups have been so classified. Public enterprises and the activities of government departments concerned with education, health, transport, communication, marketing, the operation of financial institutions, etc., are classified along with the corresponding private activities in these fields so that from the standpoint of the ISIC and the domestic product classification based on it no distinction is made between private and public activities. Public administration thus covers only a narrowly defined range of governmental operations such as the armed forces and police, parliament, the regular administrative departments involved in tax administration, the control of business and foreign relations, and administration connected with public health, education and other activities of general government.

Operationally, perhaps the least satisfactory aspect of this classification of government is the attempt to separate education, health and other services of general government from the administration or regulation connected with them. Nevertheless, the treatment as a whole does divide up government cleanly and assists in achieving a classification which is satisfactory for showing the contribution of each activity. Certainly regarding the whole complex of general government (i.e., excluding government enterprises) as forming a single industry, as is sometimes done, is less satisfactory.

It would, of course, be possible to show the cost structure of public administration and defence in its column instead of showing only factor payments, as is often done where government activity is distributed in the manner described. Purchases of food and clothing for the armed forces, for example, would then be recorded in this column rather than in autonomous government consumption. Total input and output of the industry would be raised accordingly; since government is the only buyer the row would remain empty except for the sale to government of the entire output, valued now at cost inclusive of non-factor payments. This procedure, by furnishing a more adequate record of information for a major productive activity, would improve the usefulness of the input-output table for analytical purposes. Indeed, considering the scale of defence expenditures in many countries and the interest centring on economic issues in this area, it would be even better to distinguish the civil and military components and to treat each as a separate industry with its own input structure.

As regards the industry group 'banks and other financial institutions', it has to be recognized that if the value added by banking is not to be negative, or at any rate negligible, it cannot be taken as the difference between actual service charges and intermediate costs. In SNA account is taken of the fact that banks maintain themselves chiefly by virtue of the margin between the income from invested deposits and the interest paid to depositors by imputing to depositors a service charge equal to this excess and at the same time imputing to them a corresponding amount of interest. The justification for this step is the assumption that depositors receive bank services free in this amount so that the cost and benefit of these services can be entered as imputed charges and interest in the accounts of banks and depositors.

So far as this treatment of banking makes sense in national income accounting it is equally appropriate for input-output analysis. The main statistical drawback is the need to allocate total imputed charges first between business and households and then, for the business portion, among the various industries. In national income accounting it is the volume of deposits which usually forms the basis for allocating imputed charges. Inasmuch as the turnover of deposits is thus ignored — and turnover is an important cost in the handling and management of deposits — no great accuracy can be claimed for this procedure, and any other reasonable basis that proves convenient could be substituted for it in interindustry studies.

Operation of social security schemes is usually included in general government administration. The generally accepted national accounting treatment is to regard employers' and employees' contributions as part of employee compensation, and pensions and other benefits as transfers. The net output of the activity is the sum of the factor payments incurred in operating the programme, while these payments, together with the other costs of administration, are included under government expenditure. There is no reason why this treatment of social security should not be followed in interindustry studies.

The operation of private contributory pension plans can be handled along the same lines. Thus, the compensation of employees can be taken gross of the contributions of both parties, and pensions regarded as transfer payments. Since contributions cover the cost of benefits plus the cost of administration, only the difference between contributions and benefits, or administrative, charges, need be taken into account explicitly. As administrative costs are resolved into factor payments, it is necessary to include these costs in final expenditure; this can be done by including administrative charges in private consumption expenditure.

Unlike social security plans, however, private pension plans are not confined to a single industry. Unless the final demand for the output of each industry of which pension plans are a feature is to be reported gross of the costs of providing retirement security, the operation of such plans must be separated from ordinary business transactions. This could be readily accomplished in the input-output matrix by removing pension plans from the various industries which operate them and assigning them to the insurance industry, which in any case already covers annuity-type policies. Total input into insurance would thus be raised by the amount of the administrative costs of the company plans while final sales of insurance services to consumers would be increased by the same amount.

The services performed in providing life insurance can also be handled in input-output tables without showing premiums and claims. The premiums and the income earned on policy holders' savings enable life insurance companies to pay claims and other benefits, to cover operating expenses, earn profits, and accumulate savings. In national income accounting, the income earned on policy holders' savings is imputed to households as interest, premiums and claims are disregarded, and life insurance companies are regarded as charging policy holders for their services as measured by operating expenses. The treatment here is thus also suitable for interindustry investigations.

Imports as a part of interindustry relations

The application of the input-output approach to an analysis of a country's external economic relationships presents no new problems. Problems relating to the use of fixed coefficients, alternative geographic sources of supply, general substitution, the 'price-mix', and capacity limitations, among others, are present in most types of input-output analyses. Imports have attracted more attention since in many countries successful treatment of import problems is a necessary condition for the success of input-output as an analytical tool.

The traditional treatment of imports and exports, as exemplified in the early work of Leontief and the U.S. Bureau of Labour Statistics, is to incorporate foreign countries as an aggregative sector appended to the domestic economy. The output of the foreign trade sector comprises the imports of the domestic economy while its inputs are the exports of the domestic economy. Since many economic problems are concerned with changes in structural relationships rather than changes in broad aggregates, it would be advantageous to tabulate foreign trade by country of origin and country of destination. In fact, a possible objective would be a world-wide matrix in which the principal diagonal is standardized national matrices linked together by imports and exports.

Competitive and noncompetitive imports

Imports are generally divided into two categories, competitive and noncompetitive. The former include commodities and services which are similar in nature to or highly substitutable for home production; they are an alternative source to domestic supply. Noncompetitive imports comprise those foreign-produced goods and services for which there are no similar or closely substitutable commodities or services produced in the domestic economy. In addition, noncompetitives usually include net private and governmental unilateral payments abroad, and personal, governmental, and business expenditures in foreign countries. Noncompetitive imports, by definition, are not an addition to the pool of home-produced commodities since there is no counterpart home production.

This general division based on narrow technological criteria tends to break down in actual practice. Questions concerning product substitutability and potential rather than actual sources of supply immediately arise. Technology changes, as evidenced by substitution between natural and synthetic fibres and natural and synthetic rubber. In both cases, for the United States, the noncompetitive natural product became an import competitive to domestically-produced synthetics.

The distinction between the two, being technological, tends to be ambiguous in an economic context. Changes in relative prices between domestic and foreign-produced commodities, inelasticity of domestic supply in the short run, import and currency controls, as well as institutionalized practices can readily transform a competitive into a noncompetitive import. This transformation at the margin can be important. The critical question is, under what circumstances is it permissible to treat an import as an addition to home supply and when is it not? In the former case, requirements — direct and indirect — must be worked into the analysis as an offset against domestic resources; in the latter case, no adjustment is required.

Distribution of imports

The problem here is twofold and involves first the manner in which imports are charged into the domestic sectors, and second, the treatment of finished goods, that is, imported goods going directly to ultimate users in the form in which they are imported.

The manner of introducing imports into the matrix influences the meaning of the coefficients and the results of the model. Let us first consider the original treatment of imports by Leontief. Noncompetitive imports were charged directly to consuming sectors as part of their cost of materials. They had no effect on the definition of output used as the denominator in computing input ratios. Competitive imports were considered as augmenting domestic supply and were charged through the domestic industry whose products were their counterpart. The competitive import was added both to the inputs of the appropriate sector and to its output, in order to maintain equality between revenues and disbursements. The output of any sector was defined as domestic production plus competitive imports. This definition was the one utilized as the denominator for computing input coefficients. In relation to domestic production input ratios were decreased by a ratio reflecting the relative importance of competitive imports for the sector.

The above treatment is equivalent to assuming explicitly that each of the consuming industries absorbs home-produced commodities combined in a fixed proportion with their imported counterparts, the relationship being determined by the ratio of imports to domestic supply. (Note the identity with the treatment of home-produced secondary products.) As is often the case in input-output analysis, computational methods can be developed to circumvent built-in stabilities. The ratio of imports to domestic supply can be altered simply by adjusting the domestic input ratios by a scalar which reflects the changing ratio of imports to domestic supply. Again, the analyst is free to insert new information and change the structural relationships accordingly. The assumption of fixed proportions in consumption can also be avoided by changing ratios as above or by manipulating final demand.

As an example, let us examine the question of the import content of exports. Since exports are defined as exports of domestic merchandise only — re-exports are excluded — a proportional allocation of imports is clearly wrong. Two things can be done. One is to separate imports of final goods from imports of intermediate goods and allocate the former directly to type of final user. Total — foreign and domestic — purchases can be shown, element by element, in the appropriate column vector. A separate vector for imports with negative entries would offset such imports. Output would be redefined as domestic production plus imports of competitive intermediate goods. Imports would be allocated in proportion to the consumption of intermediate goods derived from the matrix plus direct estimates, if any, of finished goods.

Another method to deal with the export problem is to leave output as originally defined but to adjust either the matrix or the export vector so as to counteract the proportional consumption adjustment. Using an iterative process for solving the equation system, the first order impact is as though competitive imports did not affect the magnitude of the input ratios, i.e., as though the inputs were based on domestic production only. The adjustment could be made by inflating each sector's input by the ratio of imported plus domestic production to domestic production only. For other iterations no such adjustments are necessary. An equivalent way is to use the original ratios but to inflate each element in the final demand vector by the above ratio.

Although the stability assumption mentioned above can be modified, certain difficulties remain, especially if the analyst is concerned with domestic capacities, relative prices, and capital requirements. Adjustments are possible for these difficulties but they increase the burden of side computations. Consequently, new methods for handling competitive imports along similar lines were developed in Italy, Norway, and the United States. The basic idea of charging such imports through domestic industries is retained with the pooling of commodities independently of geographic origin. However, instead of defining output as the sum of foreign and home goods, the output concept used for computing input ratios is home production only. Competitive imports are treated in a manner analogous to inventory depletions, that is, as a negative vector of final demand. In the original treatment such imports are considered as a factor payment on the income side with exports as the corresponding commodity flow. Now, the net foreign balance for each sector (excluding noncompetitive imports) is the commodity flow with no factor cost counterpart.

Although the basic idea is the same, different tools were developed in the countries concerned. The U.S. practice is to estimate the levels of imports prior to computation and to enter them as negative final demand items. This practice stems from the detailed matrix used in the U.S., the particular model formulated for implementation which included lead times, capital requirements and capacity constraints, and the inefficiencies involved in stopping and starting the digital computers needed for the vast amount of computation. (Inverse matrices were extensively used as a computational shortcut.) In Italy and Norway the iterative method for specific solutions was used and at each stage of iteration a decision was reached as to the ratio of imports to domestic supply. The estimated level of imports, by sector, was then inserted as a negative item in the next iteration. The estimation by stage of computation does permit additional insights into determining imports for a particular problem. The choice between the two approaches is dependent on whether one can estimate level or ratio better, upon the complexities of the model, the amount of computation, and the kind of computing equipment used.

The methods described above have two elements in common: competitive imports are charged through domestic sectors, and proportional consumption of imported items is assumed unless an explicit adjustment is made. In one of his earlier articles, Leontief suggested an alternative treatment, namely to channel all imports into the domestic economy as though they were noncompetitive. This treatment calls for two separate matrices, of domestic production only, and of imports. Output is always defined as home production and all inputs, domestic and foreign, are computed with this as the denominator.

The use of two matrices describes a country's technology in a different way. The input ratios are more restrictive in that they no longer indicate total requirements by commodity (industry), but are more extensive in that they delineate consumption by geographic origin. In this formulation, intermediate and final goods are allocated separately and consumption of imported goods need not be made proportional to use of domestic commodities if differential use patterns among industries are known. A rise in consumption of imports would mean an increased offset against production (negative items in final demand); a decrease would mean the opposite.

The alternatives outlined above imply different models of how an industrial system reacts to imports. Although the methods *a priori* do not lead to identical results, adjustments can be made to bring them into close agreement. The question arises as to which method is preferable. There is no unambiguous answer, but we recommend that competitive imports be channelled as a negative final demand and that imports of intermediate goods be segregated from imports of finished goods, the latter to be charged directly to ultimate user.

This discourse on imports is intended to highlight certain critical problems, touched on throughout this paper, relating to the meaning of standardization. It is not an exaggeration to say that one may be indifferent as to how flows are treated provided the methodology is clear and auxiliary detail is published. We recommend standardized procedures, knowing that they are compromises in many instances, because they facilitate communication and use. Similar problems are present in other final demand areas, capital versus current account, treatment and valuation of inventories, and use of external scrap and used materials in general and their bearing on the meaning of the inventory column. Within the matrix itself there is the important question of imputations and their relation to practices in the standardized national accounts.

Standardization, if it is to have content, must be viewed in a broader context. Furthermore, one must distinguish problems of standardization on a conceptual level from problems of standard format, publication, and computing technique. An attempt to do so was made in this paper.

REFERENCE

[1] United Nations, *A System of National Accounts and Supporting Tables*, New York, 1960.

FOR A MORE MODEST START

by MORRIS R. GOLDMAN

In principle, some form of standardization is desirable, and for three main reasons: (1) it would permit the development of multi-regional tables, (2) it would provide a common language which would permit technicians in each country to understand and use the tables prepared in the other countries, and (3) it could improve the quality of the work in individual countries. The question is how to achieve the objective.

Cao-Pinna and du Vivier attempt to develop a specific set of proposals for standardizing input-output tables. This is indeed a difficult task, for what is feasible and meaningful for one nation is not necessarily so for others. They propose that each country prepare three types of tables, for 100–200 sectors, for 50–70 sectors, and for 25 sectors respectively. A specific set of rules, definitions and classifications are proposed which would be universally followed.

I find myself in disagreement with this basic approach for two reasons. First, I think it would cause undue rigidity in the work of the individual nations, and secondly, no one set of rules is equally advisable for all nations. This is so because problems to which input-output will be applied, the underlying statistical programmes, and the relative importance of various sectors and institutions, differ from one economy to another.

To illustrate, I should like to turn to several of the specific recommendations made. It is suggested that input-output tables in the different countries should be prepared for the same base year. While I agree with this proposal in principle, I find it somewhat unrealistic as the construction of input-output tables greatly depends on the availability of basic statistics. In those countries where input-output tables are based on annual data, there is, of course, flexibility in the selection of the benchmark year. However, in countries such as the United States, where a major portion of the necessary data is collected at less frequent intervals, flexibility is limited. To standardize the year covered by input-output tables, it is first necessary to standardize the periods covered by basic statistical collection programmes of all countries; the Statistical Office of the United Nations can testify to the difficulties in achieving such standardization.

Then there is the suggestion that the tables should do away with 'omnibus' headings, such as industries not elsewhere specified or miscellaneous services. Again, while desirable in principle, I suggest that the proposal is unrealistic. In the United States, the industry classification system for manufacturing industries identifies approximately 450 separate industries. Even in this detail there are many miscellaneous or not elsewhere specified types of industries. Also, the proposal that industries producing raw materials should be kept separate from those producing manufactured products is not always appropriate. For example, in some countries, selected industries are interconnected in such a way that the entire output of a specific raw materials industry flows to an industry producing manufactured products. In such cases, it seems to me that there is strong argument for combining the two industries.

To one who has been confronted by the problems of estimating a single column for households, a single column for public administration, and a single column for producers' durable equipment, the thought of attempting to break these columns down to the extent suggested by Cao-Pinna and du Vivier is overwhelming. Apart from practical considerations on data limitations, it is unwise to build into an international standard anything more than the traditional major components of final demand. I do not mean to suggest that additional detail may not be desirable. This is an area, however, where flexibility is very important. There are a number of possible breakdowns for each of the final demand categories and the interest in and significance of alternative breakdowns may vary from country to country and from period to period.

If the particular approach to standardization suggested is not feasible, what are the alternatives? First, I support the proposal that a manual of input-output terminology and procedures be prepared. This manual should cover alternative procedures and the relative advantages or different situations under which each is desirable. Secondly, an equal effort should be devoted to developing standards for a systematic publication package of which the final table would be only one part. The package should include subsidiary tables, supporting material and related data, all in sufficient detail to provide flexibility in using the tables for various purposes including the subsequent development of multi-regional tables. Thirdly, a classification system which provides for successive stages of aggregation should be adopted. Such a classification system would permit countries to select the level of detail necessary for their national problems which is consistent with the means available for the work. In this connection, I might note that the race for more detailed input-output tables reminds me a little of the horsepower race among United States automobile manufacturers during the last decade.

The additional horsepower was not often necessary, it was merely fashionable. I am not sure that the additional cost of preparing relatively large tables is always justified by the advantages gained by the additional detail. Certainly, large tables are often desirable, but the decision should be made by individual countries in light of the resources available for the work and the kinds of applications which are likely to follow. I favour standardization, but let us start modestly, with achievable goals.

DOES STANDARDIZATION STOP THINKING?

by ODD AUKRUST

I approach the problem of standardization from the national statistician's point of view and I will not come down so unreservedly in favour of standardization as Cao-Pinna and du Vivier. Rather, I feel as Abraham and Hoffenberg that 'Standardization is good, it is useful, but not at any price.'

It is necessary, perhaps, to remind the reader that input-output tables are, with a few exceptions, the work of national statistical offices. They cost money and, no less important, manpower. Occasionally they are worked out for the pleasure of intellectual satisfaction, or to follow the fashion. But this is rare. Normally they are worked out with particular national needs in mind, and they form part of a statistical system the building up of which has long traditions and has been given careful considerations. The conclusion I draw from this is that we should not expect national statistical services to be willing to replace their present systems by an internationally agreed one *unless* they can be convinced that they have something to gain from it.

This leads me to examine the question: Why standardize? One answer is that this would facilitate international comparisons of the structure of national economies. A study like the celebrated Chenery four-countries comparison has its fascination but it certainly is not the carrot which is likely to induce directors of statistical offices to alter their present system. It may very well be that, as international economic co-operation goes further, international standardization of input-output tables will be forced upon us — prematurely perhaps — in much the same way as the Standardized System of National Accounts was forced upon us — prematurely — ten years ago.

I use the word 'prematurely' because I hesitate when confronted with a proposal for standardization *at the present time*. In general, I submit that standardization has a tendency to freeze developments. It takes away a stimulus for new ideas. Sometimes one even has the feeling that when a standard is set up, thinking stops. We have seen something of this in the field of national accounting proper, where I strongly suspect that discussion, the mutual exchange of ideas, was cut off too early through the agreement of the SNA. We should, I believe, be careful so as to avoid making the same mistake again in the input-output field. The implication of this is clear. If we want to standardize our input-output tables now, we have to be reasonably sure that we know what the ideal input-output table should look like. The impression I have is that, though considerable agreement exists among input-output experts, there is, nevertheless, plenty of room for further experimentation. We are still, it seems to me, far from having *one* input-output analytical method. Further, there may be very valid reasons why countries might want to develop their input-output work differently. There are differences in economic structures, differences in institutions, differences in the analytical tools used, and differences in the data available.

The question also arises: which problem should be given priority — that of designing the all-purpose system of national accounts, or that of agreeing on the lay-out of the input-output accounts which are part of the former? There is a possibility that work might go on concurrently in both fields and that this might prove profitable. The natural order would seem to me however to be, first decide on the general lay-out of the larger system, then spell out the details. For this reason I seem to come again to the conclusion that standardization of input-output accounts should not be attempted now.

I have felt it my duty, since some of my colleagues rather indiscriminately argue for standardization, to state equally clearly some of the arguments against it. I am aware that in so doing I may have pushed some of my points too far. However, there can be no strong arguments against exploring the possibilities further, for instance through an expert group working under the auspices of the Conference of European Statisticians.

COMPARABILITY OF TABLES FOR SOCIALIST AND CAPITALIST ECONOMIES

by ZOLTÁN KENESSEY

Comparisons of interindustry relations between different countries are hindered by a great variety of factors many of which are competently discussed in the paper by Abraham and Hoffenberg. Most of these factors are of course present in any international comparison of complex economic phenomena (e.g. national income, standard of living, productivity of labour). The difficulties in all these cases are, as we know, considerable but, as experience shows, with some effort and imagination one can overcome them. I think that even the first steps in the seemingly long way of making structural comparisons between countries will give fruitful results, and therefore a cautious movement towards clarification of the methodological questions, which hinder international comparisons of the input-output tables, seems justified. In the following I shall first touch upon some questions in which I am in agreement with Abraham and Hoffenberg, and then on others in which I disagree with them.

On the basis of practical experience gained in Hungary in the last years: (*a*) I think that the authors are right in arguing that for the sake of comparability it is useful to have the 'establishment' as the unit for collecting information. (*b*) It seems justified to use already existing activity classifications for comparing tables. There is of course need for practical statistical considerations before comparability can be reached. (*c*) I feel the proposal handling secondary production is a fortunate one; the fictitious transfer approach, advocated by the authors, is the best compromise we can reach. (*d*) It is an important proposal to define 'construction' to include all work on own account, as well as contract work. In ISIC, as we know, own-account construction is part of the enterprise's output, not of the construction industry's. In Hungary for instance about one third of construction activity is own-account construction, and the importance of having this activity combined with that of the building industry proper is clear. (*e*) Lastly, may I underline the importance of the argument in favour of eliminating the so-called unallocated sector. In our first table for Hungary, 50 sectors for 1957, we included an unallocated sector and we had in total less than 2 per cent of all resources unallocated. Now in the second Hungarian table, of 109 sectors for 1959, we eliminated this sector, and we are convinced that the latter treatment is clearly preferable to the former.

Turning now to more critical comments — which stem from a sincere desire to make interindustrial relations more comparable all over the world — the treatment of two basic problems appears to be incomplete. The first concerns the concept of production which is to a considerable degree different in the various countries. The main differences between the practices adopted in socialist and capitalist countries are in the treatment of services which in socialist countries are not included among productive activities; the latter is defined to include only material production. The inclusion of services may result in a GNP 5 to 30 per cent higher. The technical coefficients and inverse matrices of input-output tables can have considerable differences, owing to the treatment of important parts of the national economy either as productive sectors or as consumption. I do not wish to discuss here which concept of production is better but it is impossible to ignore this basic conceptual problem, if there is a real wish of international comparability of input-output tables between socialist and capitalist economies. I wish to mention, that there is increasing experience in interpreting the National Accounts Systems of Eastern and Western countries. The work is done under the auspices of the U.N. Economic Commission of Europe and the main road followed so far is to try compute the national accounts of the socialist countries in terms of western national accounting and vice versa.

My second disagreement with Abraham and Hoffenberg concerns the linking of input-output tables with the present U.N. System of National Accounts. Theoretically I am absolutely in favour of a firmly established definitional and computational link between the broader system of national accounts and the interindustry relation table. Both theoretical thinking and actual practice are unquestionable along these lines in Hungary. But SNA in its present form is applicable only to capitalist economies, its principles and structure take into account only the needs and peculiarities of the western countries. There is hope for future revisions in SNA, to make possible its use for broader international comparisons as well. We should bear in our mind, when working on recommendations for comparable input-output tables, the needs for reconciliation with SNA and other systems of national accounts. But to link our work rigidly to the present SNA would be unpractical and in fact may hinder progress in this field.

Without going into detail, it is obvious that international standardization is hindered by the present treatment of the banks and other financial institutions, and of the ownership of dwellings in SNA. There are some new ways to be found if we wish to use SNA as a help to interpret the structure of various economic systems on a comparable basis. Some of the work in this direction may be done by the Conference of European Statisticians.

The Treatment of Government Activities

by ANTE NOVAK

In input-output tables 'public services' are differently treated in different countries. This is so because of (1) the different purposes of input-output analysis, (2) the difference in the importance of public services in the different countries, and (3) the divergent interpretation of the scope of public services.

Considering that the number of activities belonging to 'public services' is steadily increasing, it has become necessary to examine in detail their treatment in the input-output table. Moreover, the tables have become a subject of international comparisons and this makes it necessary to define clearly the treatment of public services in the individual tables.

In the following we wish to expound a way of the treatment of public services which, in the opinion of the Yugoslav experts, corresponds closest to the system of input-output analysis and to the inherent logic of the input-output system.

Alternative treatments of government activities

Public services are treated in input-output tables in three different ways. The first method treats public services as a separate sector of production; in the second, public services are distributed between consumption and production; and in the third method, with which I am in agreement, public services are treated on the consumption side.

These differences arise from different concepts of production. In the first case the starting-point is that public services create value and, therefore, belong to productive activities. In the second case some differentiation takes place among public services; part of them, financial and banking services for instance, are included in production, but the other part is included in final consumption. In the third conception — according to which the scope of production covers only the production of material goods — public services belong completely to public consumption. Public services do not represent any productive activity but only use commodities produced. The prices of the individual public services, expressed possibly in terms of money, do not mean that they represent a corresponding value. It cannot be stated, for instance, that the product of a school, an expert with a diploma, would be of a value equal to the sum spent on his education. It cannot be stated either that the result of the medical treatment of an individual, or the health of a given individual, is a product of a fixed value. Starting from this fact, and also according to the logic of the input-output analysis, public services have but inputs corresponding to the consumption of material goods used and have no outputs. Public services belong to final consumption.

The inclusion of public services in the scope of production causes several distortions in the structure, and the tables thus prepared reflect financial flows rather than the material, technological, relations of production. The interpretation of public services as production has a distorting effect also on the proportions between production and consumption. With the inclusion of public services in final consumption a more exact boundary line is drawn between production and consumption, and, on the other hand, we receive a clearer picture with regard to the relationship between personal and social consumption.

It should be mentioned here that personal and social consumption become more and more interrelated in modern society, especially in certain social systems. Human consumption is covered in an ever-increasing degree through the channels of social consumption. Consequently personal consumption is more and more supplemented by social consumption, independently of individual differences in making use of the different services rendered by the community to individuals (various degrees of insurance, possibilities of education, and recourse to health and social institutions). Personal consumption, in a sense, determines the personal living standard of individuals, whereas social consumption determines the social living standard of society as a whole.

The treatment of public services within final consumption is well-founded since, in the last analysis, differences between personal and social consumption lose more and more their social significance. Finally, in statistical practice it is very often only a question of convention whether the consumption of individual material goods belongs to personal or to common (collective) consumption.

The correctness of the treatment of public services within final consumption can be supported partly by the fact that the relationship of public services to production contains only a defensive and protective function (which, however, cannot be determined quantitively) and partly by the fact that public services are much more similar to personal consumption than to production.

The role and development of government activities

If public services are defined as social services securing the maintenance of society as a community, it becomes evident that there are very great differences between different social systems in the field of public services also. The degree of 'parasitism' of the state apparatus, the character of the army, the security organs and courts, the degree of development of cultural, social and similar institutions, and the accessibility of services may considerably differ from each other in different systems and different countries. Independently of the differences, however, the development of public services is advancing very rapidly, and moreover the rate of growth is different in the different fields of public services.

Public services steadily change their structure in general, for the benefit of those services that correspond better to the social interests of the communities. Due to these rapid structural changes it is necessary to divide these services into several groups when analysing the public service activities with the aid of input-output methods. Carrying out analytical studies in the case of these services, different development trends can be observed which are of great importance especially in the case of international comparisons.

Differences between countries which can be experienced in the field of public services are much more significant than possible differences in the structure of the production. Under the circumstances, general grouping as 'government' becomes undefined and unclear. Therefore, in our opinion, public services in input-output tables should be broken down into several sectors, namely: (1) administration, (2) defence, (3) social and health activities, (4) cultural, educational and scientific activities, (5) banks, finance, insurance, etc., and (6) communal services and similar activities.

A concluding remark

We have taken a stand in favour of the treatment of public services as consumption. We should like to add that in our opinion the other solutions mean only the formal use of the input-output techniques in the field of economic analysis and are not connected with the essential characteristics of the input-output table. It is a different question whether it is possible to utilize for individual analytical studies also such types of tables which, as a matter of fact, reflect partly financial processes. In my opinion, the traditional national accounts are much more fit for the purpose of similar analyses, aimed at depicting certain important financial flows of the economy.

PRINTED IN GREAT BRITAIN
BY ROBERT MACLEHOSE AND CO. LTD
THE UNIVERSITY PRESS, GLASGOW